JACQUES **DERRIDA**
basic writings

"Derrida's thought engages with an astonishingly wide variety of philosophical themes. This book offers the most convenient and encompassing collection of his most important contribution. An incredibly useful anthology."
Simon Glendinning, *London School of Economics and Political Science*, UK

Jacques Derrida is one of the most influential and controversial thinkers of the twentieth century. His ideas on deconstruction have had lasting impact on philosophy, literature and cultural studies.

Jacques Derrida: Basic Writings is the first anthology of his most important philosophical writings and provides an indispensable resource for all students and readers of his work. Barry Stocker's clear and helpful introductions set each reading in context, making the volume an ideal companion to those coming to Derrida's writings for the first time. The selections themselves span a range from his most famous works including *Speech and Phenomena* and *Writing and Difference* to lesser known discussion on aesthetics, ethics and politics, including selections from:

- *Of Grammatology*
- *Dissemination*
- *Speech and Phenomena*
- *Margins of Philosophy*
- *Writing and Difference*
- *Politics of Friendship*
- *Truth in Painting*

Barry Stocker is a lecturer in philosophy at Istanbul Technical University, Turkey and Senior Honorary Research Fellow in Philosophy at University College London. He is also author of *Derrida on Deconstruction* (Routledge 2006).

JACQUES
DERRIDA
basic writings
edited by **barry stocker**

Routledge
Taylor & Francis Group

LONDON AND NEW YORK

First published 2007
by Routledge
2 Milton Park Square, Milton Park, Abingdon, OX14 4RN

Simultaneously published in the USA and Canada
by Routledge
270 Madison Avenue, New York, NY 10016

Routledge is an imprint of the Taylor & Francis Group, an informa business

© 2007 Barry Stocker for selection and editorial matter

Typeset in Goudy and Helvetica by Taylor & Francis Books
Printed and bound in Great Britain by The Cromwell Press,
Trowbridge, Wiltshire

British Library Cataloguing in Publication Data
A catalogue record for this book is available from the British Library

Library of Congress Cataloging in Publication Data
Derrida, Jacques.
    [Selections. English. 2008]
    Jacques Derrida : Basic Writings / Edited by Barry Stocker.
        p. cm.
    Includes bibliographical references and index.
    ISBN-13: 978-0-415-36642-7 (hardback : alk. paper)
    ISBN-13: 978-0-415-36643-4 (pbk. : alk. paper) 1. Philosophy. I.
Stocker, Barry, 1966- II. Title. B2430.D482E5 2008
    194--dc22
                        200632868
ISBN: 978-0-415-36642-7 (hbk)
ISBN: 978-0-415-36643-4 (pbk)

CONTENTS

ACKNOWLEDGEMENTS

Derrida, Jacques. Translated by Gayatri Chakravorty Spivak. *Of Grammatology*, pp. 3–26. © 1977 John Hopkins University Press. Reprinted with permission of The John Hopkins University Press.

Derrida, Jacques. Translated by Barbara Johnson. *Dissemination*, pp. 95–117. © 1981, 2004 Continuum. Reprinted with permission of Continuum International Publishing.

Derrida, Jacques. Translated by David B. Allison and Newton Garver. *Speech and Phenomena*, pp. 32–47, 88–104. © 1979 Northwestern University Press. Reprinted with permission of Northwestern University Press.

Derrida, Jacques. Translated by Alan Bass. *Margins of Philosophy*, pp. 157–173, 307–330. © 1982 University of Chicago Press. Reprinted with permission of The University of Chicago Press.

Derrida, Jacques. Translated by John P. Leavey. *Edmund Husserl's Origin of Geometry: An Introduction*, pp. 87–107. © 1989 University of Nebraska Press. Reprinted with permission of University of Nebraska Press.

Derrida, Jacques. Translated by Alan Bass. *Writing and Difference*, pp. 3–30, 278–293. © 2001 Routledge. Reprinted with the permission of Taylor and Francis Books UK, and The University of Chicago Press, USA.

Derrida, Jacques. Translated by George Collins. *Politics of Friendship*, pp. 1–24. © 1997 Verso. Reprinted with the permission of Verso Press.

Derrida, Jacques. 'Onto-Theology of National-Humanism'. Translated by Geoffrey Bennington. *Oxford Literary Review* 14: 1–23 (1992). Reprinted by permission of the editors.

Derrida, Jacques. *For Nelson Mandela*, pp. 13–42. Translated by Mary Ann Caws and Isabelle Lorenz. © Henry Holt & Co. Reprinted with the permission of Henry Holt & Co.

Derrida, Jacques. Translated by G. Bennington and I. McLeod. *The Truth in Painting*, pp. 17–36. © 1987 University of Chicago Press. Reprinted with permission of The University of Chicago Press.

EDITOR'S INTRODUCTION

Life: Jacques Derrida (1930–2004)

Derrida was born into a French-Jewish family in French colonial Algeria. After studies in Algeria up to Lycée level, he took preparatory courses in Paris for the entrance exams to the Grandes Écoles, and gained entry to the École normale supérieure (ENS). From 1953 to 1954 he studied in the Edmund Husserl archives at the University of Louvain in Belgium. The result was a thesis published much later in Derrida's career (Derrida 2003). Derrida taught successively at the University of Paris, ENS, and the École des hautes études en sciences sociales (EHESS). He was the first director of the Collège international de philosophie, founded to provide a public lecture series in philosophy. Derrida also campaigned for philosophy teaching in schools. He published in great quantity, and much still remains to be published from his lectures at EHESS. Apart from all his scholarly work, and his work within academic institutions, he campaigned against Apartheid in South Africa, for human rights in Communist Czechoslovakia, and for the rights of immigrants and asylum seekers in France.

Derrida began publishing in the early 1960s, but really took off as a philosopher of major reputation in 1967 when he published three major books: *Of Grammatology* (Derrida 1997a), *Speech and Phenomena* (Derrida 1973), *Writing and Difference* (Derrida 1978). His name became famous as the author of highly original work written in a very distinctive style but also widely reviled as a pretentious impostor hiding behind an exaggeratedly obscure style. In many cases, those working in literary studies, other areas of aesthetic studies, cultural studies, and the social sciences were more sympathetic to Derrida than those working in philosophy departments. The overall effect was still of enormous influence, so enormous that 'deconstruction' has entered the language as a term for any kind of criticism or exposure of assumptions, or disruptions of discourse. Despite the continuing unfavourable response from many philosophers, Derrida is now taught in many philosophy departments and at the very least is now recognised as one of the major figures in the history of Continental European philosophy since Kant, a field increasingly recognised by English language philosophers as a legitimate field, and even as a necessary point of reference.

Derrida's increasing fame across the world in many fields, and his prolific output led to constant publications, translations, interviews and conferences across the world. His publications are influential in phenomenology (the description of consciousness), hermeneutics (philosophy of interpretation), aesthetics, ethics, political philosophy, philosophy of law, as well as a wide range of related work across the social sciences and humanities. Despite the widespread hostility, some mainstream English medium philosophers took up Derrida as a contributor to debates in the philosophy of language and metaphysics. His teaching and graduate supervision left a legacy outside Paris during his many visits to universities in many countries, including a particularly close and regular relationship with the University of California at Irvine. Outside the academic world, Derrida was published in newspapers, took part in French election campaigns, organised an exhibition at the Louvre, and was the subject of a cinema film. This extraordinary range of achievements was in the end recognized by the French state, in the most solemn manner, when the office of the President of the Republic announced Derrida's death to the world in October 2004. He left a widow and two sons.

Derrida's influences, legacy and reputation
In the English-speaking world, the dominant mode of analytic philosophy emphasises logical precision, conceptual clarity and a direct literal style of argument that strongly contrasts with Derrida's own inclination to write in a literary style rich with allusion, playfulness and indirectness exploiting all the resources of language. Continental European departments were dominated by history of philosophy, in a form orientated to disciplined textual and historical studies aiming at accurate reconstruction of texts. Derrida's texts look closer to the second school as he frequently quotes at length from the history of philosophy with full attention to linguistic and etymological issues. Nevertheless his texts are devoted to arguments putting forward the philosophy of paradox, anti-formalism, critique of metaphysics, and radical empiricism usually

known as 'deconstruction'. His arguments, and particularly his style, were and often still are received, with incomprehension mingled with hostility in both schools.

In other areas of the humanities and social sciences, Derrida's philosophy could be received in relation to established work using psychoanalysis; structuralist theories of texts, communications and culture; modernist and avant-garde aesthetics. Those philosophers who were most open to Derrida in the first place were those who had worked on the philosophers in the tradition Derrida drew on: Hegel, Kierkegaard, Nietzsche, Husserl, Heidegger, Sartre, Merleau-Ponty. This reception of Derrida was intertwined with a number of French philosophers roughly contemporary with him: Althusser, Foucault, Lévinas, Blanchot, Lyotard, Deleuze, Cixous, Irigary, Ricoeur, Marion. Louis Althusser and Michel Foucault were amongst Derrida's teachers at the ENS. Derrida had friendly relations with most if not all of the others. Emmanuel Lévinas appears to have been a particular friend, and their work bears important traces of the other's influence. All of these influential philosophers engaged with Derrida's work, though in the case of Foucault and Paul Ricoeur largely through criticism. The debate with Ricoeur focused on metaphor. Derrida's 1971 paper 'White Mythology: Metaphor in the Text of Philosophy' (in *Margins of Philosophy*, Derrida 1982 [originally published 1972]), one of his best known, developed at some length the view that metaphor cannot be eliminated from language, and that this is true of philosophical texts, despite efforts to make philosophy non-metaphorical. Derrida focused on a reading of Aristotle in which he argued that even as Aristotle tried to reduce metaphor to a secondary aspect of language in relation to the 'proper' meaning of names, he had to resort to metaphor. In *The Rule of Metaphor* (Ricoeur 2005 [first published in 1975]), Ricoeur claimed that Derrida had reduced all language to metaphor. Derrida forcefully rejected this interpretation in the 1978 paper 'The Retrait of Metaphor' (Derrida 1998b), where he argued that the irreducibility of metaphor from language is not the same as arguing that language is primarily metaphor, the argument is rather that language cannot escape the equivocation between the proper meaning and the metaphorical meaning.

The strongest positive examples are to be found in Lévinas and Blanchot, and it is their work which was most important for Derrida in formulating his own position. Blanchot's work covers literary fiction and literary journalism in addition to philosophy and literary aesthetics. Lévinas and Blanchot were also mutual influences. Lévinas and Blanchot both drew on Hegel and Heidegger. Lévinas puts them in the context of Husserl's phenomenology and Judaic traditions of religious ethics and interpretative reading of religious texts. Derrida is mostly concerned with phenomenology, particularly in his earlier publications. However, Judaism and issues of religion in general do appear in Derrida from the 1964 paper 'Edmond Jabès and the Question of the Book' (in Derrida 1978) onwards. The issues Derrida raises there of interpretation, law and poetry are anticipated from the beginning of his work. Lévinas is concerned to elevate a presumed Judaic tradition of ethics to first philosophy, in place of ontology (philosophy of being, kinds of thing). This challenges Aristotle's assumption in his *Metaphysics* that ontological questions are questions of first philosophy. Lévinas makes the bold claim that all Western philosophy is rooted in a Greek elevation of Being which finds expression in the Germanic tradition of Hegel, Husserl and Heidegger. Lévinas was very familiar with this tradition, he was a Husserl specialist who had studied with both Husserl and Heidegger, and his texts are full of the language of all three. Lévinas used the language of German philosophy against itself with a reading of Jewish tradition as primarily ethical, concerned with obligations to the stranger, the orphan and the widow. The Jewish tradition of interpretation of the Torah (the main texts of Judaic law, particularly the first five 'Mosaic' books of the Old Testament and commentaries on them) allows argument about ethics and law as the primary preoccupation of Jewish tradition. The Mosaic books of the Old Testament even show Moses arguing with God about the ethics of God's behaviour towards the Biblical Jews. Lévinas brings these concerns into phenomenology by constituting the Same, the I, as what is dependent on the Other. That is, I can only grasp myself in the transcendence of myself by what is Other to myself. The Other refers to God and to the face of the other individual. Without that relation to what is outside myself, there is no I. From this point of view, Lévinas criticises the violence of Being in Heidegger which excludes otherness, and the subjectivity of Kierkegaard as denying the presence of the Other in myself. Lévinas most famously put these views forward in *Totality and Infinity* (Lévinas 1999 [originally published in 1961]). Derrida subjected this book, and other works of Lévinas, to a vigorous but sympathetic critique in the 1963 essay, 'Violence and Metaphysics' (in Derrida 1978). Lévinas's best known book after *Totality and Infinity*, *Otherwise than Being, Or Beyond Essence* (Lévinas 1998 [originally published in 1974]), is in part a response to Derrida's critique. Derrida had argued that Lévinas is violent and reductive with regard to the positions that he criticises, that the peace Lévinas argues for is impossible and requires violence against otherness, that Lévinas' position is largely constituted through the German tradition he claims to reject, and that the transcendence of myself by the Other is a metaphysical moment of the pure presence of Being. While Derrida was concerned with his own Jewish heritage, he was not religious and did not support any view in which Judaism is privileged in any way. He was very interested in the status of religious concepts, at the unavoidable limits of language and experience.

Blanchot was concerned with literature since Romantic Symbolism and the experience of nothingness. Like Lévinas, his work contains a questioning of the sovereignty of the ego and the ways in which the self can only exist through its experience of a limit to the self and a beyond of the self. There was mutual influence between the two, though Blanchot had been a supporter of the anti-Semitic extreme right before the Second World War. What Blanchot focuses on is the literary experience as the experience of death, nothingness or a neutral emptiness of subjectivity. This largely came about through a reading of literary texts since the Romantic Symbolist poets of the nineteenth century in terms of Hegel and Heidegger: in particular the discussion of death in Hegel's *Phenomenology of Spirit* (Hegel 1977 [first published in 1807]), in the context of the struggle between master and slave; and the discussion of 'being-towards-death' in Heideger's *Being and Time* (Heidegger 1962 [first published in 1927]). These passages were also important for Lévinas, and then for Derrida. The way in which consciousness and language is conditioned by the possibility of death is a constant motif in his texts. In Blanchot's thought, these moments in Hegel and Heidegger enable us to write on the death and nothingness which are at the limit of experience and conceivability, and where the self lacks sovereignty. Writing, particularly of literature, is an experience and manifestation of that experience at the limits of experience; the experience of creating something which can only essentially communicate lack of meaning, disintegration, contradiction, death and nothingness. Blanchot also developed ethical positions out of this loss of sovereignty, as we can only experience our own self properly in a passivity before the other person, in an unwillingness to assert our mastery over another person or in any way. Blanchot responds to Derrida's development of his own themes in *Writing the Disaster* (Blanchot 1986 [first published in 1980]).

The context for Derrida's philosophy can be partly understood by describing some main points, necessarily very briefly, in the work of his contemporaries listed above, and in that of other figures, as will be discussed below. Louis Althusser developed a version of Marxist philosophy, emphasising a scientific, non-humanistic, interpretation in which history and social structures are grasped through processes which do not have a human subject, structures lacking a determining whole or centre, and ideology produced by social structures and so not just existing as subjective illusion. Althusser's last work was concerned with chance and indeterminacy and may in some part owe something to Derrida. Derrida's own attitude to Marxism was of interest rather than one of being a Marxist. Michel Foucault worked on the histories of institutions and discourses in very philosophical ways, that show knowledge and subjectivity as the products of underlying structures of thought and the interests of power. Jean-François Lyotard was concerned with desire and with the paradoxical nature of judgements. Gilles Deleuze wrote on the production of desire, power and concepts emphasising the superiority of material change over abstract representation. Hélène Cixous writes literature and is a feminist philosopher orientated towards psychoanalysis and literary texts in exploring sexual difference. Luce Irigary works on feminist philosophy with regard to feminine writing and language, using psychoanalytic ideas of sexual difference. Paul Ricouer wrote on hermeneutics with regard to language, time, consciousness, literature and religion. Jean-Luc Marion is a phenomenologist who has made major contributions to the history of philosophy and the philosophy of religion.

The main aim is to situate Derrida with regard to the history of philosophy since Kant and the analytic mode of philosophy which already dominates the English-speaking world, and is becoming increasingly influential in philosophy as it exists throughout the world. First the French philosophers above will be situated with regard to philosophy, humanities and social science in France. Derrida's own philosophy emerged from widespread interests in phenomenology in philosophy and structuralism in the humanities and social sciences. More will be said about phenomenology below, but it should be noted at this point that Husserl's phenomenology had an enormous presence in French philosophy of the 1950s, when Derrida was being formed as a philosopher, along with Heidegger's phenomenologically-influenced philosophy and Hegel, who in some respects established a phenomenological approach of describing the structures and contents of consciousness, though Hegelianism was rejected by Husserl and the other early phenomenologists. The most important and original French philosophical work from the 1930s to the 1960s includes a series of major works on phenomenology by Jean-Paul Sartre and Maurice Merleau-Ponty. Lyotard began in philosophy through phenomenology; Foucault was deeply affected by the work of the Hegelian Jean Hyppolite; the whole French philosophical scene was deeply affected by the lectures Alexandre Kojève gave on Hegel in Paris in the 1930s. Blanchot, the philosopher and writer Georges Bataille and the psychoanalyst Jacques Lacan were amongst the audience. Structuralism had an enormous presence in the humanities and social sciences, largely with reference to the work of the anthropologist

Claude Lévi-Strauss. Lévi-Strauss's structuralism compared kinship rules, myths, cuisine and other aspects of human culture, with reference to primary organising oppositions which establish 'structures' underneath the empirical phenomena of culture. These oppositions rested on the elemental origin between nature and culture. Lévi-Strauss's structuralist model, which Derrida discusses in 'Structure, Sign and Play in the Discourse of the Human Sciences' (Chapter 8 in this collection), is based on the linguistics of Ferdinand de Saussure, the Swiss originator of structuralist linguistics and semiology, that is the study of the sign. Structuralism as a movement of post-war thought has other origins, in the psychological study of relations between elements of consciousness and the biological study of elements and wholes in organisms. Derrida refers briefly to the latter in his 1963 discussion of literary structuralism in 'Force and Signification' (Chapter 13 in this collection). The main thrust was an interest in Saussure's theory of the sign, with regard to its non-referential aspects: the sign as having a meaning determined by its relations with other elements in a system rather than as a tie with an object in the world. Structuralism was brought into psychoanalysis by Jacques Lacan and into literary studies by Roland Barthes and Gérard Genette, along with others mentioned by Derrida in 'Force and Signification'. Lacan, Barthes and Genette did not always fly the flag of Structuralism and it would be inaccurate to define them as structuralists, but structuralism was dominant in some stages of their thought. The structuralist label was also applied to Althusser and Foucault, although they never used it themselves, and their work evolved away from abstract structures to an emphasis on empirical heterogeneity. Their decisive intellectual moments included encounters with Hegel's philosophy and with the philosophy of science in Georges Bachelard and Georges Canguilhelm, and will be briefly discussed below. Lacan was of major interest for Derrida, as was psychoanalysis in general. Derrida found psychoanalysis to be permeated with metaphysics but sought to overcome that in various places including the 1966 essay 'Freud and the Scene of Writing' (in Derrida 1978) and the whole of *The Post Card* (Derrida 1987a [first published 1980]. For Derrida, structuralism in general both contained metaphysical assumptions and contradicted itself in its emphasis on abstract structure, but was an important source of thought on wholes and the relations between elements of a system.

Derrida's ideas about knowledge are strongly conditioned by Althusser and Foucault, and by their predecessors Bachelard and Canguilhelm, along with Jean Cavaillès. Derrida's own relation with Foucault was one of conflict stemming from Derrida's critical but appreciative discussion of Foucault's *Madness and Civilisation* (Foucault 2001 [originally published in 1961] in the 1963 paper 'Cogito and the History of Madness' (in Derrida 1978). Foucault, who generally does not seem to have taken criticism well, appeared to take considerable offence, and more importantly replied to Derrida 'My Body, This Paper, This Fire' (Foucault 2000) in 1971, having had a long time to reflect on the apparently unpleasant experience of listening to Derrida's criticisms at ENS in 1963. Nevertheless, Foucault's later tendencies to emphasise the irreducibility of the body and an empiricism of chance, seem broadly in line with Derrida's philosophy. The point of the dispute is that Derrida found Foucault's contrast between 'madness' and 'reason' too absolute, though Foucault here, as in all his work was trying to show that opposing categories of knowledge are constructed in the context of discourse and society. Derrida concentrated on the reading of Descartes in Foucault, where he suggested that Descartes' famous hypothesis of a deceiving demon in 'Meditation One' of the *Meditations on First Philosophy*, is read by Foucault in a way which excludes unreason from the self, instead of allowing this necessary otherness within rational consciousness.

Bachelard worked on the history and philosophy of science in early twentieth-century France, and also on the poetics of experience. His most famous idea of the 'epistemological break' was mentioned occasionally, but significantly, by Derrida. The 'epistemological break' was fundamental for Althusser and Foucault. It appears in Althusser as a way of referring to the point of emergence of a science. For Althusser, the science of society appears in Marx in the transition from humanism of the young Marx to the scientific position of the mature Marx. Humanity, or the human individual, is the source of social process in early Marx, while the later Marx is concerned with structures of capitalism autonomous from human intentions. Concepts themselves change in meaning after an epistemological break, which may conceal the existence of the break. For Foucault, the concern is with establishing the conditions for a new discourse in which concepts are organised in a new way; he never had Althusser's belief in absolutely objective science. Canguilhelm in some ways carried on Bachelard's work, particulary in the history of medicine, concerning himself with the history and ordering of concepts, including the contrast between the normal and the pathological in medicine. Foucault was also engaged with the work of Jean Cavaillès, a resistance martyr, who had worked on the philosophy of mathematics in relation to Husserlian phenomenology, investigating the relations between singularity and universality in the layers of consciousness described in phenomenology. Foucault took this up in the discussion of archaeology and orders of knowledge and discourse. Derrida took it up with regard to the tensions in phenomenology between the immediacy of consciousness and layers of ideas in memory, a guiding concern in his early essays on Husserl. The work of Bachelard and Canguilhelm may anticipate and parallel work in history and philosophy of science in analytic philosophy since Thomas Kuhn. That issue will be taken up below when Derrida is situated with regard to analytic philosophy. The 'epistemological break' is present indirectly in Derrida's first major publication *Edmund Husserl's Origin of Geometry: An Introduction* (Derrida 1989 [first published in 1962]), which won a French prize for epistemology, in Jean Cavaillès' name. Husserl was concerned with the relation between the empirical conditions for the emergence of geometrical theorems and their claims to transcendental universal content. The emergence of geometrical principles is a break caught up in the relativity that infects universal truth claims, when they have merged at a particular point in time. They do not precede history as truths known absolutely already to the human mind, even if in principle the human mind can deduce the whole of geometry from self-evident axioms. The account of the *Introduction* will be expanded below with regard to the section included in this collection.

The major reference to the 'epistemological break' is in the 1968 paper, 'The Linguistic Circle of Geneva' (in Derrida 1982). Derrida suggests that Rousseau's *Essay on the Origin of Languages* could be conveniently referred to as an 'epistemological break' (Derrida 1982: 140). The context is very significant: Derrida is taking up the account of Rousseau's linguistics in Noam Chomsky's *Cartesian Linguistics* (Chomsky 2003), with regard to Rousseau's roots in seventeenth-century Cartesian rationalist thought about logic and grammar. Chomsky, a Professor at MIT, has a highly influential body of work in linguistics, cognitive psychology and philosophy (along with many well-known political polemics). He is not an obvious point of reference for Derrida, since Chomsky is associated with the naturalistic branch of analytic philosophy which regards philosophy as the continuation of science, particularly cognitive psychology. Nevertheless, in Cartesian Linguistics and elsewhere, Chomsky emphasises Wilhelm von Humboldt as anticipating his own work of universal grammar. Humboldt's work in language, and other fields, is closely linked with German idealist philosophy, particularly that of his friend Hegel. There is evidence here of overlaps between analytic and Continental European philosophy, an issue that will be further explored in relation to Derrida in more detail in the individual chapter introductions. Derrida's discussion of the 'epistemological break' in Rousseau suggests that Rousseau is claiming to have broken with all previous discussion of language by putting it on a new properly general basis. That claim itself is a claim that language marks the move from nature to history, that language is the institution that establishes society. In some respects Derrida is sympathetic to such a claim. He recognises language as a special field which is present in all fields of knowledge, since all knowledge is embedded in language. This is part of the structuralist influence on Derrida, and this is apparent in 'Force and Signification' and *Of Grammatology* including the excerpt in Chapter 1 of this collection. What Derrida emphasises is that the claim to have a general theory of language as social, is the claim that language itself as social must exclude natural forces. This is a necessarily impossible claim, since language itself must exist interlaced with material forces which most notably include speech and writing but also include computer encoding and are continuous with natural biological encoding within a cell, as Derrida notes in the excerpted section from *Of Grammatology*. The 'epistemological break' in Bachelard, which may be taken as comparable with the 'paradigm shift' in Thomas Kuhn, appears in the formation of linguistics as a discipline; it is the equivocation within the foundational moment between the empirical moment and the universal claims that emerge in that moment. That is the equivocation that Derrida establishes for geometry through the reading of Husserl. Both structuralism and phenomenology are conditioned by an equivocation between pure ideas with universal content and the empirical conditions for their appearance and application. The study of structuralism and phenomenology in Derrida is therefore the study of equivocations which condition all philosophical systems and all systematic knowledge claims.

The emphasis on language does not only tie Derrida to structuralism. In Continental European philosophy, Humboldt, Nietzsche and Heidegger all gave language a special status. The same applies to much analytic philosophy. On some definitions analytic philosophy is a philosophy of linguistic analysis, although the rise of naturalism in analytic philosophy may challenge that. Even in the key naturalists, like Chomsky and W. V. O. Quine, language appears as central. Derrida himself wrote one of his most famous papers, 'Signature Event Context', which appeared in 1971, (see Chapter 4 in this collection) with reference to the analytic linguistic philosopher J. L. Austin, also taking structuralism into account. Derrida's attitude to language is often compared with Ludwig Wittgenstein's and there is also a body of work comparing Derrida with Quine and with Donald Davidson, for whom all philosophical questions are intertwined questions of truth, belief and meaning. Derrida does not just see structuralism as a position on the primacy of language, he also discusses it as a form of metaphysics, exemplifying metaphysical tradition going back to Aristotle.

There is no 'linguistic idealism' in Derrida. The claim that Derrida has a metaphysical position according to which the only reality is that of language, or the text, picks up on what has become a legendary line from Derrida in *Of Grammatology* 'there is nothing outside of the text' (Derrida 1997a: 158). The line is taken out of a context in which Derrida is discussing Rousseau's *Confessions*, with regard to the impossibility of getting outside the text in discussing the characters who appear in Rousseau's autobiography. There is a broader point being made, but it is important to grasp that the line has a context that has nothing to do with the rather peculiar claim that existence is linguistic. It is not clear that anyone has ever believed this, and there is no more reason to suppose that Derrida holds such a position than there is with regard to Wittgenstein and Austin, Quine and Davidson. The broader point is one of 'supplementarity'. 'Supplementarity' is one way in which Derrida argues that we never grasp a referent in itself. The word is always a substitute for the referent, the thing named by the word. The word can only be a supplement for the referent, something to substitute for the referent in its absence. Since no one claimed that the thing named is present in the word, Derrida's claim is not extraordinary in what it says about words and things. What is significant is what Derrida is saying about meaning and interpretation, which is that interpretation is always the interpretation of interpretations, since language never disappears to leave us with the reality of the referent. Language, even in its simplest naming functions, is always a way of defining a word in the context of other words. This is not to say that there are no real referents out there, it is to say that we can only talk about referents through language as a whole. We do not take the whole of language at any one time, but we always put words in a context and the contextualisation has no necessary end. It could always encompass the whole of language, even if that is not what we do in practice. There is nothing extraordinary about this in terms of analytic philosophy. Derrida's position may not be exactly the same as any particular analytic philosopher. His one discussion of an analytic philosopher in 'Signature Event Context' suggests that Austin always resorts to a moment of certainty in determining meaning around sincere intentionality. Derrida argues that no such moment can ever be definitely established. An interest in context for analytic philosophers usually includes ways of determining the certainty of isolated names or sentences, as will be discussed in more detail in relation to comments on 'Signature Event Context'. Nevertheless, the claim that no name or word can be defined outside a linguistic context is not outrageous for analytic philosophy, and no one would deny that context is necessary to fix meaning, even if we may believe that the meaning itself is given by the object named in pure reference, denotation or designation. Writing and language are themselves conceived as material by Derrida. Part of the point of his discussion of Rousseau is to insist that language emerges from, and contains, natural material forces.

Derrida does belong to Continental European philosophy, a tradition which comes out of German Idealism. We should not necessarily see German idealist philosophy – Kant, Fichte, Schelling and Hegel – as primarily concerned with claiming that the only real world is an ideal world, the world of mental constructions. The Idealists did assume an identity between structures of the mind and the structures of reality. That is not the same as claiming that reality is just ideal or mental. It is more the claim that if reality is rational then it must have the same structure as the rational intelligence of the mind, and that is the only way we can perceive the world. Derrida resists this absolute rationalism, but it is important to appreciate that the Continental European tradition as a whole is not concerned with the denial of reality. It is not even concerned with claiming that reality is radically different from what we normally assume. Derrida certainly does not deny the importance of experience: he defined himself as a 'radical empiricist' and wished to emphasise what had been repressed and ignored by metaphysical philosophy. Derrida draws strongly on Nietzsche, who aimed to take a scientific empirical point of view to its furthest extreme in undermining all abstract claims about reality, and who attempted to find purpose rather than chance in the natural world.

Analytic philosophers typically reject Derrida on the grounds that he represents self-contradictory extreme forms of scepticism and relativism. He is an extreme sceptic on this account, because he casts doubt on truth and reality to the point where no sentence is true and there is no reality outside our subjective beliefs. At such an extreme point of scepticism, scepticism may contradict itself, because if I do not know the truth of anything I do not know the truth of the claim that such is the case. If I am a sceptic I must reject the claims made by scepticism, as well as every other position. Relativism may contradict itself if I claim that every truth is only relative to the position of the person who accepts a truth. If I am a relativist, I must accept that my own relativist claim is only true relative to my own point of view, and may be even only my point of view at one moment. In that case I must reject relativism as a purely relative truth. Sceptical and relativist positions can both be found in analytic philosophy however. Peter Unger, an influential professor at New York University, one of the main centres of analytic philosophy, has advocated both scepticism (Unger 1978) and relativism (Unger 2002). His arguments depend heavily on the context principle, which

Derrida uses. The difference is that Derrida never uses the context principle to advocate scepticism and relativism. Paul Feyerabend, one of the major figures in philosophy of science, who had major appointments in the USA and Britain, advocated relativism in science and knowledge (Feyerabend 1993 [first published 1975]). Neither philosopher is a minor or marginal figure. Their arguments are based in central work in analytic philosophy. They both changed their minds about scepticism and relativism, but when they held those positions no one denied that they were analytic philosophers with strong arguments. Much of the most influential work in analytic philosophy has been open to charges of relativism and scepticism, for various reasons which include: reduction of knowledge and meaning to subjective experience; defining scientific truths as varying according to the framework adopted; reducing meta-physical questions of reality to questions of changeable frameworks; denying that the word 'truth' has any substance at all beyond a kind of emphasis; ethical nihilism in which it is believed that there is no ethics because we live in an infinity of possible worlds in which all possibilities are actualised in some world so that our actions make no difference to the sum of good and evil in all possible worlds; scientific instrumentalism in which it is claimed that scientific theories are not true, they are just useful instruments for interpreting data; our awareness of our own mind tells us nothing about the real causes of our actions; mathematics only exists as constructed by the mind; numbers have no reality outside our numerical symbols. In comparison, Derrida is a moderate and even conservative common sense philosopher. The extraordinarily bitter attacks on Derrida sometimes made by analytic philosophers, who have only read a small, or even tiny, proportion of Derrida's work, can only reflect inner anxieties about the presence of scepticism and relativism in analytic philosophy.

One source of misunderstanding may be the ignorance of many analytic philosophers of texts in the tradition that Derrida inherited. In Hegel, Heidegger and Merleau-Ponty in particular, a very strong position is taken against scepticism on the grounds that we cannot begin to make the world of our experience intelligible except as the experience of a world, a world in which we always find ourselves before we begin to reflect on philosophy. Of Derrida's major references, Nietzsche may sometimes seem sceptical or relativist, but Nietzsche was also an enthusiast for scientific truth and universality in human values. Like Kierkegaard, Nietzsche thought that scepticism is only of value when it reflects a determination to live a life based on denial of certain assumptions, which is how they understood Antique scepticism. While Derrida may seem sceptical and relativist, it is important to remember that the tradition that preceded him and which he assumes his reader has read, was already full of arguments against scepticism.

It is clear then that reading Derrida fully requires a survey of the European tradition since Kant, with regard to what Derrida took from various philosophers in that tradition. What Derrida took from Kant is an interest in the nature of judgement itself. When Kant takes judgements as autonomous, he finds that they are reflective so that they do not just bring a particular thing under a general concept. The reflective judgement, as subjective, comes from the play of the faculties of understanding (concepts) and sensibility (sensation), and in its subjective aspect essentially forms aesthetic judgements of the beautiful and the sublime. These judgements refer to inner play of faculties and the communicability of judgements between individuals in a community, rather than to the existence of objects or the rules of morality, where judgement is determinant. Derrida takes from Hegel a concern with my possible death as intrinsic to consciousness. I only have consciousness and thought because I am absent from the contents of consciousness. My own consciousness is where I find myself limited by the otherness of the thoughts and perceptions, which fill my consciousness. My existence as a self depends on incorporating that otherness instead of the self-destructive drive to isolate a pure me. Nevertheless, we are always caught between a sense of myself and what I grasp within consciousness as outside myself. Judgements always exist in a context, which limits and negates the simple judgement. Derrida appears to have read Kierkegaard as he first became interested in philosophy. However, he did not write on Kierkegaard directly apart from 'Whom to Give To (Knowing Not to Know)' in *The Gift of Death* (Derrida 1996b [first published 1992]) and scattered remarks. From what there is, we can say that Derrida took from Kierkegaard concerns with a deep subjectivity which still requires a relation with something outside itself, the paradox of justifying pure decisions between opposed positions, the irreducible irrationality of pure subjectivity and pure decisions, along with the paradoxes of trying to follow moral rules consistently. As has been noted above, Derrida follows Nietzsche's empirical anti-transcendental tendencies. He also follows up Nietzsche's concern to establish ethics on something other than abstract obligation, his commitment to a way of writing philosophy that resists system, examining the history and contradictions of concepts, and an emphasis on differences disrupting all Being and identity. Husserl was the starting point for Derrida, because his concern with identifying pure structures of consciousness draws attention to the impossibility of Husserl's attempts to exclude the empirical, the material, the social and the historical from consciousness and language. Husserl's later reflections, on the difficulty of reconciling the historical conditions of knowledge with its universal claims, also opened an understanding of necessary equivocation in knowledge claims for Derrida. Heidegger is taken up with regard to the end attempt to end metaphysics and the attempt to find a pure Being before abstract concepts, which parallels the natural in Rousseau. Heidegger's desire for pure Being is anti-metaphysical and deconstructive because no system or abstraction can capture Being itself.

After the German philosophers, the twentieth-century French philosophers who followed the Germans are the major influence on Derrida. However, first we should briefly consider Henri Bergson who Derrida mentions very little, if at all. Bergson was not following any German thinkers, he had his own reactions to Darwinian evolution, psychology and social science in which he emphasised will, memory and inner experience. Bergson was not taken up by major French philosophers until Deleuze, but his work still anticipates much later French work on the phenomenological and material aspects of consciousness, in relation to inner time and outer objects. Despite the lack of overt interest in Bergson by later French philosophers, he certainly needs to be studied for a full understanding of what came later, including Derrida.

Husserl's phenomenology had a major impact in France, and stimulated original work by two major philosophers: Sartre and Merleau-Ponty. Derrida also refers to the work of Jean Cavaillès and Tran Duc Thao with regard respectively to the philosophy of mathematics in phenomenology and a Marxist materialist version of phenomenology, but their work is not as well known as that of Sartre and Merleau-Ponty and it is on the latter that we must concentrate. Derrida's remarks on Sartre are few and rather critical. The most notable discussion is in the 1968 paper, 'The Ends of Man' (in Derrida 1982), where Sartre is brought up to stand for an uncritical subjective metaphysical humanism which has reduced Heidegger's Being and Time to its own terms, instead of recognizing the ways in which it questions the absoluteness of human experience. Sartre is condemned for using 'lived human reality' as a translation for 'Being-in-the-world' in Heidegger, which Heidegger establishes as a characteristic of Dasein (the kind of being that asks the question of Being), and which refers to ways in which experience is a standing outside of the self. Much later Derrida suggested that there might be some continuity between his own work and Sartre's in an article in Les Temps Modernes. Les Temps Modernes itself was founded by Sartre, Merleau-Ponty and Sartre's companion, the feminist philosopher Simone de Beauvoir. In an issue commemorating the 50th anniversary of its foundation, Derrida wrote a long essay '"Il courait mort": salut, salut. Notes pour un courier aux Temps Modernes' (Derrida 1996a), which takes a more generous view on continuities between his own work and Sartre's versions of phenomenology. Unfortunately no translation appears to be available at present and it does not appear to be available in any form outside the original magazine edition. Sartre's direct contribution in the field of phenomenology belongs to the early part of his career, particularly in his lengthy book *Being and Nothingness: An Essay On Phenomenological Ontology* (Sartre 2003a [first published in 1943]). In comparison with Husserl, Sartre emphasises the empirical subjective aspects of the phenomenology of consciousness, along with the role of interpersonal and social relations and the body. He establishes a rather Hegelian distinction between Being-in-itself, which is inert materiality and Being-for-itself which is consciousness aware of its own intentions and freedom. He describes human consciousness as conditioned by an unavoidable structure of bad faith, in which consciousness denies the freedom of 'Being-for-itself' in regarding itself as 'Being-in-itself' which is the product of external circumstances. Humans interact through the Look, in which someone becomes the object of someone else's vision. Human subjectivity and intersubjectivity is structured by a struggle between becoming an object and turning another consciousness into an object which is partly explained through a form of Hegel's master–slave struggle. A full introduction to Sartre can be found in an earlier book in the series to which this book belongs, *Jean-Paul Sartre: Basic Writings* (Sartre 2003b). The elements of contradiction and external context for consciousness do anticipate Derrida, though the absolutes of Being and Nothingness; Being-in-itself and Being-for-itself are metaphysical by Derrida's standards.

Merleau-Ponty receives slightly more favourable acknowledgement in Derrida's earlier texts, as in 'Force and Signification' (Chapter 13 in this collection). However, it is only much later in *Memoirs of the Blind* (Derrida 1993 [first published 1990]) and *On Touching–Jean-Luc Nancy* (Derrida 2005b [first published in 2000]), that Derrida gives anything like a full account of the relationship. He appears to have had a particular anxiety in the earlier part of his career about acknowledging Sartre and Merleau-Ponty, presumably because they were so influential in French philosophy, then so out of favour for a while, and they in some respects anticipated his own work on phenomenology. Merleau-Ponty's biggest contribution to phenomenology, *Phenomenology of Perception* (Merleau-Ponty 1962 [first published 1945]) is comparable in size and scope to *Being and Nothingness* and was published shortly afterwards. It makes much more reference than Sartre to scientific psychology and in that respect anticipates analytic naturalistic work on the philosophy of mind. Merleau-Ponty criticises the absolute opposition between in-itself and for-itself, without naming Sartre. Nevertheless the target is clear and anticipates Derrida's approach to absolute oppositions in philosophy. Merleau-Ponty emphasises the embodied nature of perception in which we orientate towards the world we are in, so that we do not stand aside from our own body or from the external world. Consciousness can never grasp itself completely because it is a flow over time, in which we lose a moment of consciousness before we can grasp it. Perception exists as a field in which a figure stands out against a background itself circumscribed by a horizon at the edge of perception. These three elements keep changing in relation to each other, and this undermines any sense that perception is the perception of moments of immediate sensation, which stand individually as unchallengeable moments of experience. Here Merleau-Ponty anticipates Derrida's thoughts about experience and time in phenomenology. The book Merleau-Ponty was still working on at the time of his regrettably early death in 1960, *The Visible and the Invisible* (Merleau-Ponty 1969), seems to overlap even more clearly with Derrida's philosophy. At this point Merleau-Ponty is less concerned with scientific psychology and the description of perception, and is more concerned with establishing constitutive conditions of perception. This leads him the consideration of the 'chiasm' in which consciousness of the visible turns inwards and cannot find an origin in consciousness, encountering body as 'flesh', where there is the invisible. Consciousness intertwines with a world from which it cannot be isolated, and with the 'flesh' that appears in its own invisibility. As with Sartre, a survey of Merleau-Ponty can be found in an earlier volume in the present series, *Maurice Merleau-Ponty: Early Writings* (Merleau-Ponty 2004).

The emphasis on the chiasm in The Visible and the Invisible generally anticipates Derrida's concern with moments of contradiction and aporia. In particular it anticipates his discussion of 'chiasmic double invagination' in the 1980 paper 'The Law of Genre' (in Derrida 1992). Derrida's strange-looking phrase combines concerns with language, narrative and gender difference. In French, 'genre' refers both to genre in the English sense and gender in the sexual sense. Derrida is discussing a short story by Blanchot, 'Madness of the Day', in terms of a double aporia, double uncertainty or chiasm. The double uncertainty applies to the Blanchot narrative, because the narrator casts doubt on the reality of the 'I' that narrates and on the narrative that the 'I' narrates. For Derrida this is a constitutive condition of literature which Blanchot has drawn attention to in his literary fictions and in his literary criticisms. The 'invagination' refers to a fold in the line of the narrative, if we are thinking of it in diagrammatic terms. The 'invagination' also refers to the female vagina, with the aim of providing an alternative to the 'phallocentric' which

Derrida regards as an example of 'logocentrism'. Logocentrism is a discourse which claims to be grounded by the pure presence of truth, the word which reveals truth. Here Derrida is referring to psychoanalysis, particularly as it appears in Lacan where it is defined through language and the sign, and it is where Derrida deals with the concerns of feminist philosophers like Luce Irigaray who seek a feminine writing distinct from a masculine metaphysical tradition. The suggestion is that a subjective way of writing which enjoys the flow of language is both non-metaphysical and feminine. This is some extrapolation from Merleau-Ponty, and as far as the present author is concerned, the attempt to define questions of narrative and discourse in such reductive psychoanalytic terms is not the best way to deal with narrative and discourse; or gender and psychoanalysis. Nevertheless, the discussion of the conditions for the existence of literature is a strong argument with important consequences in understanding language and consciousness, which is always a consciousness which experiences itself through language when it is a linguistically competent subject. There is no explicit reference to Merleau-Ponty, but it is clear enough that Merleau-Ponty is part of the context of Derrida's philosophy.

Before finishing the survey of French philosophy in the background of Derrida's thought, some mention must be made of Georges Bataille. One paper from 1967, 'From Restricted to General Economy: A Hegelianism without Reserve' (in Derrida 1978) focuses on Bataille. Bataille was in the surrealist circle in Paris in the 1920s and continued as an active literary and intellectual figure in France until the 1960s. In his literature, his writings on literature, on philosophy and on society he emphasised transgression of boundaries as the way to the deepest inner experience; he advocated the pure gift as a model of social relations, along with the loss of self-sovereignty in pure expenditure with no hope of return: expenditure applied to economic relations and all natural forces present in the individual. Nietzsche, and then Hegel, are the most important philosophical references. In Bataille, Derrida finds a model of anti-metaphysical thinking but also an emphasis on pure force and pure loss which would take us beyond thought of any kind. Reaching that boundary is necessary, but there is always transcendence and Being in Derrida. They are never absolute but they always emerge within empirical forces, in their generalisation and abstraction in thought and the systemisation which must be embedded in thought. The combination of philosophical and literary achievements parallels Blanchot and at least one other French writer of that time to whom Derrida sometimes refers, Pierre Klossowski, along with the achievements of Antonin Artaud as dramatist and writer on the theatre of cruelty, that is pure physicality. Literature dealing with limits of conceivability and narrative coherence was always important for Derrida, as can be seen in his discussions of the poets Stéphane Mallarmé, Lautréamont, Paul Valéry; and the fictions of James Joyce, Franz Kafka and François Ponge.

After situating Derrida with regard to the history of Continental European philosophy since Kant, and French thought since Bergson, we will try to define Derrida in relation to analytic philosophy. Derrida is in many ways the antithesis of the analytic mode, as in all cases he argues in a way that uses all the metaphorical, figurative and stylistic aspects of language. He never wrote papers on standard analytic topics, and never really wrote papers on some strictly defined and delimited philosophical question. He moves through discussions of texts guided by philosophical strategies which aim to shake metaphysics and release empirical forces, showing their multiplicity and diversity.

However, Derrida is not completely distinct from analytic philosophy. His research as a graduate student and many of his early publications deal with Edmund Husserl. Husserl's work, particularly *Logical Investigations* (Husserl 2001 [first published 1901) has become of increasing interest to analytic philosophers, and there is really no clear reason for saying that *Logical Investigations* is Continental European philosophy rather than analytic philosophy. It is not a book about formal logic, the logic in the title really refers to kinds of judgement, but it is a book which has inspired logically orientated philosophers. For example, the discussion of wholes and parts has strongly influenced technically orientated analytic discussions of rules for combining parts into wholes. The whole book has inspired analytic discussions of propositions, relations, possibility and essence. Some of the analytic Husserlians, such as Kevin Mulligan, are very strongly opposed to Derrida, claiming that his readings are subjective and arbitrary, and are based on a wildly relativistic philosophical position, that it is a position which denies objectivity and universality for any claim about the world. Mulligan's paper 'Searle, Derrida and the Ends of Phenomenology' (Mulligan 2003) and his journal article 'How Not to Read: Derrida on Husserl' (Mulligan 1991) is a very polemical and uncompromising version of this kind of argument. The trouble with this kind of argument is that it is too tied up with the idea that Husserl must be doing the same things as current analytic philosophers to even try to reconstruct Derrida's argument or to consider what there is in Husserl that might attract Derrida's emphasis on equivocation and contradiction in Husserl's phenomenology. Mulligan, and others, may not like Derrida's attempt to uncover metaphysical assumptions in Husserl; but they have only proved that they have a different way of reading Husserl and they have not proved anything illegitimate in Derrida's reading of Husserl as concerned with questions of transcendental metaphysics or ontology. Their assumption that Derrida is an extreme relativist and subjectivist shows their failure to read Derrida with discernment.

One thing that comes out of Derrida's reading of Husserl is a brief acknowledgement of Gottlob Frege, one of the foundational figures in analytic philosophy. In 'Sign and Signs', the first chapter of *Speech and Phenomena* (Derrida 1973), Derrida outlines the different ways in which Frege and Husserl deal with the difference between 'Sinn' and 'Bedeutung', and also does so in the 1967 paper 'Form and Meaning: A Note on the Phenomenology of Language' (in Derrida 1982). In one of the foundational papers of analytic philosophy, published by Frege in 1892, usually translated as 'On Sense and Reference' (Frege 1997), Frege argues that words, phrases and sentences have two fundamental aspects: the object referred to and the general sense communicated in language. The nature of this distinction is not at all self-evident and there is a vast literature on it, but for our purposes it is sufficient to note that Frege thought that the 'Bedeutung' (translated as 'reference' or 'meaning') of a linguistic expression is an object, while the 'Sinn' (translated as 'sense' or 'meaning') is the objective communicable content of the linguistic expression itself. For Husserl, in 'Investigation I: Expression and Meaning' in *Logical Investigations* (Husserl 2001 [first published in 1901]), there is no distinction between 'meaning' and 'sense' though it is possible to distinguish between 'meaning' and 'fulfilling sense intentions' which make judgements meaningful; and the argument moves to a distinction between 'expression' as pure meaning and 'indication' as material means of communication. While in Section 124 of *Ideas* (Husserl 1962 [first published in 1913]), Husserl suggests a distinction between meaning as the meaning for concepts, and sense as meaning in its most general sense. This discussion is really completed by Derrida in 'Signature Event Context' (Chapter 4 of this collection), where he refers to the equivocations in Husserl around sentences which are syntactic (formed according to grammatical rules) but which lack meaning. The Frege moments are fleeting, but in context we can say that Derrida clarifies a distinction between Husserl and Frege and that if we extrapolate, we can say that a Derridean view of Frege is that he idealises fixed sense and meaning for linguistic expressions, in contrast to the contextuality he recognises is necessary for defining the parts of a proposition. For Frege, the proposition as a whole must be more than a simple sum of its parts. The idealisation for Derrida would be a necessary stage, but misleading from the point of view of the empirical indeterminacy of meaning outside a context. Such a view does not look far from that of Wittgenstein in *Philosophical Investigations* (Wittgenstein 2001 [written 1951]).

Derrida also makes fleeting references to a founding figure of analytic philosophy in the brief comments on Charles Peirce's semiotics (Peirce 1991) in *Of Grammatology* (Derrida 1997a). The American philosopher Peirce developed both semiotics and pragmatist philosophy in the nineteenth century. As he was dissatisfied with the subjectivist direction some Pragmatists gave to the idea, he later adopted the label of Pragmaticism to distinguish himself. Many very different American philosophers put themselves in the Pragmatist tradition including W. V. O. Quine, Hilary Putnam and Richard Rorty. Pragmatism is an empiricist philosophy which defines and tests beliefs and meanings with regard to experience, denying that they can have any content. However, pragmatism is not a reductionist empiricism, that is it does not reduce meaning and knowledge to separate individual moments. Pragmatism is contextual: an experience has meaning and cognitive content according to our whole body of beliefs and meanings. Peirce largely took this from Hegel. It can be seen that the origins of analytic philosophy are intertwined with the history of Continental European philosophy, which is something to be taken into account when discussing Derrida. The main point of Derrida's account of Peirce's semiotics is to be less caught in metaphysics than Saussure's semiology or Husserl's theory of the sign. The subtitle of *Speech and Phenomena* is concerned with the latter. Unlike Husserl or Saussure, Peirce allows for the infinite substitutability of the sign:

> Peirce goes very far in the direction that I have called deconstruction of the transcendental signified, which, at one time or another, would place a reassuring end to the reference from sign to sign. I have identified logocentrism and the metaphysics of presence as the exigent, powerful, systematic, and irrepressible desire for such a signified. Now Peirce considers the indefiniteness of reference as the criterion that allows us to recognise that we are indeed dealing with a system of signs. What broaches the movement of signification is what makes its interruption impossible. The thing itself is a sign.
>
> (Derrida 1997a: 49)

This is one way of explaining what Derrida means by 'nothing outside of the text', along with his main objects of criticism: metaphysics of presence, transcendental signified and logocentrism, and what deconstructive philosophy in general is. And this succinct explanation of Derrida's fundamental terms occurs in a discussion on the founder of American analytic philosophy.

Derrida's other remarks on analytic philosophy are discussed above with regard to Chomsky and with regard to Austin in introductory remarks on 'Signature Event Context' in Chapter 4. Scattered allusions to Austin occur in various places including *Glas* (Derrida 1986 [first published in 1974]) and 'Envois', the main section of *The Post Card* (Derrida 1987a). The only other reference is to Gilbert Ryle's 'Theory of Meaning' (Ryle 1953), which Derrida refers to allusively in his particularly fragmented and allusive text, 'Envois'. It is a strange choice for someone not versed in analytic philosophy since it is not the best known of Ryle's papers. Derrida brings it in through playful references to 'Fido-Fido'. This refers to Ryle's criticism of a theory of the meaning of names he attributes to John Stuart Mill and Wittgenstein in the *Tractatus Logico-Philosophicus* (Wittgenstein 1961 [first published in 1921]), according to which the meaning of a name is the object it names, or the bearer of that name. In that case the meaning of 'Fido' is the dog called 'Fido'. Ryle criticises the view that names, or any part of language, can be defined by reference to an object, rather than their contextual place in language, the role a word has in language. Along with Derrida's discussion of Austin, this is evidence that we can regard Derrida as continuing the work of those analytic philosophers concerned with context and rules of use for words, including P. F. Strawson and Wittgenstein, as well as Austin and Ryle. These philosophers are often known as 'Ordinary Language Philosophers'. Such a label would not do for Derrida though who is concerned with extraordinary and contradictory aspects of language. Derrida is a linguistic and semantic contextualist, but in a radical way which excludes the view that rules of use make up a fixed, stable and consistent system. In that case, Derrida's views may be close to Saul Kripke's version of Wittgenstein, who, according to Wittgenstein on *Rules and Private Language* (Kripke 1982), was concerned with the groundlessness of any rule for the use of a word, so that no rule has completely sure criteria for following it successfully and we never have completely secure criteria for knowing which rule is at work.

Derrida has often been treated as the complete antithesis of analytic philosophy, to the extent that some well-known analytic philosophers have campaigned against any recognition of Derrida as an academic philosopher, or as a thinker who deserves to be taken seriously in any context. Nevertheless some analytic philosophers have thought it appropriate to take Derrida seriously. Much of this will be discussed in my introductions to the Derrida extracts in the following chapters. In general it should be pointed out that Richard Rorty, who certainly thinks Derrida is an important and serious philosopher, is rooted in analytic philosophy. Although he has moved away from a pure analytic approach as he has combined pragmatism with Continental philosophy to arrive at neo-pragmatism, he has had a major impact on analytic philosophy. Donald Davidson and John McDowell, for example, pay great tribute to Rorty's presence in philosophy and the importance of his work for their own. Rorty takes an anti-transcendental view according to which all purely philosophical positions are to be rejected in favour of pragmatic recognition of context. He justifies this in arguments that analytic philosophy itself has undermined claims that there could be any foundations to knowledge or that knowledge could be a reflecting mirror of objective reality in itself. What is in the mind as beliefs cannot be explained or justified by objective reality outside, but by their place in a context of other beliefs and whatever influences the mind. This is not entirely the same as Derrida, who Rorty regards as too transcendental (Rorty 1991,Rorty 1998a, and Rorty 1998b) but is certainly in line with Derrida's rejection of any claims to knowledge based on transcendental principles or on moments of pure experience. Though Rorty's position is empirical he rejects any idea according to which experiences can be isolated as pure immediate supports for beliefs. Experience is always interpreted in a context of assumptions, theories and the system of beliefs as a whole. This is all consistent with Derrida and is in part inspired by Derrida. For Derrida, there is still an interest in philosophy as an area of thought, and the need for transcendental aspects of thought, which Rorty rejects as not pragmatic enough. Rorty serves as a means for transmitting Derrida's thought into analytic philosophy but also as a Pragmatist philosopher of analytic origins who finds Derrida insufficiently pragmatic and sceptical about transcendental abstraction. The background to this is best established by considering the context for each of Derrida's texts selected, in each introductory section. This will also lead us into some issues that have been little considered above with regard to ethics, politics and aesthetics.

Further Reading

Derrida, Jacques. Translated by Gayatri Chakravorty Spivak. *Of Grammatology*, pp. 3–26. © 1977 John Hopkins University Press. Reprinted with permission of The John Hopkins University Press.

Derrida, Jacques. Translated by Barbara Johnson. *Dissemination*, pp. 95–117. © 1981, 2004 Continuum. Reprinted with permission of Continuum International Publishing.

Derrida, Jacques. Translated by David B. Allison and Newton Garver. *Speech and Phenomena*, pp 32–47, 88–104. © 1979 Northwestern University Press. Reprinted with permission of Northwestern University Press.

Part I

Metaphysics

1 'EXERGUE' AND 'THE END OF THE BOOK AND THE BEGINNING OF WRITING'

OF GRAMMATOLOGY (DERRIDA 1997A
[FIRST PUBLISHED 1967])

Translated by Gayatri Chakravorty Spivak

Themes

The extract comes from the beginning of *Of Grammatology* which may be Derrida's most widely read book. The translator Gayatri Chakravorty Spivak is a notable writer on colonialism, post-colonialism and gender. She is a leading representative of the most radical-left and Marxist orientated readings of Derrida.

The extract sets up some of Derrida's central arguments about metaphysics, writing and the nature of his own deconstructive philosophy. The reference to the 'the end of the book' is not a literal claim that books are disappearing. It refers to certain ideas of the Book, derived from religious texts, particularly the *Bible*, which refers to 'books' in its etymology. Scientific rationalist encyclopaedic texts, such as Diderot's eighteenth-century Enlightenment *Encyclopaedia*, and in particular Hegel's *Encyclopaedia of Philosophical Sciences* (1830) are seen in terms of attempts to present absolute truth. The 'Book' in that sense is metaphysical. The Book is opposed to Writing, in an opposition between logocentrism and the substitutability of signs. Logocentrism is the determination of an entity as its full presence. It relies on metaphors of what stands in the real entity, or truth, but needs to deny its reliance on metaphor. Historically these metaphors have included: the truth of the soul, the book of nature, the writing of God. The distinction between signifier and signified, exemplified by Saussure's linguistics, is an example of logocentrism because it assumes that the signifier, the material existence of a sign, merely stands for the signified, the pure ideas or concepts contained in words. Writing reveals itself as the signifier of the signifier, in which words are only defined by other words; a signifier only stands for another signifier and not something behind signification. This is a comment on how language works freed of metaphysical assumptions, it is in no way a metaphysical claim that language of any kind is more real than the physical world. Derrida makes clear here his adherence to a Nietzschean kind of empiricism in which the empirical, or the non-philosophical, always exceeds abstractions in their content, in a focus on perspective, evaluation, difference.

Logocentism turns writing, the signifier of the signifier, into something secondary in its 'phonocentrism'. Phonocentrism makes speech and the voice metaphysically primary. Logocentrism looks for a living presence of truth and finds it in speech which is understood as the immediate presence of the soul, or the consciousness, that speaks. Phonocentrism emphasises: the presence of the thing to sight as *eidos*, or form; pure presence as the presence of substance, existence, and *ousia*, or spirit; the point of the now in temporal presence; the self-presence of consciousness; the co-presence of the other and the self; intersubjectivty as an intentional phenomenon of the Ego. Phonocentism is threatened by the emphasis on logical forms and pure symbolism of ideas outside normal language, which can be found in Leibniz. Then growth of recorded speech threatens the assumption of phonocentrism that speech is always the immediate expression of an inner intention. The growth of the language of computer programming and biological awareness of programming in cells has a similar effect, because it shows forms of language and communication of information which do not refer to speech at all.

Metaphysics claims to be scientific and to provide foundations for science. However, science is not governed by logic. The laws of science are not derived from logical laws, and therefore refer to an empirical diversity which cannot be reduced to a pure system of rules or incorporated into a total system. Science is always concerned with the empirical world and that always exceeds abstract unities.

Context

Derrida's view on metaphysics is an explicit rejection, but that does not exclude metaphysics, since in rejecting metaphysical positions a metaphysical position is taken. Derrida recognizes that deconstruction always falls back into metaphysics. Anti-metaphysical thought goes back to the

Ancient Greek sceptics (most notably Sextus Empiricus), and has always been caught in the paradox that it offers another metaphysics. Anti-metaphysical metaphysics, in Derrida, and elsewhere, is nominalist. Nominalism is the position according to which names of types of things (common nouns) and types of property (adjectives) are just names grouping objects and do not refer to any underlying real kinds. Nominalism as an explicit tradition goes back to the Medieval philosopher, William of Ockham. In recent analytic philosophy Nelson Goodman is its most distinguished representative, though Quine started as a nominalist and the position he eventually adopted of 'conceptualism' retained nominalist aspects. Not all empiricist philosophers are nominalists, Charles Peirce for example was a strong realist. Some of Derrida's predecessors in Continental European philosophy were strongly anti-nominalist, including Hegel, Husserl and Heidegger. Derrida distanced himself from all three in the respect that he insisted on a Nietzschean empiricism which is implicitly nominalist. The paradox of adopting a metaphysical position in rejecting metaphysics was one felt deeply by the logical positivists who gathered in the Vienna Circle after the First World War. The logical positivist began with the belief that they could eliminate metaphysics through the reduction of all knowledge and all meaning to logic and empirical observation. This heroic empiricism did not last, partly because of the ambiguities entailed around the reality of scientific laws, or laws in general, can bring both laws of logic and empirical science into question; and the ambiguity of 'anti' metaphysics having to take up metaphysical positions. Struggles with these problems are very noticeable in the classical logical positivist texts of Rudolf Carnap and Moritz Schlick. Carnap, contrary to Derrida, regards philosophy as the logic of science, and in a completely opposite approach to Derrida focuses on issues of logical structure in language and knowledge. His progress towards a more pragmatic and historical version of his thesis might be taken to confirm Derrida's scepticism about a logic of science. Carnap's focus on logic and logic of language leads him to pose questions of knowledge and of ontological assumptions in terms of what language we are using, again converging with Derrida in the belief that there is no clear separation to be made between the assumptions of language and assumptions about knowledge and metaphysics made in that language. This aspect of Carnap is taken further by Quine in 'On What There Is' (1948) and 'Ontological Relativity' (1969) which both emphasise that ontological questions are pragmatic and formal questions of what kind of entities are assumed in the language we have.

A stronger 'analytic' precedent for Derrida might be found in Ludwig Wittgenstein. Wittgenstein was close to the Vienna Circle for a while, and his form of anti-metaphysics belongs with them in some respects, but Wittgenstein was also deeply impressed by Kierkegaard and Nietzsche, and his philosophy must therefore be seen in the context of Continental European philosophy. In the *Tractatus Logico-Philosophicus* (Wittgenstein 1961 [first published 1921]) Wittgenstein advocates pure logical and pure empirical science, but also deals with the question of what can be shown but not said and the paradoxes of communicating anti-metaphysical positions. The structure of reality and language are seen as the same, in a way which is logocentric from Derrida's point of view, but which does not make any attempt to bring the structure into presence except in the way that the *Tractatus* is composed and in the style of its lapidiary propositions. This is Derrida's territory. The later Wittgenstein of the *Philosophical Investigations* himself acknowledges metaphysical aspects of the *Tractatus*. The alternative is still rooted in the *Tractatus*, the assumption that the structure of reality is described in describing the structure of language. The structure becomes complicated and ramified, so that it is no longer a unified architectural monument, through an emphasis on perspectives, evaluations and differences within language in its different language games which provide context for words and the plurality of meanings they contain. As with the *Tractatus* the philosophy is partly communicated by style and a fragmentation of the text into short aphoristic passages.

OF GRAMMATOLOGY: EXERGUE

1. The one who will shine in the science of writing will shine like the sun. A scribe (*EP*, p. 87).
   O Samas (sun-god), by your light you scan the totality of lands as if they were cuneiform signs (ibid.).
2. These three ways of writing correspond almost exactly to three different stages according to which one can consider men gathered into a nation. The depicting of objects is appropriate to a savage people; signs of words and of propositions, to a barbaric people; and the alphabet to civilized people. J.-J. Rousseau, *Essai sur l'origine des langues*.
3. Alphabetic script is in itself and for itself the most intelligent. Hegel, *Enzyklopädie*.

This triple exergue is intended not only to focus attention on the *ethnocentrism* which, everywhere and always, had controlled the concept of writing. Nor merely to focus attention on what I shall call *logocentrism*: the metaphysics of phonetic writing (for example, of the alphabet) which was fundamentally—for enigmatic yet essential reasons that are inaccessible to a simple historical relativism—nothing but the most original and powerful ethnocentrism, in the process of imposing itself upon the world, controlling in one and the same *order*:

1. *the concept of writing* in a world where the phoneticization of writing must dissimulate its own history as it is produced;

2. *the history of* (the only) *metaphysics*, which has, in spite of all differences, not only from Plato to Hegel (even including Leibniz) but also,

beyond these apparent limits, from the pre-Socratics to Heidegger, always assigned the origin of truth in general to the logos: the history of truth, of the truth of truth, has always been—except for a metaphysical diversion that we shall have to explain—the debasement of writing, and its repression outside "full" speech.

3. *the concept of science* or the scientificity of science—what has always been determined as *logic*—a concept that has always been a philosophical concept, even if the practice of science has constantly challenged its imperialism of the logos, by invoking, for example, from the beginning and ever increasingly, nonphonetic writing. No doubt this subversion has always been contained within a system of direct address [*système allocutoire*] which gave birth to the project of science and to the conventions of all nonphonetic characteristics. It could not have been otherwise. Nonetheless, it is a peculiarity of our epoch that, at the moment when the phoneticization of writing—the historical origin and structural possibility of philosophy as of science, the condition of the *epistémè*—begins to lay hold on world culture, science, in its advancements, can no longer be satisfied with it. This inadequation had always already begun to make its presence felt. But today something lets it appear as such, allows it a kind of takeover without our being able to translate this novelty into clear cut notions of mutation, explicitation, accumulation, revolution, or tradition. These values belong no doubt to the system whose dislocation is today presented as such, they describe the styles of an historical movement which was meaningful—like the concept of history itself—only within a logocentric epoch.

By alluding to a science of writing reined in by metaphor, metaphysics, theology, this exergue must not only announce that the science of writing—*grammatology*—shows signs of liberation all over the world, as a result of decisive efforts. These efforts are necessarily discreet, dispersed, almost imperceptible; that is a quality of their meaning and of the milieu within which they produce their operation. I would like to suggest above all that, however fecund and necessary the undertaking might be, and even if, given the most favorable hypothesis, it did overcome all technical epistemological obstacles as well as all the theological and metaphysical impediments that have limited it hitherto, such a science of writing runs the risk of never being established as such and with that name. Of never being able to define the unity of its project or its object. Of not being able either to write its discourse on method or to describe the limits of its field. For essential reasons: the unity of all that allows itself to be attempted today through the most diverse concepts of science and of writing, is, in principle, more or less covertly yet always, determined by an historico-metaphysical epoch of which we merely glimpse the *closure*. I do not say the *end*. The idea of science and the idea of writing—therefore also of the science of writing—is meaningful for us only in terms of an origin and within a world to which a certain concept of the sign (later I shall call it *the* concept of sign) and a certain concept of the relationships between speech and writing, have *already* been assigned. A most determined relationship, in spite of its privilege, its necessity, and the field of vision that it has controlled for a few millennia, especially in the West, to the point of being now able to produce its own dislocation and itself proclaim its limits.

Perhaps patient meditation and painstaking investigation on and around what is still provisionally called writing, far from falling short of a science writing or of hastily dismissing it by some obscurantist reaction, letting it rather develop its positivity as far as possible, are the wanderings of a way of thinking that is faithful and attentive to the ineluctable world of the future which proclaims itself at present, beyond the closure of knowledge.

The future can only be anticipated in the form of an absolute danger. It is that which breaks absolutely with constituted normality and can only be proclaimed, *presented*, as a sort of monstrosity. For that future world and for that within it which will have put into question the values of sign, word, and writing, for that which guides our future anterior, there is as yet no exergue.

The end of the book and the beginning of writing

Socrates, he who does not write—Nietzsche[1]

However the topic is considered, the *problem of language* has never been simply one problem among others. But never as much as at present has it invaded, *as such*, the global horizon of the most diverse researches and the most heterogeneous discourses, diverse and heterogeneous in their intention, method, and ideology. The devaluation of the word "language" itself, and how, in the very hold it has upon us, it betrays a loose vocabulary, the temptation of a cheap seduction, the passive yielding to fashion, the consciousness of the avant-garde, in other words—ignorance—are evidences of this effect. This inflation of the sign "language" is the inflation of the sign itself, absolute inflation, inflation itself. Yet, by one of its aspects or shadows, it is itself still a sign: this crisis is also a symptom. It indicates, as if in spite of itself, that a historico-metaphysical epoch *must* finally determine as language the totality of its problematic horizon. It must do so not only because all that desire had wished to wrest from the play of language finds itself recaptured within that play but also because, for the same reason, language itself is menaced in its very life, helpless, adrift in the threat of limitlessness, brought back to its own finitude at the very moment when its limits seem to disappear, when it ceases to be self-assured, contained, and *guaranteed* by the infinite signified which seemed to exceed it.

The program

By a slow movement whose necessity is hardly perceptible, everything that for at least some twenty centuries tended toward and finally succeeded in being gathered under the name of language is beginning to let itself be transferred to, or at least summarized under, the name of writing. By a hardly perceptible necessity, it seems as though the concept of writing—no longer indicating a particular, derivative, auxiliary form of language in general (whether understood as communication, relation, expression, signification, constitution of meaning or thought, etc.), no longer designating the exterior surface, the insubstantial double of a major signifier, *the signifier of the signifier*—is beginning to go beyond the extension of language. In all senses of the word, writing thus *comprehends* language. Not that the word "writing" has ceased to designate the signifier of the signifier, but it appears, strange as it may seem, that "signifier of the signifier" no longer defines accidental doubling and fallen secondarity. "Signifier of the signifier" describes on the contrary the movement of language: in its origin, to be sure, but one can already suspect that an origin whose structure can be expressed as "signifier of the signifier" conceals and erases itself in its own production. There the signified always already functions as a signifier. The secondarity that it seemed possible to ascribe to writing alone affects all signifieds in general; affects them always already, the moment they *enter the game*. There is not a single signified that escapes, even if recaptured, the play of signifying references that constitute language. The advent of writing is the advent of this play; today such a play is coming into its own, effacing the limit starting from which one had thought to regulate the circulation of signs, drawing along with it all the reassuring signifieds, reducing all the strongholds, all the out-of-bounds shelters that watched over the field of language. This, strictly speaking, amounts to destroying the concept of "sign" and its entire logic. Undoubtedly it is not by chance that this *overwhelming* supervenes at the moment when the extension of the concept of language effaces all its limits. We shall see that this overwhelming and this effacement have the same meaning, are one and the same phenomenon. It is as if the Western concept of language (in terms

of what, beyond its plurivocity and beyond the ⸱
opposition of speech [*parole*] and language [*langue*],
to phonematic or glossematic production, to lan⸠
hearing, to sound and breadth, to speech) were rev
guise or disguise of a primary writing:[1] more funda
which, before this conversion, passed for the simple
the spoken word" (Rousseau). Either writing was never ⸱
ment," or it is urgently necessary to construct a ne⸢   ⸣the
"supplement." It is this urgency which will guide us furt..er in reading
Rousseau.

These disguises are not historical contingencies that one might admire
or regret. Their movement was absolutely necessary, with a necessity
which cannot be judged by any other tribunal. The privilege of the *phonè*
does not depend upon a choice that could have been avoided. It
responds to a moment of *economy* (let us say of the "life" of "history" or
of "being as self-relationship"). The system of "hearing (understanding)-
oneself-speak" through the phonic substance—which *presents itself* as the
nonexterior, nonmundane, therefore nonempirical or noncontingent
signifier—has necessarily dominated the history of the world during an
entire epoch, and has even produced the idea of the world, the idea of
world-origin, that arises from the difference between the worldly and the
non-worldly, the outside and the inside, ideality and nonideality,
universal and nonuniversal, transcendental and empirical, etc.

With an irregular and essentially precarious success, this movement
would apparently have tended, as toward its *telos*, to confine writing to a
secondary and instrumental function: translator of a full speech that was
fully *present* (present to itself, to its signified, to the other, the very
condition of the theme of presence in general), technics in the service of
language, *spokesman*, interpreter of an originary speech itself shielded
from interpretation.

Technics in the service of language: I am not invoking a general
essence of technics which would be already familiar to us and would help
us in *understanding* the narrow and historically determined concept of
writing as an example. I believe on the contrary that a certain sort of
question about the meaning and origin of writing precedes, or at least
merges with, a certain type of question about the meaning and origin of
technics. That is why the notion of technique can never simply clarify
the notion of writing.

It is therefore as if what we call language could have been in its origin
and in its end only a moment, an essential but determined mode, a
phenomenon, an aspect, a species of writing. And as if it had succeeded
in making us forget this, and *in wilfully misleading us*, only in the course of

nture: as that adventure itself. All in all a short enough adventure. ...erges with the history that has associated technics and logocentric metaphysics for nearly three millennia. And it now seems to be approaching what is really its own *exhaustion;* under the circumstances—and this is no more than one example among others—of this death of the civilization of the book, of which so much is said and which manifests itself particularly through a convulsive proliferation of libraries. All appearances to the contrary, this death of the book undoubtedly announces (and in a certain sense always has announced) nothing but a death of speech (of a *so-called* full speech) and a new mutation in the history of writing, in history as writing. Announces it at a distance of a few centuries. It is on that scale that we must reckon it here, being careful not to neglect the quality of a very heterogeneous historical duration: the acceleration is such, and such its qualitative meaning, that one would be equally wrong in making a careful evaluation according to past rhythms. "Death of speech" is of course a metaphor here: before we speak of disappearance, we must think of a new situation for speech, of its subordination within a structure of which it will no longer be the archon.

To affirm in this way that the concept of writing exceeds and comprehends that of language, presupposes of course a certain definition of language and of writing. If we do not attempt to justify it, we shall be giving in to the movement of inflation that we have just mentioned, which has also taken over the word "writing," and that not fortuitously. For some time now, as a matter of fact, here and there, by a gesture and for motives that are profoundly necessary, whose degradation is easier to denounce than it is to disclose their origin, one says "language" for action, movement, thought, reflection, consciousness, unconsciousness, experience, affectivity, etc. Now we tend to say "writing" for all that and more: to designate not only the physical gestures of literal pictographic or ideographic inscription, but also the totality of what makes it possible; and also, beyond the signifying face, the signified face itself. And thus we say "writing" for all that gives rise to an inscription in general, whether it is literal or not and even if what it distributes in space is alien to the order of the voice: cinematography, choreography, of course, but also pictorial, musical, sculptural "writing." One might also speak of athletic writing, and with even greater certainty of military or political writing in view of the techniques that govern those domains today. All this to describe not only the system of notation secondarily connected with these activities but the essence and the content of these activities themselves. It is also in this sense that the contemporary biologist speaks of writing and *pro-gram* in relation to the most elementary processes of information within the living cell. And, finally, whether it has essential limits or not, the entire field covered by the cybernetic *program* will be the field of writing. If the theory of cybernetics is by itself to oust all metaphysical concepts—including the concepts of soul, of life, of value, of choice, of memory—which until recently served to separate the machine from man, it must conserve the notion of writing, trace, *grammè* [written mark], or grapheme, until its own historico-metaphysical character is also exposed. Even before being determined as human (with all the distinctive characteristics that have always been attributed to man and the entire system of significations that they imply) or nonhuman, the *grammè*—or the grapheme—would thus name the element. An element without simplicity. An element, whether it is understood as the medium or as the irreducible atom, of the arche-synthesis in general, of what one must forbid oneself to define within the system of oppositions of metaphysics, of what consequently one should not even call *experience* in general, that is to say the origin of *meaning* in general.

This situation has always already been announced. Why is it today in the process of making itself known *as such* and *after the fact*? This question would call forth an interminable analysis. Let us simply choose some points of departure in order to introduce the limited remarks to which I shall confine myself. I have already alluded to *theoretical* mathematics; its writing—whether understood as a sensible *graphie* [manner of writing] (and that already presupposes an identity, therefore an ideality, of its form, which in principle renders absurd the so easily admitted notion of the "sensible signifier"), or understood as the ideal synthesis of signifieds or a trace operative on another level, or whether it is understood, more profoundly, as the *passage* of the one to the other—has never been absolutely linked with a phonetic production. Within cultures practicing so-called phonetic writing, mathematics is not just an enclave. That is mentioned by all historians of writing; they recall at the same time the imperfections of alphabetic writing, which passed for so long as the most convenient and "the most intelligent" writing. This enclave is also the place where the practice of scientific language challenges intrinsically and with increasing profundity the ideal of phonetic writing and all its implicit metaphysics (metaphysics *itself*, particularly, that is, the philosophical idea of the *epistémè*; also of *istoria* a concept profoundly related to it in spite of the dissociation or opposition which has distinguished one from the other during one phase of their common progress. History and knowledge, *istoria* and *epistémè* have always been determined (and not only etymologically or philosophically) as detours *for the purpose of* the reappropriation of presence.

But beyond theoretical mathematics, the development of the *practical methods* of information retrieval extends the possibilities of the "message" vastly to the point where it is no longer the "written" translation of a language, the transporting of a signified which could remain spoken in its integrity. It goes hand in hand with an extension of phonography and of all the means of conserving the spoken language, of making it function without the presence of the speaking subject. This development, coupled with that of anthropology and of the history of writing, teaches us that phonetic writing, the medium of the great metaphysical, scientific, technical, and economic adventure of the West, is limited in space and time and limits itself even as it is in the process of imposing its laws upon the cultural areas that had escaped it. But this nonfortuitous conjunction of cybernetics and the "human sciences" of writing leads to a more profound reversal.

The signifier and truth

The "rationality"—but perhaps that word should be abandoned for reasons that will appear at the end of this sentence—which governs a writing thus enlarged and radicalized, no longer issues from a logos. Further, it inaugurates the destruction, not the demolition but the de-sedimentation, the de-construction, of all the significations that have their source in that of the logos. Particularly the signification of *truth*. All the metaphysical determinations of truth, and even the one beyond metaphysical onto-theology that Heidegger reminds us of, are more or less immediately inseparable from the instance of the logos, or of a reason thought within the lineage of the logos, in whatever sense it is understood: in the pre-Socratic or the philosophical sense, in the sense of God's infinite understanding or in the anthropological sense, in the pre-Hegelian or the post-Hegelian sense. Within this logos, the original and essential link to the *phonè* has never been broken. It would be easy to demonstrate this and I shall attempt such a demonstration later. As has been more or less implicitly determined, the essence of the *phonè* would be immediately proximate to that which within "thought" as logos relates to "meaning," produces it, receives it, speaks it, "composes" it. If, for Aristotle, for example, "spoken words (ta en tē phonē) are the symbols of mental experience (pathēmata tes psychēs) and written words are the symbols of spoken words" (*De interpretatione*, 1, 16a 3) it is because the voice, producer of *the first symbols*, has a relationship of essential and immediate proximity with the mind. Producer of the first signifier, it is not just a simple signifier among others. It signifies "mental experiences" which themselves reflect or mirror things by natural resemblance.

Between being and mind, things and feelings, there would be a relationship of translation or natural signification; between mind and logos, a relationship of conventional symbolization. And the *first* convention, which would relate immediately to the order of natural and universal signification, would be produced as spoken language. Written language would establish the conventions, interlinking other conventions with them.

> Just as all men have not the same writing so all men have not the same speech sounds, but mental experiences, of which these are the *primary symbols* (*semeîa prótos*), are the same for all, as also are those things of which our experiences are the images (*De interpretatione*, 1, 16a. Italics added).

The feelings of the mind, expressing things naturally, constitute a sort of universal language which can then efface itself. It is the stage of transparence. Aristotle can sometimes omit it without risk. In every case, the voice is closest to the signified, whether it is determined strictly as sense (thought or lived) or more loosely as thing. All signifiers, and first and foremost the written signifier, are derivative with regard to what would wed the voice indissolubly to the mind or to the thought of the signified sense, indeed to the thing itself (whether it is done in the Aristotelian manner that we have just indicated or in the manner of medieval theology, determining the *res* as a thing created from its *eidos*, from its sense thought in the logos or in the infinite understanding of God). The written signifier is always technical and representative. It has no constitutive meaning. This derivation is the very origin of the notion of the "signifier." The notion of the sign always implies within itself the distinction between signifier and signified, even if, as Saussure argues, they are distinguished simply as the two faces of one and the same leaf. This notion remains therefore within the heritage of that logocentrism which is also a phonocentrism: absolute proximity of voice and being, of voice and the meaning of being, of voice and the ideality of meaning. Hegel demonstrates very clearly the strange privilege of sound in idealization, the production of the concept and the self-presence of the subject.

> This ideal motion, in which through the sound what is as it were the simple subjectivity [*Subjektivität*], the soul of the material thing expresses itself, the ear receives also in a theoretical [*theoretisch*] way, just as the eye shape and colour, thus allowing the interiority of the object to become interiority itself [*läßt dadurch das Innere der Gegenstände für das Innere selbst werden*] (*Esthétique*, III. I

tr. fr. p. 16).[2] . . . The ear, on the contrary, perceives [*vernimmt*] the result of that interior vibration of material substance without placing itself in a practical relation toward the objects, a result by means of which it is no longer the material form [*Gestalt*] in its repose, but the first, more ideal activity of the soul itself which is manifested [*zum Vorschein kommt*] (p. 296).[3]

What is said of sound in general is a fortiori valid for the *phonè* by which, by virtue of hearing (understanding)-oneself-speak—an indissociable system—the subject affects itself and is related to itself in the element of ideality.

We already have a foreboding that phonocentrism merges with the historical determination of the meaning of being in general as *presence*, with all the subdeterminations which depend on this general form and which organize within it their system and their historical sequence (presence of the thing to the sight as *eidos*, presence as substance/essence/existence [*ousia*], temporal presence as point [*stigmè*] of the now or of the moment [*nun*], the self-presence of the cogito, consciousness, subjectivity, the co-presence of the other and of the self, intersubjectivity as the intentional phenomenon of the ego, and so forth). Logocentrism would thus support the determination of the being of the entity as presence. To the extent that such a logocentrism is not totally absent from Heidegger's thought, perhaps it still holds that thought within the epoch of onto-theology, within the philosophy of presence, that is to say within philosophy *itself*. This would perhaps mean that one does not leave the epoch whose closure one can outline. The movements of belonging or not belonging to the epoch are too subtle, the illusions in that regard are too easy, for us to make a definite judgment.

The epoch of the logos thus debases writing considered as mediation of mediation and as a fall into the exteriority of meaning. To this epoch belongs the difference between signified and signifier, or at least the strange separation of their "parallelism," and the exteriority, however extenuated, of the one to the other. This appurtenance is organized and hierarchized in a history. The difference between signified and signifier belongs in a profound and implicit way to the totality of the great epoch covered by the history of metaphysics, and in a more explicit and more systematically articulated way to the narrower epoch of Christian creationism and infinitism when these appropriate the resources of Greek conceptuality. This appurtenance is essential and irreducible; one cannot retain the convenience or the "scientific truth" of the Stoic and later medieval opposition between *signans* and *signatum* without also bringing with it all its metaphysico-theological roots. To these roots adheres not only the distinction between the sensible and the intelligible—already a great deal—with all that it controls, namely, metaphysics in its totality. And this distinction is generally accepted as self-evident by the most careful linguists and semiologists, even by those who believe that the scientificity of their work begins where metaphysics ends. Thus, for example:

> As modern structural thought has clearly realized, language is a system of signs and linguistics is part and parcel of the science of signs, or semiotics (Saussure's *sémiologie*). The mediaeval definition of sign—"*aliquid stat pro aliquo*" has been resurrected and put forward as still valid and productive. Thus the constitutive mark of any sign in general and of any linguistic sign in particular is its twofold character: every linguistic unit is bipartite and involves both aspects—one sensible and the other intelligible, or in other words, both the *signans* "signifier" (Saussure's *signifiant*) and the *signatum* "signified" (*signifié*). These two constituents of a linguistic sign (and of sign in general) necessarily suppose and require each other.

But to these metaphysico-theological roots many other hidden sediments cling. The semiological or, more specifically, linguistic "science" cannot therefore hold on to the difference between signifier and signified—the very idea of the sign—without the difference between sensible and intelligible, certainly, but also not without retaining, more profoundly and more implicitly, and by the same token the reference to a signified able to "take place" in its intelligibility, before its "fall," before any expulsion into the exteriority of the sensible here below. As the face of pure intelligibility, it refers to an absolute logos to which it is immediately united. This absolute logos was an infinite creative subjectivity in medieval theology: the intelligible face of the sign remains turned toward the word and the face of God.

Of course, it is not a question of "rejecting" these notions; they are necessary and, at least at present, nothing is conceivable for us without them. It is a question at first of demonstrating the systematic and historical solidarity of the concepts and gestures of thought that one often believes can be innocently separated. The sign and divinity have the same place and time of birth. The age of the sign is essentially theological. Perhaps it will never *end*. Its historical *closure* is, however, outlined.

Since these concepts are indispensable for unsettling the heritage to which they belong, we should be even less prone to renounce them. Within the closure, by an oblique and always perilous movement, constantly risking falling back within what is being deconstructed, it is necessary to surround the critical concepts with a careful and thorough discourse—to mark the conditions, the medium, and the limits of their effectiveness and to designate rigorously their intimate relationship to the machine whose deconstruction they permit; and, in the same process, designate the crevice through which the yet unnameable glimmer beyond the closure can be glimpsed. The concept of the sign is here exemplary. We have just marked its metaphysical appurtenance. We know, however, that the thematics of the sign have been for about a century the agonized labor of a tradition that professed to withdraw meaning, truth, presence, being, etc., from the movement of signification. Treating as suspect, as I just have, the difference between signified and signifier, or the idea of the sign in general, I must state explicitly that it is not a question of doing so in terms of the instance of the present truth, anterior, exterior or superior to the sign, or in terms of the place of the effaced difference. Quite the contrary. We are disturbed by that which, in the concept of the sign—which has never existed or functioned outside the history of (the) philosophy (of presence)—remains systematically and genealogically determined by that history. It is there that the concept and above all the work of deconstruction, its "style," remain by nature exposed to misunderstanding and nonrecognition.

The exteriority of the signifier is the exteriority of writing in general, and I shall try to show later that there is no linguistic sign before writing. Without that exteriority, the very idea of the sign falls into decay. Since our entire world and language would collapse with it, and since its evidence and its value keep, to a certain point of derivation, an indestructible solidity, it would be silly to conclude from its placement within an epoch that it is necessary to "move on to something else," to dispose of the sign, of the term and the notion. For a proper understanding of the gesture that we are sketching here, one must understand the expressions "epoch," "closure of an epoch," "historical genealogy" in a new way; and must first remove them from all relativism.

Thus, within this epoch, reading and writing, the production or interpretation of signs, the text in general as fabric of signs, allow themselves to be confined within secondariness. They are preceded by a truth, or a meaning already constituted by and within the element of the logos. Even when the thing, the "referent," is not immediately related to the logos of a creator God where it began by being the spoken/thought sense, the signified has at any rate an immediate relationship with the logos in general (finite or infinite), and a mediated one with the signifier, that is to say with the exteriority of writing. When it seems to go otherwise, it is because a metaphoric mediation has insinuated itself into the relationship and has simulated immediacy; the writing of truth in the soul, opposed by *Phaedrus* (278a) to bad writing (writing in the "literal" [*propre*] and ordinary sense, "sensible" writing, "in space"), the book of Nature and God's writing, especially in the Middle Ages; all that functions as *metaphor* in these discourses confirms the privilege of the logos and founds the "literal" meaning then given to writing: a sign signifying a signifier itself signifying an eternal verity, eternally thought and spoken in the proximity of a present logos. The paradox to which attention must be paid is this: natural and universal writing, intelligible and nontemporal writing, is thus named by metaphor. A writing that is sensible, finite, and so on, is designated as writing in the literal sense; it is thus thought on the side of culture, technique, and artifice; a human procedure, the ruse of a being accidentally incarnated or of a finite creature. Of course, this metaphor remains enigmatic and refers to a "literal" meaning of writing as the first metaphor. This "literal" meaning is yet unthought by the adherents of this discourse. It is not, therefore, a matter of inverting the literal meaning and the figurative meaning but of determining the "literal" meaning of writing as metaphoricity itself.

In "The Symbolism of the Book," that excellent chapter of *European Literature and the Latin Middle Ages*, E. R. Curtius describes with great wealth of examples the evolution that led from the *Phaedrus* to Calderon, until it seemed to be "precisely the reverse" (tr. fr. p. 372)[4] by the "newly attained position of the book" (p. 374) [p. 306]. But it seems that this modification, however important in fact it might be, conceals a fundamental continuity. As was the case with the Platonic writing of the truth in the soul, in the Middle Ages too it is a writing understood in the metaphoric sense, that is to say a *natural*, eternal, and universal writing, the system of signified truth, which is recognized in its dignity. As in the *Phaedrus*, a certain fallen writing continues to be opposed to it. There remains to be written a history of this metaphor, a metaphor that systematically contrasts divine or natural writing and the human and laborious, finite and artificial inscription. It remains to articulate rigorously the stages of that history, as marked by the quotations below, and to follow the theme of God's book (nature or law, indeed natural law) through all its modifications.

> Rabbi Eliezer said: "If all the seas were of ink, and all ponds planted with reeds, if the sky and the earth were parchments and if all human beings practised the art of writing—they would not exhaust the Torah I have learned, just as the Torah itself would not be diminished any more than is the sea by the water removed by a paint brush dipped in it."

Galileo: "It [the book of Nature] is written in a mathematical language."[5]

Descartes: "to read in the great book of Nature . . ."[6]

Demea, in the name of natural religion, in the *Dialogues*, . . . of Hume: "And this volume of nature contains a great and inexplicable riddle, more than any intelligible discourse or reasoning."[7]

Bonnet: "It would seem more philosophical to me to presume that our earth is a book that God has given to intelligences far superior to ours to read, and where they study in depth the infinitely multiplied and varied characters of His adorable wisdom."

G. H. von Schubert: "This language made of images and hieroglyphs, which supreme Wisdom uses in all its revelations to humanity—which is found in the inferior [*nieder*] language of poetry—and which, in the most inferior and imperfect way [*auf der allerniedrigsten und unvollkommensten*], is more like the metaphorical expression of the dream than the prose of wakefulness, . . . we may wonder if this language is not the true and wakeful language of the superior regions. If, when we consider ourselves awakened, we are not plunged in a millennial slumber, or at least in the echo of its dreams, where we only perceive a few isolated and obscure words of God's language, as a sleeper perceives the conversation of the people around him."[8]

Jaspers: "The world is the manuscript of an other, inaccessible to a universal reading, which only existence deciphers."[9]

Above all, the profound differences distinguishing all these treatments of the same metaphor must not be ignored. In the history of this treatment, the most decisive separation appears at the moment when, at the same time as the science of nature, the determination of absolute presence is constituted as self-presence, as subjectivity. It is the moment of the great rationalisms of the seventeenth century. From then on, the condemnation of fallen and finite writing will take another form, within which we still live: it is non-self-presence that will be denounced. Thus the exemplariness of the "Rousseauist" moment, which we shall deal with later, begins to be explained. Rousseau repeats the Platonic gesture by referring to another model of presence: self-presence in the senses, in the sensible cogito, which simultaneously carries in itself the inscription of divine law. On the one hand, *representative*, fallen, secondary, instituted writing, writing in the literal and strict sense, is condemned in *The Essay on the Origin of Languages* (it "enervates" speech; to "judge genius" from books is like "painting a man's portrait from his corpse," etc.). Writing in the common sense is the dead letter, it is the carrier of death. It exhausts life. On the other hand, on the other face of the same proposition, writing in the metaphoric sense, natural, divine, and living writing, is venerated; it is equal in dignity to the origin of value, to the voice of conscience as divine law, to the heart, to sentiment, and so forth.

> The Bible is the most sublime of all books, . . . but it is after all a book. . . . It is not at all in a few sparse pages that one should look for God's law, but in the human heart where His hand deigned to write (*Lettre à Vernes*).[10]
>
> If the natural law had been written only in the human reason, it would be little capable of directing most of our actions. But it is also engraved in the heart of man in ineffacable characters. . . . There it cries to him (*L'état de guerre.*)[11]

Natural writing is immediately united to the voice and to breath. Its nature is not grammatological but pneumatological. It is hieratic, very close to the interior holy voice of the *Profession of Faith*, to the voice one hears upon retreating into oneself: full and truthful presence of the divine voice to our inner sense: "The more I retreat into myself, the more I consult myself, the more plainly do I read these words written in my soul: be just and you will be happy. . . . I do not derive these rules from the principles of the higher philosophy, I find them in the depths of my heart written by nature in characters which nothing can efface."[12]

There is much to say about the fact that the native unity of the voice and writing is *prescriptive*. Arche-speech is writing because it is a law. A natural law. The beginning word is understood, in the intimacy of self-presence, as the voice of the other and as commandment.

There is therefore a good and a bad writing: the good and natural is the divine inscription in the heart and the soul; the perverse and artful is technique, exiled in the exteriority of the body. A modification well within the Platonic diagram: writing of the soul and of the body, writing of the interior and of the exterior, writing of conscience and of the passions, as there is a voice of the soul and a voice of the body. "Conscience is the voice of the soul, the passions are the voice of the body" [p. 249]. One must constantly go back toward the "voice of nature," the "holy voice of attire," that merges with the divine inscription and prescription; one must encounter oneself within it, enter into a dialogue within its signs, speak and respond to oneself in its pages.

> It was as if nature had spread out all her magnificence in front of our eyes to offer its text for our consideration. . . . I have therefore closed all the books. Only one is open to all eyes. It is the

> book of Nature. In this great and sublime took I learn to serve and
> adore its author.

The good writing has therefore always been *comprehended*. Comprehended
as that which had to be comprehended: within a nature or a natural
law, created or not, but first thought within an eternal presence.
Comprehended, therefore, within a totality, and enveloped in a volume
or a book. The idea of the book is the idea of a totality, finite or infinite,
of the signifier; this totality of the signifier cannot be a totality, unless a
totality constituted by the signified preexists it, supervises its inscriptions
and its signs, and is independent of it in its ideality. The idea of the
book, which always refers to a natural totality, is profoundly alien to
the sense of writing. It is the encyclopedic protection of theology and
of logocentrism against the disruption of writing, against its aphoristic
energy, and, as I shall specify later, against difference in general. If I
distinguish the text from the book, I shall say that the destruction of
the book, as it is now under way in all domains, denudes the surface of the
text. That necessary violence responds to a violence that was no less
necessary.

The written being/the being written

The reassuring evidence within which Western tradition had to organize
itself and must continue to live would therefore be as follows: the order
of the signified is never contemporary, is at best the subtly discrepant
inverse or parallel—discrepant by the time of a breath—from the order
of the signifier. And the sign must be the unity of a heterogeneity, since
the signified (sense or thing, noeme or reality) is not in itself a signifier,
a *trace*: in any case is not constituted in its sense by its relationship with
a possible trace. The formal essence of the signified is *presence*, and the
privilege of its proximity to the logos as *phonè* is the privilege of presence. This is the inevitable response as soon as one asks: "what is the
sign?," that is to say, when one submits the sign to the question of
essence, to the "ti esti." The "formal essence" of the sign can only be
determined in terms of presence. One cannot get around that response,
except by challenging the very form of the question and beginning to
think that the sign is that ill-named thing, the only one, that escapes the
instituting question of philosophy: "what is . . . ?"

Radicalizing the concepts of *interpretation, perspective, evaluation,
difference*, and all the "empiricist" or nonphilosophical motifs that have
constantly tormented philosophy throughout the history of the West,
and besides, have had nothing but the inevitable weakness of being

produced in the field of philosophy, Nietzsche, far from remaining *simply* (with Hegel and as Heidegger wished) *within* metaphysics, contributed a great deal to the liberation of the signifier from its dependence or derivation with respect to the logos and the related concept of truth or the primary signified, in whatever sense that is understood. Reading, and therefore writing, the text were for Nietzsche "originary" operations (I put that word within quotation marks for reasons to appear later) with regard to a sense that they do not first have to transcribe or discover, which would not therefore be a truth signified in the original element and presence of the logos, as *topos noetos*, divine understanding, or the structure of a priori necessity. To save Nietzsche from a reading of the Heideggerian type, it seems that we must above all not attempt to restore or make explicit a less naive "ontology," composed of profound ontological intuitions acceding to some originary truth, an entire fundamentality hidden under the appearance of an empiricist or metaphysical text. The virulence of Nietzschean thought could not be more completely misunderstood. On the contrary, one must *accentuate* the "naiveté" of a breakthrough which cannot attempt a step outside of metaphysics, which cannot *criticize* metaphysics radically without still utilizing in a certain way, in a certain type or a certain style of *text*, propositions that, read within the philosophic corpus, that is to say according to Nietzsche ill-read or unread, have always been and will always be "naivetés," incoherent signs of an absolute appurtenance. Therefore, rather that [sic] protect Nietzsche from the Heideggerian reading, we should perhaps offer him up to it completely, underwriting that interpretation without reserve; in a *certain way* and up to the point where, the content of the Nietzschean discourse being almost lost for the question of being, its form regains its absolute strangeness, where his text finally invokes a different type of reading, more faithful to his type of writing: Nietzsche has *written what* he has written. He has written that writing—and first of all his own—is not originarily subordinate to the logos and to truth. And that this subordination has *come into being* during an epoch whose meaning we must deconstruct. Now in this direction (but only in this direction, for read otherwise the Nietzschean demolition remains dogmatic and, like all reversals, a captive of that metaphysical edifice which it professes to overthrow. On that point and in that *order of reading*, the conclusions of Heidegger and Fink are irrefutable), Heideggerian thought would reinstate rather than destroy the instance of the logos and of the truth of being as "primum signatum:" the "transcendental" signified ("transcendental" in a certain sense, as in the Middle Ages the transcendental—*ens, unum, verum, bonum*—was said to be the "primum cognitum") implied by all categories or all determined significations, by all lexicons and all syntax, and therefore by all linguistic signifiers, though not to be identified simply with any one of those signifiers, allowing itself to be precomprehended through each of them, remaining irreducible to all the epochal determinations that it nonetheless makes possible, thus opening the history of the logos, yet itself being only through the logos; that is, *being nothing* before the logos and outside of it. The logos *of* being, "Thought obeying the Voice of Being," is the first and the last resource of the sign, of the difference between *signans* and *signatum*. There has to be a transcendental signified for the difference between signifier and signified to be somewhere absolute and irreducible. It is not by chance that the thought of being, as the thought of this transcendental signified, is manifested above all in the voice: in a language of words [*mots*]. The voice is *heard* (understood)— that undoubtedly is what is called conscience—closest to the self as the absolute effacement of the signifier: pure auto-affection that necessarily has the form of time and which does not borrow from outside of itself, in the world or in "reality," any accessory signifier, any substance of expression foreign to its own spontaneity. It is the unique experience of the signified producing itself spontaneously from within the self, and nevertheless, as signified concept, in the element of ideality or universality. The unworldly character of this substance of expression is constitutive of this ideality. This experience of the effacement of the signifier in the voice is not merely one illusion among many—since it is the condition of the very idea of truth—but I shall elsewhere show in what it does delude itself. This illusion is the history of truth and it cannot be dissipated so quickly. Within the closure of this experience, the word [*mot*] is lived as the elementary and undecomposable unity of the signified and the voice, of the concept and a transparent substance of expression. This experience is considered in its greatest purity—and at the same time in the condition of its possibility—as the experience of "being." The word "being," or at any rate the words designating the sense of being in different languages, is, with some others, an "originary word" (*"Urwort"*), the transcendental word assuring the possibility of being-word to all other words. As such, it is precomprehended in all language and—this is the opening of *Being and Time*—only this precomprehension would permit the opening of the question of the sense of being in general, beyond all regional ontologies and all metaphysics: a question that broaches philosophy (for example, in the *Sophist*) and lets itself be taken over by philosophy, a question that Heidegger repeats by submitting the history of metaphysics to it. Heidegger reminds us constantly that the sense of being is neither the word "being" nor the concept of being. But as that sense is nothing outside of language and the language of words, it is tied, if not to a particular word or to a particular system of language (concesso non dato), at least to the possibility of the word in general. And to the possibility of its irreducible simplicity. One could thus think that it remains only to choose between two possibilities. (1) Does a modern linguistics, a science of signification breaking the unity of the word and breaking with its alleged irreducibility, still have anything to do with "language?" Heidegger would probably doubt it. (2) Conversely, is not all that is profoundly meditated as the thought or the question of being enclosed within an old linguistics of the word which one practices here unknowingly? Unknowingly because such a linguistics, whether spontaneous or systematic, has always had to share the presuppositions of metaphysics. The two operate on the same grounds.

It goes without saying that the alternatives cannot be so simple.

On the one hand, if modern linguistics remains completely enclosed within a classical conceptuality, if especially it naively uses the word *being* and all that it presupposes, that which, within this linguistics, deconstructs the unity of the word in general can no longer, according to the model of the Heideggerian question, as it functions powerfully from the very opening of *Being and Time*, be circumscribed as ontic science or regional ontology. In as much as the question of being unites indissolubly with the precomprehension of the word *being*, without being reduced to it, the linguistics that works for the deconstruction of the constituted unity of that word has only, in fact or in principle, to have the question of being posed in order to define its field and the order of its dependence.

Not only is its field no longer simply ontic, but the limits of ontology that correspond to it no longer have anything regional about them. And can what I say here of linguistics, or at least of a certain work that may be undertaken within it and thanks to it, not be said of all research *in as much as and to the strict extent that* it would finally deconstitute the founding concept-words of ontology, of being in its privilege? Outside of linguistics, it is in psychoanalytic research that this breakthrough seems at present to have the greatest likelihood of being expanded.

Within the strictly limited space of this breakthrough, these "sciences" are no longer *dominated* by the questions of a transcendental phenomenology or a fundamental ontology, One may perhaps say, following the order of questions inaugurated by *Being and Time* and radicalizing the questions of Husserlian phenomenology, that this breakthrough does not belong to science itself, that what thus seems to be produced within an ontic field or within a regional ontology, does not belong to them by rights and leads back to the question of being itself.

Because it is indeed the *question* of being that Heidegger asks metaphysics. And with it the question of truth, of sense, of the logos. The incessant meditation upon that question does not restore confidence. On the contrary, it dislodges the confidence at its own depth, which, being a matter of the meaning of being, is more difficult than is often believed. In examining the state just before all determinations of being, destroying the securities of onto-theology, such a meditation contributes, quite as much as the most contemporary linguistics, to the dislocation of the unity of the sense of being, that is, in the last instance, the unity of the word.

It is thus that, after evoking the "voice of being," Heidegger recalls that it is silent, mute, insonorous, wordless, originarily *a-phonic* (*die Gewähr der lautlosen Stimme verborgener Quellen . . .*). The voice of the sources is not heard. A rupture between the originary meaning of being and the word, between meaning and the voice, between "the voice of being" and the "*phonè*," between "the call of being," and articulated sound; such a rupture, which at once confirms a fundamental metaphor, and renders it suspect by accentuating its metaphoric discrepancy, translates the ambiguity of the Heideggerian situation with respect to the metaphysics of presence and logocentrism. It is at once contained within and transgresses it. But it is impossible to separate the two. The very movement of transgression sometimes holds it back short of the limit. In opposition to what we suggested above, it must be remembered that, for Heidegger, the sense of being is never simply and rigorously a "signified." It is not by chance that that word is not used; that means that being escapes the movement of the sign, a proposition that can equally well be understood as a repetition of the classical tradition and as a caution with respect to a technical or metaphysical theory of signification. On the other hand, the sense of being is literally neither "primary," nor "fundamental," nor "transcendental," whether understood in the scholastic, Kantian, or Husserlian sense. The restoration of being as "transcending" the categories of the entity, the opening of the fundamental ontology, are nothing but necessary yet provisional moments. From *The Introduction to Metaphysics* onward, Heidegger renounces the project of and the word ontology. The necessary, originary, and irreducible dissimulation of the meaning of being, its occultation within the very blossoming forth of presence, that retreat without which there would be no history of being which was completely *history* and history of *being*, Heidegger's insistence on noting that being is produced as history only through the logos, and is nothing outside of it, the difference between being and the entity—all this clearly indicates that fundamentally nothing escapes the movement of the signifier and that, in the last instance, the difference between signified and signifier is *nothing*. This proposition of transgression not yet integrated into a careful discourse runs the risk of formulating regression itself. One must therefore go by way of the question of being as it is directed by Heidegger and by him alone, at and beyond onto-theology, in order to reach the rigorous thought of that strange nondifference and in order to determine it correctly. Heidegger occasionally reminds us that "being," as it is fixed in its general syntactic and lexicological forms within linguistics and Western philosophy, is not a primary and absolutely, irreducible signified, that it is still rooted in a system of languages and an historically determined "significance," although strangely privileged as the virtue of disclosure and dissimulation; particularly when he invites us to meditate on the "privilege" of the "third person singular of the present indicative" and the "infinitive." Western metaphysics, as the limitation of the sense of being within the field of presence, is produced as the domination of a linguistic form. To question the origin of that domination does not amount to hypostatizing a transcendental signified, but to a questioning of what constitutes our history and what produced transcendentality itself. Heidegger brings it up also when in *Zur Seinsfrage*, for the same reason, he lets the word "being" be read only if it is crossed out (*kreuzweise Durchstreichung*). That mark of deletion is not, however, a "merely negative symbol" (p. 31) [p. 83]. That deletion is the final writing of an epoch. Under its strokes the presence of a transcendental signified is effaced while still remaining legible. Is effaced while still remaining legible, is destroyed while making visible the very idea of the sign. In as much as it de-limits onto-theology, the metaphysics of presence and logocentrism, this last writing is also the first writing.

To come to recognize, not within but on the horizon of the Heideggerian paths, and yet in them, that the sense of being is not a transcendental or trans-epochal signified (even if it was always dissimulated within the epoch) but already, in a truly *unheard of* sense, a determined signifying trace, is to affirm that within the decisive concept of ontico-ontological difference, *all is not to be thought at one go*; entity and being, ontic and ontological, "ontico-ontological," are, in an original style, *derivative* with regard to difference; and with respect to what I shall later call *différance*, an economic concept designating the production of differing/deferring. The ontico-ontological difference and its ground (*Grund*) in the "transcendence of Dasein" (*Vom Wesen des Grundes* [Frankfurt am Main, 1955], p. 16 [p. 29]) are not absolutely originary. *Différance* by itself would be more "originary," but one would no longer be able to call it "origin" or "ground," those notions belonging essentially to the history of onto-theology, to the system functioning as the effacing of difference. It can, however, be thought of in the closest proximity to itself only on one condition: that one begins by determining it as the ontico-ontological difference before erasing that determination. The necessity of passing through that erased determination, the necessity of that *trick of writing* is irreducible. An unemphatic and difficult thought that, through much unperceived mediation, must carry the entire burden of our question, a question that I shall provisionally call *historial* [*historiale*]. It is with its help that I shall later be able to attempt to relate *différance* and writing.

The hesitation of these thoughts (here Nietzsche's and Heidegger's) is not an "incoherence": it is a trembling proper to all post-Hegelian attempts and to this passage between two epochs. The movements of deconstruction do not destroy structures from the outside. They are not possible and effective, nor can they take accurate aim, except by inhabiting those structures. Inhabiting them *in a certain way*, because one always inhabits, and all the more when one does not suspect it. Operating necessarily from the inside, borrowing all the strategic and economic resources of subversion from the old structure, borrowing them structurally, that is to say without being able to isolate their elements and atoms, the enterprise of deconstruction always in a certain way falls prey to its own work. This is what the person who has begun the same work in another area of the same habitation does not fail to point out with zeal. No exercise is more widespread today and one should be able to formalize its rules.

Hegel was already caught up in this game. *On the one hand*, he undoubtedly *summed up* the entire philosophy of the logos. He determined ontology as absolute logic; he assembled all the delimitations of philosophy as presence; he assigned to presence the eschatology of parousia, of the self-proximity of infinite subjectivity. And for the same reason he had to debase or subordinate writing. When he criticizes the Leibnizian characteristic, the formalism of the understanding, and mathematical symbolism, he makes the same gesture: denouncing the being-outside-of-itself of the logos in the sensible or the intellectual abstraction. Writing is that forgetting of the self, that exteriorization, the contrary of the interiorizing memory, of the *Erinnerung* that opens the history of the spirit. It is this that the *Phaedrus* said: writing is at once mnemotechnique and the power of forgetting. Naturally, the Hegelian critique of writing stops at the alphabet. As phonetic writing, the alphabet is at the same time more servile, more contemptible, more secondary ("alphabetic writing expresses *sounds* which are themselves signs. It consists therefore of the signs of signs ['*aus Zeichen der Zeichen*,'" *Enzyklopädie*, § 459])[13] but it is also the best writing, the mind's writing; its effacement before the voice, that in it which respects the ideal interiority of phonic signifiers, all that by which it sublimates space and sight, all that makes of it the writing of history, the writing, that is, of the infinite spirit relating to itself in its discourse and its culture:

> It follows that to learn to read and write an alphabetic writing should be regarded as a means to infinite culture (*unendliches Bildungsmittel*) that is not enough appreciated; because thus the mind, distancing itself from the concrete sense-perceptible, directs its attention on the more formal moment, the sonorous word and its abstract elements, and contributes essentially to the founding and purifying of the ground of interiority within the subject.

In that sense it is the *Aufhebung* of other writings, particularly of hieroglyphic script and of the Leibnizian characteristic that had been criticized previously through one and the same gesture. (*Aufhebung* is, more or less implicitly, the dominant concept of nearly all histories of writing, even today. It is *the* concept of history and of teleology.) In fact, Hegel continues: "Acquired habit later also suppresses the specificity of alphabetic writing, which consists in seeming to be, in the interest of sight, a detour [*Umweg*] through hearing to arrive at representations, and makes it into a hieroglyphic script for us, such that in using it, we do not need to have present to our consciousness the mediation of sounds."

It is on this condition that Hegel subscribes to the Leibnizian praise of nonphonetic writing. It can be produced by deaf mutes, Leibniz had said. Hegel:

> Beside the fact that, by the practice which transforms this alphabetic script into hieroglyphics, the aptitude for abstraction acquired through such an exercise *is conserved* [italics added], the reading of hieroglyphs is for itself a deaf reading and a mute writing (*ein taubes Lesen und ein stummes Schreiben*). What is audible or temporal, visible or spatial, has each its proper basis and in the first place they are of equal value; but in alphabetic script there is only *one* basis and that following a specific relation, namely, that the visible language is related only as a sign to the audible language; intelligence expresses itself immediately and unconditionally through speech (ibid.).

What writing itself, in its nonphonetic moment, betrays, is life. It menaces at once the breath, the spirit, and history as the spirit's relationship with itself. It is their end, their finitude, their paralysis. Cutting breath short, sterilizing or immobilizing spiritual creation in the repetition of the letter, in the commentary or the *exegesis*, confined in a narrow space, reserved for a minority, it is the principle of death and of difference in the becoming of being. It is to speech what China is to Europe: "It is only to the exegeticism of Chinese spiritual culture that their hieroglyphic writing is suited. This type of writing is, besides, the part reserved for a very small section of a people, the section that possesses the exclusive domain of spiritual culture. . . . A hieroglyphic script would require a philosophy as exegetical as Chinese culture generally is" (ibid.).

If the nonphonetic moment menaces the history and the life of the spirit as self-presence in the breath, it is because it menaces substantiality, that other metaphysical name of presence and of *ousia*. First in the form of the substantive. Nonphonetic writing breaks the noun apart. It describes relations and not appellations. The noun and the word, those unities of breath and concept, are effaced within pure writing. In that regard, Leibniz is as disturbing as the Chinese in Europe: "This situation, the analytic notation of representations in hieroglyphic script, which seduced Leibniz to the point of wrongly preferring this script to the alphabetic, rather contradicts the fundamental exigency of language in general, namely the noun. . . . All difference [*Abweichung*] in analysis would produce another formation of the written substantive."

The horizon of absolute knowledge is the effacement of writing in the logos, the retrieval of the trace in parousia, the reappropriation of difference, the accomplishment of what I have elsewhere called the *metaphysics of the proper* [*le propre*—self-possession, propriety, property, cleanliness].

Yet, all that Hegel thought within this horizon, all, that is, except eschatology, may be reread as a meditation on writing. Hegel is also the thinker of irreducible difference. He rehabilitated thought as the *memory productive* of signs. And he reintroduced, as I shall try to show elsewhere, the essential necessity of the written trace in a philosophical—that is to say Socratic—discourse that had always believed it possible to do without it; the last philosopher of the book and the first thinker of writing.

Notes

1 "Aus dem Gedankenkreise der Geburt der Tragödie," I.3. *Nietzsche Werke* (Leipzig, 1903), vol. 9, part 2, i, p. 66.
2 Georg Wilhelm Friedrich Hegel, *Werke*, Suhrkamp edition (Frankfurt am Main, 1970), vol. 14, p. 256; translated as *The Philosophy of Fine Art* by F. P. Osmaston (London, 1920), vol. 3, pp. 15–16.
3 Hegel, p. 134; Osmaston, p. 341.
4 Ernst Robert Curtius, "Das Buch als Symbol," *Europäische Literatur und lateinisches Mittelalter* (Bern, 1948), p. 307. French translation by Jean Brejoux (Paris, 1956): translated as *European Literature and the Latin Middle Ages*, by Willard R. Trask, Harper Torchbooks edition (New York, 1963), pp. 305, 306.

5 Quoted in Curtius, op. cit. (German), p. 326, (English), p. 324; Galileo's word is "philosophy" rather than "nature."
6 Ibid. (German) p. 324, (English) p. 322.
7 David Hume, *Dialogues Concerning Natural Religion*, ed. Norman Kemp Smith (Oxford, 1935), p. 193.
8 Gotthilf Heinrich von Schubert, *Die Symbolik des Traumes* (Leipzig, 1862), pp. 23–24.
9 Quoted in P. Ricoeur, *Gabriel Marcel et Karl Jaspers* (Paris, 1947), p. 45.
10 *Correspondance complète de Jean Jacques Rousseau*, ed. R. A. Leigh (Geneva, 1967), vol. V, pp. 65–66. The original reads "l' évangile" rather than "la Bible."
11 Rousseau, *Oeuvres complètes*, Pléiade edition, vol. III, p. 602.
12 Derrida's reference is *Emile*, Pléiade edition, vol. 4, pp. 589, 594. My reference is *Emile*, tr. Barbara Foxley (London, 1911), pp. 245, 249. Subsequent references to this translation are placed within brackets.
13 *Enzyklopädie der philosophischen Wissenschaften in Grundrisse*, Suhrkamp edition (Frankfurt am Main, 1970), pp. 273–76.

2 'THE PHARMAKON'

DISSEMINATION (DERRIDA 2004 [FIRST PUBLISHED 1972])

Translated by Barbara Johnson

Themes

Derrida discusses 'the *pharmakon*' in Plato's dialogue *Phaedrus*, with regard to Plato's criticism of writing as a means of communication in comparison with speech. In Derrida's argument, language contains cultural references and verbal patterns which interact in ways that cannot be reduced to the intentions of the author. We cannot decide which possible meanings and interpretations of the text belong to Plato's intentions and which are accidentally present. Textuality is constituted by differences between meanings and differences from differences, so that the text is absolutely heterogeneous within itself. The text is composed with the forces of difference that tend to annihilate the text. There is only textuality where there is difference between signs, and the necessity of difference threatens to destroy the unity and identity of the text. Derrida focuses discussion of these themes on Plato's use of the word 'pharmakon' in *Phaedrus* and other dialogues. In Ancient Greek 'pharmakon' refers both to a medical remedy and to a poison. These represent in some respects contradictory meanings: the thing that damages the body and the thing that heals the body. The contradictory meanings provide a particularly convenient example for Derrida of the contradictions that condition all language and all meaning. There is no possibility of communication in language without the possibility of contradiction. In the context of Plato's philosophy the contradictory meanings contained by 'pharmakon', bring out contradictory attitudes to

Socrates, particularly in the context of *The Laws* where Plato favours the punishment of magicians as a kind of 'pharmakon', which has resonance with regard to Socrates in the *Meno* and the *Symposium* as a kind of 'pharmakon' in his powers of argument. The interactions of cultural references and verbal patterns, which feature in the underlying equivocation about Socrates, are themselves embedded in the citational nature of language. Much of language contains clearly deliberate and explicit citations of phrases and passages in existing texts and tradition. In addition any use of words could be a citation, whether through hidden intentions of the author, unconscious memory, or pure accident. From Derrida's point of view, it is not important which of the three is the case as they are all aspects of the necessarily citational nature of language, and that is what is important.

Derrida looks at how Plato's philosophy rests on a series of metaphysical oppositions. Metaphysics itself can be defined as the thought that relies on absolute oppositions. In Plato these oppositions include: good and evil; true and false; essence and appearance; inside and outside. Derrida considers the determining opposition to be that of inside and outside. Metaphysics is what emphasises the internal, the inner, what belongs inside inner mental space as prior to the external, the outside and what belongs outside mental space. The value judgement of all oppositions rests on: what comes from inside me; and confirms my identity with myself as superior to what comes from outside me, and threatens my identity with myself. Plato's condemnation of writing depends on an opposition between: speech immediately derived from my inner thoughts and writing which has some origin in my inner thoughts, but becomes separated from them as an enduring physical trace of inscription. Writing is external to me, while speech is the product of the internal. Writing survives my own death and can have interpretations imposed on it which I will not be able to resist. For Derrida, inner consciousness is already conditioned by the possibility of death.

The problem here, for Plato, according to Derrida is that the purity of the internal cannot be maintained. Speech requires memory. Plato shows great suspicion of aids to memory discussed by the Sophists. But his own philosophy at some points explicitly allows for a form of recollection or reminiscence outside normal memory, when he suggests that knowledge comes from embedded memories of the forms of things. Although he stages his attack on writing as an attack on the Sophists, they had already made similar comments about writing themselves. In general there is no way of identifying a pure internal memory. Memory must be what comes from outside this moment, and is therefore external to my inner self at this moment. There is no memory without externality, and there is no consciousness without memory, therefore there is consciousness with externality within consciousness itself. The very notion of harming the inner self through writing, when the writing is taken as a 'pharmakon', presumes the possibility of external writing affecting the inside of the self, in which case the absolute opposition between the internal and the external is undermined. Writing rests on a repetition which denies the self-contained nature of consciousness at any one moment, and which shows that immediate unity to be impossible.

Context

Derrida's emphasis on inevitable contradiction in metaphysics seems at odds with the more logically orientated kinds of philosophy, since Derrida does not demand the elimination of contradiction. We are always caught in contradiction for Derrida, the point is to make these contradictions explicit. We can struggle with metaphysical assumptions, but we can never completely defeat since we just cannot avoid the abstraction nature of concepts, abstract systems of concepts in their necessary rules and differences between concepts defined as oppositions. The role of contradiction has precedents in the Continental European tradition. Kant conceived of reason as inherently prone to create contradictions, which can be eliminated but which must be encountered where reason explores reason itself without reference to knowledge of objects. That is the subject matter of the dialectical sections in Kant's three great critiques: *Critique of Pure Reason* (Kant 1998 [first published 1781]), *Critique of Practical Reason* (in Kant 1996 [first published 1788]), *Critique of the Power of Judgement* (Kant 2000 [first published 1790]). Hegel's philosophy deals with differences that become oppositions that are reconciled in the full dialectical grasp of a concept. Kierkegaard referred to philosophy as a passion for paradox, and expanded this in discussion of the 'dialectic of the absurd' and other forms of contradiction. Nietzsche thought that contradictions are only eliminated by rationalist metaphysics; in contrast a strong anti-metaphysical philosophy will grasp contradictions which exist in the nature of the universe as composed of conflicting forces.

This is not just an interest of Continental philosophers since Kant. In recent years some analytic philosophers have concerned themselves with contradiction as something that cannot always be eliminated. One philosopher, Graham Priest, has even established a position of 'dialetheism' which argues that contradictions cannot be eliminated. He has developed these positions with reference to Derrida in *Beyond the Limits of Thought* (Priest 2002 [first published 1995]) and 'Derrida and

Self-Reference' (Priest 1994). The position is very much a minority one in current philosophy on Priest's own account. Nevertheless his work is respected even by many who reject his claim, including the highly distinguished and influential analytic metaphysician David Lewis, who helped to get Priest's work published. Those who support Priest in advocating dialetheism of some kind include J. C. Beall, Edwin D. Meares, Jay Garfield, Frederick Kroon, Vann McGee and John Cogburn. Priest, and other supporters of dialetheism, are very orientated towards formal logic, philosophy of mathematics and formal semantics (logical work on meaning). Part of Priest's arguments depend on discussion of logical and mathematical paradoxes. The general starting point for all work on logical paradoxes is the 'lair paradox' which has the general form 'Everything I say is false' or 'This statement is false'. In both cases, if the statement is true then it is false, and if it is false it is true, because what it says of itself is that it is false. Priest also draws on paradoxes of infinity, which refer to the difficulty of establishing an absolute infinity. This sounds an odd problem to many but it is very easy to think of an infinite series of numbers, such as all odd numbers, rather than a larger infinite series which includes that series, such as all the positive numbers, which can itself be part of a larger series, or all rational numbers, and so on. Any infinite we can define always turns out to be 'transfinite' only, as there is always a larger infinite. Hegel had a version of this, which is the distinction between the 'Bad Infinite' and an absolute infinite. Priest deals with Hegel in his central work, *Beyond the Limits of Thought* (Priest 2002), along with Aristotle and Kant in the history of Western philosophy. He deals with paradoxes of infinity in modern mathematics and logical philosophy, and with East Asian philosophy. He also deals with Derrida in a respectful way as continuing the discussion of these problems.

The other obvious examples of analytic philosophers who think that contradictions cannot be eliminated are Nicholas Rescher and Robert Brandom in their co-authored work *The Logic of Inconsistency* (Rescher and Brandom 1979). What Rescher and Brandom argue is based on modal logic and possible worlds semantics. Modal logic is logic which includes operators for possibility and necessity as well as for true and false. Possible world semantics is the view that we can interpret any statement of possibility as a statement that is true in at least one possible world, while statements of necessity are statements that are true in all possible worlds. Possible worlds other than our own may be regarded as purely abstract constructs, but in David Lewis's case they may be regarded as real. In Rescher and Brandom's version of possible world semantics, if we can say something is true of an object in one world but not in another world then we have generated an inconsistency which cannot be eliminated.

An inconsistency is not the same as a contradiction, but it can lead to contraction. Both Rescher and Brandom are rooted in the Pragmatist tradition going back to Peirce, in Brandom's case this is taken in the direction of Hegel and Heidegger. Neither Brandom nor Rescher consider Derrida, but at least two philosophers have looked at Derrida's views on inconsistency and contradiction of meaning as implicitly rooted in modalism: Christopher Norris in *Language, Logic and Epistemology* (Norris 2004) and Frank Farrell in 'Iterability and Meaning' (Farrell 1988). We will return to this work in Part III on Consciousness.

Derrida's discussion of Plato includes the claim that Plato's own references to the 'pharmakon' undermine his own claims of its secondary ontological status, that is of its own non-Being. This repeats the problem that Plato himself acknowledged in *The Sophist*, that to say something about non-being, even to say it is not, is to give it being of some kind in contradiction to its non-Being. Derrida refers to this obliquely when he talks about difference in Plato and Saussure in *Of Grammatology* (Derrida 1997a: 52–53). This paradox of non-Being in Plato was very important for two of the key figures in the history of analytic philosophy: Bertrand Russell and W. V. O. Quine. In *Principles of Mathematics* (Russell 1992b [first published 1903]) Russell refers to Plato's paradox in the context of a discussion of classes in mathematics and empty classes, in the build up to Russell's own paradox of classes, which is essentially a version of the lair paradox. In his 1905 paper 'On Denoting' (in Russell 1992a), a paper of extreme influence, Russell brings up a version of Plato's paradox with regard to denoting phrases which appear to denote something that does not exist. Quine develops that aspect of Russell in another highly influential paper of 1948 'On What There Is' (in Quine 1980). Unlike Priest or Derrida, Russell and Quine are trying to eliminate contradictions as a threat to logical systems and to rationality in general. Nevertheless their approach leads us to recognise the tendency to produce contractions in language, so much so that they think ordinary language needs to be revised. If ordinary language is so prone to contradiction that it needs revision, they are not so far from Derrida in some assumptions. The subject matter of this paragraph has been discussed at greater length in 'Presence and Immediacy in Analysis and Deconstruction' (Stocker 2003).

DISSEMINATION: THE *PHARMAKON*

> This is the malady in them all for which law must find a *pharmakon*. Now it is a sound old adage that it is hard to fight against two enemies at once—even when they are enemies from opposite quarters. We see the truth of this in medicine and elsewhere.

Let us return to the text of Plato, assuming we have ever really left it. The word *pharmakon* is caught in a chain of significations. The play of that chain seems systematic. But the system here is not, simply, that of the intentions of an author who goes by the name of Plato. The system is not primarily that of what someone *meant-to-say* [*un vouloir-dire*]. Finely regulated communications are established, through the play of language, among diverse functions of the word and, within it, among diverse strata or regions of culture. These communications or corridors of meaning can sometimes be declared or clarified by Plato when he plays upon them "voluntarily," a word we put in quotation marks because what it designates, to content ourselves with remaining within the closure of these oppositions, is only a mode of "submission" to the necessities of a given "language." None of these concepts can translate the relation we are aiming at here. Then again, in other cases, Plato can *not* see the links, can leave them in the shadow or break them up. And yet these links go on working of themselves. In spite of him? thanks to him? in *his* text? *outside* his text? but then where? between his text and the language? for what reader? at what moment? To answer such questions in principle and in general will seem impossible; and that will give us the suspicion that there is some malformation in the question itself, in each of its concepts, in each of the oppositions it thus accredits. One can always choose to believe that if Plato did not put certain possibilities of passage into practice, or even interrupted them, it is because he perceived them but left them in the impracticable. This formulation is possible only if one avoids all recourse to the difference between conscious and unconscious, voluntary and involuntary, a very crude tool for dealing with relations in and to language. The same would be true of the opposition between speech—or writing—and language if that opposition, as is often the case, harked back to the above categories.

This reason alone should already suffice to prevent us from reconstituting the entire chain of significations of the *pharmakon*. No absolute privilege allows us absolutely to master its textual system. This limitation can and should nevertheless be displaced to a certain extent. The possibilities and powers of displacement are extremely diverse in nature, and, rather than enumerating here all their titles, let us attempt to produce some of their effects as we go along, as we continue our march through the Platonic problematic of writing.[1]

We have just sketched out the correspondence between the figure of Thoth in Egyptian mythology and a certain organization of concepts, philosophemes, metaphors, and mythemes picked up from what is called the Platonic text. The word *pharmakon* has seemed to us extremely apt for the task of tying all the threads of this correspondence together. Let us now reread, in a rendering derived from Robin, this sentence from the *Phaedrus* "Here, O King, says Theuth, is a discipline (*mathēma*) that will make the Egyptians wiser (*sophōterous*) and will improve their memories (*mnēmonikōterous*): both memory (*mnēmē*) and instruction (*sophia*) have found their remedy (*pharmakon*)".

The common translation of *pharmakon* by remedy [*remède*]—a beneficent drug—is not, of course, inaccurate. Not only can *pharmakon* really mean remedy and thus erase, on a certain surface of its functioning, the ambiguity of its meaning. But it is even quite obvious here, the stated intention of Theuth precisely to stress the worth of his product, that he *turns* the word on its strange and invisible pivot, presenting it from a single one, the most reassuring of its *poles*. This medicine is beneficial; it repairs and produces, accumulates and remedies, increases knowledge and reduces forgetfulness. Its translation by "remedy" nonetheless erases, in going outside the Greek language, the other pole reserved in the word *pharmakon*. It cancels out the resources of ambiguity and makes more difficult, if not impossible, an understanding of the context. As opposed to "drug" or even "medicine," remedy says the transparent rationality of science, technique, and therapeutic causality, thus excluding from the text any leaning toward the magic virtues of a force whose effects are hard to master, a dynamics that constantly surprises the one who tries to manipulate it as master and as subject.

Now, *on the one hand*, Plato is bent on presenting writing as an occult, and therefore suspect, power. Just like painting, to which he will later compare it, and like optical illusions and the techniques of *mimēsis* in general. His mistrust of the mantic and magic, of sorcerers and casters of spells, is well attested.[2] In the *Laws*, in particular, he reserves them terrible punishments. According to an operation we will have cause to remember later, he recommends that they be excluded—expelled or cut off—from the social arena. Expulsion and ostracism can even be accomplished at the same time, by keeping them in prison, where they would no longer be visited by free men but only by the slave that would bring them their food; then by depriving them of burial: "At death he shall be cast out beyond the borders without burial, and if any free citizen has a hand in his burial, he shall be liable to a prosecution for impiety at the suit of any who cares to take proceedings" (X, 909b–c).

On the other hand, the King's reply presupposes that the effectiveness of the *pharmakon* can be reversed: it can worsen the ill instead of remedy it. Or rather, the royal answer suggests that Theuth, by ruse and/or naïveté, has exhibited the reverse of the true effects of writing. In order to vaunt the worth of his invention, Theuth would thus have denatured the *pharmakon*, said the opposite (*tounantion*) of what writing is capable of. He has passed a poison off as a remedy. So that in translating *pharmakon* by *remedy*, what one respects is not what Theuth intended, nor even what Plato intended, but rather what the King says Theuth has said, effectively deluding either the King or himself. If Plato's text then goes on to give the King's pronouncement as the truth of Theuth's production and his speech as the truth of writing, then the translation *remedy* makes Theuth into a simpleton or a flimflam artist, *from the sun's point of view*. From that viewpoint, Theuth has no doubt played on the word, interrupting, for his own purposes, the communication between the two opposing values. But the King restores that communication, and the translation takes no account of this. And all the while the two interlocutors, whatever they do and whether or not they choose, remain within the unity of the same signifier. Their discourse plays within it, which is no longer the case in translation. *Remedy* is the rendition that, more than "medicine" or "drug" would have done, obliterates the virtual, dynamic references to the other uses of the same word in Greek. The effect of such a translation is most importantly to destroy what we will later call Plato's anagrammatic writing, to destroy it by interrupting the relations interwoven among different functions of the same word in different places, relations that are virtually but necessarily "citational."

When a word inscribes itself as the citation of another sense of the same word, when the textual center-stage of the word *pharmakon*, even while it means *remedy*, cites, re-cites, and makes legible that which *in the same word* signifies, in another spot and on a different level of the stage, *poison* (for example, since that is not the only other thing *pharmakon* means), the choice of only one of these renditions by the translator has as its first effect the neutralization of the citational play, of the "anagram," and, in the end, quite simply of the very textuality of the translated text. It could no doubt be shown, and we will try to do so when the time comes, that this blockage of the passage among opposing values is itself already an effect of "Platonism," the consequence of something already at work in the translated text, in the relation between "Plato" and his "language." There is no contradiction between this proposition and the preceding one. Textuality being constituted by differences and by differences from differences, it is by nature absolutely heterogeneous and is constantly composing with the forces that tend to annihilate it.

One must therefore accept, follow, and analyze the composition of these two forces or of these two gestures. That composition is even, in a certain sense, the single theme of this essay. On the one hand Plato decides in favor of a logic that does not tolerate such passages between opposing senses of the same word, all the more so since such a passage would reveal itself to be something quite different from simple confusion, alternation, or the dialectic of opposites. And yet, on the other hand, the *pharmakon*, if our reading confirms itself, constitutes the original medium of that decision, the element that precedes it, comprehends it, goes beyond it, can never be reduced to it, and is not separated from it by a single word (or signifying apparatus), operating within the Greek and Platonic text. All translations into languages that are the heirs and depositaries of Western metaphysics thus produce on the *pharmakon* an *effect of analysis* that violently destroys it, reduces it to one of its simple elements by interpreting it, paradoxically enough, in the light of the ulterior developments it itself has made possible. Such an interpretative translation is thus as violent as it is impotent: it destroys the *pharmakon* but at the same time forbids itself access to it, leaving it untouched in its reserve.

The translation by "remedy" can thus be neither accepted nor simply rejected. Even if one intended thereby to save the "rational" pole and the laudatory intention, the idea of the *correct* use of the *science* or *art* of medicine, one would still run every risk of being deceived by language. Writing is no more valuable, says Plato, as a remedy than as a poison. Even before Thamus has let fall his pejorative sentence, the remedy is disturbing in itself. One must indeed be aware of the fact that Plato is suspicious of the *pharmakon* in general, even in the case of drugs used exclusively for therapeutic ends, even when they are wielded with good intentions, and even when they are as such effective. There is no such thing as a harmless remedy. The *pharmakon* can never be simply beneficial.

For two different reasons, and at two different depths. First of all because the beneficial essence or virtue of a *pharmakon* does not prevent it from hurting. The *Protagoras* classes the *pharmaka* among the things than can be both good (*agatha*) and painful (*aniara*) (354a). The *pharmakon* is always caught in the mixture (*summeikton*) mentioned in the *Philebus* (46a), examples of which are *hubris*, that violent, unbounded excess of pleasure that makes the profligate cry out like a madman (45e), and "relieving an itch by rubbing, and anything that can be treated by such a remedy (*ouk allēs deomena pharmaxeōs*)." This type of painful pleasure, linked as much to the malady as to its treatment, is a *pharmakon* in itself. It partakes of both good and ill, of the agreeable and the disagreeable. Or rather, it is within its mass that these oppositions are able to sketch themselves out.

Then again, more profoundly, even beyond the question of pain, the pharmaceutical remedy is essentially harmful because it is artificial. In this, Plato is following Greek tradition and, more precisely, the doctors of Cos. The *pharmakon* goes against natural life: not only life unaffected by any illness, but even sick life, or rather the life of the sickness. For Plato believes in the natural life and normal development, so to speak, of disease. In the *Timaeus*, natural disease, like *logos* in the *Phaedrus*, is compared to a living organism which must be allowed to develop according to its own norms and forms, its specific rhythms and articulations. In disturbing the normal and natural progress of the illness, the *pharmakon* is thus the enemy of the living in general, whether healthy or sick. One must bear this in mind, and Plato invites us to do so, when writing is proposed as a *pharmakon*. Contrary to life, writing—or, if you will, the *pharmakon*—can only *displace* or even *aggravate* the ill. Such will be, in its logical outlines, the objection the king raises to writing: under pretext of supplementing memory, writing makes one even more forgetful; far from increasing knowledge, it diminishes it. Writing does not answer the needs of memory, it aims to the side, does not reinforce the *mnēmē*, but only *hypomnēsis*. And if, in the two texts we are now going to look at together, the formal structure of the argument is indeed the same; if in both cases what is supposed to produce the positive and eliminate the negative does nothing but *displace* and at the same time *multiply* the effects of the negative, leading the lack that was its cause to proliferate, the necessity for this is inscribed in the *sign pharmakon*, which Robin (for example) dismembers, here as remedy, there as drug.

We expressly said the *sign pharmakon*, intending thereby to mark that what is in question is *indissociably* a signifier and a concept signified.

A) In the *Timaeus*, which spreads itself out, from its opening pages, in the space between Egypt and Greece as in that between writing and speech ("You Hellenes are never anything but children, and there is not an old man among you," whereas in Egypt "everything has been written down by us of old": *panta gegrammena* [22b, 23a]), Plato demonstrates that, among all the body's movements, the best is natural motion, which spontaneously, from within, "is produced in a thing by itself":

Now of all motions that is the best which is produced in a thing by itself, for it is most akin to the motion of thought and of the universe, but that motion which is caused by others is not so good, and worst of all is that which moves the body, when at rest, in parts only and by some agency alien to it. Wherefore of all modes of purifying and reuniting the body the best is gymnastics; the next best is a surging motion, as in sailing or any other mode of conveyance which is not fatiguing; the third sort of motion may be of use in a case of extreme necessity, but in any other will be adopted by no man of sense—I mean the purgative treatment (*tēs pharmakeutikēs katharseōs*) of physicians; for diseases unless they are very dangerous should not be irritated by medicines (*ouk erethisteon pharmakeiais*), since every form of disease is in a manner akin to the living being (*tēi tōn zōōn phusei*), whose complex frame (*sustasis*) has an appointed term of life. For not the whole race only, but each individual—barring inevitable accidents—comes into the world having a fixed span. . . . And this holds also of the constitution of diseases; if anyone regardless of the appointed time tries to subdue them by medicine (*pharmakeiais*), he only aggravates and multiplies them. Wherefore we ought always to manage them by regimen, as far as a man can spare the time, and not provoke a disagreeable enemy by medicines (*pharmakeuonta*). (89a–d)

The reader will have noted that:

1. The noxiousness of the *pharmakon* is indicted at the precise moment the entire context seems to authorize its translation by "remedy" rather than poison.

2. The natural illness of the living is defined in its essence as an *allergy*, a reaction to the aggression of an alien element. And it is necessary that the most general concept of disease should be allergy, from the moment the natural life of the body ought only to follow its own endogenous motions.

3. Just as health is auto-nomous and auto-matic, "normal" disease demonstrates its autarky by confronting the pharmaceutical aggres-

sion with *metastatic* reactions which displace the site of the disease, with the eventual result that the points of resistance are reinforced and multiplied. "Normal" disease defends itself. In thus escaping the supplementary constraints, the superadded pathogeny of the *pharmakon*, the disease continues to follow its own course.

4.   This schema implies that the living being is finite (and its malady as well): that it can have a relation with its other, then, in the allergic reaction, that it has a limited lifetime, that death is already inscribed and prescribed within its structure, in its "constitutive triangles." ("The triangles in us are originally framed with the power to last for a certain time beyond which no man can prolong his life." Ibid.) The immortality and perfection of a living being would consist in its having no relation at all with any outside. That is the case with God (cf. *Republic* II, 381b–c). God has no allergies. Health and virtue (*hugieia kai aretē*), which are often associated in speaking of the body and, analogously, of the soul (cf. *Gorgias*, 479b), always proceed from within. The *pharmakon* is that which, always springing up from without, acting like the outside itself, will never have any definable virtue of its own. But how can this supplementary parasite be excluded by maintaining the boundary, or, let us say, the triangle?

B) The system of these four features is reconstituted when, in the *Phaedrus*, King Thamus depresses and depreciates the *pharmakon* of writing, a word that should thus not too hastily be considered a metaphor, unless the metaphorical possibility is allowed to retain all its power of enigma. Perhaps we can now read the King's response:

> But the king said, "Theuth, my master of arts (*Ō tekhnikōtate Theuth*), to one man it is given to create the elements of an art, to another to judge the extent of harm and usefulness it will have for those who are going to employ it. And now, since you are father of written letters (*patēr ōn grammatōn*), your paternal goodwill has led you to pronounce the very opposite (*tounantion*) of what is their real power. The fact is that this invention will produce forgetfulness in the souls of those who have learned it because they will not need to exercise their memories (*lēthēn men en psuchais parexei mnēmēs ameletēsiai*), being able to rely on what is written, using the stimulus of external marks that are alien to themselves (*dia pistin graphēs exōthen hup' allotriōn tupōn*) rather than, from within, their own unaided powers to call things to mind (*ouk endothen autous huph' hautōn anamimnēskomenous*). So it's not a remedy for memory, but for reminding, that you have discovered

(*oukoun mnēmēs, alla hupomnēseōs, pharmakon hēures*). And as for wisdom (*sophias de*), you're equipping your pupils with only a semblance (*doxan*) of it, not with truth (*alētheian*). Thanks to you and your invention, your pupils will be widely read without benefit of a teacher's instruction; in consequence, they' ll entertain the delusion that they have wide knowledge, while they are, in fact, for the most part incapable of real judgment. They will also be difficult to get on with since they will be men filled with the conceit of wisdom (*doxosophoi*), not men of wisdom (*anti sophōn*)." (274*e*–275*b*)

The king, the father of speech, has thus asserted his authority over the father of writing. And he has done so with severity, without showing the one who occupies the place of his son any of that paternal good will exhibited by Theuth toward his own children, his "letters." Thamus presses on, multiplies his reservations, and visibly wants to leave Theuth no hope.

In order for writing to produce, as he says, the "opposite" effect from what one might expect, in order for this *pharmakon* to show itself, with use, to be injurious, its effectiveness, its power, its *dunamis* must, of course, be ambiguous. As is said of the *pharmakon* in the *Protagoras*, the *Philebus*, the *Timaeus*. It is precisely this ambiguity that Plato, through the mouth of the King, attempts to master, to dominate by inserting its definition into simple, clear-cut oppositions: good and evil, inside and outside, true and false, essence and appearance. If one rereads the reasons adduced by the royal sentence, one will find this series of oppositions there. And set in place in such a way that the *pharmakon*, or, if you will, writing, can only go around in circles: writing is only apparently good for memory, seemingly able to help it from within, through its own motion, to know what is true. But in truth, writing is essentially bad, external to memory, productive not of science but of belief, not of truth but of appearances. The *pharmakon* produces a play of appearances which enable it to pass for truth, etc.

But while, in the *Philebus* and the *Protagoras*, the *pharmakon*, because it is painful, seems bad whereas it is beneficial, here, in the *Phaedrus* as in the *Timaeus*, it is passed off as a helpful remedy whereas it is in truth harmful. Bad ambiguity is thus opposed to good ambiguity, a deceitful intention to a mere appearance. Writing's case is grave.

It is not enough to say that writing is conceived out of this or that series of oppositions. Plato thinks of writing, and tries to comprehend it, to dominate it, on the basis of *opposition* as such. In order for these contrary values (good/evil, true/false, essence/appearance, inside/outside, etc.) to be in opposition, each of the terms must be simply *external* to the other, which means that one of these oppositions (the opposition between inside and outside) must already be accredited as the matrix of all possible opposition. And one of the elements of the system (or of the series) must also stand as the very possibility of systematicity or seriality in general. And if one got to thinking that something like the *pharmakon*—or writing—far from being governed by these oppositions, opens up their very possibility without letting itself be comprehended by them; if one got to thinking that it can only be out of something like writing—or the *pharmakon*—that the strange difference between inside and outside can spring; if, consequently, one got to thinking that writing as a *pharmakon* cannot simply be assigned a site within what it situates, cannot be subsumed under concepts whose contours it draws, leaves only its ghost to a logic that can only seek to govern it insofar as logic arises from it—one would then have to *bend* (*plier*) into strange contortions what could no longer even simply be called logic or discourse. All the more so if what we have just imprudently called a *ghost* can no longer be distinguished, with the same assurance, from truth, reality, living flesh, etc. One must accept the fact that here, for once, to leave a ghost behind will in a sense be to salvage nothing.

This little exercise will no doubt have sufficed to warn the reader: to come to an understanding with Plato, as it is sketched out in this text, is already to slip away from the recognized models of commentary, from the genealogical or structural reconstitution of a system, whether this reconstitution tries to corroborate or refute, confirm or "overturn," mark a return-to-Plato or give him a "send-off" in the quite Platonic manner of the *khairein*. What is going on here is something altogether different. That too, of course, but still completely other. If the reader has any doubt, he is invited to reread the preceding paragraph. Every model of classical reading is exceeded there at some point, precisely at the point where it attaches to the inside of the series—it being understood that this excess is not a simple exit out of the series, since that would obviously fall under one of the categories of the series. The excess—but can we still call it that?—is only a *certain* displacement of the series. And a certain *folding back* [*repli*]—which will later be called a *re-mark*—of opposition within the series, or even within its dialectic. We cannot qualify it, name it, comprehend it under a simple concept without immediately being off the mark. Such a functional displacement, which concerns differences (and, as we shall see, "simulacra") more than any conceptual identities signified, is a real and necessary challenge. It writes itself. One must therefore begin by reading it.

If writing, according to the king and under the sun, produces the opposite effect from what is expected, if the *pharmakon* is pernicious, it is because, like the one in the *Timaeus*, it doesn't come from around here. It comes from afar, it is external or alien: to the living, which is the right-here of the inside, to *logos* as the *zōon* it claims to assist or relieve. The imprints (*tupoi*) of writing do not inscribe themselves this time, as they do in the hypothesis of the *Theaetetus*, in the wax of the soul *in intaglio*, thus corresponding to the spontaneous, autochthonous motions of psychic life. Knowing that he can always leave his thoughts outside or check them with an external agency, with the physical, spatial, superficial marks that one lays flat on a tablet, he who has the *tekhnē* of writing at his disposal will come to rely on it. He will know that he himself can leave without the *tupoi*'s going away, that he can forget all about them without their leaving his service. They will represent him even if he forgets them; they will transmit his word even if he is not there to animate them. Even if he is dead, and only a *pharmakon* can be the wielder of such power, *over* death but also in cahoots with it. The *pharmakon* and writing are thus always involved in questions of life and death.

Can it be said without conceptual anachronism—and thus without serious interpretative error—that the *tupoi* are the representatives, the *physical* surrogates of the *psychic* that is absent? It would be better to assert that the written traces no longer even belong to the order of the *phusis*, since they are not alive. They do not grow; they grow no more than what could be sown, as Socrates will say in a minute, with a reed (*kalamos*). They do violence to the natural, autonomous organization of the *mnēmē*, in which *phusis* and *psuchē* are not opposed. If writing does belong to the *phusis*, wouldn't it be to that moment of the *phusis*, to that necessary movement through which its truth, the production of its appearing, tends, says Heraclitus, to take shelter in its crypt? "Cryptogram" thus condenses in a single word a pleonastic proposition.

If one takes the king's word for it, then, it is this life of the memory that the *pharmakon* of writing would come to hypnotize: fascinating it, taking it out of itself by putting it to sleep in a monument. Confident of the permanence and independence of its types (*tupoi*), memory will fall asleep, will not keep itself up, will no longer keep to keeping itself alert, present, as close as possible to the truth of what is. Letting itself get stoned [*médusée*] by its own signs, by its own guardians, by the types committed to the keeping and surveillance of knowledge, it will sink down into the *lēthē*, overcome by non-knowledge and forgetfulness.[3] Memory and truth cannot be separated. The movement of *alētheia* is a deployment of *mnēmē* through and through. A deployment of living memory, of memory as psychic life in its self-presentation to itself. The powers of *lēthē* simultaneously increase the domains of death, of nontruth, of nonknowledge. This is why writing, at least insofar as it sows "forget-fulness in the soul," turns us toward the inanimate and toward nonknowledge. But it cannot be said that its essence simply and *presently* confounds it with death or nontruth. For writing *has* no essence or value of its own, whether positive or negative. It plays within the simulacrum. It is in its type the mime of memory, of knowledge, of truth, etc. That is why men of writing appear before the eye of God not as wise men (*sophoi*) but in truth as fake or self-proclaimed wise men (*doxosophoi*).

This is Plato's definition of the sophist. For it is above all against sophistics that this diatribe against writing is directed: it can be inscribed within the interminable trial instituted by Plato, under the name of philosophy, against the sophists. The man who relies on writing, who brags about the knowledge and powers it assures him, this simulator unmasked by Thamus has all the features of a sophist: "the imitator of him who knows," as the Sophist puts it (*mimētēs tou sophou*, 268c). He whom we would call the graphocrat is as much like the sophist Hippias as a brother. Like the Hippias we see in the *Lesser Hippias*, he boasts about knowing and doing all. And mainly—which Socrates twice, in two different dialogues, ironically pretends he has forgotten to include in his list—about having a better understanding than anyone else of mnemonics and mnemotechnics. This is indeed the power he considers his pride and joy:

SOCRATES   Then in astronomy also, the same man will be true and false?
HIPPIAS   It would seem so.
SOCRATES   And now, Hippias, consider the question at large about all the sciences, and see whether the same principle does not always hold. I know that in most arts you are the wisest (*sophōtatos*) of men, as I have heard you boasting in the Agora at the tables of the money-changers, when you were setting forth the great and enviable stores of your wisdom. . . . Moreover, you told us that you had brought with you poems, epic, tragic, and dithyrambic, as well as prose writings of the most various kinds, and you said that your skill was also pre-eminent in the arts which I was just now mentioning, and in the true principles of rhythm and harmony and of orthog-raphy. And, if I remember rightly, there were a great many other accomplishments in which you excelled. I have forgotten to mention your art of memory, which you regard as your special glory, and I dare say that I have forgotten many other things, but, as I was saying, only look to your own arts—and there are plenty of them—and to those of others, and tell me, having regard to the admissions which you and I have made, whether you discover any department

of art or any description of wisdom or cunning, whichever name you use, in which the true and false are different and not the same. Tell me, if you can, of any. But you cannot.

HIPPIAS Not without consideration, Socrates.

SOCRATES Nor will consideration help you, Hippias, as I believe, but then if I am right, remember what the consequence will be.

HIPPIAS I do not know what you mean, Socrates.

SOCRATES I suppose that you are not using your art of memory . . .
(368a–d).

The sophist thus sells the signs and insignia of science: not memory itself (*mnēmē*), only monuments (*hypomnēmata*), inventories, archives, citations, copies, accounts, tales, lists, notes, duplicates, chronicles, genealogies, references. Not memory but memorials. He thus answers the demands of the wealthy young men, and that is where he is most warmly applauded. After admitting that his young admirers cannot stand to hear him speak of the greater part of his knowledge (*Greater Hippias*, 285c–d), the sophist must tell Socrates all:

SOCRATES What then are the subjects on which they listen to you with pleasure and applause? Pray enlighten me; I cannot see.

HIPPIAS They delight in the genealogies of heroes and of men and in stories of the foundations of cities in olden times, and, to put it briefly, in all forms of antiquarian lore, so that because of them I have been compelled to acquire a thorough comprehension and mastery of all that branch of learning.

SOCRATES Bless my soul, you have certainly been lucky that the Lacedaemonians do not want to hear a recital of the list of our archons, from Solon downward; you would have had some trouble learning it.

HIPPIAS Why? I can repeat fifty names after hearing them once.

SOCRATES I am sorry, I quite forgot about your mnemonic art . . .
(285d–e).

In truth, the sophist only pretends to know everything; his "polymathy" (*The Sophist*, 232a) is never anything but pretense. Insofar as writing *lends a hand* to hypomnesia and not to live memory, it, too, is foreign to true science, to anamnesia in its properly psychic motion, to truth in the process of (its) presentation, to dialectics. Writing can only *mime* them. (It could be shown, but we will spare ourselves the development here, that the problematic that today, and in this very spot, links writing with the (putting in) question of truth—and of thought and speech, which are informed by it—must necessarily exhume, without remaining at that, the conceptual monuments, the vestiges of the battlefield (*champ de bataille*), the signposts marking out the battle lines between sophistics and philosophy, and, more generally, all the buttresses erected by Platonism. In many ways, and from a viewpoint that does not cover the entire field, we are today on the eve of Platonism. Which can also, naturally, be thought of as the morning after Hegelianism. At that specific point, the *philosophia*, the *epistēmē* are not "overturned," "rejected," "reined in," etc., in the name of something like writing; quite the contrary. But they are, according to a relation that philosophy would call *simulacrum*, according to a more subtle excess of truth, assumed and at the same time displaced into a completely different field, where one can still, but that's all, "mime absolute knowledge," to use an expression coined by Bataille, whose name will enable us here to dispense with a whole network of references.)

The front line that is violently inscribed between Platonism and its closest other, in the form of sophistics, is far from being unified, continuous, as if stretched between two homogeneous areas. Its design is such that, through a systematic indecision, the parties and the party lines frequently exchange their respective places, imitating the forms and borrowing the paths of the opponent. These permutations are therefore possible, and if they are obliged to inscribe themselves within some common territory, the dissension no doubt remains internal and casts into absolute shadow some entirely-other of *both* sophistics *and* Platonism, some resistance having no common denominator with this whole commutation.

Contrary to what we have indicated earlier, there are also good reasons for thinking that the diatribe against writing is not aimed first and foremost at the sophists. On the contrary: sometimes it seems to proceed *from* them. Isn't the stricture that one should exercise one's memory rather than entrust traces to an outside agency the imperious and classical recommendation of the sophists? Plato would thus be appropriating here, once again, as he so often does, one of the sophists' argumentations. And here again, he will use it against them. And later on, after the royal judgment, Socrates' whole discourse, which we will take apart stitch by stitch, is woven out of schemes and concepts that issue from sophistics.

One must thus minutely recognize the crossing of the border. And be fully cognizant that this reading of Plato is at no time spurred on by some slogan or password of a "back-to-the-sophists" nature.

Thus, in both cases, on both sides, writing is considered suspicious and the alert exercise of memory prescribed. What Plato is attacking in sophistics, therefore, is not simply recourse to memory but, within such recourse, the substitution of the mnemonic device for live memory, of the prosthesis for the organ; the perversion that consists of replacing a limb by a thing, here, substituting the passive, mechanical "by-heart" for the active reanimation of knowledge, for its reproduction in the present. The boundary (between inside and outside, living and nonliving) separates not only speech from writing but also memory as an unveiling (re-)producing a presence from re-memoration as the mere repetition of a monument; truth as distinct from its sign, being as distinct from types. The "outside" does not begin at the point where what we now call the psychic and the physical meet, but at the point where the *mnēmē*, instead of being present to itself in its life as a movement of truth, is supplanted by the archive, evicted by a sign of re-memoration or of commemoration. The space of writing, space *as* writing, is opened up in the violent movement of this surrogation, in the difference between *mnēmē* and *hypomnēsis*. The outside is already *within* the work of memory. The evil slips in within the relation of memory to itself, in the general organization of the mnesic activity. Memory is finite by nature. Plato recognizes this in attributing life to it. As in the case of all living organisms, he assigns it, as we have seen, certain limits. A limitless memory would in any event be not memory but infinite self-presence. Memory always therefore already needs signs in order to recall the nonpresent, with which it is necessarily in relation. The movement of dialectics bears witness to this. Memory is thus contaminated by its first substitute: *hypomnēsis*. But what Plato *dreams* of is a memory with no sign. That is, with no supplement. A *mnēmē* with no *hypomnēsis*, no *pharmakon*. And this at the very moment and for the very reason that he calls *dream* the confusion between the hypothetical and the anhypothetical in the realm of mathematical intelligibility (*Republic*, 533b).

Why is the surrogate or supplement dangerous? It is not, so to speak, dangerous in itself, in that aspect of it that can present itself as a thing, as a being-present. In that case it would be reassuring. But here, the supplement is not, is not a being (*on*). It is nevertheless not a simple nonbeing (*mēon*), either. Its slidings slip it out of the simple alternative presence/absence. *That* is the danger. And that is what enables the type always to pass for the original. As soon as the supplementary outside is opened, its structure implies that the supplement itself can be "typed," replaced by its double, and that a supplement to the supplement, a surrogate for the surrogate, is possible and necessary. Necessary because this movement is not a sensible, "empirical" accident: it is linked to the ideality of the *eidos* as the possibility of the repetition of the same. And writing appears to Plato (and after him to all of philosophy, which is as such constituted in this gesture) as that process of redoubling in which we are fatally (en)trained: the supplement of a supplement, the signifier, the representative of a representative. (A series whose first term or rather whose first structure does not yet—but we will do it later—have to be *kicked up* [*faire sauter*] and its irreducibility made apparent.) The structure and history of *phonetic* writing have of course played a decisive role in the determination of writing as the doubling of a sign, the sign of a sign. The signifier of a phonic signifier. While the phonic signifier would remain in animate proximity, in the living presence of *mnēmē* or *psuchē*, the graphic signifier, which reproduces it or imitates it, goes one degree further away, falls outside of life, entrains life out of itself and puts it to sleep in the type of its double. Whence the *pharmakon*'s two misdeeds: it dulls the memory, and if it is of any assistance at all, it is not for the *mnēmē* but for *hypomnēsis*. Instead of quickening life in the original, "in person," the *pharmakon* can at best only restore its monuments. It is a debilitating poison for memory, but a remedy or tonic for its external signs, its *symptoms*, with everything that this word can connote in Greek: an empirical, contingent, superficial event, generally a fall or collapse, distinguishing itself like an index from whatever it is pointing to. Your writing cures only the symptom, the King has already said, and it is from him that we know the unbridgeable difference between the essence of the symptom and the essence of the signified; and that writing belongs to the order and exteriority of the symptom.

Thus, even though writing is external to (internal) memory, even though hypomnesia is not in itself memory, it affects memory and hypnotizes it in its very inside. That is the effect of this *pharmakon*. If it were purely external, writing would leave the intimacy or integrity of psychic memory untouched. And yet, just as Rousseau and Saussure will do in response to the same necessity, yet without discovering *other* relations between the intimate and the alien, Plato maintains *both* the exteriority of writing *and* its power of maleficent penetration, its ability to affect or infect what lies deepest inside. The *pharmakon* is that dangerous supplement[4] that breaks into the very thing that would have liked to do without it yet lets itself *at once* be breached, roughed up, fulfilled, and replaced, completed by the very trace through which the present increases itself in the act of disappearing.

If, instead of meditating on the structure that makes such supplementarity possible, if above all instead of meditating on the reduction by which "Plato—Rousseau—Saussure" try in vain to master it with an odd kind of "reasoning," one were to content oneself with pointing to the "logical contradiction," one would have to recognize here an instance of that kind of "kettle-logic" to which Freud turns in the *Traumdeutung* in order to illustrate the logic of dreams. In his attempt to arrange everything in his favor the defendant piles up contradictory arguments: 1. The kettle I am returning to you is brand new; 2. The holes were already in it when you lent it to me; 3. You never lent me a kettle, anyway. Analogously: 1. Writing is rigorously exterior and inferior to living memory and speech, which are therefore undamaged by it. 2. Writing is harmful to them because it puts them to sleep and infects their very life which would otherwise remain intact. 3. Anyway, if one has resorted to hypomnesia and writing at all, it is not for their intrinsic value, but because living memory is finite, it already has holes in it before writing ever comes to leave its traces. Writing has no effect on memory.

The opposition between *mnēmē* and *hypomnēsis* would thus preside over the meaning of writing. This opposition will appear to us to form a system with the great structural oppositions of Platonism. What is played out at the boundary line between these two concepts is consequently something like the major decision of philosophy, the one through which it institutes itself, maintains itself, and contains its adverse deeps.

Nevertheless, between *mnēmē* and *hypomnēsis*, between memory and its supplement the line is more than subtle; it is hardly perceptible. On both sides of that line, it is a question of *repetition*. Live memory repeats the presence of the *eidos*, and truth is also the possibility of repetition through recall. Truth unveils the *eidos* or the *ontōs on*, in other words, that which can be imitated, reproduced, repeated in its identity. But in the anamnesic movement of truth, what is repeated must present itself as such, as what it is, in repetition. The true is repeated; it is what is repeated in the repetition, what is represented and present in the representation. It is not the repeater in the repetition, nor the signifier in the signification. The true is the presence of the *eidos* signified.

Sophistics—the deployment of hypomnesia—as well as dialectics—the deployment of anamnesia—both presuppose the possibility of repetition. But sophistics this time keeps to the other side, to the other face, as it were, of repetition. And of signification. What is repeated is the repeater, the imitator, the signifier, the representative, in the absence, as it happens, of *the thing itself*, which these appear to reedit, and without psychic or mnesic animation, without the living tension of dialectics. Writing would indeed be the signifier's capacity to repeat itself by itself, mechanically, without a living soul to sustain or attend it in its repetition, that is to say, without truth's *presenting itself* anywhere. Sophistics, hypomnesia, and writing would thus only be separated from philosophy, dialectics, anamnesis, and living speech by the invisible, almost nonexistent, thickness of that *leaf* between the signifier and the signified. The "leaf": a significant metaphor, we should note, or rather one taken from the signifier face of things, since the leaf with its recto and verso first appears as a surface and support for writing. But by the same token, doesn't the unity of this leaf, of the system of this difference between signified and signifier, also point to the inseparability of sophistics and philosophy? The difference between signifier and signified is no doubt the governing pattern within which Platonism institutes itself and determines its opposition to sophistics. In being inaugurated in this manner, philosophy and dialectics are determined in the act of determining their other.

This profound complicity in the break has a first consequence: the argumentation against writing in the *Phaedrus* is able to borrow all its resources from Isocrates or Alcidamas at the moment it turns their own weapons, "transposing" them,[5] against the sophists. Plato imitates the imitators in order to restore the truth of what they imitate: namely, truth itself. Indeed, only truth as the presence (*ousia*) of the present (*on*) is here discriminative. And its power to discriminate, which commands or, as you will, is commanded by the difference between signified and signifier, in any case remains systematically inseparable from that difference. And this discrimination itself becomes so subtle that eventually it separates nothing, in the final analysis, but the same from itself, from its perfect, almost indistinguishable double. This is a movement that produces itself entirely within the structure of ambiguity and reversibility of the *pharmakon*.

How indeed does the dialectician simulate him whom he denounces as a simulator, as the simulacrum-man? On the one hand, the sophists advised, as does Plato, the exercise of memory. But, as we have seen, it was in order to enable themselves to speak without knowing, to recite without judgment, without regard for truth, in order to give signs. Or rather in order to sell them. Through this economy of signs, the sophists are indisputably men of writing at the moment they are protesting they are not. But isn't Plato one, too, through a symmetrical effect of reversal? Not only because he is actually a writer (a banal argument we will specify later on) and cannot, whether *de facto* or *de jure*, explain what dialectics is without recourse to writing; not only because he judges that the repetition of the same is necessary in anamnesis; but also because he judges it indispensable as an inscription in the type. (It is notable that *tupos* applies with equal pertinence to the graphic impression and to the *eidos* as model. (Among many other examples, cf. *Republic*, 402d.) This necessity belongs to the order of the law and is posited by the *Laws*. In this instance, the immutable, petrified identity of writing is not simply added to the signified law or prescribed rule like a mute, stupid simulacrum: it assures the law's permanence and identity with the vigilance of a guardian. As another sort of guardian of the laws, writing guarantees the means of returning at will, as often as necessary, to that ideal object called the law. We can thus scrutinize it, question it, consult it, make it talk, without altering its identity. All this, even in the same words (notably *boētheia*), is the other side, exactly opposite, of Socrates' speech in the *Phaedrus*.

> CLINIAS   And, mark you, such argument will be a most valuable aid to intelligent legislation (*nomothesia*), because legal prescriptions (*prostagmata*), once put into writing (*en grammasi tethenta*), remain always on record, as though to challenge the question of all time to come. Hence we need feel no dismay if they should be difficult on a first hearing, since even the dull student may return to them for reiterated scrutiny. Nor does their length, provided they are beneficial, make it less irrational than it is impious, in my opinion at least, for any man to refuse such discourse his heartiest support (*to mē ou boēthein toutois tois logois*). (X, 891*a*. I am still quoting from an authorized translation,[6] including the Greek where pertinent, and leaving the reader to appreciate the usual effects of translation. On the relation between written and unwritten laws, see notably VII, 7935*b–c*).

The italicized Greek words amply demonstrate it: the *prostagmata* of the law can be *posited* only in writing (*en grammasi tethenta*). *Nomothesia* is engrammatical. The legislator is a writer. And the judge a reader. Let us skip to book XII: "He that would show himself a righteously equal judge must keep these matters before his eyes; he must procure books (*grammata*) on the subject, and must make them his study. There is, in truth, no study whatsoever so potent as this of law, if the law be what it should be, to make a better man of its student" (957c).

Inversely, symmetrically, the rhetors had not waited around for Plato in order to *translate writing into judgment*, For Isocrates,[7] for Alcidamas, *logos* was also a living thing (*zōon*) whose vigor, richness, agility, and flexibility were limited and constrained by the cadaverous rigidity of the written sign. The type does not adapt to the changing givens of the present situation, to what is unique and irreplaceable about it each time, with all the subtlety required. While *presence* is the general form of what is, the *present*, for its part, is always different. But writing, in that it repeats itself and remains identical in the type, cannot flex itself in all senses, cannot bend with all the differences among presents, with all the variable, fluid, furtive necessities of psychagogy. He who speaks, in contrast, is not controlled by any preestablished pattern; he is better able to conduct his signs; he is there to accentuate them, inflect them, retain them, or set them loose according to the demands of the moment, the nature of the desired effect, the hold he has on the listener. In attending his signs in their operation, he who acts by vocal means penetrates more easily into the soul of his disciple, producing effects that are always unique, leading the disciple, as though lodged within him, to the intended goal. It is thus not its pernicious violence but its breathless impotence that the sophists held against writing. In contrast to this blind servant with its haphazard, clumsy movements, the Attic school (Gorgias, Isocrates, Alcidamas) extolled the force of living *logos*, the great master, the great power: *logos dunastēs megas estin*, says Gorgias in his *Encomium of Helen*. The dynasty of speech may be just as violent as that of writing, but its infiltration is more profound, more penetrating, more diverse, more assured. The only ones who take refuge in writing are those who are no better speakers than the man in the street. Alcidamas recalls this in his treatise "on those who write speeches" and "on the Sophists." Writing is considered a consolation, a compensation, a remedy for sickly speech.

Despite these similarities, the condemnation of writing is not engaged in the same way by the rhetors as it is in the *Phaedrus*. If the written word is scorned, it is not as a *pharmakon* coming to corrupt memory and truth. It is because *logos* is a more effective *pharmakon*. This is what Gorgias calls it. As a *pharmakon*, *logos* is at once good and bad; it is not at the outset governed exclusively by goodness or truth. It is only within this ambivalence and this mysterious indetermination of *logos*, and after these have been recognized, that Gorgias *determines* truth as a *world*, a structure or order, the counterpart (*kosmos*) of *logos*. In so doing he no doubt prefigures the Platonic gesture. But before such a determination, we are in the ambivalent, indeterminate space of the *pharmakon*, of that which in *logos* remains potency, potentiality, and is not yet the transparent language of knowledge. If one were justified in trying to capture it in categories that are subsequent to and dependent upon the history thus opened up, categories arising precisely *in the aftermath of decision*, one would have to speak of the "irrationality" of living *logos*, of its spellbinding powers of enchantment, mesmerizing fascination, and alchemical transformation, which make it kin to witchcraft and magic. Sorcery (*goēteia*), psychagogy, such are the "facts and acts" of speech, the most fearsome of *pharmaka*. In his *Encomium of Helen*, Gorgias used these very words to qualify the power of speech.

> Sacred incantations sung with words (*hai gar entheoi dia logōn epōidai*) are bearers of pleasure and banishers of pain, for, merging with opinion in the soul, the power of incantation is wont

to beguile it (*ethelxe*) and persuade it and alter it by witchcraft (*goēteiai*). There have been discovered two arts of witchcraft and magic: one consists of errors of soul and the other of deceptions of opinion. . . . What cause then prevents the conclusion that Helen similarly, against her will, might have come under the influence (*humnos*) of speech, just as if ravished by the force of the mighty? . . . For speech constrained the soul, persuading it which it persuaded, both to believe the things said and to approve the things done. The persuader, like a constrainer, does the wrong and the persuaded, like the constrained, in speech is wrongly charged.[8]

Persuasive eloquence (*peithō*) is the power to break in, to carry off, to seduce internally, to ravish invisibly. It is furtive force per se. But in showing that Helen gave in to the violence of speech (would she have yielded to a letter?), in disculpating this victim, Gorgias indicts *logos* in its capacity to lie. "By introducing some reasoning (*logismon*) into speech (*tōi logōi*)," he wishes "to free the accused of blame and, having reproved her detractors as prevaricators and proved the truth, to free her from their ignorance."

But before being reined in and tamed by the *kosmos* and order of truth, *logos* is a wild creature, an ambiguous animality. Its magical "pharmaceutical" force derives from this ambivalence, which explains the disproportion between the strength of that force and the inconsiderable thing speech seems to be:

But if it was speech which persuaded her and deceived her heart, not even to this is it difficult to make an answer and to banish blame as follows. Speech is a powerful lord, which by means of the finest and most invisible body effects the divinest words: it can stop fear and banish grief and create joy and nurture pity.

Such persuasion entering the soul through speech is indeed a *pharmakon*, and that is precisely what Gorgias calls it:

The effect of speech (*tou logou dunamis*) upon the condition of the soul (*pros tēn tēs psuchēs taxis*) is comparable (*ton auton de logon*) to the power of drugs (*tōn pharmakōn taxis*) over the nature of bodies (*tēn tōn somatōn phusin*). For just as different drugs dispel different secretions from the body, and some bring an end to disease and others to life, so also in the case of speeches, some distress, others delight, some cause fear, others make the hearers bold, and some drug and bewitch the soul with a kind of evil persuasion (*tēn psuchēn epharmakeusan kai exegoēteusan*).

The reader will have paused to reflect that the relation (the analogy) between the *logos*/soul relation and the *pharmakon*/body relation is itself designated by the term *logos*. The name of the relation is the same as that of one of its terms. The *pharmakon* is *comprehended* in the structure of *logos*. This comprehension is an act of both *domination* and *decision*.

Notes

1 I take the liberty of referring the reader, in order to give him a preliminary, indicative direction, to the "Question of Method" proposed in *De la grammatologie* [translated by Gayatri Spivak as *Of Grammatology* (Baltimore: The Johns Hopkins University Press, 1976)]. With a few precautions, one could say that *pharmakon* plays a role analogous, in this reading of Plato, to that of *supplément* in the reading of Rousseau.

2 Cf. in particular *Republic* II, 364 ff; Letter VII, 333e. The problem is raised with copious and useful references in E. Moutsopoulos, *La Musique dans l'œuvre de Platon* (Paris: Presses Universitaires de France, 1959), pp. 13 ff.

3 We would here like to refer the reader in particular to the extremely rich text by Jean-Pierre Vernant (who deals with these questions with quite different intentions): "Aspects mythiques de la mémoire et du temps," in *Mythe et pensée chez les Grecs* (Paris: Maspéro, 1965). On the word *tupos*, its relations with *perigraphē* and *paradeigma*, cf. A. von Blumenthal, *Tupos und Paradeigma*, quoted by P. M. Schuhl, in *Platon et l'art de son temps* (Paris: Presses Universitaires de France, 1952), p. 18, n. 4.

4 TN. The expression "that dangerous supplement," used by Rousseau in his *Confessions* to describe masturbation, is the title of that chapter in *Of Grammatology* in which Derrida follows the consequences of the way in which the word *supplément*'s two meanings in French—"addition" and "replacement"—complicate the logic of Rousseau's treatment of sex, education, and writing. Writing, pedagogy, masturbation, and the *pharmakon* share the property of being—with respect to speech, nature, intercourse, and living memory—at once something secondary, external, and compensatory, and something that substitutes, violates, and usurps.

5 We are here using Diès's word, referring to his study of *La transposition platonicienne*, more precisely to his first chapter, "La Transposition de la rhétorique," in *Autour de Platon* II, 400.

6 TN. Derrida is quoting from Diès; I am quoting from A. E. Taylor. Interestingly, another of these "effects of translation" is precisely the *difficulty* involved in translating a discussion of effects of translation.

7 If one holds, as does Robin, that the *Phaedrus* is, despite certain appearances, "an indictment against the rhetoric of Isocrates" (Introduction to the *Phaedrus*, Bode edition, p. clxxiii) and that the latter is more concerned, whatever he may say, with *doxa* than with *epistēmē* (p. clxviii), one will not be surprised by the title of his discourse, "Against the Sophists." Neither will one be amazed to find, for example, this passage, whose formal resemblance

with Socrates' argumentation is blinding: "But it is not these sophists alone who are open to criticism, but also those who profess to teach political discourse (*tous politikous logous*). For the latter have no interest whatever in the truth, but consider that they are masters of an art if they can attract great numbers of students by the smallness of their charges . . . [One should note that Isocrates charged very high fees, and know what the price of truth was when it was speaking through his mouth] . . . For they are themselves so stupid and conceive others to be so dull that, although the speeches which they compose are worse than those which some laymen improvise, nevertheless they promise to make their students such clever orators that they will not overlook any of the possibilities which a subject affords. More than that, they do not attribute any of this power either to the practical experience or to the native ability of the student, but undertake to transmit the science of discourse (*tēn tōn logōn epistēmēn*) as simply as they would teach the letters of the alphabet. . . . But I marvel when I observe these men setting themselves up as instructors of youth who cannot see that they are applying the analogy of an art with hard and fast rules to a creative process. For, excepting these teachers, who does not know that the art of using letters remains fixed and unchanged, so that we continually and invariably use the same letters for the same purposes, while exactly the reverse is true of the art of discourse? For what has been said by one speaker is not equally useful for the speaker who comes after him; on the contrary, he is accounted most skilled in this art who speaks in a manner worthy of his subject and yet is able to discover in it topics which are nowise the same as those used by others. But the greatest proof of the difference between these two arts is that oratory is good only if it has the qualities of fitness for the occasion, propriety of style, and originality of treatment, while in the case of letters there is no such need whatsoever." The conclusion: one ought to pay in order to write. Men of writing should never be paid. The ideal would be that they would always put their pockets on the line. That they would pay, since they are in such need of the help of the masters of *logos*. "So that those who make use of such analogies (*paradeigmasin*: letters) ought more justly to pay out than to accept fees, since they attempt to teach others when they are themselves in great need of instruction" (*Kata tōn sophistōn* XIII 9, 10, 12, 13 [trans. George Norlin, in *Isocrates*, Loeb Classical Library (New York: G. P. Putnam's Sons, 1929) II, 169–71.].

8 [English translation by George Kennedy, in *The Older Sophists*, ed. R. K. Sprague (Columbia, S.C.: University of South Carolina Press, 1972), pp. 50–54.] On this passage of the *Encomium*, on the relations of *thelgō* and *peithō*, of charm and persuasion, on their use in Homer, Aeschylus, and Plato, see Diès, pp. 116–17.

Part II
Language and meaning

3 'MEANING AS SOLILOQUY'

SPEECH AND PHENOMENA (DERRIDA 1973 [FIRST PUBLISHED 1967])

Translated by David B. Allison and Newton Garver

Themes

Husserl discusses language and the sign in the context of a phenomenology which is quite Platonist in various respects, including the foundational role of the distinction between the Inside and the Outside, Internal and External. For Husserl sense in language is rooted in an inner mental life, which as it is purely internal must be solitary. The internal mental life is that of transcendental phenomenology, according to which expression is always animated by meaning and the meaning is always understood as the intention internal consciousness has towards an object. This turns the phenomenology that Husserl claims is transcendental and impersonal into philosophy of how expressions are willed; it becomes a voluntaristic philosophy, that is a philosophy which defines inner will as the final source. Husserl's intentionalism turns transcendental phenomenology into transcendental voluntarism, which takes will as the absolute and universal principle. Husserl thinks of expressive experience as sense that wants to be signified.

Husserl divides language into the expressive and the indicative. The expressive refers to meanings which exist in a transcendental manner distinct from any specific material circumstance. That is the content of communication according to Husserl. The indicative refers to material signs of communication. Footsteps in the earth are indicative of feet walking in Husserl's account. The indicative is non-expressive because it is a material trace, but for Derrida such a distinction is impossible and the indicative is necessarily within language. Husserl draws the boundary of language as a boundary between expression and indication, however expression must always have an indicative aspect according to Derrida. Husserl regards all signs as indicative and therefore as external to language, but we cannot separate signs from language. There can be no communication which is not embedded in the materiality of speech and writing.

Speech must be understood with reference to its indicative material side and not through the kind of 'interior monologue' constructed by Husserl. Husserl's interior monologue is a product of his view of expression as above, and excluding, indication. The interior monologue is free of signs since it is just consciousness speaking to itself. However, for Derrida the inner voice must still be in language that is material, intersubjective, social and historical. In Husserl's transcendental approach it might look as if language originates in transcendence, but that relies on accepting Husserl's transcendental approach. The language of the interior monologue is dependent on there being signs in: phonemes – the sounds in which we articulate words; and in graphemes – the marks which make up writing. Language is what communicates a meaning and that presumes communication with another subjectivity, so intersubjectivity is necessary for language. Intersubjective communication is communication in a community of language speakers, the social side of language. Social language varies over time, between historical epochs and so language is tied up with history and historical variation. These are all empirical factors which cannot be excluded from language, but which Husserl needs to exclude from language.

For Derrida, language is necessarily material, contextual, and intersubjective. It cannot be within consciousness in any kind of primary way. We have inner states of consciousness which contain linguistic meaning. But they only have meaning as the kind of thing which can be communicated. Communication is not reliable but there is no language without the possibility of communication. All language theories which focus on the ideal content of language, whether as mental states or as transcendental abstractions, must deny the materiality and communicability of language. The sign always exists as a material sign, it is not just a disguise for an abstract or mental content of a linguistic concept. The abstract aspects of language meaning themselves rest on the material differences between material signs. There could be no differences between concepts without the differences between material signs.

Language cannot be just a matter of self-affection within consciousness. Either nothing happens because consciousness is undifferentiated, or consciousness is differentiated allowing communication within communication. However, if there is communication within consciousness there is heterogeneity and otherness within consciousness. For Derrida, the latter must be the case. Even in our most private thoughts, thoughts are emerging from the otherness within consciousness and communicate with the otherness in consciousness.

Context

The issue of interior monologue strongly parallels a major issue in Wittgenstein, namely that of 'private language'. In *Philosophical Investigations* (Wittgenstein 2001 [written 1951]), Wittgenstein discusses the possibility of a language which is logically private, in which I name objects with names that I do not communicate to anyone else. This is usually taken as a discussion of the possibility that experience occurs as private impressions or ideas of the contents of consciousness, with reference to the empiricism of David Hume or of the logical positivists. Another possibility is that Wittgenstein is referring to Frege's notion of 'grasping' a thought, in which thoughts, existing as abstract entities according to Frege, enter consciousness through a private psychological act of grasping. The second possibility would be the one that corresponds most carefully with Derrida's reflections on Husserl.

For Wittgenstein, there can be no logically private language. I can make up a private language and I can avoid teaching it to anyone else, but any language I invent can be communicated and taught if I so choose. In that case the privacy is only contingent and not logical. Wittgenstein looks at the claim that any idea I have of an object of experience must be private to me. There is no sure way of knowing that when other people use the names I use that they are having the same experiences. These kinds of privacy cannot be the foundation of language according to Wittgenstein. Language exists in 'games', different rule-governed contexts in which words get meaning from their rules of use in that context. A rule-governed activity is one that can be repeated. The rule must apply to more than one occasion. The question of whether the name I have for a certain object is being used in the same way by other people does not arise, because the use of names is determined by public rule-governed situations or 'games', not by internal experience. Wittgenstein's argument partly depends on behaviourist claims, since he argues that we should see language as a form of behaviour rather than as an expression of inner mental states.

Wilfrid Sellars develops a related line of argument in *Empiricism and the Philosophy of Mind* (Sellars 1997 [originally published 1956]) in his discussion of 'inner' or 'private' episodes. This is the problem of immediate experience or impressions, which is part of Sellars' general problem of the 'Myth of the Given'. The 'given' refers to the idea that I receive impressions from outside in a passive way without reference to already existing concepts and rules. The structural problem that Sellars thinks sums up the question is the problem of how we get from seeing that something has a quality to seeing that something exists that has that property. According to Sellars we should resist thinking that we derive knowledge of objects from inner episodes. We need to say that the language of the properties of objects depends on theories about objects. It is not the case that knowledge of objects is derived from observation of properties, without any prior assumptions about what objects are and how they interact. His position has Hegelian undertones, because it suggests that knowledge of general relations is assumed in knowledge of particulars. We can never grasp properties as pure impressions given to us without reference to the general categories of objects and different kinds of objects.

The critical accounts of Wittgenstein and Sellars with regard to a purely private mental inner life, deal with different issues from Derrida's criticisms of privacy. Derrida is not concerned with empiricist theories of immediate experience as the foundation of knowledge, or with the relation between properties and objects. Nevertheless, both Wittgenstein and Sellars emphasise that language exists under external causes and material conditions, rather than in an abstracted inner mental life. Derrida does not share Wittgenstein's behaviourist leanings, or Sellars's concern with empirical impressions as given or immediate. Derrida does have in common with behaviourism a resistance to a transcendental mind; and he does have in common with Sellars a resistance to the immediacy of private episodes. There is no immediacy for Derrida, we are always already in a system of thought, when we have inner experiences. Ruth Sonderegger offers an important reading of the relations and differences between Wittgenstein and Derrida on private language in 'A Critique of Pure Meaning' (Sonderegger 1997).

Richard Rorty who has written much on Sellars, including an introduction to the 1997 reissue of *Empiricism and the Philosophy of Language* which also has a study guide by Robert Brandom, has also written much about Derrida. In *Philosophy and the Mirror of Nature* (Rorty 1980) Rorty thinks of linguistic philosophy since Wittgenstein as undermining 'foundationalism' in philosophy. By foundationalism, he means a philosophical position according to which there are absolute foundations for knowledge, which enable our mind to mirror the world. Once philosophy starts to introduce language into its foundations, the world starts to become something created in language. According to Rorty, the Sellars type of argument about private language marks a decisive blow against foundationalism in knowledge, because that rests on the assumption that our perceptions exist as private mental contents from which we derive all knowledge. If all our perceptions are perceptions of things that are named, then the perception is not private since the naming is not private.

SPEECH AND PHENOMENA: MEANING AS SOLILOQUY

Let us suppose that indication is excluded; expression remains. What is expression? It is a sign charged with meaning. Husserl undertakes to define meaning (*Bedeutung*) in section 5 of the First Investigation: "Expressions as Meaningful Signs" (*Ausdrücke als bedeutsame Zeichen*). Expressions are signs which "want to say," which "mean."

A) Meaning doubtless comes to the sign and transforms it into expression only by means of speech, oral discourse. "From indicative signs we distinguish *meaningful* signs, i.e., *expressions*" (§5; ET, p. 275).[1] But why "expressions" and why "meaningful" signs? This can only be explained by bringing together a whole sheaf of reasons, unified by a single underlying intention.

1. Expression is exteriorization. It imparts to a certain outside a sense which is first found in a certain inside. We suggested above that this outside and this inside were absolutely primordial: the outside is neither nature, nor the world, nor a real exterior relative consciousness. We can now be more precise. The meaning *bedeuten* intends an outside which is that of an ideal ob-ject. This outside is then ex-pressed and goes forth beyond itself into another outside, which is always "in" consciousness. For, as we shall see, the expressive discourse, as such and in essence, has no need of being effectively uttered in the world. Expressions as meaningful signs are a twofold going-forth beyond itself of the sense (*Sinn*) in itself, existing in consciousness, in the with-oneself or before-oneself which Husserl first determined as "solitary mental life." Later, after the discovery of the transcendental reduction, he will describe this solitary life of the soul as the noetic—noematic sphere of consciousness. If, by anticipation and for greater clarity, we refer to the corresponding

sections in *Ideas I*, we see how the "unproductive" stratum of expression comes to reflect, "to mirror" (*widerzuspiegeln*) every other intentionality in both its form and its content. The relation to objectivity thus denotes a "preexpressive" (*vorausdrücklich*) intentionality aiming at a sense which is to be transformed into meaning and expression. It is not self-evident, however, that this repeated and reflected "going-forth" toward the noematic sense and then toward expression is an unproductive reduplication, especially if we consider that by being "unproductive" Husserl understands the "*productivity that exhausts itself in expressing*, and in the *form of the conceptual* introduced with this function."[2]

We shall have to return to this. We only wanted to note here what "expression" means for Husserl: the going-forth-beyond-itself of an act, then of a sense, which can remain in itself, however, only in speech, in the "phenomenological" voice.

2. The word "expression" is already required in the *Investigations* for another reason. Expression is a voluntary exteriorization; it is meant, conscious through and through, and intentional. There is no expression without the intention of a subject animating the sign, giving it a *Geistigkeit*. In indication the animation has two limits: the body of the sign, which is not merely a breath, and that which is indicated, an existence in the world. In expression the intention is absolutely explicit because it animates a voice which may remain entirely internal and because the expressed is a meaning (*Bedeutung*), that is, an ideality "existing" nowhere in the world.

3. That there can be no expression without voluntary intention can be confirmed from another point of view. If expression is always inhabited and animated by a meaning (*bedeuten*), as *wanting* to say, this is because, for Husserl, the *Deutung* (the interpretation or the understanding of the *Bedeutung*) can never take place outside oral discourse (*Rede*). Only such discourse is subject to a *Deutung*, which is never primarily reading, but rather listening. What "means," i.e., *that which* the meaning means to say—the meaning, *Bedeutung*—is left up to whoever is speaking, insofar as he says what he *wants* to say, what he *means* to say—expressly, explicitly, and consciously. Let us examine this.

Husserl recognizes that his use of the word "expression" is somewhat "forced." But the constraint thus exercised over language clears up his own intentions and at the same time reveals a common fund of metaphysical implications.

> We shall lay down, for provisional intelligibility, that all speech (*Rede*) and every part of speech (*Redeteil*), as also each sign that is essentially of the same sort, shall count as an expression,

whether or not such speech is actually uttered (*wirklich geredet*), or addressed with communicative intent to any persons or not (§5; ET, p. 275).

Thus everything that constitutes the effectiveness of what is uttered, the physical incarnation of the meaning, the body of speech, which in its ideality belongs to an empirically determined language, is, if not outside discourse, at least foreign to the nature of expression as such, foreign to that pure intention without which there could be no speech. The whole stratum of empirical effectiveness, that is, the factual totality of speech, thus belongs to indication, which is still more extensive than we had realized. The effectiveness, the totality of the events of discourse, is indicative, not only because it is in the world, but also because it retains in itself something of the nature of an *involuntary* association.

For if intentionality never simply meant will, it certainly does seem that in the order of expressive experiences (supposing it to be limited) Husserl regards intentional consciousness and voluntary consciousness as synonymous. And if we should come to think—as Husserl will authorize us to do in *Ideas I*—that every intentional lived experience may in principle be taken up again in an expressive experience, we would perhaps have to conclude that, in spite of all the themes of receptive or intuitive intentionality and passive genesis, the concept of intentionality remains caught up in the tradition of a voluntaristic metaphysics—that is, perhaps, in metaphysics *as such*. The explicit teleology that commands the whole of transcendental phenomenology would be at bottom nothing but a transcendental voluntarism. Sense wants to be signified; it is expressed only in a meaning [*vouloir-dire*] which is none other than a wanting-to-tell-itself proper to the presence of sense.

This explains why everything that escapes the pure spiritual intention, the pure animation by *Geist*, that is, the will, is excluded from meaning (*bedeuten*) and thus from expression. What is excluded is, for example, facial expressions, gestures, the whole of the body and the mundane register, in a word, the whole of the visible and spatial as such. As such: that is, insofar as they are not worked over by *Geist*, by the will, by the *Geistigkeit* which, in the word just as in the human body, transforms the *Körper* into *Leib* (into flesh). The opposition between body and soul is not only at the center of this doctrine of signification, it is confirmed by it; and, has always been at bottom the case in philosophy, it depends upon an interpretation of language. Visibility and spatiality as such could only destroy the self-presence of will and spiritual animation which opens up discourse. *They are literally the death of that self-presence.* Thus:

Such a definition excludes (from expression) facial expression and the various gestures which involuntarily (*unwillkürlich*) accompany speech without communicative intent, or those in which a man's mental states achieve understandable "expression" for his environment, without the added help of speech. Such "utterances" (*Äusserungen*) are not expressions in the sense in which a case of speech (*Rede*) is an expression, they are not phenomenally one with the experiences made manifest in them in the consciousness of the man who manifests them, as is the case with speech. In such manifestations one man communicates nothing to another: their utterance involves no intent to put certain "thoughts" on record expressively (*in ausdrücklicher Weise*), whether for the man himself, in his solitary state, or for others. Such "expressions," in short, have properly speaking, *no meaning* (*Bedeutung*) (§5; ET, p. 275).

They do not have anything to *say*, for they do not *want* to say anything. In the order of signification, explicit intention is an intention to express. What is implicit does not belong to the essence of speech. What Husserl here affirms concerning gestures and facial expressions would certainly hold *a fortiori* for preconscious or unconscious language.

That one may eventually "interpret" gesture, facial expression, the nonconscious, the involuntary, and indication in general, that one may sometime take them up again and make them explicit in a direct and discursive commentary—for Husserl this only confirms the preceding distinctions. This interpretation (*Deutung*) makes a latent expression *heard*, brings a meaning (*bedeuten*) out from what was still held back. Nonexpressive signs mean (*bedeuten*) only in the degree to which they can be made to say what was murmuring in them, in a stammering attempt. Gestures mean something only insofar as we can hear them, interpret (*deuten*) them. As long as we identify *Sinn* and *Bedeutung*, nothing that resists the *Deutung* can have sense or be language in the strict sense. The essence of language is in its *telos*; and its *telos* is voluntary consciousness as meaning [*comme vouloir-dire*]. The indicative sphere which remains outside expression so defined circumscribes the failure of this *telos*. However interwoven with expression, the indicative sphere represents everything that cannot itself be brought into deliberate and meaningful speech.

For all these reasons, the distinction between indication and expression cannot rightfully be made as one between a nonlinguistic and linguistic sign. Husserl draws a boundary which passes, not between language and the nonlinguistic, but, within language in general, between the explicit and nonexplicit (with all their connotations). For it would be difficult—and in fact impossible—to exclude all the indicative forms from language.

At most, then, we can distinguish with Husserl between linguistic signs "in the strict sense" and linguistic signs in the broader sense. For, justifying his exclusion of gestures and facial expressions, Husserl concludes:

> It is not to the point that another person may interpret (deuten) our involuntary manifestations (unwillkürlichen Äusserungen), e.g., our "expressive movements," and that he may thereby become deeply acquainted with our inner thoughts and emotions. They [these manifestations or "utterances"] "mean" (bedeuten) something to him in so far as he interprets (deutet) them, but even for him they are without meaning (Bedeutungen) in the special sense in which verbal signs have meaning (im prägnanten Sinne sprachlicher Zeichen): they only mean in the sense of indicating (§5; ET, p. 275).

This leads us to seek the limit of the indicative field still further. Even for him who finds something discursive in another person's gestures, the indicative manifestations of the other are not thereby transformed into expressions. It is he, the interpreter, who expresses himself about them. In the relation to the other perhaps there is something that makes indication irreducible.

B) It does not suffice, in short, to recognize oral discourse as the medium of expressivity. Once we have excluded all the nondiscursive signs immediately given as extrinsic to speech (gestures, facial expressions, etc.), there still remains a considerable sphere of the nonexpressive within speech itself. This nonexpressiveness is not only restricted to the physical aspect of expression ("the sensible sign, the articulate sound-complex, the written sign on paper"). "A mere distinction between physical signs and sense-giving experiences is by no means enough, and not at all enough for logical purposes" (§6; ET, p. 276).

Considering now the nonphysical side of speech, Husserl excludes from it, as belonging to indication, everything that belongs to the *communication* or *manifestation* of mental experiences. The move which justifies this exclusion should teach us a great deal about the metaphysical tenor of this phenomenology. The themes which will arise therein will never again be re-examined by Husserl; on the contrary, they will repeatedly be confirmed. They will lead us to think that in the final analysis what separates expression from indication could be called the immediate nonself-presence of the living present. The elements of worldly existence, of what is natural or empirical, of sensibility, of association, etc., which determined the concept of indication, will perhaps (certainly across a number of mediations we can anticipate) find their ultimate unity in this nonpresence. And this nonpresence to itself of the living present will simultaneously qualify the relation to others in general as well as the relation to the self involved in temporalization.

This takes form slowly, prudently, but rigorously in the *Investigations*. We have seen that the difference between indication and expression was functional or intentional, and not substantial. Husserl can thus think that some elements of a substantially discursive order (words, parts of speech in general) function in certain cases as indicative signs. And this indicative function of speech is everywhere at work. All *speech inasmuch as it is engaged in communication and manifests lived experience operates as indication*. In this way words act like gestures. Or rather, the very concept of gesture would have to be determined on the basis of indication as what is not expressive.

Husserl indeed admits that expression is "originally framed" to serve the function of communication (First Investigation, §7). And yet expression itself is never purely expression as long as it fulfills this original function; only when communication is suspended can pure expression appear.

What in effect happens in communication? Sensible phenomena (audible or visible, etc.) are animated through the sense-giving acts of a subject, whose intention is to be simultaneously understood by another subject. But the "animation" cannot be pure and complete, for it must traverse, and to some degree lose itself in, the opaqueness of a body:

> Such sharing [of communication] becomes a possibility if the auditor also understands the speaker's intention. He does this inasmuch as he takes the speaker to be a person, who is not merely uttering sounds but *speaking to him*, who is accompanying those sounds with certain sense-giving acts, which the sounds reveal to the hearer, or whose sense they seek to communicate to him. What first makes mental commerce possible, and turns connected speech into discourse, lies in the correlation among the corresponding physical and mental experiences of communicating persons which is effected by the physical side of speech (§7; ET, p. 277).

Everything in my speech which is destined to manifest an experience to another must pass by the mediation of its physical side; this irreducible mediation involves every expression in an indicative operation. The manifesting function (*kundgebende Funktion*) is an indicative function. Here we find the core of indication: indication takes place whenever the sense-giving act, the animating intention, the living spirituality of the meaning-intention, is not fully present.

When I listen to another, his lived experience is not present to me "in person," in the original. Husserl thinks I may have a primordial intuition, that is, an immediate perception of what is exposed of the other in the world: the visibility of his body, his gestures, what may be understood of the sounds he utters. But the subjective side of his experience, his consciousness, in particular the acts by which he gives sense to his signs, are not immediately and primordially present to me as they are for him and mine are for me. Here there is an irreducible and definitive limit. The lived experience of another is made known to me only insofar as it is mediately indicated by signs involving a physical side. The very idea of "physical," "physical side," is conceivable in its specific difference only on the basis of this movement of indication.

To explain the irreducibly indicative character of manifestation, even in speech, Husserl already proposes certain themes which will be meticulously and systematically elaborated in the fifth *Cartesian Meditation*: outside the transcendental monadic sphere of what is my own (*mir eigenes*), the ownness of my own (*Eigenheit*), my own self-presence, I only have relations of *analogical appresentation, of mediate and potential intentionality*, with the other's ownness, with the self-presence of the other; its primordial presentation is closed to me. What will there be described under the surveillance of a differentiated, bold, and rigorous transcendental reduction is here, in the *Investigations*, sketched out in the "parallel" dimension of the mental.

> The hearer perceives the intimation in the same sense in which he perceives the intimating person—even though the mental phenomena which make him a person cannot fall, for what they are, in the intuitive grasp of another. Common speech credits us with percepts even of other people's inner experiences; we "see" their anger, their pain, etc. Such talk is quite correct, as long as, e.g., we allow outward bodily things likewise to count as perceived, and as long as, in general, the notion of perception is not restricted to the adequate, the strictly intuitive percept. If the essential mark of perception lies in the intuitive persuasion (Vermeinen) that a thing or event is itself before us (gegenwärtigen) for our grasping—such a persuasion is possible, and in the main mass of cases actual, without verbalized, conceptual apprehen-

sion—then the receipt of such an intimation (Kundnahme) is the mere perceiving of it. . . . The hearer perceives the speaker as manifesting certain inner experiences, and to that extent he also perceives these experiences themselves: he does not, however, himself experience them, he has not an "inner" but an "outer" percept of them. Here we have the big difference between the real grasp of what is in adequate intuition, and the putative (vermeintlichen) grasp of what is on a basis of inadequate, though intuitive, presentation. In the former case we have to do with an experienced, in the latter case with a presumed (supponiertes) being, to which no truth corresponds at all. Mutual understanding demands a certain correlation among the mental acts mutually unfolded in intimation and in the receipt of such intimation, but not at all their exact resemblance (§7; ET, p. 278).

The notion of *presence* is the core of this demonstration. If communication or intimation (*Kundgabe*) is essentially indicative, this is because we have no primordial intuition of the presence of the other's lived experience. Whenever the immediate and full presence of the signified is concealed, the signifier will be of an indicative nature. (This is why *Kundgabe*, which has been translated a bit loosely by "manifestation" ["intimation" in Findlay's English translation], does not manifest, indeed, renders nothing manifest, if by manifest we mean evident, open, and presented "in person." The *Kundgabe* announces and at the same time conceals what it informs us about.)

All speech, or rather everything in speech which does not restore the immediate presence of the signified content, is inexpressive. Pure expression will be, the pure active intention (spirit, *psychē*, life, will) of an act of meaning (*bedeuten*) that animates a speech whose content (*Bedeutung*) is present. It is present not in nature, since only indication takes place in nature and across space, but in consciousness. Thus it is present to an "inner" intuition or perception. We have just understood why the intuition to which it is present cannot be that of the other person in communication. The meaning is therefore *present to the self* in the life of a present that has not yet gone forth from itself into the world, space, or nature. All these "goings-forth" effectively exile this life of self-presence in indications. We know now that indication, which thus far includes practically the whole surface of language, is the process of death at work in signs. As soon as the other appears, indicative language—another name for the relation with death—can no longer be effaced.

The relation with the other as nonpresence is thus impure expression. To reduce indication in language and reach pure expression at last, the relation with the other must perforce be suspended. I will no longer then have to pass through the mediation of the physical side, or any appresentation whatever. Section 8, "Expressions in Solitary Life," thus follows a path which is, from two points of view, parallel to that of the reduction to the monadic sphere of *Eigenheit* in the *Cartesian Meditations*: the psychic is parallel to the transcendental, and the order of expressive experiences is parallel to the order of experiences in general.

> So far we have considered expressions as used in communication, which last depends essentially on the fact that they operate indicatively. But expressions also play a great part in uncommunicated, interior mental life. This change in function plainly has nothing to do with whatever makes an expression an expression. Expressions continue to have meanings (*Bedeutungen*) as they had before, and the same meanings as in dialogue. A word only ceases to be a word when our interest stops at its sensory contour, when it becomes a mere sound-pattern. But when we live in the understanding of a word, it expresses something and the same thing, whether we address it to anyone or not. It seems clear, therefore, that an expression's meaning (*Bedeutung*), and whatever else pertains to it essentially, cannot coincide with its feats of intimation (§8; ET, pp. 278–79).

The first advantage of this reduction to the interior monologue is that the physical event of language there seems absent. Insofar as the unity of the word—what lets it be recognized as a word, *the same* word, the unity of a sound-pattern and a sense—is not to be confused with the multiple sensible events of its employment or taken to depend on them, the *sameness* of the word is ideal; it is the ideal possibility of repetition, and it loses nothing by the reduction of *any* empirical event marked by its appearance, nor all of them. Although "what we are to use as an indication [the distinctive sign] must be perceived by us as *existent*," the unity of a word owes nothing to its *existence* (*Dasein, Existenz*). Its being an expression owes nothing to any worldly or empirical existence, etc.; it needs no empirical body but only the ideal and identical form of this body insofar as this form is animated by a meaning. Thus in "solitary mental life" the pure unity of expression as such should at last be restored to me.

Is this to say that in speaking to myself I communicate nothing to myself? Are the *"Kundgabe"* (the manifesting) and *"Kundnahme"* (the cognizance taken of the manifested) suspended then? Is nonpresence reduced and, with it, indication, the analogical detour, etc.? Do I not then modify myself? Do I learn nothing about myself?

Husserl considers the objection and then dismisses it: "Shall one say that in soliloquy one speaks to oneself, and employs words as signs (*Zeichen*), i.e., as indications (*Anzeichen*) of one's own inner experiences? I cannot think such a view acceptable" (§8; ET, p. 279).

Husserl's argumentation is decisive here; we must follow it closely. The whole theory of signification introduced in this first chapter devoted to essential distinctions would collapse if the *Kundgabe/Kundnahme* function could not be reduced in the sphere of my own lived experiences—in short, if the ideal or absolute solitude of subjectivity "proper" still needed indications to constitute its own relation to itself. We see unmistakably that in the end the need for indications simply means the need for signs. For it is more and more clear that, despite the initial distinction between an indicative sign and an expressive sign, only an indication is truly a sign for Husserl. The full expression—that is, as we shall see later on, the meaning-filled intention—departs in a certain manner from the concept of the sign. In the phrase just quoted, we can read: "as signs, i.e., as indications." But for the moment let us consider that as a slip of the tongue, the truth of which will be revealed only as we go on. Rather than say "as signs, i.e., as indications" (*als Zeichen, nämlich als Anzeichen*), let us say "signs, namely, signs in the form of indications." For on the surface of his text Husserl continues for the moment to respect the initial distinction between two kinds of signs.

To demonstrate that indication no longer functions in solitary mental life, Husserl begins by noting the difference between two kinds of "reference": reference as *Hinzeigen* (which we must avoid translating as "indication," for reasons of convention, as well as for fear of destroying the coherence of the text; let us say, arbitrarily, "showing"), and reference as *Anzeigen* (indication). If in the silent monologue, "as everywhere else, words function as signs," and if "everywhere they can be said to show something (*Hinzeigen*)," then in this case, Husserl tells us, the passage from expression to sense, from the signifier to the signified, is no longer indication. The *Hinzeigen* is not an *Anzeigen*, for this passage, or this reference, occurs without any existence (*Dasein, Existenz*), whereas in indication an existing sign or empirical event refers to a content whose existence is at least presumed, and it motivates our anticipation or conviction of the existence of what is indicated. An indicative sign cannot be conceived without the category of empirical, which is to say only probable, existence (Husserl will thus define worldly existence in contrast to the existence of the *ego cogito*).

The reduction to the monologue is really a putting of empirical worldly existence between brackets. In "solitary mental life" we no longer use real (*wirklich*) words, but only imagined (*vorgestellt*) words.

And lived experience—about which we were wondering whether it might not be "indicated" to the speaking subject by himself—does not have to be so indicated because it is immediately certain and present to itself. While in real communication existing signs *indicate* other existences which are only probable and mediately evoked, in the monologue, when expression is *full*,[3] nonexistent signs *show* significations (*Bedeutungen*) that are ideal (and thus nonexistent) and certain (for they are presented to intuition). The certitude of inner existence, Husserl thinks, has no need to be signified. It is immediately present to itself. It is living consciousness.

In the interior monologue, a word is thus only represented. It can occur in the imagination (*Phantasie*). We content ourselves with imagining the word, whose existence is thus neutralized. In this imagination, this imaginary representation (*Phantasievorstellung*) of the word, we no longer need the empirical occurrence of the word; we are indifferent to its existence or nonexistence. For if we need the *imagination* of the word, we can do without the *imagined word*. The imagination of the word, the imagined, the word's being-imagined, its "image," is not the (imagined) word. In the same way as, in the perception of the word, the word (perceived or appearing) which is "in the world" belongs to a radically different order from that of the perception or appearing of the word, the word's being perceived, so the (imagined) word is of a radically heterogeneous order from that of the imagination of the word. This simple and subtle difference shows what is irreducibly specific to phenomena; and unless one lends a constant and vigilant attention to differences such as these, one can understand nothing of phenomenology.

But why is Husserl not content with the difference between the existing (or perceived) word and the perception or being-perceived, the phenomenon, of the word? It is because in the phenomenon of perception reference is made, within its phenomenal being, to the existence of the word. The sense of "existence" thus belongs to the phenomenon. This is no longer the case in the phenomenon of imagination. In imagination the existence of the word is not implied, even by virtue of intentional sense. There *exists* only the imagination of the word, which is absolutely certain and self-present insofar as it is lived. This, then, is already a phenomenological reduction which isolates the subjective experience as the sphere of absolute certainty and absolute existence.

This absolute existence only appears by reducing the relative existence of the transcendent world. And the imagination, that "vital element of phenomenology" (*Ideas I*), already grants this move its privileged medium. Here, in solitary discourse,

---

we are in general content with imagined rather than with actual words. In imagination a spoken or printed word floats before us, though in reality it has no existence. We should not, however, confuse imaginative representations (*Phantasievorstellungen*), and still less the image-contents they rest on, with their imagined objects. The imagined verbal sound, or the imagined printed word, does not exist, only its imaginative representation does so. The difference is the difference between imagined centaurs and the imagination of such beings. The word's nonexistence (*Nicht-Existenz*) neither disturbs nor interests us, since it leaves the word's expressive function unaffected (§8; ET, p. 279, modified).

This argumentation would be fragile indeed if it merely appealed to a classical psychology of the imagination, but it would be most imprudent to understand it in this way. For such a psychology, the image is a picture-sign whose *reality* (whether it be physical or mental) would serve to indicate the imagined object. Husserl will show in *Ideas I* what problems such a conception leads to.[4] Although it belongs to the existent and absolutely certain sphere of consciousness, an image, being an intentional or noematic sense, is not one reality duplicating another reality. This is not only because it is not a reality (*Realität*) in nature, but because the noema is a nonreal (*reell*) component of consciousness.

Saussure was also careful to distinguish between the real word and its image. He also saw the expressive value of a "signifier" only in the form of the "sound-image."[5] "Signifier" means "sound-image." But, not taking the "phenomenological" precaution, Saussure makes the sound-image, the signifier as "mental impression," into a reality whose sole originality is to be internal, which is only to shift the problem without resolving it.

But if in the *Investigations* Husserl conducts his description within the realm of the mental rather than the transcendental, he nonetheless distinguishes the essential components of a structure that will be delineated in *Ideas I*: phenomenal experience does not belong to reality (*Realität*). In it, certain elements really (*reell*) belong to consciousness (*hylē*, *morphē*, and *noēsis*), but the noematic content, the sense, is a nonreal (*reell*) component of the experience.[6] The irreality of inner discourse is thus a most differentiated structure. Husserl writes with precision, though without emphasis: "a spoken or printed word floats before us, though in reality it has no existence. We should not, however, confuse imaginative representations (*Phantasievorstellungen*) and still less [our underlining] the image-contents they rest on, with their imagined objects." Not only, then, does the imagination of the word, which is not the word imagined, not exist, but the *content* (the noema) of this imagination exists *even less* than the act.

Notes

1 [Unless otherwise indicated, all quotations from Husserl are from the First Investigation.—Translator.]
2 *Ideas I*, §124; ET, p. 321. Elsewhere we examine more closely the problem of meaning and expression in *Ideas I*; cf. "La Forme et le vouloir-dire: Note sur la phénoménologie du langage," *Revue internationale de philosophie*, LXXXI (September 1967), 277–99.
3 To avoid confusing and multiplying the difficulties, we shall here consider only the perfect expression, that by which the "*Bedeutungsintention*" is "filled." We can do this to the extent that this fullness is, as we shall see, the *telos* and completion of what Husserl wants to isolate here by the terms "meaning" and "expression." Nonfulfillment of expressions will give rise to new problems that we shall encounter later on.
   Here is the passage we are referring to: "But if we reflect on the relation of expression to meaning (*Bedeutung*), and to this end break up our complex, intimately unified experience of the sense-filled expression, into the two factors of word and sense, the word comes before us as intrinsically indifferent, whereas the sense seems the thing aimed at by the verbal sign and meant by its means: the expression seems to direct interest away from itself towards its sense (*von sich ab und auf den Sinn hinzulenken*), and to point (*hinzuzeigen*) to the latter. But this pointing (*Hinzeigen*) is not an indication (*das Anzeigen*) in the sense previously discussed. The existence (*Dasein*) of the sign neither 'motivates' the existence of the meaning (*Bedeutung*), nor, properly expressed, our belief in the meaning's existence. What we are to use as an indication [the distinctive sign] must be perceived by us as existent (*als daseiend*). This holds also of expressions used in communication, but not for expressions used in soliloquy" (§8; ET, p. 279).
4 Cf. *Ideas I*, §90 and the whole of Chapter IV of Section III, particularly §§99, 109, 111 and especially 112: "That attitude will not be changed until practice in general phenomenological analysis is more widespread than is the case at present. So long as one treats experiences as 'contents' or as mental 'elements,' which in spite of all the fashionable attacks against atomizing and hypostatizing psychology are still looked upon as a kind of minute matter (*Sächelchen*), so long as the belief accordingly prevails that it is possible to fix the difference between 'contents of sensation' and the corresponding 'contents of imagination' only through material characters of 'intensity,' 'fullness,' and the like, no improvement is to be looked for" (ET, p. 312).
   The original phenomenological data that Husserl thus wants to respect lead him to posit an absolute heterogeneity between perception or primordial presentation (*Gegenwärtigung, Präsentation*) and representation or representative reproduction, also translated as presentification (*Vergegenwärtigung*). Memory, images, and signs are representations in this sense. Properly speaking, Husserl is not *led* to recognize this heterogeneity, for it is this which constitutes the very possibility of phenomenology. For phenomenology can only make sense if a pure and primordial presentation is possible and

given in the original. This distinction (to which we must add that between positional [*setzende*] re-presentation, which posits the having-been-present in memory, and the imaginary re-presentation [*Phantasie-Vergegenwärtigung*], which is neutral in that respect), part of a fundamental and complex system, which we cannot directly investigate here, is the indispensable instrument for a critique of classical psychology, and, in particular, the classical psychology of the imagination and the sign.

But can't one assume the necessity for this critique of naïve psychology only up to a certain point? What if we were to show, finally, that the theme or import of "pure presentation," pure and primordial perception, full and simple presence, etc., makes of phenomenology an accomplice of classical psychology—indeed constitutes their common metaphysical presupposition? In affirming that *perception does not exist* or that what is called perception is not primordial, that somehow everything "begins" by "re-presentation" (a proposition which can only be maintained by the elimination of these last two concepts: it means that there is no "beginning" and that the "representation" we were talking about is not the modification of a "re-" that has *befallen* a primordial presentation) and by reintroducing the difference involved in "signs" at the core of what is "primordial," we do not retreat from the level of transcendental phenomenology toward either an "empiricism" or a "Kantian" critique of the claim of having primordial intuition; we are here indicating the prime intention—and the ultimate scope—of the present essay.

5   This text of the *Logical Investigations* should be compared with the following passage from the *Course in General Linguistics*: "The linguistic sign unites, not a thing and a name, but a concept and a sound-image. The latter is not the material sound, a purely physical thing, but the psychological imprint of the sound, the impression that it makes on our senses. The sound-image is sensory, and if I happen to call it 'material,' it is only in that sense, and by way of opposing it to the other term of the association, the concept, which is generally more abstract. The psychological character of our sound-images becomes apparent when we observe our own speech. *Without moving our lips or tongue, we can talk to ourselves or recite mentally a selection of verse*" (*Cours de linguistique générale* [Paris: Payot, 1916], p. 98; italics added, ET, by Wade Baskin [New York: Philosophical Library, 1959], p. 66).

And Saussure adds this caution, which has been quickly forgotten: "Because we regard the words of our language as sound-images, we must avoid speaking of the 'phonemes' that make up the words. This term, which suggests vocal activity, is applicable to the spoken word only, to the realization of the inner image in discourse." This remark was no doubt forgotten because Saussure's proposed thesis only aggravates the difficulty: "We can avoid that misunderstanding by speaking of the *sounds* and *syllables* of a word provided we remember that the names refer to the sound-image." But that is easier to remember when speaking in terms of phonemes rather than sounds. Sounds are conceivable outside real vocal activity only insofar as they can be taken as objects in nature more easily than can phonemes.

To avoid other misunderstandings, Saussure concludes: "Ambiguity would disappear if the three notions involved here were designated by three names, each suggesting and opposing the others. I propose to retain the word *sign* to designate the whole and to replace *concept* and *sound-image* respectively by *signified* and *signifier*" (p. 67).

The equivalencies signifier/expression and signified/*Bedeutung* could be posited were not the *bedeuten*/*Bedeutung*/sense/object structure much more complex for Husserl than for Saussure. The operation by which Husserl proceeds in the First Investigation would also have to be systematically compared with Saussure's delimitation of the "internal system" of language.

6 On the nonreality of the noema in the case of the image and the sign, cf., in particular, *Ideas I*, §102.

4 'SIGNATURE EVENT CONTEXT'

MARGINS OF PHILOSOPHY (DERRIDA 1982 [FIRST PUBLISHED 1972])

Translated by Alan Bass

Themes

'signature Event Context' is one of Derrida's best-known texts, and has provoked the greatest reaction from analytic philosophers. The latter is largely due to its status as the one place in which Derrida devotes much attention to an example of analytic philosophy. The text deals with the work of J. L. Austin, though not right from the beginning. It starts with the problem of defining communication. Defining communication presents the problem that the definition assumes the meaning of communication, because the definition assumes the act of communication. All the problems of circularity in philosophy arise here. While meaning requires context for definition, context is never absolutely deterministic. The use of context in fixing meaning depends on intrinsic equivocation in language about meaning. In that case context is conditioned by equivocation and there is a structural non-saturation, that is a necessary lack of fully determined meaning. All communication is the sending of a message for which the addressee is missing, since the intended receiver is always absent in the sending of the message.

There is always representation standing in for and supplementing the lack of presence. Writing depends on distance, delay, division and 'différance'. 'Différance' refers to a combination of temporal deferral and difference within a system, and is the conditioning form of difference. There is always distance between sender and receiver, delay in the arrival of the message and division of the message because it can be received by different addresses, or the same receiver can interpret it in more than one way.

Writing must remain legible: legible even when all the determined addresses have disappeared. Writing must be repeatable, or iterable, in that situation. With the 'iterable', Derrida introduces the issue of ethics, since 'iterable' comes from the Sanksrit word 'itera' which can be translated as other. The issue of the 'interior monologue' is revived in the suggestion that there is no code which is structurally secret. The claim is that no code is absolutely secret, we can create a secret code but that code can always be decoded with sufficient work and patience. All language is a code since there is authority present for deciding the meaning of words. The addressee may die while the message is being sent, the sender may die before the message is received and interpreted. A written sign can never be completely reduced to its context, since the context requires context itself. There is always the possibility of citation, or grafting, in which we can lift any part of language from its context and find another context to determine its meaning. Even the sentences which Husserl identifies as completely lacking in meaning can be given a meaning in that way. The context principle undermines the idea of an unequivocal boundary between meaningless signs and meaningful signs.

The paper includes a discussion of J. L. Austin, with regard to the account of the performative and the perlocutionary in *How to do Things with Words* (Austin 1975 [first published 1961]). Derrida defines the performative, or perlocutionary, as the communication by force or effect in a general theory of action. In Derrida's account, Austin frees the performative from the value of truth and the opposition of truth and falsity. Austin's discussion of possible failures of the performative in language gives us an idea of the general possibility of failure in language. However, Austin does not take this in the way that Derrida does. Derrida goes beyond Austin in defining language as what necessarily fails in communication, because of the necessary possibilities of failure which mean we never know if we have received the right message. If we do not know then we have never fully received the message. As a condition of language this is positive not negative for language, because it is a structural condition of language and is therefore what allows there to be language.

The phenomenological idea of a semantic horizon, a determination of pure transcendental meaning, which is implicit in all philosophies that assume a fixity of meaning, including Austin's philosophy, is punctured by 'writing'. What Derrida is concerned with in 'writing' is not just the written parts of language but the way that all of language is conditioned by what philosophers such as Plato rejected as negative aspects of writing: the absence of the sender and the receiver; the division and delay of the message which in some sense never arrives.

The supposedly 'parasitical' aspects of writing come to the fore in this way, and with regard to the way that all writing is citation. All language could be the citation of words in irony, fiction or lies, rather than the literal assertion of what is said. There is no guarantee that any signature, including a spoken assurance of sincerity, is valid. The signature, or assertion of sincerity, is itself conditioned by difference and citationality.

Derrida develops a definition of deconstruction in this paper. Deconstruction identifies opposition in which one term is placed above the other, such as when speech is placed above writing. The strategy of deconstruction is to turn the value judgement upside down so that the inferior one comes first. The goal is not to assert a new hierarchy but to undermine the old hierarchy in a general displacement of concepts following from the reversal of the hierarchy.

Context

There is an explicit engagement with Austin, and an implicit engagement with Wittgenstein, in the criticisms of the 'structurally secret code'. This was probably written in reaction to Husserl, the explicit target of comparable comments in 'Meaning as Soliloquy' (see Chapter 3). The reading of Austin was attacked as obscure and mistaken by John Searle who had written his Oxford doctorate partly under the supervision of Austin, in 'Reiterating the Differences: A Reply to Derrida'. Derrida's essay and Searle's reply both appeared in the first issue of the now defunct literary theory journal *Glyph*. Derrida himself replied to Searle later the same year in *Limited Inc.* (Derrida 1977). It was a very bad-tempered exchange. However this was not the only result for the analytic discussion of Derrida. Stanely Cavell, who like Searle had written on Austin and had some personal communication with him, had a much more positive reaction to Derrida's use of Austin though he had some criticisms, in *Philosophical Passages* (Cavell 1995). Cavell was also deeply concerned with Wittgenstein, suggesting that Derrida's work has points of contact with both Austin and Wittgenstein. Though Cavell's general approach has some eccentricities by analytic standards – i.e. it is literary, subjective and sometimes autobiographical in approach – the importance of his work is acknowledged by many analytic philosophers including Thomas Kuhn, a great figure in philosophy of science, who acknowledges Cavell's influence in his 1962 masterpiece *The Structure of Scientific Revolutions* (Kuhn 1996 [first published 1962]). Other positive accounts by analytic philosophers include Frank Farrell's 'Iterability and Meaning' (Farrell 1988), A. W. Moore's 'Arguing with Derrida' (Moore 2000) and Sarah Richmond's 'Derrida and Analytical Philosophy' (Richmond 1996). The controversy largely centres on whether Derrida is correct to think of indeterminacy, failure and plurality of possible meaning as conditions for language. Though Derrida's reading of Austin lacks grounding in general knowledge of analytic philosophy, apart from Searle, most analytic commentators have found his understanding adequate and clear after sufficient work in reading Derrida's text. Cavell's reading of Derrida, however, makes the strange claim that Derrida is not concerned with the absence of the speaker in communication and, in particular, that Derrida is not concerned with the ethical implications. Cavell is lacking a grasp of the context of French philosophy, just as Derrida lacks a grasp of the context of analytic philosophy. The idea of 'iteration' is concerned with the necessary presence of the Other in all language. That is to say, there is no way of eliminating the presence of other speakers in my own use of language. My use of language is conditioned by the attempt to communicate with others, and the language of others. That has strong ethical implications for Derrida, which leads him to emphasise the value issues in Austin's theory of utterances. That is, for Austin utterances are always an example of social contract. This fits with Derrida's own extensive writing on Rousseau's language theory in the context of his ethical and political views. Grasping this element of 'Signature Event Context' partly rests on grasping what Derrida takes from Lévinas, in identifying ethics with the constant presence of the Other. In general, Derrida's views on force in 'Signature Event Context' feed into his political and ethical philosophy. The view that all law rests on force, just as all apparently abstract language rests on the empirical force of communication, is the topic of his 1989 paper 'Force of Law: The "Mystical Foundation of Authority"' (in Derrida 2002). The theme is also picked up in texts in Parts V and VI on ethics and politics.

Derrida's emphasis on contextuality in determining meaning puts him in the same company as many analytic philosophers, who work on the context and pragmatics of meaning. H. Paul Grice is the figure whose work perhaps comes closest to Derrida in taking the possibilities of pragmatic context to the extreme. In work going back to the 1950s, collected in *Studies in the Way of Words* (Grice 1989), he discusses the role of 'implicature' in communication. What Grice means by this is that the meaning of an utterance may be very different from the explicit meaning of the words in the utterance. Grice's most memorable example is of the American officer captured in Italy during the Second World

War. In Grice's example, which emerges in a debate with Searle, the American utters the German sentence, 'Kennst du das Land wo die Zitronen blühen'. The literal meaning is 'Do you know the country where the lemon trees bloom'. However, the officer is not asking this question of the Italian officers. He wants them to believe that he is a German officer. He brings about the belief that he is a German officer by uttering the one line of German he remembers from school. That is meaning for Grice, the belief that the utterer intends to bring about in the listener. The emphasis on intention is far from what Derrida has to say, since for Derrida there is no way of determining intentions in consciousness or in language. Nevertheless, the emphasis on the difference between average literal meaning and the meanings that may be taken up depending on context is very much in line with Derrida. It is surely significant that Derrida's critic Searle should criticise Grice's theory of implicature in *Speech Acts* (Searle 1969) in an argument that anticipates his criticisms of Derrida in 'Reiterating the Differences'.

SIGNATURE EVENT CONTEXT

> Still confining ourselves for simplicity, to *spoken* utterance.
> (Austin, *How to Do Things with Words,* p. 113 n.2)

Is it certain that there corresponds to the word *communication* a unique, univocal concept, a concept that can be rigorously grasped and transmitted: a communicable concept? Following a strange figure of discourse, one first must ask whether the word or signifier "communication" communicates a determined content, an identifiable meaning, a describable value. But in order to articulate and to propose this question, I already had to anticipate the meaning of the word *communication*: I have had to predetermine communication as the vehicle, transport, or site of passage of a *meaning,* and of a meaning that is *one.* If *communication* had several meanings, and if this plurality could not be reduced, then from the outset it would not be justified to define communication *itself* as the transmission of a meaning, assuming that we are capable of understanding one another as concerns each of these words (transmission, meaning, etc.). Now, the word *communication,* which nothing initially authorizes us to overlook as a word, and to impoverish as a polysemic word, opens a semantic field which precisely is not limited to semantics, semiotics, and even less to linguistics. To the semantic field of the word *communication* belongs the fact that it also designates nonsemantic movements. Here at least provisional recourse to ordinary language and to the equivocalities of natural language teaches us that one may, for example, *communicate a movement,* or that a tremor, a shock, a displacement of *force* can be communicated—that is, propagated, transmitted. It is also said that different or distant places can communicate between each other by means of a given passageway or opening. What happens in this case, what is transmitted or communicated, are not phenomena of meaning or signification. In these cases we are dealing neither with a semantic or conceptual content, nor with a semiotic operation, and even less with a linguistic exchange.

Nevertheless, we will not say that this nonsemiotic sense of the word *communication*, such as it is at work in ordinary language, in one or several of the so-called natural languages, constitutes the *proper* or *primitive* meaning, and that consequently the semantic, semiotic, or linguistic meaning corresponds to a derivation, an extension or a reduction, a metaphoric displacement. We will not say, as one might be tempted to do, that semiolinguistic communication is *more metaphorico* entitled "communication," because by analogy with "physical" or "real" communication it gives passage, transports, transmits something, gives access to something. We will not say so:

1. because the value of literal, *proper meaning* appears more problematical than ever,
2. because the value of displacement, of transport, etc., is constitutive of the very concept of metaphor by means of which one allegedly understands the semantic displacement which is operated from communication as a nonsemiolinguistic phenomenon to communication as a semiolinguistic phenomenon.

(I note here between parentheses that in this communication the issue will be, already is, the problem of polysemia and communication, of dissemination—which I will oppose to polysemia—and communication. In a moment, a certain concept of writing is bound to intervene, in order to transform itself, and perhaps in order to transform the problematic.)

It seems to go without saying that the field of equivocality covered by the word *communication* permits itself to be reduced massively by the limits of what is called a *context* (and I announce, again between parentheses, that the issue will be, in this communication, the problem of context, and of finding out about writing as concerns context in general). For example, in a *colloquium* of *philosophy* in the *French language*, a conventional context, produced by a kind of implicit but structurally vague consensus, seems to prescribe that one propose "communications" on communication, communications in discursive form, colloquial, oral communications destined to be understood and to open or pursue dialogues within the horizon of an intelligibility and truth of meaning, such that in principle a general agreement may finally be established.

These communications are to remain within the element of a determined "natural" language, which is called French, and which commands certain very particular uses of the word *communication*. Above all, the object of these communications should be organized, by priority or by privilege, around communication as *discourse*, or in any event as signification. Without exhausting all the implications and the entire structure of an "event" like this one, which would merit a very long preliminary analysis, the prerequisite I have just recalled appears evident; and for anyone who doubts this, it would suffice to consult our schedule in order to be certain of it.

But are the prerequisites of a context ever absolutely determinable? Fundamentally, this is the most general question I would like to attempt to elaborate. Is there a rigorous and scientific concept of the *context*? Does not the notion of context harbor, behind a certain confusion, very determined philosophical presuppositions? To state it now in the most summary fashion, I would like to demonstrate why a context is never absolutely determinable, or rather in what way its determination is never certain or saturated. This structural nonsaturation would have as its double effect:

1. a marking of the theoretical insufficiency of the *usual concept of* (the linguistic or nonlinguistic) *context* such as it is accepted in numerous fields of investigation, along with all the other concepts with which it is systematically associated;

2. a rendering necessary of a certain generalization and a certain displacement of the concept of writing. The latter could no longer, henceforth, be included in the category of communication, at least if communication is understood in the restricted sense of the transmission of meaning. Conversely, it is within the general field of writing thus defined that the effects of semantic communication will be able to be determined as particular, secondary, inscribed, supplementary effects.

Writing and telecommunication

If one takes the notion of writing in its usually accepted sense—which above all does not mean an innocent, primitive, or natural sense—one indeed must see it as a *means of communication*. One must even acknowledge it as a powerful means of communication which *extends* very far, if not infinitely, the field of oral or gestural communication. This is banally self-evident, and agreement on the matter seems easy. I will not describe all the *modes* of this extension in time and in space. On the other hand I will pause over the value of *extension* to which I have just had recourse. When we say that writing *extends* the field and powers of a locutionary or gestural communication, are we not presupposing a kind of *homogenous* space of communication? The range of the voice or of gesture certainly appears to encounter a factual limit here, an empirical boundary in the form of space and time; and writing, within the same time, within the same space, manages to loosen the limits, to open the *same field* to a much greater range. Meaning, the content of the semantic message, is thus transmitted, *communicated*, by different *means*, by technically more powerful mediations, over a much greater distance, but within a milieu that is fundamentally continuous and equal to itself, within a homogenous element across which the unity and integrity of meaning is not affected in an essential way. Here, all affection is accidental.

The system of this interpretation (which is also in a way *the* system of interpretation, or in any event of an entire interpretation of hermeneutics), although it is the usual one, or to the extent that it is as usual as common sense, has been *represented* in the entire history of philosophy. I will say that it is even, fundamentally, the properly philosophical interpretation of writing. I will take a single example, but I do not believe one could find, in the entire history of philosophy as such, a single counterexample, a single analysis that essentially contradicts the one proposed by Condillac, inspired, strictly speaking, by Warburton, in the *Essay on the Origin of Human Knowledge* (*Essai sur l'origine des connaissances humaines*).[1] I have chosen this example because an *explicit* reflection on the origin and function of the written (this explicitness is not encountered in all philosophy, and one should examine the conditions of its emergence or occultation) is organized within a philosophical discourse which like all philosophy presupposes the simplicity of the origin and the continuity of every derivation, every production, every analysis, the homogeneity of all orders. Analogy is a major concept in Condillac's thought. I choose this example also because the analysis which "retraces" the origin and function of writing is placed, in a kind of noncritical way, *under the authority of the category of communication.*[2] If men write, it is (1) because they have something to communicate; (2) because what they have to communicate is their "thought," their "ideas," their representations. Representative thought precedes and governs communication which transports the "idea," the signified content; (3) because men are already capable of communicating and of communicating their thought to each other when, in continuous fashion, they invent the means of communication that is writing. Here is a passage from chapter 13 of part 2 ("On Language and On Method"), section 1 ("On the Origin and Progress of Language"), (writing is thus a modality of language and marks a continuous progress in a communication of linguistic essence), section 13, "On Writing": "Men capable of communicating their thoughts to each other by sounds felt the necessity of imagining new signs apt to perpetuate them and to make them *known* to *absent* persons" (I italicize this value of *absence*, which, if newly reexamined, will risk introducing a certain break in the homogeneity of the system). As soon as men are capable of "communicating their thoughts," and of doing so by sounds (which is, according to Condillac, a secondary stage, articulated language coming to "supplement" the language of action, the unique and radical principle of all language), the birth and progress of writing will follow a direct, simple, and continuous line. The history of writing will conform to a law of mechanical economy: to gain the most space and time by means of the most convenient abbreviation; it will never have the least effect on the structure and content of the meaning (of ideas) that it will have to vehiculate. The same content, previously communicated by gestures and sounds, henceforth will be transmitted by writing, and successively by different modes of notation, from pictographic writing up to alphabetic writing, passing through the hieroglyphic writing of the Egyptians and the ideographic writing of the Chinese. Condillac continues: "Imagination then will represent but the *same* images that they had already expressed by actions and words, and which had, from the beginnings, made language figurative and metaphoric. *The most natural means* was therefore to draw the pictures of things. To *express the idea* of a man or a horse the form of one or the other will be represented, and the first attempt at writing was but a simple painting" (p. 252; my italics).

The representative character of written communication—writing as picture, reproduction, imitation of its content—will be the invariable trait of all the progress to come. The concept of *representation* is indissociable here from the concepts of *communication* and *expression* that I have underlined in Condillac's text. Representation, certainly, will be complicated, will be given supplementary way-stations and stages, will become the representation of representation in hieroglyphic and ideographic writing, and then in phonetic-alphabetic writing, but the representative structure which marks the first stage of expressive communication, the idea/sign relationship, will never be suppressed or transformed. Describing the history of the kinds of writing, their continuous derivation on the basis of a common radical which is never displaced and which procures a kind of community of analogical participation between all the forms of writing, Condillac concludes (and this is practically a citation of Warburton, as is almost the entire chapter): "This is the general history of writing conveyed by a *simple gradation* from the state of painting through that of the letter; for letters are *the last steps* which remain to be taken after the Chinese marks, which partake of letters precisely as hieroglyphs partake equally of Mexican paintings and of Chinese characters. These characters are so close to our writing that an alphabet *simply diminishes* the confusion of their number, and is their *succinct abbreviation*" (pp. 254–53).

Having placed in evidence the motif of the economic, *homogenous, and mechanical* reduction, let us now come back to the notion of *absence* that I noted in passing in Condillac's text. How is it determined?

1. First, it is the absence of the addressee. One writes in order to communicate something to those who are absent. The absence of the sender, the addressor, from the marks that he abandons, which are cut off from him and continue to produce effects beyond his presence and beyond the present actuality of his meaning, that is, beyond his life itself, this absence, which however belongs to the structure of all writing—and I will add, further on, of all language in general—this absence is never examined by Condillac.
2. The absence of which Condillac speaks is determined in the most classical fashion as a continuous modification, a progressive extenuation of presence. Representation regularly *supplements* presence. But this operation of supplementation ("to supplement" is one of the most decisive and frequently employed operative concepts on Condillac's *Essai*)[3] is not exhibited as a break in presence, but rather as a reparation and a continuous, homogenous modification of presence in representation.

Here, I cannot analyze everything that this concept of absence as a modification of presence presupposes, in Condillac's philosophy and elsewhere. Let us note merely that it governs another equally decisive operative concept (here I am classically, and for convenience, opposing *operative* to *thematic*) of the *Essai: to trace* and *to retrace*. Like the concept of supplementing, the concept of trace could be determined otherwise than in the way Condillac determines it. According to him, to trace means "to express," "to represent," "to recall," "to make present" ("in all likelihood painting owes its origin to the necessity of thus tracing our thoughts, and this necessity has doubtless contributed to conserving the language of action, as that which could paint the most easily," p. 253). The sign is born at the same time as imagination and memory, at the moment when it is demanded by the absence of the object for present perception ("Memory, as have seen, consists only in the power of reminding ourselves of the signs of our ideas, or the circumstances which accompanied them; and this capacity occurs only by virtue of the *analogy of signs* (my italics; this concept of analogy, which organizes Condillac's entire system, in general makes certain all the continuities, particularly the continuity of presence to absence) that we have chosen, and by virtue of the order that we have put between our ideas, the objects that we wish to retrace have to do with several of our present needs" (p. 129). This is true of all the orders of signs distinguished by Condillac (arbitrary, accidental, and even natural signs, a distinction which Condillac nuances, and on certain points, puts back into question in his Letters to Cramer). The philosophical operation that Condillac also calls "to retrace" consists in traveling back, by way of analysis and continuous decomposition, along the movement of genetic derivation which leads from simple sensation and present perception to the complex edifice of representation: from original presence to the most formal language of calculation.

It would be simple to show that, essentially, this kind of analysis of written signification neither begins nor ends with Condillac. If we say now that this analysis is "ideological," it is not primarily in order to contrast its notions to "scientific" concepts, or in order to refer to the often dogmatic—one could also say "ideological"—use made of the word ideology, which today is so rarely examined for its possibility and history. If I define notions of Condillac's kind as ideological, it is that against the background of a vast, powerful, and systematic philosophical tradition dominated by the self-evidence of the *idea* (*eidos*, *idea*), they delineate the field of reflection of the French "ideologues" who, in Condillac's wake, elaborated a theory of the sign as a representation of the idea, which itself represents the perceived thing. Communication, hence, vehiculates a representation as an ideal content (which will be called meaning); and writing is a species of this general communication. A species: a communication having relative specificity within a genus.

If we ask ourselves now what, in this analysis, is the essential predicate of this *specific difference*, we once again find *absence*.

Here I advance the following two propositions or hypotheses:

1. Since every sign, as much in the "language of action" as in articulated language (even before the intervention of writing in the classical sense), supposes a certain absence (to be determined), it must be because absence in the field of writing is of an original kind if any specificity whatsoever of the written sign is to be acknowledged.
2. If, perchance, the predicate thus assumed to characterize the absence proper to writing were itself found to suit every species of sign and communication, there would follow a general displacement: writing no longer would be a species of communication, and all the concepts to whose generality writing was subordinated (the concept itself as meaning, idea, or grasp of meaning and idea, the

concept of communication, of sign, etc.) would appear as noncritical, ill-formed concepts, or rather as concepts destined to ensure the authority and force of a certain historic discourse.

Let us attempt then, while continuing to take our point of departure from this classical discourse, to characterize the absence which seems to intervene in a fashion specific to the functioning of writing.

A written sign is proffered in the absence of the addressee. How is this absence to be qualified? One might say that at the moment when I write, the addressee may be absent from my field of present perception. But is not this absence only a presence that is distant, delayed, or in one form or another, idealized in its representation? It does not seem so, or at very least this distance, division, delay, *différence*[4] must be capable of being brought to a certain absolute degree of absence for the structure of writing, supposing that writing exists, to be constituted. It is here that *différence* as writing could no longer (be) an (ontological) modification of presence. My "written communication" must, if you will, remain legible despite the absolute disappearance of every determined addressee in general for it to function as writing, that is, for it to be legible. It must be repeatable—iterable—in the absolute absence of the addressee or of the empirically determinable set of addressees. This iterability (*iter*, once again, comes from *itara*, other in Sanskrit, and everything that follows may be read as the exploitation of the logic which links repetition to alterity), structures the mark of writing itself, and does so moreover for no matter what type of writing (pictographic, hieroglyphic, ideographic, phonetic, alphabetic, to use the old categories). A writing that was not structurally legible—iterable—beyond the death of the addressee would not be writing. Although all this appears self-evident, I do not want it to be assumed as such, and will examine the ultimate objection that might be made to this proposition. Let us imagine a writing with a code idiomatic enough to have been founded and known, as a secret cipher, only by two "subjects." Can it still be said that upon the death of the addressee, that is, of the two partners, the mark left by one of them is still a writing? Yes, to the extent to which, governed by a code, even if unknown and nonlinguistic, it is constituted, in its identity as a mark, by its iterability in the absence of whoever, and therefore ultimately in the absence of every empirically determinable "subject." This implies that there is no code—an organon of iterability—that is structurally secret. The possibility of repeating, and therefore of identifying, marks is implied in every code, making of it a communicable, transmittable, decipherable grid that is iterable for a third party, and thus for any possible user in general. All writing, therefore, in order to be what it is, must be able to function in the radical absence of every empirically determined addressee in general. And this absence is not a continuous modification of presence; it is a break in presence, "death," or the possibility of the "death" of the addressee, inscribed in the structure of the mark (and it is at this point, I note in passing, that the value or effect of transcendentality is linked necessarily to the possibility of writing and of "death" analyzed in this way). A perhaps paradoxical consequence of the recourse I am taking to iteration and to the code: the disruption, in the last analysis, of the authority of the code as a finite system of rules; the radical destruction, by the same token, of every context as a protocol of a code. We will come to this in a moment.

What holds for the addressee holds also, for the same reasons, for the sender or the producer. To write is to produce a mark that will constitute a kind of machine that is in turn productive, that my future disappearance in principle will not prevent from functioning and from yielding, and yielding itself to, reading and rewriting. When I say "my future disappearance," I do so to make this proposition more immediately acceptable. I must be able simply to say my disappearance, my nonpresence in general, for example the nonpresence of my meaning, of my intention-to-signify, of my wanting-to-communicate-this, from the emission or production of the mark. For the written to be the written, it must continue to "act" and to be legible even if what is called the author of the writing no longer answers for what he has written, for what he seems to have signed, whether he is provisionally absent, or if he is dead, or if in general he does not support, with his absolutely current and present intention or attention, the plenitude of his meaning, of that very thing which seems to be written "in his name." Here, we could reelaborate the analysis sketched out above for the addressee. The situation of the scribe and of the subscriber, as concerns the written, is fundamentally the same as that of the reader. This essential drifting, due to writing as an iterative structure cut off from all absolute responsibility, from *consciousness* as the authority of the last analysis, writing orphaned, and separated at birth from the assistance of its father, is indeed what Plato condemned in the *Phaedrus*. If Plato's gesture is, as I believe, the philosophical movement par excellence, one realizes what is at stake here.

Before specifying the inevitable consequences of these nuclear traits of all writing—to wit: (1) the break with the horizon of communication as the communication of consciousnesses or presences, and as the linguistic or semantic transport of meaning; (2) the subtraction of all writing from the semantic horizon or the hermeneutic horizon which, at least as a horizon of meaning, lets itself be punctured by writing; (3) the necessity of, in a way, *separating* the concept of polysemia from the concept I have elsewhere named *dissemination*, which is also the concept of writing; (4) the disqualification or the limit of the concept of the "real" or "linguistic" context, whose theoretical determination or empirical saturation are, strictly speaking, rendered impossible or insufficient by writing—I would like to demonstrate that the recognizable traits of the classical and narrowly defined concept of writing are generalizable. They would be valid not only for all the orders of "signs" and for all languages in general, but even, beyond semiolinguistic communication, for the entire field of what philosophy would call experience, that is, the experience of Being: so-called "presence."

In effect, what are the essential predicates in a minimal determination of the classical concept of writing?

1. A written sign, in the usual sense of the word, is therefore a mark which remains, which is not exhausted in the present of its inscription, and which can give rise to an iteration both in the absence of and beyond the presence of the empirically determined subject who, in a given context, has emitted or produced, it. This is how, traditionally at least, "written communication" is distinguished from "spoken communication."

2. By the same token, a written sign carries with it a force of breaking with its context, that is, the set of presences which organize the moment of its inscription. This force of breaking is not an accidental predicate, but the very structure of the written. If the issue is one of the so-called "real" context, what I have just proposed is too obvious. Are part of this alleged real context a certain "present" of inscription, the presence of the scriptor in what he has written, the entire environment and horizon of his experience, and above all the intention, the meaning which at a given moment would animate his inscription. By all rights, it belongs to the sign to be legible, even if the moment of its production is irremediably lost, and even if I do not know what its alleged author-scriptor meant consciously and intentionally at the moment he wrote it, that is abandoned it to its essential drifting. Turning now to the semiotic and internal context, there is no less a force of breaking by virtue of its essential iterability; one can always lift a written syntagma from the interlocking chain in which it is caught or given without making it lose every possibility of functioning, if not every possibility of "communicating,'" precisely. Eventually, one may recognize other such possibilities in it by inscribing or *grafting* it into other chains. No context can enclose it. Nor can any code, the code being here both the possibility and impossibility of writing, of its essential iterability (repetition/alterity).

3. This force of rupture is due to the spacing which constitutes the written sign: the spacing which separates it from other elements of the internal contextual chain (the always open possibility of its extraction and grafting), but also from all the forms of a present referent (past or to come in the modified form of the present past or to come) that is objective or subjective. This spacing is not the simple negativity of a lack, but the emergence of the mark. However, it is not the work of the negative in the service of meaning, or of the living concept, the *telos*, which remains *relevable* and reducible in the *Aufhebung* of a dialectics.[5]

Are these three predicates, along with the entire system joined to them, reserved, as is so often believed, for "written" communication, in the narrow sense of the word? Are they not also to be found in all language, for example in spoken language, and ultimately in the totality of "experience," to the extent that it is not separated from the field of the mark, that is, the grid of erasure and of difference, of unities of iterability, of unities separable from their internal or external context, and separable from themselves, to the extent that the very iterability which constitutes their identity never permits them to be a unity of self-identity?

Let us consider any element of spoken language, a large or small unity. First condition for it to function: its situation as concerns a certain code; but I prefer not to get too involved here with the concept of code, which does not appear certain to me; let us say that a certain self-identity of this element (mark, sign, etc.) must permit its recognition and repetition. Across empirical variations of tone, of voice, etc., eventually of a certain accent, for example, one must be able to recognize the identity, shall we say, of a signifying form. Why is this identity paradoxically the division or dissociation from itself which will make of this phonic sign a grapheme? It is because this unity of the signifying form is constituted only by its iterability, by the possibility of being repeated in the absence not only of its referent, which goes without saying, but of a determined signified or current intention of signification, as of every present intention of communication. This structural possibility of being severed from its referent or signified (and therefore from communication and its context) seems to me to make of every mark, even if oral, a grapheme in general, that is, as we have seen, the nonpresent *remaining* of a differential mark cut off from its alleged "production" or origin. And I will extend this law even to all "experience" in general, if it is granted that there is no experience of *pure* presence, but only chains of differential marks.

Let us remain at this point for a while, and come back to the absence of the referent and even of the signified sense, and therefore of the correlative intention of signification. The absence of the referent is a possibility rather easily admitted today. This possibility is not only an empirical eventuality. It constructs the mark; and the eventual presence of the referent at the moment when it is designated changes nothing about the structure of a mark which implies that it can do without the referent. Husserl, in the *Logical Investigations*, had very rigorously analyzed this possibility. It is double:

1. A statement whose object is not impossible but only possible might very well be proffered and understood without its real object (its referent) being present, whether for the person who produces the statement, or for the one who receives it. If I say, while looking out the window, "The sky is blue;" the statement will be intelligible (let us provisionally say, if you will, communicable), even if the interlocutor does not see the sky; even if I do not see it myself, if I see poorly, if I am mistaken, or if I wish to trick my interlocutor. Not that it is always thus; but the structure of possibility of this statement includes the capability of being formed and of functioning either as an empty reference, or cut off from its referent. Without this possibility, which is also the general, generalizable, and generalizing iteration of every mark, there would be no statements.

2. The absence of the signified. Husserl analyzes this too. He considers it always possible, even if, according to the axiology and teleology which govern his analysis, he deems this possibility inferior, dangerous, or "critical": it opens the phenomenon of the crisis of meaning. This absence of meaning can be layered according to three forms:

   a. I can manipulate symbols without in active and current fashion animating them with my attention and intention to signify (the crisis of mathematical symbolism, according to Husserl). Husserl indeed stresses the fact that this does not prevent the sign from functioning: the crisis or vacuity of mathematical meaning does not limit technical progress. (The intervention of writing is decisive here, as Husserl himself notes in *The Origin of Geometry*.)

   b. Certain statements can have a meaning, although they are without *objective* signification. "The circle is square" is a proposition invested with meaning. It has enough meaning for me to be able to judge it false or contradictory (*wider-sinnig* and not *sinnlos*, says Husserl). I am placing this example under the category of the absence of the signified, although the tripartition signifier/signified/referent does not pertinently account for

Husserl's analysis. "Square circle" marks the absence of a referent, certainly, and also the absence of a certain signified, but not the absence of meaning. In these two cases, the crisis of meaning (nonpresence in general, absence as the absence of the referent—of perception—or of meaning—of the actual intention to signify) is always linked to the essential possibility of writing; and this crisis is not an accident, a factual and empirical anomaly of spoken language, but also the positive possibility and "internal" structure of spoken language, from a certain outside.

c. Finally there is what Husserl calls *Sinnlosigkeit* or agrammaticality. For example, "green is or" or "abracadabra." In the latter cases, as far as Husserl is concerned, there is no more language, or at least no more "logical" language, no more language of knowledge as Husserl understands it in teleological fashion, no more language attuned to the possibility of the intuition of objects given in person and signified in *truth*. Here, we are confronted with a decisive difficulty. Before pausing over it, I note, as a point which touches upon our debate on communication, that the primary interest of the Husserlian analysis to which I am referring here (precisely by extracting it, up to a certain point, from its teleological and metaphysical context and horizon, an operation about which we must ask how and why it is always possible) is that it alleges, and it seems to me arrives at, a rigorous dissociation of the analysis of the sign or expression (*Ausdruck*) as a signifying sign, a sign meaning something (*bedeutsame Zeichen*), from all phenomena of communication.[6]

Let us take once more the case of agrammatical *Sinnlosigkeit*. What interests Husserl in the *Logical Investigations* is the system of rules of a universal grammar, not from a linguistic point of view, but from a logical and epistemological point of view. In an important note from the second edition,[7] he specifies that from his point of view the issue is indeed one of a purely *logical* grammar, that is the universal conditions of possibility for a morphology of significations in the relation of knowledge to a possible object, and not of a pure grammar in *general*, considered from a psychological or linguistic point of view. Therefore, it is only in a context determined by a will to know, by an epistemic intention, by a conscious relation to the object as an object of knowledge within a horizon of truth—it is in this oriented contextual field that "green is or" is unacceptable. But, since "green is or" or "abracadabra" do not constitute their context in themselves, nothing prevents their functioning in another context as signifying marks (or indices, as Husserl would say). Not only in the contingent case in which, by means of the translation of German into French "*le vert est ou*" might be endowed with grammaticality, *ou* (*oder*, or) becoming when heard *où* (where, the mark of place): "Where has the green (of the grass) gone (*le vert est où*)?, "Where has the glass in which I wished to give you something to drink gone (*le verre est où*)." But even "green is or" still signifies an *example of agrammaticality*. This is the possibility on which I wish to insist: the possibility of extraction and of citational grafting which belongs to the structure of every mark, spoken or written, and which constitutes every mark as writing even before and outside every horizon of semiolinguistic communication; as writing, that is, as a possibility of functioning cut off, at a certain point, from its "original" meaning and from its belonging to a saturable and constraining context. Every sign, linguistic or nonlinguistic, spoken or written (in the usual sense of this opposition), as a small or large unity, can be *cited*, put between quotation marks; thereby it can break with every given context, and engender infinitely new contexts in an absolutely nonsaturable fashion. This does not suppose that the mark is valid outside its context, but on the contrary that there are only contexts without any center of absolute anchoring. This citationality, duplication, or duplicity, this iterability of the mark is not an accident or an anomaly, but is that (normal/abnormal) without which a mark could no longer even have a so-called "normal" functioning. What would a mark be that one could not cite? And whose origin could not be lost on the way?

The parasites. Iter, of writing: that perhaps it does not exist
I now propose to elaborate this question a little further with help from— but in order to go beyond it too—the problematic of the *performative*. It has several claims to our interest here.

1. Austin,[8] by his emphasis on the analysis of perlocution and especially illocution, indeed seems to consider acts of discourse only as acts of communication. This is what his French translator notes, citing Austin himself: "It is by comparing the *constative* utterance (that is, the classical 'assertion,' most often conceived as a true or false 'description' of the facts) with the *performative* utterance (from the English *performative*, that is, the utterance which allows us to do something by means of speech itself) that Austin has been led to consider *every* utterance worthy of the name (that is, destined to

communicate, which would exclude, for example, reflex-exclamations) as being first and foremost a *speech act* produced in the *total* situation in which the interlocutors find themselves (*How to Do Things With Words*, p. 147)."[9]

2. This category of communication is relatively original. Austin's notions of illocution and perlocution do not designate the transport or passage of a content of meaning, but in a way the communication of an original movement (to be defined in a *general theory of action*), an operation, and the production of an effect. To communicate, in the case of the performative, if in all rigor and purity some such thing exists (for the moment I am placing myself within this hypothesis and at this stage of the analysis), would be to communicate a force by the impetus of a mark.

3. Differing from the classical assertion, from the constative utterance, the performative's referent (although the word is inappropriate here, no doubt, such is the interest of Austin's finding) is not outside it, or in any case preceding it or before it. It does not describe something which exists outside and before language. It produces or transforms a situation, it operates; and if it can be said that a constative utterance also effectuates something and always transforms a situation, it cannot be said that this constitutes its internal structure, its manifest function or destination, as in the case of the performative.

Austin had to free the analysis of the performative from the authority of the *value of truth*, from the opposition true/false,[10] at least in its classical form, occasionally substituting for it the value of force, of difference of force (*illocutionary or perlocutionary force*). (It is this, in a thought which is nothing less than Nietzschean, which seems to me to beckon toward Nietzsche; who often recognized in himself a certain affinity with a vein of English thought.)

For these four reasons, at least, it could appear that Austin has exploded the concept of communication as a purely semiotic, linguistic, or symbolic concept. The performative is a "communication" which does not essentially limit itself to transporting an already constituted semantic content guarded by its own aiming at truth (truth as an *unveiling* of that which is in its Being, or as an *adequation* between a judicative statement and the thing itself).

And yet—at least this is what I would like to attempt to indicate now—all the difficulties encountered by Austin in an analysis that is patient, open, aporetic, in constant transformation, often more fruitful in the recognition of its impasses than in its positions, seem to me to have a common root. It is this: Austin has taken into account that which in the structure of *locution* (and therefore before any illocutory or perlocutory determination) already bears within itself the system of predicates that I call *graphematic in general*, which therefore confuses all the ulterior oppositions whose pertinence, purity, and rigor Austin sought to establish in vain.

In order to show this, I must take as known and granted that Austin's analyses permanently demand a value of *context*, and even of an exhaustively determinable context, whether de jure or teleologically; and the long list of "infelicities" of variable type which might affect the event of the performative always returns to an element of what Austin calls the total context.[11] One of these essential elements—and not one among others—classically remains consciousness, the conscious presence of the intention of the speaking subject for the totality of his locutory act. Thereby, performative communication once more becomes the communication of an intentional meaning,[12] even if this meaning has no referent in the form of a prior or exterior thing or state of things. This conscious presence of the speakers or receivers who participate in the effecting of a performative, their conscious and intentional presence in the totality of the operation, implies teleologically that no *remainder* escapes the present totalization. No remainder, whether in the definition of the requisite conventions, or the internal and linguistic context, or the grammatical form or semantic determination of the words used; no irreducible polysemia, that is no "dissemination" escaping the horizon of the unity of meaning. I cite the first two lectures of *How to Do Things with Words*: "Speaking generally, it is always necessary that the *circumstances* in which the words are uttered should be in some way, or ways, *appropriate*, and it is very commonly necessary that either the speaker himself or other persons should *also* perform certain *other* actions, whether 'physical' or 'mental' actions or even acts of uttering further words. Thus, for naming the ship, it is essential that I should be the person appointed to name her, for (Christian) marrying, it is essential that I should not be already married with a wife living, sane and undivorced, and so on; for a bet to have been made, it is generally necessary for the offer of the bet to have been accepted by a taker (who must have done something, such as to say 'Done'), and it is hardly a gift if I say 'I give it you' but never hand it over. So far, well and good" (pp. 8–9).

In the Second Lecture, after having in his habitual fashion set aside the grammatical criterion, Austin examines the possibility and origin of the failures or "infelicities" of the performative utterance. He then defines the six indispensable, if not sufficient, conditions for success. Through the values of "conventionality," "correctness," and "completeness" that intervene in the definition, we necessarily again find those of an exhaustively definable context, of a free consciousness present for the totality of the operation, of an absolutely full meaning that is master of itself: the teleological jurisdiction of a total field whose *intention* remains the organizing center (pp. 12–16). Austin's procedure is rather remarkable, and typical of the philosophical tradition that he prefers to have little to do with. It consists in recognizing that the possibility of the negative (here, the *infelicities*) is certainly a structural possibility, that failure is an essential risk in the operations under consideration; and then, with an almost *immediately simultaneous* gesture made in the name of a kind of ideal regulation, an exclusion of this risk as an accidental, exterior one that teaches us nothing about the language phenomenon under consideration. This is all the more curious, and actually rigorously untenable, in that Austin denounces with irony the "fetish" of opposition *value/fact*.

Thus, for example, concerning the conventionality without which there is no performative, Austin recognizes that *all* conventional acts are *exposed* to failure: "It seems clear in the first place that, although it has excited us (or failed to excite us) in connexion with certain acts which are or are in part acts of *uttering words*, infelicity is an ill to which *all* acts are heir which have the general character of ritual or ceremonial, all *conventional* acts: not indeed that *every* ritual is liable to every form of infelicity (but then nor is every performative utterance)" (pp. 18–19; Austin's italics).

Aside from all the questions posed by the very historically sedimented notion of "convention," we must notice here: (1) That in this specific place Austin seems to consider only the conventionality that forms the *circumstance* of the statement, its contextual surroundings, and not a certain intrinsic conventionality of that which constitutes locution itself, that is, everything that might quickly be summarized under the problematic heading of the "arbitrariness of the sign"; which extends, aggravates, and radicalizes the difficulty. Ritual is not an eventuality, but, as iterability, is a structural characteristic of every mark. (2) That the value of risk or of being open to failure, although it might, as Austin recognizes, affect the totality of conventional acts, is not examined as an essential predicate or law. Austin does not ask himself what consequences derive from the fact that something possible—a possible risk—is *always* possible, is somehow a necessary possibility. And if, such a necessary possibility of failure being granted, it still constitutes an accident. What is a success when the possibility of failure continues to constitute its structure?

Therefore the opposition of the success/failure of illocution or perlocution here seems quite insufficient or derivative. It presupposes a general and systematic elaboration of the structure of locution which avoids the endless alternation of essence and accident. Now, it is very significant that Austin rejects this "general theory," defers it on two occasions, notably in the Second Lecture. I leave aside the first exclusion. ("I am not going into the general doctrine here: in many such cases we may even say the act was 'void' (or voidable for duress or undue influence) and so forth. Now I suppose that some very general high-level doctrine might embrace both what we have called infelicities *and* these other 'unhappy' features of the doing of actions—in our case actions containing a performative utterance—in a single doctrine: but we are not including this kind of unhappiness—we must just remember, though, that features of this sort can and do *constantly obtrude* into any case we are discussing. Features of this sort would normally come under the heading of 'extenuating circumstances' or of 'factors reducing or abrogating the agent's responsibility,' and so on"; p. 21; my italics). The second gesture of exclusion concerns us more directly here. In question, precisely, is the possibility that every performative utterance (and a priori every other utterance) may be "cited." Now, Austin excludes this eventuality (and the general doctrine which would account for it) with a kind of lateral persistence, all the more significant in its off-sidedness. He insists upon the fact that this possibility remains *abnormal, parasitical*, that it constitutes a kind of extenuation, that is an agony of language that must firmly be kept at a distance, or from which one must resolutely turn away. And the concept of the "ordinary," and therefore of "ordinary language," to which he then has recourse is indeed marked by this exclusion. This makes it all the more problematic, and before demonstrating this, it would be better to read a paragraph from this Second Lecture:

(ii) Secondly, as *utterances* our performatives are *also* heir to certain other kinds of ill which infect *all* utterances. And these likewise, though again they might be brought into a more general account, we are deliberately at present excluding. I mean, for example, the following: a performative utterance will, for example, be *in a peculiar way* hollow or void if said by an actor on the stage, or if introduced in a poem, or spoken in soliloquy. This applies in a similar manner to any and every utterance—a sea-change in special circumstances. Language in such circumstances is in special ways—intelligibly—used not *seriously* [I am italicizing here, J. D.], but in ways *parasitic* upon its normal use—ways which fall under the doctrine of the *etiolations* of language. All this we are *excluding* from consideration. Our performative utterances, felicitous or not, are to be understood as issued in ordinary circumstances" (pp. 21–22). Austin therefore excludes, along with what he calls the *sea-change*, the "non-serious," the "parasitic," the "etiolations," the "non-ordinary" (and with them the general theory which in accounting for these oppositions no longer would be governed by them), which he nevertheless recognizes as the possibility to which every utterance is open. It is also as a "parasite" that writing has always been treated by the philosophical tradition, and the rapprochement, here, is not at all fortuitous.

Therefore, I ask the following question: is this general possibility necessarily that of a failure or a trap into which language might *fall*, or in which language might lose itself, as if in an abyss situated outside or in front of it? What about *parasitism*? In other words, does the generality of the risk admitted by Austin surround language like a kind of *ditch*, a place of external perdition into which locution might never venture, that it might avoid by remaining at home, in itself, sheltered by its essence or *telos*? Or indeed is this risk, on the contrary, its internal and positive condition of possibility? this outside its inside? the very force and law of its emergence? In this last case, what would an "ordinary" language defined by the very law of language signify? Is it that in excluding the general theory of this structural parasitism, Austin, who nevertheless pretends to describe the facts and events of ordinary language, makes us accept as ordinary a teleological and ethical determination (the univocality of the statement—which he recognizes elsewhere remains a philosophical "ideal," pp. 72–73—the self-presence of a total context, the transparency of intentions, the presence of meaning for the absolutely singular oneness of a speech act, etc.)?

For, finally, is not what Austin excludes as anomalous, exceptional, "nonserious,"[13] that is, *citation* (on the stage, in a poem, or in a soliloquy), the determined modification of a general citationality—or rather, a general iterability—without which there would not even be a "successful" performative? Such that—a paradoxical, but inevitable consequence—a successful performative is necessarily an "impure" performative, to use the word that Austin will employ later on when he recognizes that there is no "pure" performative.[14]

Now I will take things from the side of positive possibility, and no longer only from the side of failure: would a performative statement be possible if a citational doubling did not eventually split, dissociate from itself the pure singularity of the event? I am asking the question in this form in order to forestall an objection. In effect, it might be said to me: you cannot allege that you account for the so-called graphematic structure of locution solely on the basis of the occurrence of failures of the performative, however real these failures might be, and however effective or general their possibility. You cannot deny that there are also performatives that succeed, and they must be accounted for: sessions are opened, as Paul Ricoeur did yesterday, one says "I ask a question," one bets, one challenges, boats are launched, and one even marries occasionally. Such events, it appears, have occurred. And were a single one of them to have taken place a single time, it would still have to be accounted for.

I will say "perhaps." Here, we must first agree upon what the "occurring" or the eventhood of an event consists in, when the event supposes in its allegedly present and singular intervention a statement which in itself can be only of a repetitive or citational structure, or rather, since these last words lead to confusion, of an iterable structure. Therefore, I come back to the point which seems fundamental to me, and which now concerns the status of the event in general, of the event of speech or by speech, of the strange logic it supposes, and which often remains unperceived.

Could a performative statement succeed if its formulation did not repeat a "coded" or iterable statement, in other words if the expressions I use to open a meeting, launch a ship or a marriage were not identifiable as *conforming* to an iterable model, and therefore if they were not identifiable in a way as "citation"? Not that citationality here is of the same type as in a play, a philosophical reference, or the recitation of a poem. This is why there is a relative specificity, as Austin says, a "relative purity" of performatives. But this relative purity is not constructed against citationality or iterability, but against other kinds of iteration within a general iterability which is the effraction into the allegedly rigorous purity of every event of discourse or every speech act. Thus, one must less oppose citation or iteration to the noniteration of an event, than construct a differential typology of forms of iteration, supposing that this is a tenable project that can give rise to an exhaustive program, a question I am holding off on here. In this typology, the category of intention will not disappear; it will have its place, but from this place it will no longer be able to govern the entire scene and the entire system of utterances. Above all, one then would be concerned with different types of marks or chains of iterable marks, and not with an opposition between citational statements on the one hand, and singular and original statement-events on the other. The first consequence of this would be the following: given this structure of iteration, the intention which animates utterance will never be completely present in itself and its content. The iteration which structures it a priori introduces an essential dehiscence and demarcation. One will no longer be able to exclude, as Austin wishes, the "non-serious," the *oratio obliqua*, from "ordinary" language. And if it is alleged that ordinary language, or the ordinary circumstance of language, excludes citationality or general iterability, does this not signify that the "ordinariness" in question, the thing and the notion, harbors a lure, the teleological lure of consciousness whose motivations, indestructible necessity, and systematic effects remain to be analyzed? Especially since this essential absence of intention for the actuality of the statement, this structural unconsciousness if you will, prohibits every saturation of a context. For a context to be exhaustively determinable, in the sense demanded by Austin, it at least would be necessary for the conscious intention to be totally present and actually transparent for itself and others, since it is a determining focal point of the context. The concept of or quest for the "context" therefore seems to suffer here from the same theoretical and motivated uncertainty as the concept of the "ordinary," from the same metaphysical origins: an ethical and teleological discourse of consciousness. This time, a reading of the connotations of Austin's text would confirm the reading of its descriptions; I have just indicated the principle of this reading.

Différance, the irreducible absence of intention or assistance from the performative statement, from the most "event-like" statement possible, is what authorizes me, taking into account the predicates mentioned just now, to posit the general graphematic structure of every "communication." Above all, I will not conclude from this that there is no relative specificity of the effects of consciousness, of the effects of speech (in opposition to writing in the traditional sense), that there is no effect of the performative, no effect of ordinary language, no effect of presence and of speech acts. It is simply that these effects do not exclude what is generally opposed to them term by term, but on the contrary presuppose it in dyssemtrical fashion, as the general space of their possibility.

Signatures

This general space is first of all spacing as the disruption of presence in the mark, what here I am calling writing. That all the difficulties encountered by Austin intersect at the point at which both presence and writing are in question, is indicated for me by a passage from the Fifth Lecture in which the divided agency of the legal *signature* emerges.

Is it by chance that Austin must note at this point: "I must explain again that we are floundering here. To feel the firm ground of prejudice slipping away is exhilarating, but brings its revenges" (p. 61). Only a little earlier an "impasse" had appeared, the impasse one comes to each time "any *single simple* criterion of grammar or vocabulary'" is sought in order to distinguish between performative or constative statements. (I must say that this critique of linguisticism and of the authority of the code, a critique executed on the basis of an analysis of language, is what most interested me and convinced me in Austin's enterprise.) He then attempts to justify, with nonlinguistic reasons, the preference he has shown until now for the forms of the first-person present indicative in the active voice in the analysis of the performative. The justification of last appeal is that in these forms reference is made to what Austin calls the *source* (origin) of the utterance. This notion of the *source*—whose stakes are so evident— often reappears in what follows, and it governs the entire analysis in the phase we are examining. Not only does Austin not doubt that the source of an oral statement in the first-person present indicative (active voice) is *present* in the utterance and in the statement, (I have attempted to explain why we had reasons not to believe so), but he no more doubts that the equivalent of this link to the source in written utterances is simply evident and ascertained in the *signature*: "Where there is not, in the verbal formula of the utterance, a reference to the person doing the uttering, and so the acting, by means of the pronoun 'I' (or by his personal name), then in fact he will be 'referred to' in one of two ways:

"(a) In verbal utterances, *by his being the person who does* the uttering— what we may call the utterance-*origin* which is used generally in any system of verbal reference-co-ordinates.
"(b) In written utterances (or 'inscriptions'), *by his appending his signature* (this has to be done because, of course, written utterances are not tethered to their origin in the way spoken ones are)" (pp. 60–61). Austin acknowledges an analogous function in the expression "hereby" used in official protocols.

Let us attempt to analyze the signature from this point of view, its relation to the present and to the source. I take it as henceforth implied in this analysis that all the established predicates will hold also for the oral "signature" that is, or allegedly is, the presence of the "author" as the "person who does the uttering," as the "origin," the source, in the production of the statement.

By definition, a written signature implies the actual or empirical nonpresence of the signer. But, it will be said, it also marks and retains his having-been present in a past now, which will remain a future now, and therefore in a now in general, in the transcendental form of nowness (*maintenance*). This general *maintenance* is somehow inscribed, stapled to present punctuality, always evident and always singular, in the form of the signature. This is the enigmatic originality of every paraph. For the attachment to the source to occur, the absolute singularity of an event of the signature and of a form of the signature must be retained: the pure reproducibility of a pure event.

Is there some such thing? Does the absolute singularity of an event of the signature ever occur? Are there signatures?

Yes, of course, every day. The effects of signature are the most ordinary thing in the world. The condition of possibility for these effects is simultaneously, once again, the condition of their impossibility, of the impossibility of their rigorous purity. In order to function, that is, in order to be legible, a signature must have a repeatable, iterable, imitable form; it must be able to detach itself from the present and singular intention of its production. It is its sameness which, in altering its identity and singularity, divides the seal. I have already indicated the principle of the analysis above.

To conclude this very *dry*[15] discourse:

1. As writing, communication, if one insists upon maintaining the word, is not the means of transport of sense, the exchange of intentions and meanings, the discourse and "communication of consciousnesses." We are not witnessing an end of writing which, to follow McLuhan's ideological representation, would restore a transparency or immediacy of social relations; but indeed a more and more powerful historical unfolding of a general writing of which the system of speech, consciousness, meaning, presence, truth, etc., would only be an effect, to be analyzed as such. It is this questioned effect that I have elsewhere called *logocentrism*.

2. The semantic horizon which habitually governs the notion of communication is exceeded or punctured by the intervention of writing, that is of a *dissemination* which cannot be reduced to a *polysemia*. Writing is read, and "in the last analysis" does not give rise to a hermeneutic deciphering, to the decoding of a meaning or truth.

3. Despite the general displacement of the classical, "philosophical," Western, etc., concept of writing, it appears necessary, provisionally and strategically, to conserve the *old name*. This implies an entire logic of *paleonymy* which I do not wish to elaborate here.[16] Very schematically: an opposition of metaphysical concepts (for example, speech/writing, presence/absence, etc.) is never the face-to-face of two terms, but a hierarchy and an order of subordination. Deconstruction cannot limit itself or proceed immediately to a neutralization: it must, by means of a double gesture, a double science, a double writing, practice an *overturning* of the classical opposition *and* a general *displacement* of the system. It is only on this condition that deconstruction will provide itself the means with which to *intervene* in the field of oppositions that it criticizes, which is also a field of nondiscursive forces. Each concept, moreover,

belongs to a systematic chain, and itself constitutes a system of predicates. There is no metaphysical concept in and of itself. There is a work—metaphysical or not—on conceptual systems. Deconstruction does not consist in passing from one concept to another, but in overturning and displacing a conceptual order, as well as the nonconceptual order with which the conceptual order is articulated. For example, writing, as a classical concept, carries with it predicates which have been subordinated, excluded, or held in reserve by forces and according to necessities to be analyzed. It is these predicates (I have mentioned some) whose force of generality, generalization, and generativity find themselves liberated, grafted onto a "new" concept of writing which also corresponds to whatever always has *resisted* the former organization of forces, which always has constituted the *remainder* irreducible to the dominant force which organized the—to say it quickly—logocentric hierarchy. To leave to this new concept the old name of writing is to maintain the structure of the graft, the transition and indispensable adherence to an effective *intervention* in the constituted historic field. And it is also to give their chance and their force, their power of *communication*, to everything played out in the operations of deconstruction.

But what goes without saying will quickly have been understood, especially in a philosophical colloquium: as a disseminating operation *separated* from presence (of Being) according to all its modifications, writing, if there is any, perhaps communicates, but does not exist, surely. Or barely, hereby, in the form of the most improbable signature.

(*Remark*: the-written-text of this-oral-communication was to have been addressed to the *Association of French Speaking Societies of Philosophy* before the meeting. Such a missive therefore had to be signed. Which I did, and counterfeit here. Where? There. J. D.)

J. DERRIDA

Notes

1 TN. *Essai sur l'origine des connaissances humaines*, with an introductory essay by Jacques Derrida (Paris: Galilee, 1973).

2 Rousseau's theory of language and writing is also proposed under the general rubric of *communication*. ("On the Various Means of Communicating Our Thoughts" is the title of the first chapter of the *Essay on the Origin of Languages*.)

3 Language supplements action or perception, articulated language supplements the language of action, writing supplements articulated language, etc.

4 TN. On the concept of *différence*, see "La différance," above, and my notes 7, 8, 9, and 10.

5 TN. On Derrida's translation of *Aufheben* as *relever*, and my maintenance of the French term, see note 23 to "La différance," above, for a system of references.

6 "So far we have considered expressions as used in communication, which last depends essentially on the fact that they operate indicatively. But expressions also play a great part in uncommunicated, interior mental life. This change in function plainly has nothing to do with whatever makes an expression an expression. Expressions continue to have *Bedeutungen* as they had before, and the same *Bedeutungen* as in dialogue." *Logical Investigations*, trans. J. N. Findlay (London: Routledge and Kegan Paul, 1970), p. 278. What I am asserting here implies the interpretation I proposed of Husserlian procedure on this point. Therefore, I permit myself to refer to *Speech and Phenomena*.

7 "In the First Edition I spoke of 'pure grammar,' a name conceived and expressly devised to be analogous to Kant's 'pure science of nature.' Since it cannot, however, be said that pure formal semantic theory comprehends the entire *a priori* of general grammar—there is, e.g., a peculiar *a priori* governing relations of mutual understanding among minded persons, relations very important for grammar—talk of pure logical grammar is to be preferred." *Logical Investigations*, vol. 2, p. 527. [In the paragraph that follows I have maintained Findlay's translation of the phrase Derrida plays upon, i.e. "green is or," and have given the French necessary to comprehend this passage in parentheses.]

8 TN. J. L. Austin, *How to Do Things with Words* (New York: Oxford University Press, 1962). Throughout this section I have followed the standard procedure of translating *enoncé* as statement, and *énonciation* as utterance.

9 G. Lane, Introduction to the French translation of *How to Do Things with Words*.

10 " . . . two fetishes which I admit to an inclination to play Old Harry with, viz., 1) the true/false fetish, 2) the value/fact fetish" (p. 150).

11 See e.g. pp. 52 and 147.

12 Which sometimes compels Austin to reintroduce the criterion of truth into the description of performatives. See e.g. pp. 51–52 and 89–90.

13 The very suspect value of the "non-serious" is a frequent reference (see e.g. pp. 104, 121). It has an essential link with what Austin says elsewhere about the *oratio obliqua* (pp. 70–71) and about *mime*.

14 From this point of view one might examine the fact recognized by Austin that "the *same* sentence is used on different occasions of utterance in *both* ways, performative and constative. The thing seems hopeless from the start, if we are to leave utterances *as they stand* and seek for a criterion" (p. 67). It is the graphematic root of citationality (iterability) that provokes this confusion, and makes it "not possible," as Austin says, "to lay down even a list of all possible criteria" (ibid.).

15 TN. Derrida's word here is *sec*, combining the initial letters of three words that form his title, Signature, Event, Context.

16 See *Dissemination* and *Positions*.

Part III

Consciousness

5 'THE SUPPLEMENT OF ORIGIN'

SPEECH AND PHENOMENA (DERRIDA 1973 [FIRST PUBLISHED 1967])

Translated by David B. Allison and Newton Garver

Themes

Derrida sets up the concept, or quasi-concept, of 'différance' in this paper, which became the topic of a paper in its own right in 1968, 'Différance', and appears in both the English edition of *Speech and Phenomena* (Derrida 1973) as well as in *Margins of Philosophy* (Derrida 1982), which is where Derrida placed it. 'Différance' is a term invented by Derrida that sounds exactly the same as 'différence', the normal French word for 'difference'. The difference between the two words in French can be seen in written form but not heard in speech. One aspect of this is to emphasise that meanings in words are dependent on the written form as well as on the spoken form. Derrida also suggests that 'différence' contains reference to 'deferral', that is to what comes in the future. His sense of difference is not just of static differences within an atemporal system, but also of difference in time. What is also captured here is: Heidegger's 'ontological difference' between Being as such and the being of particular beings or entities; difference in Hegel's logic; differences between psychic and neural forces in the mind, partly with reference to Freud. That is an issue for consciousness, because the idea of a transparent consciousness completely present to itself is undermined by the way in which the contents of consciousness can only be defined with regard to what is not there. In that case, there is no pure presence of consciousness since what is present in consciousness depends on absence. That structure of consciousness is also the supplementary, and substitutive, structure of the sign. The sign is only defined through substitution by other signs. The substitutions show the need for the supplementation of the original sign. The substitutability of the sign and its supplementary nature are present in consciousness. This is not an example of 'linguistic idealism' or the supremacy of the sign though. The supplementary and substitutive structure characterise psychic forces of the mind and the neural forces of the brain, in an intertwined way, according to Derrida.

Derrida establishes these themes in 'The Supplement of Origin' through the close and critical reading of Husserl. His own commitment to the ideal aspect of meaning, and all intentions of consciousness, in expression, precludes the idea that meaning depends on the presence of the object meant. In this way, Husserl undermines his own suggestion that 'intuitive cognitions' fulfil meaning. The meaning of an object cannot be fulfilled by the empirical acts of intuitive cognition, because Husserl regards the objects of meaning as what goes beyond the intuitions of objects. Meanings are ideal; intuitions are empirical.

The way in which meaning excludes the intuition of the object must refer to the 'I' of consciousness. A contradiction is created, because the 'I', which refers to itself, refers to itself as referring and does not refer to anything. It does not refer to any object, because there is no object to which it can refer given that there is no object which satisfies the infinite possibilities contained within meaning. However, since there is an 'I' that is referring, 'I' must refer to an object. In that case, there is an unavoidable contradiction infecting the 'I' of consciousness, the 'I' which constitutes consciousness. This puzzle of the 'I' goes back to the relation between transcendental and empirical ego in Kant's *Critique of Pure Reason* [1781]; and the relation between 'I' and not 'I' in Fichte's *Science of Knowledge* [1794].

Notions of sense, intentionality, and the presence of an object are tied together in consciousness and in a particular structure of consciousness in Husserl's phenomenology, but in a contradictory way. The object, including the meaning-object of language, is required to be the empirical object of empirical intuitions-sensations and to be the abstract object of sense as pure meaning. That contradiction is one way of dealing with the differences of forces which make up meaning, consciousness and the physical processes of the brain, which Derrida refers to Nietzsche and to Freudian psychoanalysis.

Context
Derrida is concerned with questioning a metaphysical tradition in which the interior is valued over the exterior. That is the starting point for a

series of oppositions: truth over falsity; essence over appearance; being over becoming; good over evil. These oppositions have dominated metaphysical philosophy, and given the necessary tendency of language towards abstractions which are metaphysical, even the most empiricist philosophy cannot be completely free of such oppositions. The oppositions start with an opposition between what is inside and what is outside. That clearly applies to all conceptions of consciousness and mind. What is internal to consciousness is placed over what is external to consciousness. The language of the 'internal' and the 'external' has become established in recent analytic philosophical with regard to mind, meaning and knowledge. To a large degree the idea of externalism goes back to Saul Kripke's theory of reference in *Naming and Necessity* (Kripke 1981 [first published 1972]). Kripke has a causal theory of naming according to which I use a name for an object, because of a chain of causes external to myself which link the name back to the moment it was first applied to the object. Pure internalism is usually traced back to Descartes' claim that the mind is a different kind of substance from matter, so that the thinking self is cut off from the external material world. Wittgenstein's 'private language argument', along with analogous arguments in Quine and Sellars are usually taken to have defeated pure internalism. Kripke along with logical and metaphysical arguments of Tye Burge, and arguments about cognitive psychology in Stephen Stich, provide a source for pure externalism. Given Derrida's objections to the metaphysics of the internal, there may be a case for seeing Derrida as a pure externalist. However, in Derrida's strategies of deconstruction, the reversal of the hierarchy of two terms may be a strategy but cannot be the end goal. The reality defended by Derrida is that the two opposites contain each other and are mutually dependent. That does not suggest a harmonisation between them; they are always in contradiction but belong together. In that case, attempts to establish a middle way between pure internalism and externalism in Hilary Putnam and Donald Davidson may be closer to Derrida. At least a couple of Derrida commentators have found Putnam and Derrida to be close; and at least a couple have found Derrida and Davidson to be close. Frank Farrell in 'Iterability and Meaning' (Farrell 1988) and Christopher Norris in *Language, Logic and Epistemology* (Norris 2004) both emphasise a link between Putnam and Derrida. Samuel Wheeler in 'Indeterminacy of French Translation' (Wheeler 1985) and *Deconstruction as Analytic Philosophy* (Wheeler 2000); and Geoffrey Bennington briefly in his commentary on Derrida written in conjunction with him, *Jacques Derrida* (Bennington and Derrida 1993) focus on Derrida and Davidson. Wheeler focuses more on issues of truth that can be most readily discussed in the section on Knowledge; and it is that which Bennington deals with briefly.

Farrell and Norris focus on the issues raised by Hilary Putnam in 'The Meaning of "Meaning"' (Putnam 1975). Like Kripke, Putnam's arguments refer to arguments about possibility and necessity; and like Kripke, Putnam is a modal realist. That is he claims that possibilities refers to states of affairs in at least one possible world. 'Realism' here can have the Platonist sense of 'realism' as a real abstraction in the way that we might think of numbers or classes of things as real. In some recent philosophers, most notably David K. Lewis, it may mean 'real' in the sense of other worlds that exist in parallel to our own. The argument here about modal realism is neutral between these different interpretations. Putnam argues for the indeterminacy of reference of names by using a through experiment about two very similar situations on Earth and Twin Earth. Earth and Twin Earth are identical in every respect except that while on Earth 'water' refers to the chemical compound H_2O, on Twin Earth 'water' refers to a substance which is identical in every respect with H_2O, except for its chemical structure which is a completely different combination of atoms. Someone thinking about 'water' at one moment on Earth, after science has made it widely known that water molecules are made up of two atoms of hydrogen in combination with one atom of oxygen, has a different reference than an identical someone on Twin Earth thinking the same thought about 'water' at the same moment. However, the reference must be different, in which case the meaning must be different, since there cannot be sameness of meaning where there is difference in reference. In that case, the same thoughts can have a different reference and meaning depending on external context and regardless of the content of the mind. The argument in Farrell, and Norris, is that the argument is very similar to Derrida's argument that meaning cannot be determined absolutely, and that meaning is definitely not determined within inner monologue.

Putnam's line of argument is picked up by Davidson in the earlier essays in *Subjective, Objective, Intersubjective* (Davidson 2001b), where Davidson aims like Putnam for a middle way but comes closer to internalism than Putnam. Davidson's philosophy consistently tries to avoid a rift and confrontation between the internal and the external, which Davidson avoids by emphasising that inner beliefs must be mostly true and must be true of the world in a way which means that they are not beliefs in a pure inner space. Davidson, and others, find modalism to be redundant in explaining situations of indeterminacy. Arguments for indeterminacy of reference can be found in W. V. O. Quine who was a strong opponent of modalism. In a book based on lectures of 1968,

Ontological Relativity and Other Essays (Quine 1977), he argues for 'Inscrutability of Reference', on the grounds that a term could apply to an object, a part of an object, a type, the background to an object and so on, with no definite way of determining the reference. The argument is set up in relation to Wittgenstein's private language argument but Quine argues that a better precedent exists in the work of the pragmatist philosopher John Dewey.

THE SUPPLEMENT OF ORIGIN

Thus understood, what is supplementary is in reality *différance*, the operation of differing which at one and the same time both fissures and retards presence, submitting it simultaneously to primordial division and delay. *Différance* is to be conceived prior to the separation between deferring as delay and differing as the active work of difference. Of course this is inconceivable if one begins on the basis of consciousness, that is, presence, or on the basis of its simple contrary, absence or nonconsciousness. It is also inconceivable as the mere *homogeneous* complication of a diagram or line of time, as a complex "succession." The supplementary difference vicariously stands in for presence due to its primordial self-deficiency. Going *through* the First Investigation, we must try to ascertain how far these concepts respect the relations between signs in general (indicative as well as expressive) and presence in general. When we say *through* Husserl's text, we mean a reading that can be neither simple commentary nor simple interpretation.

Let us note first that this concept of primordial supplementation not only implies nonplenitude of presence (or, in Husserl's language, the nonfulfillment of an intuition); it designates this function of substitutive supplementation [*suppléance*] in general, the "in the place of" (*für etwas*) structure which belongs to every sign in general. We were surprised, above, that Husserl did not submit the possibility of this structure to any critical questioning, that he assumed it as a matter of course when he distinguished between indicative and expressive signs. What we would ultimately like to draw attention to is that the for-itself of self-presence (*für-sich*)—traditionally determined in its dative dimension as phenomenological self-giving, whether reflexive or prereflexive—arises in the role of supplement as primordial substitution, in the form "in the place of" (*für etwas*), that is, as we have seen, in the very operation of significance in general. The *for-itself* would be *an in-the-place-of-itself*: put *for itself*, instead of itself. The strange structure of the supplement appears here: by delayed reaction, a possibility produces that to which it is said to be added on.

This structure of supplementation is quite complex. As a supplement, the signifier does not represent first and simply the absent signified. Rather, it is substituted for another signifier, for another type of signifier that maintains another relation with the deficient presence, one more highly valued by virtue of the play of difference. It is more highly valued because the play of difference is the movement of idealization and because, the more ideal the signifier is, the more it augments the power to repeat presence, the more it keeps, reserves, and capitalizes on its sense. Thus an indication is not merely a substitute that makes up for [*suppplée*] the absence or invisibility of the indicated term. The latter, it will be remembered, is always an *existent*. An indicative sign also replaces another kind of signifier, an expressive sign, a signifier whose signified (*Bedeutung*) is ideal. In real communicative speech, expression gives way to indication because, we saw, the sense aimed at by the other and, more generally, his experience are not presented to me in person and never can be. This is why Husserl says that, in such cases, expression functions "like indication."

It now remains to be seen—and this is most important—in what respect expression itself implies, in its very structure, a nonplenitude. It is known as being more full than indication, since the appresentational detour is no longer necessary here, and since it can function as such in the alleged self-presence of solitary speech.

It is important to see how from a distance—an articulated distance— an intuitionistic theory of knowledge determines Husserl's conception of language. The whole originality of this conception lies in the fact that its ultimate subjection to intuitionism does not oppress what might be called the freedom of language, the candor of speech, even if it is false and contradictory. One can speak without knowing. And against the whole philosophical tradition Husserl shows that in that case speech is still genuinely speech, provided it obeys certain rules which do not immediately figure as rules for knowledge. Pure logical grammar, pure formal semantic theory, must tell us *a priori* on what conditions speech can be speech, even where it makes no knowledge possible.

We must here consider the last exclusion—or reduction—to which Husserl invites us, so as to isolate the specific purity of expression. It is the most audacious one; it consists in putting out of play, as "nonessential components" of expression, the acts of intuitive cognition which "fulfill" meaning.

We know that the act of meaning, the act that confers *Bedeutung* (*Bedeutungsintention*), is always the aim of a relation with an object. But it is enough that this intention animates the body of a signifier for speech to take place. The fulfillment of the aim by an intuition is not indispensable. It belongs to the original structure of expression to be able to dispense with the full presence of the object aimed at by intuition. Once again evoking the confusion that arises from the intertwining (*Verflechtung*) of relations, Husserl writes in the First Investigation, §9:

> If we seek a foothold in pure description, the concrete phenomenon of the sense-informed (*sinnebelebten*) expression breaks up, on the one hand, into the *physical phenomenon* forming the physical side of the expression, and, on the other hand, into the *acts* which give it *meaning* and possibly also *intuitive fulness*, in which its relation to an expressed object is constituted. In virtue of such acts, the expression is more than a merely sounded word. It *means* something, and in so far as it means something, it relates to what is objective (ET, p. 280).[1]

Fullness therefore is only contingent. The absence of the object aimed at does not compromise the meaning, does not reduce the expression to its unanimated, and in itself meaningless, physical side.

> This objective somewhat [i.e., what was meant or intended] can either be actually present (*aktuell gegenwärtig*), through accompanying intuitions, or may at least appear in representation (*vergegenwärtigt*) e.g., in a mental image, and where this happens the relation to an object is realized. Alternatively this need not occur: the expression functions significantly (*fungiert sinnvoll*), it remains more than mere sound of words, but it lacks any basic intuition that will give it its object (ET, p. 280).

The "fulfilling" intuition therefore is not essential to expression, to what is aimed at by the meaning. The latter part of this chapter is wholly devoted to accumulating proofs of this difference between intention and intuition. Because they were blind in this respect, all the classical theories of language were unable to avoid aporias or absurdities,[2] which Husserl locates along the way. In the course of subtle and decisive analyses, which we cannot follow up here, he demonstrates the ideality of

Bedeutung and the noncoincidence between the *expression,* the *Bedeutung* (both as ideal unities), and the *object.* Two identical expressions may have the same *Bedeutung,* may mean the same thing, and yet have different objects (for example, the two propositions, "Bucephalus is a horse" and "This steed is a horse"). Two different expressions may have different *Bedeutungen* but refer to the same object (for example, the two expressions, "The victor at Jena" and "The vanquished at Waterloo"). Finally, two different expressions may have the same *Bedeutung* and the same object (London, *Londres; zwei,* two, *duo,* etc.).

Without such distinctions, no pure logical grammar would be possible. The possibility of a theory of the pure forms of judgments, which supports the entire structure of the *Formal and Transcendental Logic,* would be blocked. We know that pure logical grammar depends entirely on the distinction between *Widersinnigkeit* and *Sinnlosigkeit.* If it obeys certain rules, an expression may be *widersinnig* (contradictory, false, absurd according to a certain kind of absurdity) without ceasing to have an intelligible sense that permits normal speech to occur, without becoming nonsense (*Unsinn*). It may have no possible object for empirical reasons (a golden mountain) or for *a priori* reasons (a square circle) without ceasing to have an intelligible sense, without being *sinnlos.* The absence of an object (*Gegenstandslosigkeit*) is hence not the absence of meaning (*Bedeutungslosigkeit*). Pure logical grammar, then, excludes from normal discourse only what is nonsense in the sense of *Unsinn* ("Abracadabra," "Green is where"). If we were not able to understand what a "square circle" or "golden mountain" means, how could we come to a conclusion about the absence of a possible object for such expressions? It is this modicum of comprehension that is denied us in the *Unsinn,* in the ungrammaticalness of nonsense.

Following the logic and necessity of these distinctions, we might be tempted to maintain not only that meaning does not imply the intuition of the object but that it essentially excludes it. What is structurally original about meaning would be the *Gegenstandslosigkeit,* the absence of any object given to intuition. In the full presence that comes to fill the meaning's aim, intuition and intention are melted together, "forming an intimately blended unity (*eine innig verschmolzene Einheit*) of an original character."[3] This is to say that the language that speaks in the presence of its object effaces its own originality or lets it melt away; the structure peculiar to language alone, which allows it to function entirely *by itself* when its intention is cut off from intuition, here dissolves. Here, instead of suspecting that Husserl began his analysis and dissociation too soon, we could ask if he does not unify them too much and too soon. Are not two possibilities excluded from the start, namely, that the unity of intuition and intention can ever be homogeneous at all and that meaning can be fused into intuition without disappearing? And are they not excluded for reasons that are essential and structural, reasons that Husserl himself has adduced? To take up Husserl's language, are we not in principle excluded from ever "cashing in the draft made on intuition" *in expression?*

Let us consider the extreme case of a "statement about perception." Let us suppose that it is produced at the very moment of the perceptual intuition: I say, "I see a particular person by the window" while I really do see him. It is structurally implied in my performance that the content of this expression is ideal and that its unity is not impaired by the absence of perception here and now.[4] Whoever hears this proposition, whether he is next to me or infinitely removed in space and time, should, by right, understand what I mean to say. Since this possibility is constitutive of the possibility of speech, it should structure the very act of him who speaks while perceiving. My nonperception, my nonintuition, my *hic et nunc* absence are expressed by that very thing that I say, by *that* which I say and *because* I say it. This structure will never form an "intimately blended unity" with intuition. The absence of intuition— and therefore of the subject of the intuition—is not only *tolerated* by speech; it is *required* by the general structure of signification, when considered *in itself.* It is radically requisite: the total absence of the subject and object of a statement—the death of the writer and/or the disappearance of the objects he was able to describe—does not prevent a text from "meaning" something. On the contrary, this possibility gives birth to meaning as such, gives it out to be heard and read.

Let us go further. How is writing—the common name for signs which function despite the total absence of the subject because of (beyond) his death—involved in the very act of signification in general and, in particular, in what is called "living" speech? How does writing inaugurate and complete idealization when it itself is neither real nor ideal? And why, finally, are death, idealization, repetition, and signification intelligible, as pure possibilities, only on the basis of one and the same openness? This time let us take the example of the personal pronoun *I.* Husserl classes it among "essentially occasional" expressions. It shares this character with a whole "conceptually unified group of possible meanings (*Bedeutungen*), in whose case it is essential [each time] to orient actual meaning (*Bedeutung*) to the occasion, the speaker and the situation" (§26; ET, p. 315). This group is to be distinguished both from the group of expressions whose multiplicity of meanings is contingent and reducible by a convention (the word "rule," for example, means both a wooden instrument and a prescription) and from the group of "objective" expressions where the circumstances of the utterance, the context, and the situation of the speaking subject do not affect their univocal meaning (for example, "all expressions in theory, expressions out of which the principles and theorems, the proofs and theories of the 'abstract' sciences are made up" [ET, p. 315]. Mathematical expression would be the model for such expressions.) Objective expressions alone are absolutely pure expressions, free from all indicative contamination. An essentially occasional expression is recognizable in that it cannot in principle be replaced in speech by a permanent objective conceptual representation without distorting the meaning (*Bedeutung*) of the statement. If, for example, I tried to substitute, for the word *I* as it appears in a statement, what I take to be its objective conceptual content ("whatever speaker is designating himself"), I would end up in absurdities. Instead of "I am pleased," I would have "Whatever speaker is now designating himself is pleased." Whenever such a substitution distorts the statement, we have to do with an essentially subjective and occasional expression which functions indicatively. Indication thus enters into speech whenever a reference to the subject's situation is not reducible, wherever this subject's situation is designated by a personal pronoun, a demonstrative pronoun, or a "subjective" adverb such as *here, there, above, below, now, yesterday, tomorrow, before, after,* etc. This massive return of indication into expression forces Husserl to conclude:

> An essentially indicating character naturally spreads to all expressions which include these and similar presentations as parts: this includes all the manifold speech-forms where the speaker gives normal expression to something concerning himself, or which is thought of in relation to himself. All expressions for percepts, beliefs, doubts, wishes, fears, commands belong here (§26; ET, p. 318).

We quickly see that the root of all these expressions is to be found in the zero-point of the subjective origin, the *I*, the *here*, the *now*. The meaning (*Bedeutung*) of these expressions is carried off into indication whenever it animates real intended speech for someone else. But Husserl seems to think that this *Bedeutung*, as a relationship with the object (*I, here, now*), is "realized" *for the one who is speaking.*[5] "'In solitary speech the meaning of 'I' is essentially realized in the immediate idea of one's own personality" (ET, p. 316).

Is this certain? Even supposing that such an immediate representation is possible and actually given, does not the appearance of the word *I* in solitary speech (a supplement whose *raison d'être* is not clear if immediate representation is possible) already function as an ideality? Doesn't it give itself out as capable of remaining *the same* for an I-here-now in general, keeping its sense even if my empirical presence is eliminated or radically modified? When I say *I*, even in solitary speech, can I give my statement meaning without implying, there as always, the possible absence of the object of speech—in this case, myself? When I tell myself "I am," this expression, like any other according to Husserl, has the status of speech only if it is intelligible in the absence of its object, in the absence of intuitive presence—here, in the absence of myself. Moreover, it is in this way that the *ergo sum* is introduced into the philosophical tradition and that a discourse about the transcendental ego is possible. Whether or not I have a present intuition of myself, "I" expresses something; whether or not I am alive, *I am* "means something." Here also the fulfilling intuition is not an "essential component" of expression. Whether or not the *I* functions in solitary speech, with or without the self-presence of the speaking subject, it is *sinnvoll*. And there is no need to know who is speaking in order to understand or even utter it. Once again the border seems less certain between solitary speech and communication, between the reality and the representation of speech. Does not Husserl contradict the difference he established between *Gegenstandslosigkeit* and *Bedeutungslosigkeit* when he writes, "The word 'I' names a different person from case to case, and does so by way of an ever altering meaning (*Bedeutung*)"? Does not speech and the ideal nature of every *Bedeutung* exclude the possibility that a *Bedeutung* is "ever altering"? Does not Husserl contradict what he has asserted about the independence of the intention and fulfilling intuition when he writes,

> What its meaning [*Bedeutung*—that of the word "I"] is at the moment can be gleaned only from the living utterance and from the intuitive circumstances which surround it. If we read this word without knowing who wrote it, it is perhaps not meaningless (*bedeutungslos*) but is at least estranged from its normal meaning (*Bedeutung*) (ET, p. 315).

Husserl's premises should sanction our saying exactly the contrary. Just as I need not perceive in order to understand a statement about perception, so there is no need to intuit the object *I* in order to understand the word *I*. The possibility of this nonintuition constitutes the *Bedeutung* as such, the *normal Bedeutung* as such. When the word *I* appears, the ideality of its *Bedeutung*, inasmuch as it is distinct from its "object," puts us in what Husserl describes as an abnormal situation—just as if *I* were written by someone unknown. This alone enables us to account for the fact that we understand the word *I* not only when its "author" is unknown but when he is quite fictitious. And when he is dead. The ideality of the *Bedeutung* here has by virtue of its structure the value of a testament. And just as the import of a statement about perception did not depend on there being actual or even possible perception, so also the signifying function of the *I* does not depend on the life of the speaking subject. Whether or not perception accompanies the statement about perception, whether or not life as selfpresence accompanies the uttering of the *I*, is quite indifferent with regard to the functioning of meaning. My death is structurally necessary to the pronouncing of the *I*. That I am also "alive" and certain about it figures as something that comes over and above the appearance of the meaning. And this structure is operative, it retains its original efficiency, even when I say "I am alive" at the very moment when, if such a thing is possible, I have a full and actual intuition of it. The *Bedeutung* "I am" or "I am alive" or "my living present is" is what it is, has the ideal identity proper to all *Bedeutung*, only if it is not impaired by falsity, that is, if I can be dead at the moment when it is functioning. No doubt it will be different from the *Bedeutung* "I am dead," but not necessarily from the fact that "I am dead." The statement "I am alive" is accompanied by my being dead, and its possibility requires the possibility that I be dead; and conversely. This is not an extraordinary tale by Poe but the ordinary story of language. Earlier we reached the "I am mortal" from the "I am"; here we understand the "I am" out of the "I am dead." The anonymity of the written *I*, the impropriety of the *I am writing*, is, contrary to what Husserl says, the "normal situation." The autonomy of meaning with regard to intuitive cognition, what Husserl established and we earlier called the freedom or "candor" [*franc-parler*] of language, has its norm in writing and in the relationship with death. This writing cannot be added to speech because, from the moment speech awakens, this writing has duplicated it by animating it. Here indication neither degrades nor diverts expression; it dictates it. We draw this conclusion, then, from the idea of a pure logical grammar, from the sharp distinction between the meaning-intention (*Bedeutungsintention*), which can always function "emptily," and its "eventual" fulfillment by the intuition of the object. This conclusion is again reinforced by the supplementary distinction, equally sharp, between fulfillment by "sense" and the fulfillment by the "object." The former does not necessarily demand the latter, and one could draw the same lesson from an attentive reading of §14 ("Content as Object, Content as Fulfilling Sense, and Content as Sense or Meaning *Simpliciter*").

From the same premises, why does Husserl refuse to draw these conclusions? It is because the theme of full "presence," the intuitionistic imperative, and the project of knowledge continue to command—at a distance, we said—the whole of the description. Husserl describes, and in one and the same movement effaces, the emancipation of speech as nonknowing. The originality of meaning as an aim is limited by the *telos* of vision. To be radical, the difference that separates intention from intuition would nonetheless have to be *pro-visional*. And yet this provision would constitute the essence of meaning. The *eidos* is determined in depth by the *telos*. The "symbol" always points to [*fait signe vers*] "truth"; it is itself constituted as a lack of "truth."

> If "possibility" or "truth" is lacking, an assertion's intention can only be carried out symbolically: it cannot derive any "fulness" from intuition or from the categorial functions performed on the latter, in which "fulness" its value for knowledge consists. It then lacks, as one says, a "true," a "genuine" meaning (*Bedeutung*) (§11; ET, pp. 285–86).

In other words, the genuine and true meaning is the will to say the truth. This subtle shift incorporates the *eidos* into the *telos*, and language into knowledge. A speech could well be in conformity with its essence as speech when it was false; it nonetheless attains its entelechy when it is true. One can well *speak* in saying "The circle is square"; one speaks *well*, however, in saying that it is not. There is already sense in the first proposition, but we would be wrong to conclude from this that sense *does not wait upon* truth. It does not await truth as expecting it; it only precedes truth as its anticipation. *In truth*, the *telos* which announces the fulfillment, promised for "later," has already and beforehand opened up sense as a relation with the object. This is what is meant by the concept of *normality* each time it occurs in Husserl's description. The norm is knowledge, the intuition that is adequate to its object, the evidence that is not only distinct but also "clear." It is the full presence of sense to a consciousness that is itself self-present in the fullness of its life, its living present.

Thus, without disregarding the rigor and boldness of "pure logical grammar," without forgetting the advantages it has over the classical projects of rational grammar, we must clearly recognize that its "formality" is limited. We could say as much about the pure morphology of *judgments*, which, in the *Formal and Transcendental Logic*, determines pure logical grammar or pure morphology of *significations*. The purification of the formal is guided by a concept of *sense* which is itself determined on the basis of a *relation with an object*. Form is always the form of a sense, and sense opens up only in the knowing intentionality relating to an object. Form is but the emptiness and pure intention of this intentionality. Perhaps no project of pure grammar can escape this object-related intentionality, perhaps the *telos* of knowing rationality is the irreducible origin of the idea of pure grammar, and perhaps the semantic theme, "empty" as it is, always limits the formalist project. In any case transcendental intuitionism still weighs very heavily upon the formalist theme in Husserl. Apparently independent from fulfilling intuitions, the "pure" forms of signification, as "empty" or canceled sense, are always governed by the epistemological criterion of the relation with objects. The difference between "The circle is square" and "Green is where" or "Abracadabra" (and Husserl links up these last two examples somewhat hastily; he is perhaps not attentive enough to their difference) is that the form of the relation with an object and of a unitary intuition appears only in the first example. Here this aim will always be disappointed, yet this proposition makes *sense* only because *another content*, put in this form (S is *p*), *would be able* to let us know and see an object. "The circle is square," an expression that has sense (*sinnvoll*), has no possible object, but it makes sense only insofar as its grammatical form tolerates the possibility of a relation with the object. The efficiency and the form of signs that do not obey these rules, that is, that do not promise any knowledge, can be determined as nonsense (*Unsinn*) only if one has antecedently, and according to the most traditional philosophical move, defined sense in general on the basis of truth as objectivity. Otherwise we would have to relegate to absolute nonsense all poetic language that transgresses the laws of this grammar of cognition and is irreducible to it. In the forms of nondiscursive signification (music, nonliterary arts generally), as well as in utterances such as "Abracadabra" or "Green is where," there are modes of sense which do not point to any possible objects. Husserl would not deny the signifying force of such formations: he would simply refuse them the formal quality of being expressions endowed with *sense*, that is, of being logical, in the sense that they have a relation with an *object*. All of which amounts to recognizing an initial limitation of sense to knowledge, of logos to objectivity, of language to reason.

We have experienced the systematic interdependence of the concepts of sense, ideality, objectivity, truth, intuition, perception, and expression. Their common matrix is being as *presence*: the absolute proximity of self-identity, the being-in-front of the object available for repetition, the maintenance of the temporal present, whose ideal form is the self-presence of transcendental *life*, whose ideal identity allows *idealiter* of infinite repetition. The living present, a concept that cannot be broken down into a subject and an attribute, is thus the conceptual foundation of phenomenology as metaphysics.

While everything that is *purely* thought in this concept is thereby determined as *ideality*, the living present is nevertheless *in fact*, really, effectively, etc., deferred *ad infinitum*. This *différance* is the difference between the ideal and the nonideal. Indeed, this is a proposition which could already have been verified at the start of the *Logical Investigations*, from the point of view we are advancing. Thus, after having proposed an essential distinction between objective expressions and essentially subjective expressions, Husserl shows that absolute ideality can only be on the side of objective expressions. There is nothing surprising in that. But he immediately adds that, even in essentially subjective expressions, the fluctuation is not in the objective content of the expression (the *Bedeutung*) but only in the act of meaning (*bedeuten*). This allows him to conclude, apparently against his former demonstration, that, in a subjective expression, the *content* may always be replaced by an objective and therefore ideal content: only the act then is lost for ideality. But this substitution (which, let us note in passing, would again confirm what we said about the play of life and death in the *I*) is ideal. As the ideal is always thought by Husserl in the form of an Idea in the Kantian sense, this substitution of ideality for nonidentity, of objectivity for non-objectivity, is infinitely *deferred*. Assigning a subjective origin to fluctuation, and contesting the theory which claims it would belong to the objective content of *Bedeutung* and so impair its ideality, Husserl writes:

> We shall have to look on such a notion as invalid. The content meant by the subjective expression, with sense oriented to the occasion, is an ideal unit of meaning (*Bedeutung*) in precisely the same sense as the content of a fixed expression. This is shown by the fact that, *ideally* speaking, each subjective expression is replaceable by an objective expression which will preserve the identity of each momentary meaning (*Bedeutung*) intention.
>
> *We shall have to concede that such replacement is not only impracticable, for reasons of complexity, but that it cannot in the vast majority of cases, be carried out at all, will, in fact, never be so capable.*
>
> Clearly, in fact, to say that each subjective expression could be replaced by an objective expression, is no more than to assert the *unbounded range (Schrankenlosigkeit) of objective reason.* Everything that is, can be known "in itself." Its being is a being definite in content, and documented in such and such "truths in themselves." ... But what is objectively quite definite, must permit *objective* determination, and what permits objective determination, must,

ideally speaking, permit expression through wholly determinate word-meanings (*Bedeutungen*). . . .

We are infinitely removed from this ideal. . . . *Strike out the essentially occasional expressions from one's language, try to describe any subjective experience in unambiguous, objectively fixed fashion: such an attempt is always plainly vain* (§28; ET, pp. 321–22; italics added).

These theses concerning the unambiguous objective expression as an inaccessible ideal will be taken up again in *The Origin of Geometry* in a literally identical form.

In its ideal value, then, the whole system of "essential distinctions" is a purely teleological structure. By the same token, the possibility of distinguishing between the sign and the nonsign, linguistic sign and nonlinguistic sign, expression and indication, ideality and nonideality, subject and object, grammaticalness and nongrammaticalness, pure grammaticalness and empirical grammaticalness, pure general grammaticalness and pure logical grammaticalness, intention and intuition, etc., is deferred *ad infinitum*. Thus these "essential distinctions" are caught up in the following aporia: *de facto* and *realiter* they are never respected, and Husserl recognizes this. *De jure* and *idealiter* they vanish, since, as distinctions, they live only from the difference between fact and right, reality and ideality. Their possibility is their impossibility.

But how can we conceive this difference? What does "*ad infinitum*" mean here? What does presence mean, taken as *différance ad infinitum*? What does the life of the living present mean as *différance ad infinitum*?

That Husserl always thought of infinity as an Idea in the Kantian sense, as the indefiniteness of an "*ad infinitum*," leads one to believe that he never *derived* difference from the fullness of a *parousia*, from the full presence of a positive infinite, that he never believed in the accomplishment of an "absolute knowledge," as the self-adjacent presence of an infinite concept in Logos. What he shows us of the movement of temporalization leaves no room for doubt on this subject: although he had not made a theme of "articulation," of the "diacritical" work of difference in the constitution of sense and signs, he at bottom recognized its necessity. And yet, the whole phenomenological discourse is, we have sufficiently seen, caught up within the schema of a metaphysics of presence which relentlessly exhausts itself in trying to make difference derivative. Within this schema Hegelianism seems to be more radical, especially at the point where it makes clear that the positive infinite must be thought through (which is possible only if it thinks *itself*) in order that the indefiniteness of *différance* appear *as such*. Hegel's critique of Kant would no doubt also hold against Husserl. But this appearing of the Ideal as an infinite *différance* can only be produced within a relationship with death in general. Only a relation to my-death could make the infinite differing of presence appear. By the same token, compared to the ideality of the positive infinite, this relation to my-death becomes an accident of empirical finitude. The appearing of the infinite *différance* is itself finite. Consequently, *différance*, which does not occur outside this relation, becomes the finitude of life as an essential relation with oneself and one's death. *The infinite differance is finite.* It can therefore no longer be conceived within the opposition of finiteness and infinity, absence and presence, negation and affirmation.

In this sense, *within* the metaphysics of presence, within philosophy as knowledge of the presence of the object, as the being-before-oneself of knowledge in consciousness, we believe, quite simply and literally, in absolute knowledge as the *closure* if not the end of history. And we believe *that such a closure has taken place.* The history of being as presence, as self-presence in absolute knowledge, as consciousness of self in the infinity of *parousia*—this history is closed. The history of presence is closed, for "history" has never meant anything but the presentation (*Gegenwärtigung*) of Being, the production and recollection of beings in presence, as knowledge and mastery. Since absolute self-presence in consciousness is the infinite vocation of full presence, the achievement of absolute knowledge is the end of the infinite, which could only be the unity of the concept, logos, and consciousness in a voice without *différance. The history of metaphysics therefore can be expressed as the unfolding of the structure or schema of an absolute will-to-hear-oneself-speak.* This history is closed when this infinite absolute appears to itself as its own death. *A voice without différance, a voice without writing, is at once absolutely alive and absolutely dead.*

As for what "begins" then—"beyond" absolute knowledge—*unheard-of* thoughts are required, sought for across the memory of old signs. As long as we ask if the concept of differing should be conceived on the basis of presence or antecedent to it, it remains one of these old signs, enjoining us to continue indefinitely to question presence within the closure of knowledge. It must indeed be so understood, but also understood differently: it is to be heard in the openness of an unheard-of question that opens neither upon knowledge nor upon some nonknowledge which is a knowledge to come. In the openness of this question *we no longer know.* This does not mean that we know nothing but that we are beyond absolute knowledge (and its ethical, aesthetic, or religious system), approaching that on the basis of which its closure is announced and decided. Such a question will legitimately be understood as *meaning* nothing, as no longer belonging to the system of meaning.

Thus we no longer know whether what was always presented as a derived and modified re-presentation of simple presentation, as "supplement," "sign," "writing," or "trace," "is" not, in a necessarily, but newly, ahistorical sense, "older" than presence and the system of truth, older than "history." Or again, whether it is "older" than sense and the senses: older than the primordial dator intuition, older than the present and full perception of the "thing itself," older than seeing, hearing, and touching, even prior to the distinction between their "sensible" literalness and their metaphorical elaboration staged throughout the history of philosophy. We therefore no longer know whether what has always been reduced and abased as an accident, modification, and re-turn, under the old names of "sign" and "re-presentation," has not repressed that which related truth to its own death as it related it to its origin. We no longer know whether the force of the *Vergegenwärtigung*, in which the *Gegenwärtigung* is de-presented so as to be re-presented as such, whether the repetitive force of the living present, which is re-presented in a *supplement*, because it has never been present to itself, or whether what we call with the old names of force and *différance* is not more "ancient" than what is "primordial."

In order to conceive of this age, in order to "speak" about it, we will have to have other names than those of sign or representation. New names indeed will have to be used if we are to conceive as "normal" and preprimordial what Husserl believed he could isolate as a particular and accidental experience, something dependent and secondary—that is, the indefinite drift of signs, as errance and change of scene (*Verwandlung*), linking re-presentations (*Vergegenwärtigungen*) one to another without beginning or end. There never was any "perception"; and "presentation" is a representation of the representation that yearns for itself therein as for its own birth or its death.

Everything has, no doubt, begun in the following way:

> A name on being mentioned reminds us of the Dresden gallery. . . .
> We wander through the rooms. . . . A painting by Teniers . . .
> represents a gallery of paintings. . . . The paintings of this gallery
> would represent in their turn paintings, which on their part exhib-
> ited readable inscriptions and so forth (*Ideas I*, §100; ET, p. 293,
> modified).

Certainly nothing has preceded this situation. Asssuredly nothing will suspend it. It is not *comprehended*, as Husserl would want it, by intuitions or presentations. Of the broad daylight of presence, outside the gallery, no perception is given us or assuredly promised us. The gallery is the labyrinth which includes in itself its own exits: we have never come upon it as upon a particular *case* of experience—that which Husserl believes he is describing.

It remains, then, for us to *speak*, to make our voices *resonate* throughout the corridors in order to make up for [*suppléer*] the breakup of presence. The phoneme, the *akoumenon*, is the *phenomenon of the labyrinth*. This is the *case* with the *phōnē*. Rising toward the sun of presence, it is the way of Icarus.

And contrary to what phenomenology—which is always phenomenology of perception—has tried to make us believe, contrary to what our desire cannot fail to be tempted into believing, the thing itself always escapes.

Contrary to the assurance that Husserl gives us a little further on, "the look" cannot "abide."

Notes

1 [Unless otherwise indicated, all quotations from Husserl in this chapter are from the First Investigation.—Translator.]

2 That is, according to Husserl. No doubt this is more true of the modern theories he refutes than, for example, certain mediaeval attempts which he hardly ever refers to. One exception to this is a brief allusion to Thomas of Erfurt's *Grammatica speculativa* in the *Formal and Transcendental Logic*.

3 "In the realized relation of the expression to its objective correlate, the sense-informed expression becomes one (*eint sich*) with the act of meaning-fulfilment. The sounded word is first made one with (*ist einst mit*) the meaning-intention, and this in its turn is made one (as intentions in general are made one with their fulfilments) with its corresponding meaning-fulfilment" (§9; ET, p. 281).

4 "We distinguish, in a perceptual statement, as in every statement, between *content* and *object*; by the 'content' we understand the self-identical meaning that the hearer can grasp even if he is not a percipient" (§14; ET, p. 290).

5 "In solitary speech the meaning (Bedeutung) of 'I' is essentially realized in the immediate idea of one's own personality, which is also the meaning (Bedeutung) of the word in communicated speech. Each man has his own I-presentation (and with it his individual notion of I) and this is why the word's meaning (Bedeutung) differs from person to person." One can't help being astonished at this individual concept and this "Bedeutung" which differs with each individual. And it is Husserl's premises themselves that give rise to this astonishment. Husserl continues, "But since each person, in speaking of himself, says 'I,' the word has the character of a universally operative indication of this fact" (§27; ET, p. 316).

MARGINS OF PHILOSOPHY (DERRIDA 1982 [FIRST
PUBLISHED 1972])

Translated by Alan Bass

Themes

Form is not accepted by Derrida as ontologically neutral, or as neutral
with regard to the contents of consciousness. Husserl's emphasis on pure,
a priori and transcendental forms of consciousness contains an implicit
subordination of sense to sight. Form refers to what can be seen and has
done so at least since Plato who thought of forms, or ideas, as objects of
intellectual vision. Husserl's phenomenology of consciousness rests on
strata of consciousness. Consciousness can never be simply a matter of
the contents of consciousness at one moment. Every moment contains
residues of previous experience which form the strata of consciousness.
The most abstract, and general, form the basic strata in Husserl's
phenomenology, just as Plato thought that consciousness contains
memory of the most abstract and general truths. The ground stratum in
Husserl is one of logos, the word of truth appearing as truth itself in
Husserl's assumptions. That is the truth of forms. Meanings are formed
from something other than meaning, in the pure logos which provides
unity. The transcendental conditions of meaning in Husserl require
meanings to rest on the pure form of the essential unity of meaning as
what transcends particular meanings. Husserl cannot maintain the purity
of the transcendental. Language is always interwoven with the other
threads of experience. In that case all experience is caught up in the

intersubjective, substitutional, supplementary and historical aspects of language; and all language is caught up in the empirical contents of consciousness so that no pure meaning is left in language.

In explaining the strata of consciousness, Husserl uses metaphors of foundation and of interweaving. That is he uses the metaphor of a foundation for experience in general, following a model of foundations of knowledge which goes back to Descartes. He also needs to explain the relations between different strata of more general and particular contents of consciousness, of what comes from the now and what comes from memory, and so on. In explaining the relations he uses metaphors of interweaving. However, such metaphors come into conflict with the metaphor of foundation which assumes strict hierarchy of, and separation between, strata.

The discussion of consciousness returns to language as it always must for Derrida. There is no linguistic idealism in Derrida, but everything we can discuss in language is necessarily embedded in language. Our consciousness, of our own consciousness is, a linguistically embedded consciousness, conscious in language, of linguistically embedded consciousness. The consideration of language in Husserl's phenomenology includes Husserl's view of the distinction between two aspects of sense or meaning: 'Sinn' and 'Bedeutung'; and the distinction between Husserl's view of the distinction and Frege's view. For Frege it is the distinction between mode of expression and object; for Husserl it is the distinction between particularity and universality in the contents of consciousness, that is the distinction between pure expression and the fulfilling conditions of expression. That distinction in Husserl generates the distinction between expression as pure inner form and the external material conditions for expression in indication. However, the pre-expressive is always imprinted in the expressive, as part of the inescapable interweaving of the strata of consciousness. There is no pure expressive inner consciousness that transcends the material and the empirical.

Husserl relies on conceptual fictions and imagination to transform the material intuitions of sense into the generality of concepts. The metaphors that Husserl uses of foundations and interweaving are not something accidental in relation to consciousness. Metaphorical displacement, and imaginative unities, are necessary to conceive of the contents of consciousness in a way that closely relates to the work of the psychic and neural forces of consciousness. The metaphorical and literary aspects of Derrida's philosophy are there in part, because that is how to explain the actual working of consciousness and of language.

All Husserl's attempts to describe ideal discourse and an expressive stratum are interwoven with the pre-expressive, the empirical and the material. In his drive for the purely expressive, he attempts an account of pure self-presence in consciousness which can only be described with reference to pure transcendental forms of consciousness. However, those forms can never be pure forms, they are always embedded, and continuous with indication and relativity of meaning.

Derrida's views on consciousness are partly informed by Freudian psychoanalysis. Psychoanalysis was a persistent interest for Derrida which he focuses on in his 1966 paper 'Freud and the Scene of Writing' (in Derrida 1978) and *The Post Card* (1987a [first published 1980]). 'Fors' (in Derrida 2005b [first published 1976]), was written by Derrida as a foreword to the work of the psychoanalysts Nicholas Abraham and Maria Torok, which emphasises crypts, that is hidden structures of the mind. In these texts Derrida looks at the metaphysical presuppositions in Freud's work and tries to separate psychoanalysis from any presence of truth, logocentrism, behind consciousness. The elements or infinite repeatability and substitution, differences of forces, in Freud are emphasised.

Context
Though Derrida does not deal with precedents for his reading of Husserl in the selected text, he is clearly anticipated by Merleau-Ponty's discussion of 'interweaving' in *The Visible and the Invisible* (Merleau-Ponty 1969 [unfinished on Merleau-Ponty's death in 1960]). Merelau-Ponty's discussion of interweaving follows on from his criticisms of Husserl's form of phenomenology in *Phenomenology of Perception* (Merleau-Ponty 1962 [first published 1945]), where Merleau-Ponty criticises both empiricism and intellectualism. Husserl's emphasis on transcendental forms and intellectual judgement is targeted. Though Merleau-Ponty was a critic of Sartre's phenomenology, his own evolution was clearly related with Sartre's work on a more concrete form of phenomenology than that of Husserl, culminating in *Being and Nothingness* (Sartre 2003a [first published 1943]) which itself follows on from *Sketch for the Theory of Emotions* (Sartre 2002 [first published 1939]) and *The Imaginary* (Sartre 2004 [first published 1940]). Both were drawing on Heidegger's *Being and Time* (Heidegger 1962 [first published 1927]), which formulates a phenomenology concerned with being-in-the-world, in which things are present-at-hand or ready-to-hand so that we are always already thrown into the world. Heidegger elaborates a structural description of involvement in the world which we understand on the basis of interpretation, seeing-as, which preceded explicit intellectual understanding.

The precedents for Derrida's view of phenomenology lie within Continental European philosophy, but that work itself has been absorbed into analytic philosophy including work on consciousness and cognition. Husserl himself has been taken up with regard to formal metaphysical problems, the attempts to make him more concrete in Heidegger, Sartre and Merleau-Ponty have had great influence in philosophy of mind. Hubert Dreyfus's commentary on the first division of *Being and Time*, *Being-in-the-World* (Dreyfus 1991) emphasises anti-representationalism in Heidegger. That is, Heidegger does not conceive the phenomenology of consciousness on the basis of representations in the mind but as a description of the structure of being-in-the-world, which includes action, discourse, and care as structures preceding representation. There is no distinction between subjective inwardness and environment: Heidegger strongly criticises Descartes on that basis, because Descartes turns the mind into something hidden from the world trying to grab booty from it.

Dreyfus also works on cognitive science and these aspects of Heidegger are consistent with, and provide a philosophical framework for, the results of cognitive psychology, artificial intelligence and neurology. Cognitive psychology suggests that possession of knowledge is not the same as a conscious grasp that we know something, leading in the direction of Heidegger's emphasis on the implicit in interpretation and understanding. Artificial intelligence research looks at the mind on the model of computer programs, which displaces the centrality of consciousness in favour of the unconscious structures of inference necessary to thought and action. Neurology studies the relations between nerve cells, and that includes work on neural networks in which it can be seen that knowledge is encoded in evolving networks of neurons outside, and preceding, conscious representations. While Derrida never had much to say about such technical subjects, he does explicitly refer to programming and cybernetics as undermining a metaphysics of presence, in which consciousness is reduced to conscious representations completely present to consciousness.

Other independent work on these lines includes that of Andy Clark in *Being There* (Clark 1997), which also strongly emphasises Merleau-Ponty's development of Heidegger's insights; and Michael Wheeler in *Reconstructing the Cognitive World* (Wheeler 2005), which emphasises the Heideggerian embodiment of cognition in contrast to the Dreyfus school. Clarke emphasises the idea of the 'extended mind', which refers to the mind which does not just exist within the brain or some inner space of consciousness. In the perspective of the extended mind, the mind is everywhere that the self is interacting with the world. The mind exists in the operations of the body. If it cannot be separated from the body, then it cannot be separated from all the ways in which the body is in the world and does things in the world. The mind even extends beyond the body to what the body touches.

This kind of approach to philosophy of mind has been extended to French philosophy after Merleau-Ponty in the work of Shaun Gallagher and Dan Zahavi, with reference to Lévinas and Lyotard as well as Derrida. Gallagher, who is currently one of the main editors of the journal *Phenomenology and the Cognitive Sciences*, has written on this at greatest length in *How the Body Shapes the Mind* (Gallagher 2005): while Zahavi, who currently directs the Centre for Subjectivity Research in Copenhagen, has written at length on similar concerns in *Self-Awareness and Alterity* (Zahavi 1999). The overlap between their approaches will be explored in the forthcoming book *The Phenomenological Mind* (Gallagher and Zahavi forthcoming). They have dealt with issues of alterity in consciousness. That is the way in which the consciousness cannot be reduced to a single transparent unity. Issues explored by Husserl and Sartre of pre-reflective consciousness, are followed up by Zahavi. That means the way in which consciousness is oriented to the world before it reflects on itself. Consciousness does not exist in its ability to grasp itself explicitly, but in the ways that it is always implicitly oriented before we notice it. While Derrida never took philosophy of mind beyond his textual engagements with phenomenology, and some discussion of Freud, his work can be brought into creative relationship with phenomenologically informed work on cognitive psychology and brain science.

MARGINS OF PHILOSOPHY:
FORM AND MEANING: A NOTE ON THE PHENOMENOLOGY OF
LANGUAGE

To gar ikhnos tou amorphou morphē

Plotinus [1]

Phenomenology's critique of the state of metaphysics was aimed only at
its restoration. Phenomenology ascertained this state in order to
reawaken metaphysics to the essence of its task, the authentic originality
of its design. In its final pages, the *Cartesian Meditations* remind us of
this: as opposed to "adventurous" speculation, to "naive" and "degen-
erate" metaphysics, we must turn back to the critical project of "first
philosophy." If certain metaphysical systems awaken suspicion, and even
if the entirety of metaphysics is de facto "suspended" by phenomenology,
the latter does not exclude "metaphysics in general."[2]

The concept of *form* could serve as a thread to be followed in
phenomenology's elaboration of a purifying critique. Even if the word
"form" translates several Greek words in a highly equivocal fashion,
nevertheless one may rest assured that these words all refer to fundamental concepts of metaphysics. In reinscribing the Greek words (*eidos,
morphē,* etc.) into phenomenological language, in playing on the differences between Greek, Latin, and German, Husserl certainly wished to
deliver these concepts from the latter-day metaphysical interpretations
that had overtaken them, accusing these interpretations of having
deposited, in the word itself, the entire burden of an invisible sedimentation.[3] But Husserl always does so in order to reconstitute (and, if need

be, against the *founders*, against Plato and Aristotle), an *original* sense that *began by* being perverted immediately upon its inscription into tradition. Whether it is a question of determining *eidos* in opposition to "Platonism," or form (*Form*) (in the problematic of formal logic and ontology) or *morphē* (in the problematic of its transcendental constitution and in its relation with *hylē*) in opposition to Aristotle, the force, vigilance, and efficacy of the critique remain intrametaphysical by means of all their resources. How could it be otherwise? As soon as we utilize the concept of form—even if to criticize *an other* concept of form—we inevitably have recourse to the self-evidence of a kernel of meaning. And the medium of this self-evidence can be nothing other than the language of metaphysics. In this language we know what "form" means, how the possibility of its variations is regulated, what its limit is, and in what field all imaginable objections to it are to be maintained. The system of oppositions in which something like form, the formality of form, can be thought, is a finite system. Moreover, it does not suffice to say that "form" has a *meaning* for us, a center of self-evidence, or that its *essence* as such is given for us: in truth, this concept cannot be, and never could be, dissociated from the concept of appearing, of meaning, of self-evidence, of essence. Only a form as *self-evident*, only a form has or is an *essence*, only a form *presents itself* as such. This is an assured point, a point that no interpretation of Platonic or Aristotelian conceptuality can displace. All the concepts by means of which *eidos* or *morphē* have been translated or determined refer to the theme of *presence in general*. Form s presence itself. Formality is whatever aspect of the thing in general presents itself, lets itself be seen, gives itself to be thought. That metaphysical thought—and consequently phenomenology—is a thought of Being as form, that in metaphysics thought thinks itself as a thought of form, and of the formality of form, is nothing but what is necessary; a last sign of this can be seen in the fact that Husserl determines the *living present* (*lebendige Gegenwart*) as the ultimate, universal, absolute *form* of transcendental experience in general.

Although the privilege of *theōria*, in phenomenology, is not as simple as has sometimes been said, and although the classical theoretisms are profoundly put back into question in phenomenology, the metaphysical domination of the concept of form is bound to occasion some submission to sight. This submission always would be a submission of *sense* to sight, of sense to the sense-of-vision, since sense in general is the very concept of every phenomenological field. One could elaborate the implications of such a *placing-on-view*. One might do so in numerous directions, and based upon the most apparently diverse places of the phenomenological problematic and text: for example, by showing how this placing on view and this concept of form permit one to circulate between the project of formal ontology, the description of time or of intersubjectivity, the latent theory of the work of art, etc.

But, if sense is not discourse, their relationship, as concerns this *placing on view*, doubtless merits some particular attention. Thus have we chosen to narrow our angle here, and to approach a text concerning the status of language in *ideas*. Between the determination of this status, the privilege of the formal, and the predominance of the theoretical, a certain circulation is organized into a system. And yet coherence, here, seems to be worked upon by a certain exterior of the relation to the exterior that is the relation to form. We only wish to point out several signs of both this circularity and this uneasiness in a preliminary way, taking our authority from the assurance that not only does *Ideas* not contradict the *Logical Investigations* on this point—on the contrary, it continuously clarifies the *Investigations*—but also that nothing beyond *Ideas* ever overtly put these analyses into question.

Meaning in the text

For more than two-thirds of the book, everything occurs as if transcendental experience were silent, inhabited by no language; or rather deserted by *expressivity* as such, since, starting with the *Investigations*, Husserl in effect determined the essence or *telos* of language as *expression* (*Ausdruck*). The transcendental description of the fundamental structures of all experience is pursued up to the end of the penultimate "section" without even touching upon the problem of language. The worlds of culture and of science indeed have been evoked, but even if the predicates of culture and of science are unthinkable outside a world of language, Husserl gave himself the right, for methodological reasons, not to consider the "layer" of expression, provisionally putting it between parentheses.

Husserl can give himself this right only by supposing that expressivity constitutes an original and rigorously delimited "stratum" (*Schicht*) of experience. The *Investigations* had proposed an insistent demonstration that acts of expression are original and irreducible; and this remains presupposed in *Ideas*. Thus, at a certain moment of the descriptive itinerary, one may come to consider linguistic expressivity as a circumscribed problem. And at the point at which the problem is approached, one already knows that the "stratum of logos" will be included in the *most general structure* of experience, the structure whose poles or correlations have just been described: the parallel opposition of noesis and noema. Thus, it is already a given that however original, the stratum of the logos would have to be organized according to the parallelism of noesis and noema. The problem of "meaning" (*bedeuten*)[4] is approached in section 124, which is entitled "The Noetic-Noematic Stratum of the 'Logos.' Meaning and Meaning Something (*Bedeuten und Bedeutung*)." The metaphor of the *stratum* (*Schicht*) has two implications. On the one hand, meaning is founded on something other than itself, and this dependence will be confirmed ceaselessly by Husserl's analysis. On the other hand, meaning constitutes a stratum whose unity can be rigorously delimited. Now, if the metaphor of the stratum remains credible throughout this section, it will become suspect in the section's final lines. This suspicion is not purely rhetorical but, rather, translates a profound disquiet as concerns the descriptive fidelity of discourse. If the metaphor of the stratum does not correspond to the structure one seeks to describe, how could it have been used for so long? "For we should not hold too hard by the metaphor of stratification (*Schichtung*); expression is not of the nature of an overlaid varnish (*übergelagerter Lack*) or covering garment; it is a mental formation (*geistige Formung*), which exercises new intentional influences (*Funktionen*) on the intentional substratum (*an der intentionalen Unterschicht*) and experiences from the latter correlative intentional influences"[5] (p. 349).

This distrust of a metaphor is manifested the moment a new complication of the analysis becomes necessary. Here, I have sought only to indicate that the effort to isolate the logical "stratum" of expression encounters, even *before the difficulties of its theme*, the difficulties of its *enunciation*. The discourse on the *logic* of the discourse is entangled in a play of metaphors. The metaphor of the stratum, as we shall see, is far from being the only one.

It is apparent from the very opening of the analysis that it is a question of racking down in discourse that which assures the properly logical functioning of discourse; that the essence or *telos* of language here are determined as *logical*; that, as in the *Investigations*, the theory of discourse reduces the considerable mass of whatever is not purely *logical* in language to an *extrinsic value*. A metaphor itself betrays the difficulty of this first reduction; this difficulty is the very one which will call for new formulations and new distinctions at the end of the section. It only will have been deferred and led elsewhere. "Acts of expression, act-strata in the specific 'logical' sense, are interwoven (*verweben sich*) with all the acts hitherto considered, and in their case no less than in the others the parallelism of noesis and noema must be clearly brought out. The prevalent and unavoidable ambiguity of our ways of speaking, which is caused by this parallelism and is everywhere operative where the concomitant circumstances are mentioned, operates also of course when we talk of expression and meaning" (p. 345).

The *interweaving* (*Verwebung*) of language, the interweaving of that which is purely language in language with the other threads of experience constitutes a cloth. The word *Verwebung* refers to this metaphorical zone. The "strata" are "woven," their intercomplication is such that the warp cannot be distinguished from the woof. If the stratum of the logos were simply *founded*, one could extract it and bring to light its underlying stratum of nonexpressive acts and contents. But since this superstructure acts back upon the *Unterschicht* in an essential and decisive manner, one is indeed obliged, from the very outset of the description, to associate a properly *textual* metaphor with the geological metaphor: for cloth means *text*. *Verweben* here means *texere*. The discursive is related to the nondiscursive, the linguistic "stratum" is intermixed with the prelinguistic "stratum" according to the regulated system of a kind of *text*. We know already—and Husserl acknowledges this—that in fact, at least, the secondary threads are going to act on the primary threads; in what is *spun* (*ourdir*) in this way, it is precisely the operation of the beginning (*ordiri*) which can no longer be grasped; what is woven as language is that the discursive warp cannot be construed as warp and takes the place of a woof which has not truly preceded it. This texture is all the more inextricable in that it is highly significant: *the nonexpressive threads are not without signification*. In the *Investigations* Husserl had shown that their signification is simply of an *indicative* nature. And in the section that concerns us, he recognizes that the words *bedeuten* and *Bedeutung* can largely overflow the "expressive" field: "We restrict our glance exclusively to the 'meaning-content' (*Bedeutung*), and 'the act of meaning' (*Bedeuten*). Originally these words relate only to the sphere of speech (*sprachliche Sphäre*), that of 'expression' (*des Ausdrückens*). But it is almost inevitable, and at the same time an important step for knowledge, to extend the meaning of these words, and to modify them suitably so that they may be applied in a certain way to the whole noetico-noematic sphere, to all acts, therefore, whether these are interwoven (*verflochten*) with expressive acts or not" (p. 346).

Faced with this inextricable texture, this interlacing (*Verflechtung*)[6] which seems to defy analysis, the phenomenologist is not discouraged. His patience and scrupulousness must, in principle, undo the tangle. At stake is phenomenology's "principle of principles." If the description does not bring to light an absolutely and simply founding ground of signification, if an intuitive and perceptive ground, a pedestal of silence, does not found discourse in the originally given presence of the thing itself, if the texture of the text, in a word, is irreducible, not only will the phenomenological description have failed but the descriptive "principle" itself will have been put back into question. The stakes of this disentanglement are therefore the phenomenological motif itself.

Mirror writing

Husserl begins by delimiting the problem, by simplifying or purifying its givens. He then proceeds to a double exclusion, or if you will, to a double reduction, bowing to a necessity whose rightful status was acknowledged in the *Investigations*, and which will never again be put into question. *On the one hand*, the *sensory face* of language, its sensory and nonmaterial face, what might be called the animate "proper body" (*Leib*) of language, is put out of circulation. Since, according to Husserl, expression supposes an intention of meaning (*Bedeutungsintention*), its essential condition is therefore the pure act of animating intention, and not the body to which, in some mysterious fashion, intention unites itself and gives life. It is this enigmatic unity of informing intention and informed matter that Husserl authorizes himself to dissociate from the outset. This is why, *on the other hand*, he defers—forever, it seems—the problem of the unity of the two faces, the problem of the union of soul and body. "Let us start from the familiar distinction between the sensory, the so to speak bodily aspect (*leibliche Seite*) of expression, and its nonsensory 'mental' aspect. There is no need for us to enter more closely into the discussion of the first aspect, nor upon the way of uniting the two aspects, though we clearly have title-headings here indicated for phenomenological problems that are not unimportant" (p. 346).[7]

Having taken this double precaution, we see the contours of the problem more clearly: what are the distinctive traits that essentially separate the expressive stratum from the preexpressive stratum, and how to submit the effects of the one upon the other to an eidetic analysis? This question will receive its full formulation only after a certain progress of the analysis: "how to interpret the 'expressing' of 'what is expressed,' how expressed experiences stand in relation to those that are not expressed, and what changes the latter undergo when expression supervenes; one is then led to the question of their 'intentionality,' of their 'immanent meaning,' of their 'content' (*Materie*) and quality (i.e. the act-character of the thesis), of the distinction of this meaning and these phases of the essence which lie in the pre-expressive from the meaning of the expressing phenomenon itself and its own phases, and so forth. One gathers still in various ways from the writings of the day how little justice is apt to be done to the great problems here indicated in their full and deep-lying significance" (p. 348).

Certainly this problem already had been posed, notably at the beginning of the sixth of the *Logical Investigations*. But here, the path which leads to it is different; and not only for very general reasons (access to an openly transcendental problematic, appeal to the notion of noema, acknowledged generality of the noetico-noematic structure), but particularly because of the distinction, arisen in the interval, between the concepts of *Sinn* and *Bedeutung*. Not that Husserl now accepts this distinction proposed by Frege, one that he had objected to in the *Investigations*.[8] Rather, he simply finds it convenient to reserve the pair *bedeuten–Bedeutung* for the order of expressive meaning (*vouloir-dire*), for discourse itself, and to extend the concept of *sense* (*Sinn*) to the totality of the noematic face of experience, whether or not it is expressive.[9]

Once the extension of *sense* absolutely overflows the extension of *meaning*, discourse will always have to *draw upon its sense*. In a way, discourse will be able only to *repeat* or to *reproduce* a content of sense which does not await discourse in order to be what it is.[10] If things are thus, discourse will only transport to the exterior a sense that is constituted before it and without it. This is one of the reasons why the essence of logical meaning is determined as expression (*Ausdruck*). Discourse is expressive in its essence, because it consists in transporting to the outside, in *exteriorizing* a content of interior thought. It is never without the *sich äussern* which was spoken of in the first of the *Investigations* (§7).

Thus, we are already in possession of the first distinctive trait of the expressive stratum. If it *proffers* only a constituted sense, physically or not, it is essentially reproductive, that is, *unproductive*. Husserl's analysis is on its way to this definition in its first stage: "The stratum of expression—and this constitutes its peculiarity—apart from the fact that it lends expression to all other intentionalities, is not productive. Or if one prefers: *its productivity, its noematic service, exhausts itself in expressing*, and in the *form of the conceptual* which first comes with the expressing" (pp. 348–49).

This unproductivity of the logos is *embodied*, if we may put it thus, in the Husserlian description. It again permits itself to be *seduced* by two metaphors to which we cannot not pay attention.

The first seems to pass by Husserl unnoticed. It is displaced between a writing and a mirror. Or rather, it says mirror writing. Let us follow its constitution. In order to set forth the difference between *Sinn* and *Bedeutung*, Husserl recurs to a perceptual example, the silent perception of a "white thing." In a certain way, the statement "this is white" is perfectly independent of the perceptual experience. It is even intelligible for someone who has not had this perception. And the *Investigations* had demonstrated this rigorously. This independence of the expressive value equally implies the independence of the perceptual *sense*. We can make this *sense* explicit: "This process makes no call whatsoever on 'expression,' neither on expression in the sense of verbal sound nor on the like as verbal meaning, and here the latter can also be present independently of the verbal sound (as in the case when this sound is 'forgotten')" (p. 347).

Consequently, the transition to being stated adds nothing to sense, or in any event adds no content of sense; and yet, despite this sterility, or rather because of it, the appearance of expression is rigorously new. Because it only reissues the noematic sense, in a certain way, expression is rigorously novel. To the extent that it neither adds nor in any way deforms, expression can always in principle repeat sense, by providing access to "conceptual form": "If we have 'thought' or stated 'This is white,' a new stratum is there with the rest, and unites with the 'meant as such' in its pure perceptive form. On these lines everything remembered or fancied can, as such, have its meaning made more explicit and expressible (explizierbar und ausdrückbar). Whatever is 'meant (gemeint) as such,' every meaning (Meinung) in the noematic sense (and indeed as noematic nucleus) of any act whatsoever can be expressed conceptually (durch 'Bedeutungen')" (p. 347).

And then Husserl posits as a universal rule that logical meaning is an act of expression (Logische Bedeutung ist ein Ausdruck). Thus, everything must be capable of being said, everything must be capable of attaining the conceptual generality which properly constitutes the logic of the logos. And this not despite but because of the originality of the logical medium of expression: in effect, this originality consists in not having to erase itself as an unproductive transparency facing the passageway of sense.

But this transparency must have some consistency: not only in order to express, but primarily in order to let itself be impressed by what afterward it will give to be read: "From the noetic standpoint the rubric 'expressing' should indicate a special act-stratum to which all other acts must adjust themselves in their own way, and with which they must blend remarkably in such wise that every noematic act-sense, and consequently the relation to objectivity which lies in it, stamps itself (sich ausprägt: impresses, strikes itself) 'conceptually' (begrifflich) in the noematic phase of the expressing" (p. 347).

Thus, the preexpressive noema, the prelinguistic sense, must be imprinted in the expressive noema, must find its conceptual mark in the content of meaning. Expression, in order to limit itself to transporting a constituted sense to the exterior, and by the same token to bring this sense to conceptual generality without altering it, in order to express what is already thought (one almost would have to say written), and in order to redouble faithfully—expression then must permit itself to be imprinted by sense at the same time as it expresses sense. The expressive noema must offer itself, and this is the new image of its unproductivity, as a blank page or virgin tablet; or at least as a palimpsest given over to its pure receptivity. Once the inscription of the sense in it renders it legible, the logical order of conceptuality will be constituted as such. It then will offer itself *begrifflich*, in graspable, manipulable, conceivable, conceptual fashion. The order of the concept is inaugurated by expression, but this inauguration is the redoubling of a preexisting conceptuality, since it first will have had to imprint itself on the naked page of meaning. Following the implacable necessity of these two concepts, *production* and *revelation* are united in the impression-expression of discourse. And since Husserl, here, is not considering the verbal order, with all its "entangled" (physical and intentional) complexity, but the still silent intention of meaning (the moment when *Bedeutung* has appeared, which is more than *sense*, but has not yet effectively and physically proffered itself), it must be concluded that sense in general, the noematic sense of every experience, is something which by its nature already must be capable of *imprinting itself* in a meaning, leaving or receiving its formal mark in a *Bedeutung*. Thus, sense already would be a kind of blank and mute writing redoubling itself in meaning.

The originality of the stratum of the *Bedeutung*, therefore, would only be a kind of tabula rasa. The grave problems posed by this metaphor can already be foreseen. In particular, if there is an original history and permanence of concepts—such as they are already and uniquely inscribed in meaning, supposing that meaning can be separated from the history of language and of signifiers—concepts themselves are always older than sense, and in turn constitute a text. Even if, in principle, one could suppose that some textual virginity *in illo tempore* welcomed the first production of sense, *in fact* the systematic order of meaning in some way would have had to impose its sense upon sense, dictating the form of sense, obliging it to imprint itself according to a given rule, syntactic or otherwise. And this "in fact" is not one empirical necessity among others; it cannot be put between parentheses in order to pose transcendental questions of rightfulness, since the status of meaning cannot be fixed without simultaneously determining the status of sense. The placing of this "fact" between parentheses is a decision concerning the status of sense in general in its relations to discourse. *This gesture does not come out of phenomenology, but opens it noncritically.* And although Husserl never afterward put this juridical "anteriority" of sense in relation to meaning (of *Sinn* in relation to *bedeuten*) back into question, it is difficult to see how it can be reconciled with his future thematic, for example that of *The Origin of Geometry*. This thematic is *simultaneously*, and quite precisely, the one which we are following at the moment *and* that of a sedimented history of *bedeuten*. And even if one considers only egological history, how is the perpetual restoration of meaning in its virginity to be thought?

However, the scriptural analogy does not hold Husserl's attention here. Another metaphor demands it.

The milieu that receives the imprint would be neutral. Husserl has just evoked conceptual *Ausprägung*. He then determines the neutrality of the milieu as that of a medium without its own color, without a determined opaqueness, without power to refract. But this neutrality, then, is less that of transparency than that of specular reflection: "A peculiar intentional instrument lies before us which essentially possesses the outstanding characteristic of reflecting back as from a mirror (*widerzuspiegeln*) every other intentionality according to its form and content, of copying (*abzubilden*) it whilst colouring it in its own way, and thereby of working into (*einzubilden*) it its own form of 'conceptuality'" (pp. 347–48).

A double effect of the milieu, a double relation of logos to sense: on the one hand, a pure and simple *reflection*, a *reflection* that respects what it accepts, and refers, *de-picts*, sense as such, in its proper original colors, re-presenting it in person. This is language as *Abbildung* (copy, portrait, figuration, representation). But, on the other hand, this reproduction imposes the blank mark of the concept. It informs meaning with sense, producing a specific nonproduction which, without changing anything in sense, *paints* something in it. The concept has been produced without adding anything to sense. Here one could speak, in a sense, of a conceptual *fiction* and of a kind of *imagination* that picked up the intuition of sense in the generality of the concept. This would be language as *Einbildung*. The two words do not occur fortuitously in Husserl's description: the unproductive production of logic would be original due to this strange concurrence of *Abbildung* and *Einbildung*.

Is this a contradiction? In any event Husserl displays a certain discomfort. And there would be much to think about in Husserl's attribution of the indecision of his description to the accidental metaphoricity of language, to precisely what he calls the *Bildlichkeit* of discourse. It is because discourse occasionally must utilize images, figures, and analogies— which would be as its debris—that logos must be described simultaneously as the unproductivity of the *Abbildung* and as the productivity of the *Einbildung*. If one eliminated the *Bildlichkeit* in descriptive discourse, by the same token one would eliminate the apparent contradiction between *Abbildung* and *Einbildung*. But Husserl does not ask about this nuclear *bilden* in its relations to logos. The passage we were citing above continues this way: "Yet these figures of speech which here thrust themselves upon us, those of mirroring and copying, must be adopted with caution, as the imaginativeness (*Bildlichkeit*: metaphoricity, pictorial representation) which colours their application might easily lead one astray (*irreführen*)" (p. 348). Therefore metaphor is seductive, in every sense of the word. And phenomenological discourse is to resist this seduction.

The limiting power of form

If Husserl suspects all the predicates brought into the milieu of the logos, he never criticizes the concept of the *medium* itself. The expressive stratum is a *medium*, an ether that both accepts sense and is a means to bring it to conceptual form. The word "medium" appears often in the pages that follow. It gives its heading, precisely, to the problem of the history of concepts whose difficulty we just evoked and that we related to the future themes of *The Origin of Geometry*. Here Husserl formulates the very difficulty[11] which will constitute the central theme of *The Origin*: "Problems of exceptional difficulty beset the phenomena which find their place under the headings 'to mean' (*Bedeuten*) and 'meaning' (*Bedeutung*). Since every science, viewed from the side of its theoretical content, of all that constitutes its 'doctrine' (*Lehre*) (theorem, proof, theory), is objectified in a specific 'logical' medium, the medium of expression, it follows that for philosophers and psychologists who are guided by general logical interests the problems of expression and meaning (*Bedeutung*) lie nearest of all, and are also the first, generally speaking, which, so soon as one seeks seriously to reach their foundations, compel towards phenomenological inquiry into the essential nature of things" (p. 348).

Theory, therefore, is the name of that which can neither dispense with objectification in the medium nor tolerate the slightest deformation in its subjection to the medium. There is no scientific sense (*Sinn*) without meaning (*bedeuten*), but it belongs to the essence of science to demand an unequivocality without shadow, the absolute transparence of discourse. Science would need what it needs (discourse as pure meaning) to be useless: it is only to preserve and to glance at the sense which science confers upon it. Nowhere else can discourse simultaneously be more productive and more unproductive than as an element of theory.

Which indeed confirms—if this unproductive productivity is the *telos* of expression—that logico-scientific discourse has never ceased to function, here, as the model of every possible discourse.

The entire analysis, henceforth, will have to be displaced between two concepts or two values. On the one hand, ideal discourse will have to accomplish an overlapping or a *coincidence* (*Deckung*) of the nonexpressive stratum of sense and of the expressive stratum of meaning. But, for all the reasons we have already recognized, this overlapping can never be a *confusion*. And the work of clarification, distinction, articulation, etc. must bear upon the two strata as such. The difference between coincidence and confusion leads us back, therefore, to the very opening of our problematical space. But perhaps this formulation permits us to make some progress.

In the best of cases, that of the perfect overlapping of the two strata, there should be a *parallelism*, then. The concept of the parallel would respect at once the perfect correspondence and the nonconfusion of strata. And, following an analogy that ought to be investigated, the concept of the parallel would play as decisive a role here as when Husserl explicitly makes it intervene in order to describe the relation between the purely psychic and the transcendental.

The parallelism of the two strata can be a perfect overlapping only if meaning (if not actual discourse) reproduces the meaning of the underlying stratum *completely*. There is always a certain overlapping of the two strata, for without it the phenomenon of expression would not even occur; but this overlapping may be incomplete: "We must further lay stress on the difference between *complete* (*vollständigem*) and *incomplete* (*unvollständigem*) *expression*. The unity of the expressing and the expressed in the phenomenon is indeed that of a certain overlapping (*Deckung*), but the upper layer need not extend its expressing function over the entire lower layer. Expression is complete when the stamp of *conceptual meaning has been impressed* (*ausprägt*) *upon all the synthetic forms and matter* (*Materien*) *of the lower layer*; incomplete when this is only partially effected: as when, in regard to a complex process, the arrival of the carriage, perhaps, bringing guests that have been long expected; we call out: the carriage! The guests! This difference of completeness will naturally cut across that of relative clearness and distinctness" (p. 352).

Up to now, one might have believed that the noncompleteness of expression and the nonparallelism of the two layers have the value of a fact or an accident; and that even if such a *fact* occurs often, even if it almost always affects our discourse in its totality, it *does not belong to the essence of expression*. The example Husserl has just cited in effect belongs to the language of daily life, and it may still be assumed that the mission and power of scientific expression consist in mastering these shadows and restituting the completeness of the sense aimed at in expression.

At the risk of compromising an axiom (the unproductive and reflective value of expression), Husserl also brings to light an *essential* noncompletion of expression, an insufficiency that no effort ever will be able to overcome, precisely because it has to do with *conceptual form*, the very formality without which expression would not be what it is. Although Husserl, above, apparently wanted to stress the reflective, reproductive, repetitive nature of expression, its *Abbilden*, thereby neutralizing, in return, its effects, and its marks, its power to deform or refract, that is, its *Einbilden*, now, on the other hand, he stresses an essential displacement of expression that will forever prevent it from reissuing the stratum of sense (*Sinn*): and this difference is nothing less than the difference of the concept. We must read the entire paragraph: "An incompleteness of a totally different kind (*Eine total andere Unvollständigkeit*) from the one just discussed is that which belongs to the essential nature of the expression as such, namely, to its *generality* (*Allgemeinheit*). 'I would like,' expresses the wish in a general form; the form of command, the command; 'might very well be' the presumption, or the likely as such, and so forth. Every closer determination in the unity of the expression is itself again expressed in general form. It lies in the meaning of the generality which belongs to the essential nature of the expressing function that it would not ever be possible for all the specifications of the expressed to be reflected (*sich reflektieren*) in the expression. The stratum of the meaning function is not, and in principle is not, a sort of duplication (*Reduplikation*) of the lower stratum" (p. 352).

And referring to the entire problematic of complete and incomplete expressions in the *Logical Investigations*, Husserl then mentions the values of the underlying layer which in principle cannot be repeated in expression (the qualities of clarity, of distinction, attentional modifications, etc.).

This impoverishment is the condition for scientific formalization. Unequivocality is furthered in the extent to which the complete repetition of sense in meaning is given up. Therefore, one cannot even say that a factual, accidental, inessential noncompleteness is reduced via a teleology of scientific discourse, or that it is included as a provisional obstacle within the horizon of an infinite task. The *telos* of scientific discourse bears within itself, *as such*, a renunciation of completeness. Here, the difference is not a provisional deficiency of the *epistēmē* as discourse, but is its very resource, the positive condition for its activity and productivity. It is as much the limit of scientific power as it is the power of the scientific limit: the limiting-power of its formality.

Form "is"—its ellipsis

It seems that these propositions concerned, before anything else, the relation between the form of the statement and the content of sense, between the order of meaning and the order of the noema in general. However, they also imply an essential decision concerning the *relation of statements to each other*, within the general system of expressivity. For the relation of expression to sense to be ready to accept the determination we have just sketched out, did not an absolute privilege have to be granted to a certain type of statement? Is there not an essential relation between the value of formality and a certain structure of the sentence? And by the same token, is there not a *facility of transition* between a certain type of noema (or experience of sense) and the order of meaning which in a way would ensure the very possibility of this entire phenomenology of the logos?

With this question we are retracing our first steps: what is the status of the concept of form? How does it inscribe phenomenology within the closure of metaphysics? How does it determine the meaning of Being as presence, that is, as the present? What brings it into secret communication with the delimitation of the meaning of Being which gives us to think Being par excellence in the verbal form of the present and, more narrowly still, in the third person present indicative? What does the complicity of form in general (*eidos, morphē*) and of the "is" (*esti*) give us to think?

Let us reestablish the contact between these questions and Husserl's text at the point at which formal impoverishment has just been acknowledged as an essential rule. The problem of the relation between the different kinds of statement arises quite naturally. Is statement in the form of judgment, "it is thus," one kind of statement among others? Is there not some excellence reserved for it in the stratum of expressivity? "We must be clear about all these points if one of the oldest and hardest problems of the sphere of meaning (*Bedeutungssphäre*) is to be solved, a problem which hitherto, precisely because it lacked the requisite phenomenological insight, has remained without solution: the problem, namely, as to *how statement as the expression of judgment is related to the expressions of other acts*" (p. 353).

The answer to such a question had been prepared, and its necessity announced, at a stage of the analysis which did not yet concern the stratum of expression. There it was a question of setting forth, within practical or affective experiences, within acts of esthetic, moral, etc. evaluation, a "doxic" kernel which, while still permitting values to be thought as beings (the wished for as being-wished, the pleasant as being-pleasant, etc. (§114)), constitutes, if we may put it thus, the *logicity* of the preexpressive stratum. It is because this silent stratum always bears within it—or always has the power of restoring—a relation to form, that it can always convert its affective or axiological experience, its relation to what is not being-present, into an experience in the form of being-present (the beautiful as being-present, the desired as being-desired, the dreaded-future as being-dreaded-future, the inaccessible as being-inaccessible, and, finally, the absent as being-absent), and that it offers itself without reserve to the logical discourse watched over by predicative form, that is, by the present indicative of the verb to be.[12] From Husserl's point of view, not only would this not reduce the originality of experiences and of practical, affective, axiological discourses, but also would ensure the possibility of their formalization without limit.[13]

Having ascertained that "every act, as also every act-correlate, harbours explicitly or implicitly a 'logical' factor" (§117, p. 332), Husserl had only to draw the conclusions that concern the expressive recasting of these acts, and to confirm, rather than to discover, the privilege of the *is* or of the predicative statement. The moment he repeats[14] the question in the order of meaning, there is already, in fact, a requisite answer. Nor is there any cause for surprise or disappointment. Here, there is something like a rule of discourse or of the text: the question can be inscribed only in the form dictated by the answer that awaits it, namely, that has not awaited it. We have only to ask how the response has prescribed the form of the question: not according to the necessary, conscious, and calculated anticipation of one who conducts a systematic exposition, but, as it were, behind his back. For example, we may ask, here, to what extent the reference to the expressive stratum, before even becoming a theme, has secretly carried out analyses of the preexpressive stratum, and permitted a kernel of logical sense to be discovered in it, in the universal and allegedly silent form of being-present.

And we may ask if some irreducible complicity, between Being as being-present in the form of meaning (*bedeuten*) and Being as being-present in the so-called preexpressive form of sense (*Sinn*), has not been operative, welding the strata to each other, as well as permitting them both to be related one to the other and to be articulated within this entire problematic. Is this not the site of the decision for all the problems we have discerned thus far?[15] Does not the idea of an expressive language become problematic on the basis of this question? And, along with it, does not the possibility of a distinction between the stratum of sense and the stratum of meaning also become problematic? Above all, can the relations between the two strata be thought in the category of expression? To say, in effect, that the description of the infrastructure (of sense) has been guided secretly by the superstructural possibility of meaning, is not to contest, against Husserl, the duality of the strata and the unity of a certain transition which relates them one to the other. It is neither to wish to reduce one stratum to the other nor to judge it impossible completely to recast sense in meaning. It is neither to reconstruct the experience (of sense) as a *language*, above all if one takes this to be a *discourse*, a verbal fabric, nor to produce a critique of language on the basis of the ineffable riches of sense. It is simply to ask questions about *another relationship* between what are called, problematically, *sense* and *meaning*.

That is, about the unity of sense and the word in the "is": which in principle could promise the recasting of all language only by having already, teleologically, promised all sense to meaning. And about the relations between the *is* and formality in general: it is within the self-evidence of the (present) *is*, within *self-evidence itself*, that we find proposed all of transcendental phenomenology seen at its most ambitious, proposing both to constitute an absolutely *formal* logic and ontology, and to provide a transcendental description of self *presence* or of original consciousness.

One might think then that the *sense of Being* has been limited by the imposition of the *form* which, in its most overt value and since the origin of philosophy, seems to have assigned to Being, along with the authority of the *is*, the closure of presence, the form-of-presence, presence-in-form, form-presence.[16] One might think, on the other hand, that formality—or formalization—is limited by the sense of Being which, in fact, throughout its entire history, has never been separated from its determination as presence, beneath the excellent surveillance of the *is*: and that henceforth the thinking of form has the power to extend itself beyond the thinking of Being. But that the two limits thus denounced are *the same* may be what Husserl's enterprise illustrates: phenomenology could push to its extreme limit the *formalist demand* and could criticize all previous formalisms only on the basis of a thinking of Being as *self-presence*, on the basis of a transcendental *experience* of pure consciousness.

Thus, one probably does not have to choose between two lines of thought. Rather, one has to meditate upon the circularity which makes them pass into one another indefinitely. And also, by rigorously repeating this *circle* in its proper historical possibility, perhaps to let some *elliptical* displacement be produced in the difference of repetition: a deficient displacement, doubtless, but deficient in a way that is not yet—or is no longer—absence, negativity, non-Being, lack, silence. Neither matter nor form, nothing that could be recast by some philosopheme, that is, by some dialectics, in whatever sense dialectics may be determined. An ellipsis both of meaning and of form: neither full speech nor a perfect circle. More and less, neither more nor less. Perhaps an entirely other question.

Notes

1 TN. See "Ousia and Gramme," and note 16 below, for more on this citation from Plotinus. The reader would do well to consult these again after finishing this essay in order to understand Derrida's choice of epigraph here.
2 TN. Trans. Dorian Cairns (The Hague: Martinus Nijhoff, 1960).
3 See the Introduction to *Ideas: General Introduction to Pure Phenomenology*, trans. W. R. Boyce Gibson (New York: Humanities Press, 1969). All further references are to this edition.
4 I have attempted to justify this translation in *La voix et le phénomène* (Paris: Presses Universitaires de France, 1967; trans. David Allison as *Speech and*

Phenomena [Evanston: Northwestern University Press, 1973]), which refers especially to the first of the *Logical Investigations*. [T.N. It should be recalled throughout this essay that Derrida's translation of *bedeuten* is *vouloir-dire*, which emphasizes the relation of *meaning* to *speech*, to saying (*dire*).]

5 I refer the reader to the invaluable commentary that accompanies Ricoeur's translation of the work into French. Occasionally, for reasons due only to the intentions of the present analysis, I have had to italicize certain German words and to emphasize their metaphorical charge.

6 On the sense and importance of the *Verflechtung*, and on the functioning of this concept in the *Investigations*, see "The Reduction of Indication" in *Speech and Phenomena*.

7 In the *Investigations* these precautions had been taken and justified at length. For all that these justifications are demonstrative, of course, they are no less inherent to the interior of traditional metaphysical polarities (soul/body, psychical/physical, living/nonliving, intentionality/nonintentionality, form/matter, signified/signifier, intelligible/sensory, ideality/empiricity, etc.). These precautions are encountered particularly in the first of the *Investigations* (which in sum is nothing but a long explication of this issue), in the fifth *Investigation* (chap. 2, §19), and in the sixth (chap. 1, §7). They are confirmed unceasingly in *Formal and Transcendental Logic* and in *The Origin of Geometry*.

8 §15.

9 §124, p. 346. It goes without saying that by "discourse itself" we do not mean a discourse actually, physically, proffered, but, following Husserl's indications, the animation of verbal expression by a meaning, by an "intention" that can remain silent without being essentially affected.

10 From this point of view the entire latent aesthetics of phenomenology might be examined, the entire theory of the work of art which is discernible throughout the didactics of examples, whether the problem of the imaginary is being expounded or the status of ideality, the "once-ness" of the work, whose ideal identity can be reproduced infinitely as the *same*. A system and classification of the arts is announced in this description of the relation between archetype and reproductive examples. Can the Husserlian theory of the ideality of the work of art and of its relations to perception account for the differences between the musical and the plastic work, between the literary and the nonliterary work in general? And, moreover, do the precautions taken by Husserl concerning the originality of the imaginary, even at their most revolutionary, suffice to lift the work of art from an entire metaphysics of art as reproduction, from a *mimetics*? One could show that art, according to Husserl, always refers to perception as to its ultimate resource. And is it not already an aesthetic and metaphysical decision to offer works of art as examples in a theory of the imaginary?

11 This problem was given form in the Introduction to the *Logical Investigations* (§2).

12 Husserl wishes both to respect the novelty or originality of the (practical, affective, axiological) sense added to the kernel of sense in the naked thing (*Sache*) as such, *and*, nevertheless, to bring to light its "founded," superstructural character. "The new sense introduces a *totally new dimension of sense*: with it there is constituted no new determining marks of the mere '*material*' (*Sachen*), but *values of the materials*—qualities of value (*Wertheiten*), or

concrete objectified values (*Wertobjektitäten*): beauty and ugliness, goodness and badness; or the object for use, the work of art, the machine, the book, the action, the deed, and so forth. . . . Further, the consciousness in respect of this new character is once again a *positional* consciousness: the 'valuable' can be doxically posited as being valuable (*als wert seiend*). The 'state of being' (*seiend*) which belongs to the 'valuable' as *its* characterization can be thought of also as *modalized*, as can every 'state of being' " (§116, p. 327). "We can therefore also say: *Every act, as also every act-correlate, harbours explicitly or implicitly a 'logical' factor (ein Logisches)*. . . . It results from all this *that all acts generally—even the acts of feeling and will—are 'objectifying' ('objektivierende') acts, original factors in the 'constituting' of objects*, the necessary sources of different regions of being and of the ontologies that belong therewith. . . . Here lies the deepest of the sources for shedding light on the *universality of the logical*, in the last resort that of the predicative judgment (to which we must add the stratum of meaningful expression [*des bedeutungsmässigen Ausdrückens*] which we have not yet subjected to closer study" (§117, pp. 332–33).

13 "But therein in the last resort are grounded those analogies which have at all times been felt to hold between general logic, general theory of value, and ethics, which, when pursued into their farthest depths, lead to the constituting of general *formal* disciplines on lines parallel to the above, formal logic, formal axiology, and the formal theory of practice (*Praktik*)" (§117, p. 330).

14 "We have expressive predications in which a 'thus it is!' ('*So ist es!*') comes to expression. We have expressive presumptions, questions, doubts, expressive wishes, commands, and so forth. Linguistically we have here forms of sentence whose structure is in part distinctive, while yet they are of ambiguous interpretation: by the side of sentences that embody statements we have sentences embodying questions, presumptions, wishes, commands and so forth. The original debate bore on the issue whether, disregarding the grammatical wording and its historical forms, we had here to do with coordinate types of meaning (*gleichgeordnete Bedeutungsarten*), or whether the case was not rather that all these sentences, so far as their meaning is concerned, are not in truth sentences that state. If the latter, then all act-constructions, such, for instance, as those of the sphere of feeling, which in themselves are not acts of judgment, can achieve 'expression' only in a roundabout way (*Umweg*) through the mediation of an act of judging which is grounded in them" (§127, p. 353).

15 Even though the answer has prescribed the form of the question, or, if you will, itself has been prescribed in it, its thematic articulation is not simply redundant. It engages new concepts and encounters new difficulties, for example, at the end of Section 127, when it is a question of the *direct* or *indirect* expressions of sense, and of the status of the periphrastic detour (*Umweg*). Let us locate several points of orientation in this paragraph: "*Is the medium for the expressing of meaning, this unique medium of the Logos, specifically doxic?* . . . This would not of course exclude the possibility of there being various ways of expressing such experiences, those of feeling, for instance. A single one of these would be the *direct* [*schlicht*: our italics] plain expression of the experience (or of its noema, in the case of the correlative meaning of the term 'expression') through the *immediate* [our italics] adjustment of an articulated expression to the articulated experience of feeling

whereby doxic and doxic tally together. Thus it would have been the *doxic* form dwelling in respect of all its component aspects within the experience of feeling that made possible the adjustability of the expression, as an exclusively doxothetic (*doxothetischen*) experience, to the experience of feeling. . . . To speak more accurately, this *direct* expression, if it would be true and complete, should be applied only to the doxic *nonmodalized* experiences. . . . There exist at all times *a number of alternative indirect expressions* involving 'roundabout phrases' (*mit 'Umwegen'*)" (pp. 354–55).

16 Form (presence, self-evidence) would not be the ultimate recourse, the last analysis to which every possible sign would refer, the *archē* or the *telos*. Or rather, in a perhaps unheard-of fashion, *morphē*, *archē*, and *telos* still signal. In a sense—or a non-sense—that metaphysics would have excluded from its field, while nevertheless remaining in secret and incessant relation with this sense, form in itself already would be the *trace* (*ikhnos*) of a certain nonpresence, the vestige of the un-formed, which announces-recalls its other, as did Plotinus, perhaps, for all of metaphysics. The trace would not be the mixture, the transition between form and the amorphous, presence and absence, etc., but that which, by eluding this opposition, makes it possible in the irreducibility of its excess. Henceforth, the closure of metaphysics, the closure that the audaciousness of the *Enneads* seems to indicate by transgressing it, would not occur *around* a homogenous and continuous field of metaphysics. Rather, it would fissure the structure and history of metaphysics, *organically* inscribing and systematically *articulating* the traces of the *before* and the *after* both from within and without metaphysics. Thereby proposing an infinite, and infinitely surprising, reading. An irreducible rupture and excess can always be produced within an era, at a certain point of its text (for example, in the "Platonic" fabric of "Plotinism"). Already in Plato's text, no doubt.

Part IV
Epistemology

7 'INTRODUCTION TO THE ORIGIN OF GEOMETRY'

EDMUND HUSSERL'S ORIGIN OF GEOMETRY: *AN*
INTRODUCTION (DERRIDA 1989 [FIRST PUBLISHED 1961])

Translated by John P. Leavey

Themes

Derrida brings up issues of the philosophy of knowledge in his discussion
of Husserl's view of mathematical knowledge. This text is from Derrida's
first major publication, in which he translated Husserl's essay and pref-
aced it with a much longer introduction. Husserl aims for the absolute
objectivity of mathematical objects and establishes that in the absoluteness of tradition. The tradition of mathematical knowledge must be
embedded in writing and that raises difficulties for the ideal of non-
historical, a priori and absolute knowledge. In writing, the subjective
origin of knowledge can be presented as subjectless and transcendental.
However, Husserl's own philosophy rests on the supremacy of the intention, which must be the intention of some subject. The historical nature
of mathematical knowledge threatens the intentionality of mathematical
knowledge, which for Husserl must be concerned with objects of intentions. In Husserl, intentionality is the characteristic of the conscious act,
or judgement, that is it is directed towards something which is its object.

Writing serves as the highest possibility of all constitution of intentional objects, because it allows for permanence and preservation.
However, writing itself cannot be characterised as absolutely objective,
since it is embedded in the empirical, historical and intersubjective aspects
of language. What is contained in writing is always relative to the
context of the writing and can only be understood in context; and even

then never in a completely determinate way, since context is never completely described or certain. Writing itself is embodied since it is material and originates in an act of the body. It bridges the ideal and the embodied, which means that it is equivocal between them. In that case all knowledge embedded in writing equivocates between the embodied and the ideal. The embodiment of writing places it within the field of chance, as opposed to the immutable field of absolute mathematical objects. The book which contains knowledge itself is never purely intelligible or purely sensible. It exists in both ways, as a physical object in perception and as intelligible communication.

The historicity of mathematical knowledge is both: internal and external, ideal and factual, in Husserl, but in a way which undermines his attempted distinctions between the ideal or transcendental and the factual or empirical. From Husserl's point of view, factual knowledge should vanish leaving only ideal knowledge. That depends on his model of transcendental ideal forms of consciousness, but these can only exist in an internal way in which they must be conditioned and affected by the empirical sensibility of consciousness. For Husserl, the transcendental consciousness should be independent of the world, and rests on the possibility of surviving a fictional destruction of the factual world. For Derrida this goes to a self-contradictory extreme, since consciousness relies on there being a factual and empirical world.

Husserl's picture of knowledge is based both on a pure internal consciousness distinct from the factual, and sedimentations of sense within the ego. The ego must contain a pure internal consciousness and factual sedimentations. The drive for the univocity, and unity of pure meaning, goes together with the equivocation between the different levels of sedimentation. Husserl's account leads to contradiction. The very emphasis on pure ideas requires them to be understood as the goal of consciousness, so that they are the goal of living consciousness and therefore of life itself.

The equivocation between the univocal and the equivocal is discussed by Derrida, with regard to the grasping of culture in a general recollection within the interiority of consciousness. For Husserl, mathematics is embedded in the life of the consciousness and the cultural world of that life. The account of the history of geometry itself requires an account of culture. The goal of recollection, according to Derrida, is caught between two strategies. The first strategy is that of James Joyce's novel *Ulysses*, which incorporates a vast amount of literary, linguistic and cultural references within the minds of three characters in one day of life in Dublin. That is the strategy of the labyrinth of repetition and equivocation. The idea of the labyrinth returns in the second selected text on 'Epistemology' in Chapter 8. The second strategy is that of Husserl: the reduction of plurality to the univocal. Husserl cannot sustain the univocality, which is the univocality of any philosopher who tries to reduce the plurality of experience to general concepts. Univocality requires an objectivity before culture, or across cultures, in order to avoid splitting between the different interpretations of signs and concepts according to relative point of view.

Husserl's view of the history and origin of science assumes that the pure ideas outside history are what science is. The moment of discovery, or recollection, of principle is an empirical moment, but for Husserl one which marks an unavoidable tension between the ideal existence of the principle and the empirical moment of its discovery. Husserl tries to accommodate the tension as the relation between the finite moment and the infinite idea, which subsumes all finite moments within it. However, the moment does not belong to abstraction, and there is an unresolved contradiction in Husserl's philosophy here, which for Derrida is part of the necessary contradictions which arise in all philosophy and all thought.

Context

Derrida's reflections on the contradictions in Husserl's account of the origin and history of geometry are not just pertinent to Husserl. They continue the problem of the 'epistemological break' in Bachelard, taken up by Canguilhem and Althusser. The concern with the relation between the pre-scientific and the scientific, between different stages of science, and between the universal truth claims of science and its empirical conditions of production, are not at all unique to a French school of philosophy. Such concerns appear in one of the key works in English language philosophy and history of science, Thomas Kuhn's *Structure of Scientific Revolutions* (Kuhn 1996 [first published 1962]), which appeared only one year after Derrida published *Edmund Husserl's* Origin of Geometry: *An Introduction*. Kuhn's book emerged from the most extreme of empiricist philosophical projects. It was written as a volume in the Encyclopaedia of Unified Science, a project of the logical positivists. The logical positivists emerged in the Vienna Circle after the First World War. Their goal was to turn philosophy into logic and scientific methodology. To this end they aimed to eliminate metaphysics from philosophy through a reduction of all language to logic and reports of observation. The idea of a logic of science is certainly rejected by Derrida in *Of Grammatology* (Derrida 1997a) where he argues that the logic of science is not the same as science.

One member of the group, Rudolf Carnap, strongly condemned Heidegger in his 1932 paper 'The Elimination of Metaphysics through Logical Analysis of Language' (Carnap 1966), which did much to set up the sense of conflict between analytic and Continental European philosophy. Nevertheless, Carnap's philosophy will lead us towards Derrida's concerns. Despite some very different presuppositions from Husserl, Carnap also started with the position that philosophy can be metaphysically neutral in a purely descriptive position. The entire logical positivist project was short-lived in its pure original form. Even as it emerged, it partly referred itself to Wittgenstein's *Tractatus Logico-Philosophicus* (Wittgenstein 1961), which dealt with the problems of how a descriptive philosophy deals with the limits and goals of philosophy itself, in language which is often parallel with that of Heidegger and which anticipates Derrida's own philosophical language. The inevitable paradoxes and outright contradictions of a philosophical claim that philosophy has no philosophical subject matter ensured the short life of pure logical positivism. Nevertheless, it left a vast legacy in twentieth-century philosophy through its original texts and the later work of members of the Circle. Carnap himself moved on to consider issues of the distinction between doing science and considering the 'frame work' of science in his 1950 paper 'Empiricism, Semantics, and Ontology' (Carnap 1988). Within the framework empirical questions arise. The framework questions are questions of ontological assumptions. Semantic questions of meaning of words relate the language of science, within the framework, to the ontological language of the framework. The framework questions of ontology are not metaphysical absolutes, they are the assumptions useful and necessary for science, which may change as science evolves. This paper opens up the way for developments in the work of Carnap's student W. V.O. Quine and in Thomas Kuhn even if both seem superficially to contradict Carnap's emphasis on a strict demarcation between logic and meaning in science, and empirical questions of science. The elements of continuity between Carnap and Kuhn were firmly established by Gürol Irzik and Teo Grünberg in 'Carnap and Kuhn: Arch Enemies or Close Allies?' (Irzik and Grünberg 1995).

Quine's influence is acknowledged by Kuhn in *The Structure of Scientific Revolutions* (Kuhn 1996 [first published 1962]), and as Quine's work has itself sometimes been considered to have parallels with Derrida (Golumba 1999), it needs to be considered here. What Kuhn refers to in particular is Quine's extremely influential 1951 paper 'Two Dogmas of Empiricism' (in Quine 1980). Quine argues there that two distinctions should be eliminated from empiricist philosophy. One is the distinction between analytic and synthetic judgements, that is the distinction between judgements of what belongs to the meaning of a word and judgments of what comes from experience. According to Quine, partly contesting Carnap, there is no reliable way of establishing sameness of meaning for words, and therefore no reliable way of establishing what an analytic judgement is. In this case, there is no clear distinction between knowledge of what a scientific concept means, and what the empirical consequences are of scientific claims incorporating those concepts. It is that which Kuhn emphasises, although Quine's other attack on dogma is highly relevant to Kuhn. In the second argument, Quine denies that we can reduce science to pure observation. All science includes theoretical assumptions combined with empirical claims about observation. Therefore science exists as a whole. Scientific claims must be put in a holistic context, and scientific theories evolve in relation to both other theoretical assumptions and observation. This builds on Carnap's distinction between ontological framework and empirical contents of the framework by suggesting that there is no clear distinction and that the two kinds of question occur together and cannot be clearly separated.

Kuhn also picks up on the later Wittgenstein's comments on language games, partly with reference to Stanley Cavell who was later to write on Derrida with critical but sympathetic interest. For Kuhn, scientific knowledge is organised in paradigms which assemble basic assumptions in the same way as language games contain words used in particular ways. Words change meaning between different scientific paradigms so that concepts are incommensurable between paradigms. That is because the same word refers to concepts which are tested in different ways and link with other concepts in different ways in different paradigms. Quine did not accept the Wittgensteinian emphasis on language as an autonomous sphere. Though he had put forward arguments which parallel Wittgenstein, Quine thought they were better without the linguistic dominance they tended to have in Wittgenstein. Quine saw them as fundamentally questions about cognition and entities, rather than language in itself.

The Kuhnian combination of Carnap, Quine and Wittgenstein, in questions of the history of science, produced the claim that proper historical reconstruction of science must be in conflict with any philosophy of science that brings all science into a common logic. Science does not evolve through pure logic and isolated tests. Theories grow and are later replaced because of changes in assumptions, changes in other theories, and social relations within the scientific community. Empirical tests always occur in such a context. Therefore scientific observations never take place in a pure isolated empirical space. What tests are conducted, and how they are interpreted, depends on definitions of concepts within a paradigm, the context of science as a whole at that time, and the whole social context. 'Normal science' goes on within a paradigm but every paradigm contains anomalies, that is contradictions in the paradigm and tests which do not satisfy the predictions made by theories within that paradigm. There are moments of crisis in a paradigm which do not have a completely logical or empirical basis, in which anomalies become intolerable and scientists are increasingly willing to adopt a new paradigm before it can be confirmed empirically. No paradigm emerges simply because of the weight of empirical observation. The older paradigm will always contain more weight of experimental evidence within its tradition.

Issues that Derrida brings up in the context of phenomenology, and the epistemological tradition stemming from Bachelard, are paralleled in Kuhn and in the texts that Kuhn draws on, though Canguilhem's own repose to Kuhn was somewhat ungenerous. Canguilhem acknowledged parallels, but claimed that Kuhn was doing social psychology of science rather than looking at science itself, in Chapter 1 of *Ideology and Rationality in the History of the Life Sciences* (Canguilhem 1988 [first published 1977]). Nevertheless, for both Derrida and Kuhn there is no clear separation between questions of context, including social psychology, and the content of science. Both Derrida and Kuhn refer to the paradoxical interpenetration of the empirical and the theoretical; and both refer to the paradoxical interpenetration of the logical and the historical. In both philosophers, science does not follow logic though it often uses logic. In both philosophers, relativity cannot be eliminated from science; and for both, science cannot just be the expression for a relative point of view because of the universality inherent in scientific principles. In both cases, scientific principles cannot be abstracted from their linguistic expression, which also means that questions of context of meaning in language are present in science.

The Kuhnian concerns are also concerns of Putnam and Davidson, outlined above, with regard to consciousness of the relation between the abstract concepts we grasp in language and their empirical context. In different ways they consider the consequences of the impossibility of eliminating abstract conceptual content, empirical causality, linguistic context, history, or logic. Given that none of these can be eliminated, like Derrida, they are concerned with the consequent paradoxes; though it is Derrida alone who insists at all times on the constituent nature of paradox in philosophy and knowledge.

INTRODUCTION TO THE *ORIGIN OF GEOMETRY* VII

A decisive step remains to be taken. By itself the speaking subject, in the strict sense of the term, is incapable of absolutely grounding the ideal Objectivity of sense. Oral communication (i.e., present, immediate, and synchronic communication) among the protogeometers is not sufficient to give ideal objectivities their "continuing to be" and "*persisting factual existence*," thanks to which they perdure "even during periods in which the inventor and his fellows are no longer awake to such an exchange or even, more universally, no longer alive." To be absolutely ideal, the object must still be freed of *every* tie with an actually present subjectivity in general. Therefore, it must perdure "even when no one has actualized it in evidence" (164 [modified]). Speech [*langage oral*] has freed the object of *individual* subjectivity but leaves it bound to its beginning and to the synchrony of an exchange within the *institutive community*.

The possibility of *writing* will assure the absolute traditionalization of the object, its absolute ideal Objectivity—i.e., the purity of its relation to a universal transcendental subjectivity. Writing will do this by emancipating sense from its *actually present* evidence for a real subject and from its present circulation within a determined community. "The decisive function of written expression, of expression which documents, is that it makes communication possible without immediate or mediate address; it is, so to speak, communication become virtual" (164 [modified]).

That *virtuality* moreover, is an ambiguous value: it simultaneously makes passivity, forgetfulness, and all the phenomena of *crisis* possible.

Far from having to fall again into a real [*réale*] history, a truth that we have gained from this history – scriptural spatiotemporality (whose originality we will soon need to determine) – sanctions and completes the existence of pure transcendental historicity. Without the ultimate objectification that writing permits, all language would as yet remain captive of the de facto and actual intentionality of a speaking subject or community of speaking subjects. By absolutely virtualizing dialogue, writing creates a kind of autonomous transcendental field from which every present subject can be absent.

In connection with the general signification of the *epochē*, Jean Hyppolite invokes the possibility of a "subjectless transcendental field," one in which "the conditions of subjectivity would appear and where the subject would be constituted starting from the transcendental field."[1] Writing, as the place of absolutely permanent ideal objectivities and therefore of absolute Objectivity, certainly constitutes such a transcendental field. And likewise, to be sure, transcendental subjectivity can be fully announced and appear on the basis of this field or its possibility. Thus a subjectless transcendental field is one of the "conditions" of transcendental subjectivity.

But all this can be said only on the basis of an intentional analysis which retains from writing nothing but writing's pure relation to a consciousness which grounds it as such, and not its factuality which, left to itself, is totally without signification [*insignifiante*]. For this absence of subjectivity from the transcendental field, an absence whose possibility frees absolute Objectivity, can be only a factual absence, even if it removed for all time the totality of actual subjects. The originality of the field of writing is its ability to dispense with, *due to its sense*, every present reading in general. But if the text does not announce its own pure dependence on a writer or reader in general (i.e., if it is not haunted by a virtual intentionality), and if there is no purely juridical possibility of it being intelligible for a transcendental subject in general, then there is no more in the vacuity of its soul than a chaotic literalness or the sensible opacity of a defunct designation, a designation deprived of its transcendental function. The silence of prehistoric arcana and buried civilizations, the entombment of lost intentions and guarded secrets, and the illegibility of the lapidary inscription disclose the transcendental sense of death as what unites these things to the absolute privilege of intentionality in the very instance of its essential juridical failure [*en ce qui l'unit à l'absolu du droit intentionnel dans l'instance même de son échec*].

When considering the de jure purity of intentional animation, Husserl always says that the linguistic or graphic body is a flesh, a proper body (*Leib*), or a spiritual corporeality (*geistige Leiblichkeit*) (FTL, §2, p. 21). From then on, writing is no longer only the worldly and mnemotechnical aid to a truth whose own being-sense would dispense with all writing-down. The possibility or necessity of being incarnated in a graphic sign is no longer simply extrinsic and factual in comparison with ideal Objectivity: it is the *sine qua non* condition of Objectivity's internal completion. As long as ideal Objectivity is not, or rather, *can* not be engraved in the world—as long as ideal Objectivity is not in a position to be party to an incarnation (which, in the purity of its sense, is more than a system of signals [*signalisation*] or an outer garment)—then ideal Objectivity is not fully constituted. Therefore, the act of writing is the highest possibility of all "*constitution*," a fact against which the transcendental depth of ideal Objectivity's historicity is measured.

What Fink writes about speech in his excellent transcript of the *Origin* is *a fortiori* true for writing: "In sensible embodiment occurs the 'localization' and the 'temporalization' (*Temporalisation*) of what is, by its being-sense, unlocated and untemporal" ("Die Frage," p. 210).

Such a formulation remarkably sharpens the problem and awakens the peculiar virtue of language. It clearly translates Husserl's exacting effort to catch the ideality of thematic sense and of words [*mots*] in their relations with the linguistic event.[2] But does not this formulation permit linguistic embodiment to be understood as taking place outside the being-sense of ideal objectivity? As "occurring" or "unexpectedly happening" in addition to the being-sense? Does not this formulation give the impression that ideal objectivity is fully constituted as such *before* and *independently of* its embodiment, or rather, before and independently of its *ability to be embodied*?

But Husserl insists that truth is not fully objective, i.e., ideal, intelligible for everyone and indefinitely perdurable, as long as it cannot be said *and* written. Since this perdurability is truth's very sense, the conditions for its survival are included in those of its life. Undoubtedly, truth never keeps the ideal Objectivity or identity of any of its particular de facto linguistic incarnations; and compared to all linguistic factuality it remains "free." But this freedom is only possible precisely from the *moment* truth *can* in general be said or written, i.e., *on condition* that this *can* be done. Paradoxically, the possibility of being written [*possibilité graphique*] permits the ultimate freeing of ideality. Therefore, we could all but reverse the terms of Fink's formula: the *ability* of sense to be linguistically embodied is the only means by which sense becomes non-spatiotemporal.

Because ideal Objectivity can essentially inform or shape the body of speech and writing, and since it depends on a pure linguistic intention, it is radically independent of sensible spatiotemporality. This means that a specific spatiotemporality is prescribed for communication, and therefore for pure tradition and history, a spatiotemporality that escapes the alternative of the sensible and the intelligible, or the empirical and the metempirical. Consequently, truth is no longer *simply* exiled in the primordial event of its language. Its historical habitat authenticates this event, just as the protodocument *authenticates* whether it is the depositary of an intention, whether it refers without falsification to an original and primordial act. In other words, whether the linguistic event refers to an *authentic* act (in the Husserlian sense of the word), because it establishes a truth-value, is made responsible for it, and can appeal to the universality of its testimony.

Husserl thus indicates the direction for a phenomenology of the written thing, specifically, describing the book in its unity as a chain of significations. This unity can be more or less ideal and necessary, and therefore universal, according to the book's sense-content.[3] And not only can that ideal unity be more or less "bound" to factuality, but also according to numerous and completely original forms and modalities. Moreover, the relation of the "exemplars" to their archetypal unity is undoubtedly unique among the reproductions of other cultural formations, especially those of the nonliterary arts. Finally, the book's proper volume and duration are neither purely sensible phenomena, nor purely intelligible noumena. Their specific character seems irreducible. This "being of the book," this "instance of printed thought" whose "language is not natural," Gaston Bachelard calls a "*bibliomenon*."[4]

In the *Origin*, Husserl illuminates more directly that milieu of writing whose difficult signification and importance he had already recognized in the *Logical Investigations*.[5] The difficulty of its description is due to the fact that writing defines and completes the ambiguity of all language. As the process of that essential and constitutive capacity for embodiment, language is also where every absolutely ideal object (i.e., where truth) is factually and contingently embodied. Conversely, truth has its origin in a pure and simple right to speech and writing, but once constituted, it conditions expression, in its turn, as an empirical fact. Truth depends on the pure possibility of speaking and writing, but is independent of what is spoken or written, insofar as they are in the world. If, therefore, truth suffers in and through its language from a certain changeableness, its downfall will be less a fall toward language than a degradation within language.

From then on, in effect, as is prescribed for it, sense is gathered into a sign,[6] and the sign becomes the worldly and exposed residence of an unthought truth. We have previously seen that truth can perdure in this way without being thought in act or in fact—and that is what radically emancipates truth from all empirical subjectivity, all factual life, and the whole real world. At the same time, man's communal being "is lifted to a new level" (164): it can appear, in effect, as a transcendental community.

The authentic act of writing is a transcendental reduction performed by and toward the *we*. But since, in order to escape worldliness, sense *must* first *be able* to be set down in the world and be deposited in sensible spatiotemporality, it must put its pure intentional ideality, i.e., its truth-sense, in danger. Thus a possibility, which even here accords only with empiricism and nonphilosophy, appears in a philosophy which is (at least because of certain motifs) the contrary of empiricism: the possibility of truth's *disappearance*. We purposely use the ambiguous word disappearance. What disappears is what is annihilated, but also what ceases, intermittently or definitely, to appear *in fact* yet without affecting its being or being-sense. To determine the sense of this "disappearance" of truth is the most difficult problem posed by the *Origin* and all of Husserl's philosophy of history. Furthermore, we were unable to find in Husserl an unequivocal response to a question which only makes that of phenomenology itself return: what is the sense of its appearing? That equivocation will presently reveal both how much the author of the *Crisis* was a stranger to history or how fundamentally incapable he was of taking it seriously, and at what point (in the same moment) he strives to respect historicity's own peculiar signification and possibility and truly to penetrate them.

What then is this possibility of disappearance?

1. In the first place, let us rule out the hypothesis of a *death of sense* in general within the individual consciousness. Husserl clearly specifies in the *Origin* and elsewhere that, once sense appeared in egological consciousness, its total annihilation becomes impossible.[7] A sense that is conserved as a sedimentary habituality and whose dormant potentiality can de jure be reanimated is not returned to nothingness by the vanishing of retentions of retentions. "Far from being a phenomenological nothing," "the so-called '*unconscious*'" or "*universal substratum*" where sense is deposited is "a limit-mode of consciousness" (*FTL*, p. 319).[8] Clearly in this type of analysis, upon which formidable difficulties already weigh, Husserl is only worried about the permanence and virtual presence of sense within the monadic subject, and not about the absolutely ideal Objectivity of sense gained through speech and writing from that subjectivity. Now this Objectivity is found threatened as truth in the world. Profound *forgetfulness* therefore extends into the spaces of intersubjectivity and the distance between communities. *Forgetfulness* is a historical category.[9]

2. The graphic sign, the guarantee of Objectivity, can also *in fact* be destroyed. This danger is inherent in the factual worldliness of inscription itself, and nothing can definitively protect inscription from this. In such a *case*, because Husserl considers sense neither an in-itself nor a

pure spiritual interiority but an "object" through and through, we might first think that the forgetfulness which follows upon the destruction of Objectivity's custodial sign [*signe gardien*] would not affect (as in a "Platonism" or "Bergsonism") the surface of a sense without undermining the sense itself. Such a forgetfulness would not only suppress this sense but would annihilate it in the specific being-in-the-world to which its Objectivity is entrusted. For Husserl clearly said this: insofar as signs can be immediately perceptible by everyone in their *corporeality*; insofar as their bodies and corporeal forms are always already in an intersubjective horizon, then sense can be deposited there and communalized [*mettre en communauté*]. Corporeal exteriority undoubtedly does not *constitute* the sign as such but, in a sense that we must make clear, is *indispensable* to it.

Yet the hypothesis of such a factual destruction does not interest Husserl at all. While completely recognizing the terrifying *reality* of the current risk, he would deny it any thinkable, i.e., any philosophical significance. No doubt he would admit that a universal conflagration, a world-wide burning of libraries, or a catastrophe of monuments or "documents" in general would intrinsically ravage "bound" cultural idealities, whose notion we evoked above. By their adherence to some factuality, these idealities, *in their very sense*, would be vulnerable to that worldly accident. Death is possible for them alone and has the transcendental signification we just now granted it, but only insofar as the "bound" ideality is animated or traversed by a transcendental intention, only insofar as it is guided by the *telos* of an absolute freeing which has not been fully attained. But like that which orients Husserl's reflection (specifically, the fully freed ideality and absolute Objectivity of sense, for which mathematics is the model), the threat of an intrinsic destruction by the body of the sign can be ruled out. All factual writings, in which truth could be sedimented, will never be anything in themselves but sensible "exemplars," individual events in space and time (which is only true to a certain degree for "bound" idealities). Since truth does *not* essentially depend on *any of them*, they could *all* be destroyed without overtaking *the very sense of* absolute ideality. Undoubtedly, absolute ideality would be changed, mutilated, and overthrown *in fact*: perhaps it would disappear in fact from the surface of the world, but its sense-of-being as truth, which is not in the world—neither in our world here, nor any other—would remain intact in itself. Its being-sense would preserve its own *intrinsic* historicity, its own interconnections, and the catastrophe of worldly history would remain *exterior* to it.

That is what Husserl means when he opposes *internal* or intrinsic (*innere*) historicity to external (*aussere*) history. This distinction, which has only a phenomenological sense, is decisive.[10] It would be fruitless for him to object that historicity or being-in-history is precisely the possibility of being *intrinsically* exposed to the *extrinsic*, for then the historicity absolutely proper to any truth-sense would be missing, and Husserl's discourse would be plunged into a confusion of significations and regions. We would then be conceding that a pure ideality can be changed by a real cause, which is to lose sense. If geometry is true, its internal history must be saved integrally from all sensible aggression. Since geometry is tied neither to this moment here, nor to this territory here, nor to this world here, but to all the world (*Weltall*), nothing will ever stand between the worldly experiences which incarnated geometry and what they have begun again: discovering afresh (without any traces and after the shrouding of this world here) the paths of an adventure buried in another real history. In comparison with *veritas aeterna*, whose proper historicity Husserl wishes to grasp and about which he speaks more and more often as his thought becomes allured by history, no real development other than that of the variable example interests him. Accordingly, the hypothesis of the world-wide catastrophe could even serve as a revelatory fiction.

Thus, we should be able to repeat *analogously* the famous analysis of Section 49 of *Ideas I*.[11] The analysis concluded that, after a certain eidetic-transcendental reduction, pure consciousness is intangible, even when the existing world is annihilated or factual experience dissolved "through internal conflict . . . into illusion" (*Ideas I*, §49, p. 137 [modified]). Husserl did not dispute that under those circumstances all consciousness would *in fact* be destroyed and that its worldly existence would be engulfed with the world. In addition, the clearest intention of this analysis and fiction is to explicate a reduction which must reveal to the *Ur-Region*—transcendental consciousness—the essential relativity of the world's sense (the world being the totality of regions). Since transcendental consciousness can always and with complete freedom modify or suspend the thesis of *each* (therefore of *all*) contingent existence and of *each* (therefore of *all*) transcendence, its very sense is de jure and absolutely independent of the whole world. The situation of truth, particularly of geometrical truth, is analogous. It therefore provokes the same questions.

In fact, this eidetic independence, brought to light in a methodological idealism by a fiction, can be questioned as to its value beyond the moment of *Ideas I*; i.e., beyond the moment the eidetic-transcendental reduction has not yet attained its final radicality and is provisionally immobilized in one region. In effect, the region of pure consciousness is the "residue" of a "suspension" that still remains more eidetic than transcendental and is only the most profound of the eidetic reductions. Yet this suspension, which tends to discover the protoregion's essential structures and is certainly constitutive of the world, is constituted itself. And, as Husserl will say, it is not the "ultimate" transcendental regression (ibid., §81, p. 216).[12] Would Husserl have judged this fiction valid the moment he studied (for example, in the *Cartesian Meditations*) the genetic constitution of the *ego* in the "unity" of its "history"?[13] In a certain sense we can say yes. Through the solipsistic hypothesis in which the *Cartesian Meditations* are first couched, pure consciousness is still considered as that which no worldly factuality can penetrate as such, as "*a self-contained nexus of being*" (*Ideas I*, §49, p. 139 [modified]). Undoubtedly, the intra-egological sedimentation, the potential evidence, the "residues," and the "references"[14] that this "history" makes necessary are only a network of sense. But by the irreplaceability, irreversibility, and invariability of their interconnections, are they not also "facts" or factual structures with respect to which pure consciousness would no longer be free? Could these sedimentary structures de jure survive the annihilation, the overthrow, in a word, the complete "variation" of factuality? As sense, would they not be marked by a certain order of the factual world to which *past* consciousness is tied—a consciousness tied there by its own interconnections and structurally implicated in every present consciousness?

Husserl would probably reply that, in such a case, we are considering factual structures in the life of the *ego*—i.e., structures "bound" to some reducible contingency—and not essential ones reduced to their pure ideality. The "unity" of the *ego's* "history" is that of the *eidos* "*ego*." Husserl's description means that the essential form of every interconnection, every sedimentation, and therefore every history for every *ego* is self-sufficient. Within this *form* of historicity that we wish to attain as an invariant, all facto-historical interconnections are variable at will.

Similarly, since the interconnections and sedimentations of geometrical truth are free of all factuality, no worldly catastrophe can put *truth* itself in danger. All factual peril, therefore, stops at the threshold of its internal historicity. Even if all geometrical "documents"—and as well, all actual geometers—had to come to ruin one day, to speak of this as an event "of" geometry would be to commit a very serious confusion of sense and to abdicate responsibility for all rigorous discourse. One cannot come back to all this evidence without making the sensible the ground of geometrical truth and, therefore, without questioning once more the sense of geometry constituted as an eidetic science. Now this sense was securely decided within the static analyses that, as we saw above, were the indispensable guard rails for all genetic or historical phenomenology.

3. We would be fully convinced, if here—as in his static analyses—Husserl had considered writing to be a sensible phenomenon. But did we not just find out that writing, inasmuch as it was grounding (or contributing to the grounding of) truth's absolute Objectivity, was not *merely* a constituted sensible body (*Körper*), but was also a properly constituting body (*Leib*)—the intentional primordiality of a Here-and-Now of truth? If writing is *both* a factual event and the upsurging of sense, if it is both *Körper* and *Leib*, how would writing preserve its *Leiblichkeit* from corporeal disaster? Husserl is not going to immobilize his analysis within this *ambiguity*, which for him is only a provisional and factual confusion of regions. The phenomenologist must dissolve the ambiguity, if he does not want to be reduced to equivocation, to choose silence, or to precipitate phenomenology into *philosophy*. Husserl, therefore, maintains his dissociative analysis and disarticulates the ambiguity. In order to grasp the nature of the danger threatening truth *itself* in its constitutive speech or writing, in order not to leave "internal" historicity, he is going to track down the intention of writing (or of reading) in itself and in its purity: in a new reduction he is going to isolate the intentional act which constitutes *Körper* as *Leib* and maintain this act in its *Leiblichkeit*, in its living truth-sense. Such an analysis no longer has any need of *Körper* as such. Only in the intentional dimension of a properly animate body, of the *geistige Leiblichkeit*, more precisely, in the *Geistigkeit* of the *Leib* (to the exclusion of all factual corporeality), is sense intrinsically threatened. Although in a *word* [*mot*], *Körper* and *Leib*, body and flesh, are *in fact* numerically one and the same existent, their senses are definitively heterogeneous, and nothing can come to the latter through the former. *Forgetfulness* of truth itself will thus be nothing but the failure of an act and the abdication of a responsibility, a lapse more than a defeat—and this forgetfulness can be made to appear in person only on the basis of an intentional history.

From then on, whether it remains as the disappearance of intersubjective truth or, as we said above, a historical category, *forgetfulness* can nevertheless be described as a phenomenon of the *ego*, as one of its intentional "modifications." As intentional sense, everything can and should be described only as a modification of the pure *ego*, provided the sense of each modification is prudently respected, as Husserl tries to do, for example, concerning the difficult constitution of the *alter ego*. We also see that, for the same reason, forgetfulness will never be radical, however profound it may be, and sense can always, in principle and de jure, be reactivated.

In *Formal and Transcendental Logic* and then in the *Crisis*, linguistic objectification and mathematical symbolization were presented as the occasion of the technicist's and objectivist's alienation, which degraded science into a skill or game.[15] This accusation, taken up again in the *Origin*, is more particularly directed against the methodological and operative teaching of mathematics. One learns to use signs whose primordial sense (which is not always the logical sense that is sedimented and accessible to an *explication*) is concealed or potentialized under sedimentations. The latter, which are only intentions or intentional senses made dormant, are not only *superimposed* in the internal becoming of sense, but are more or less virtually *implicated* in their totality in each stage or step. (In the *Origin*, the notion of *Stufe* has both a structural and genetic sense and can be translated by "step" or by "stage.") The geological image of "sedimentation" translates remarkably well the style of that implication. It brings together, for all intents and purposes, the following images: The image of *level* or *stratum*—what is deposited by an inroad or a progression after the radical novelty of an irruption or *upsurge*: every advance, every proposition (*Satz*) of a new sense is *at the same time* a leap (*Satz*) and a *sedimentary* (*satzartig*) fall back of sense. Also, the image of the substantial permanence of what is then *supposed* or *situated under* the surface of actually present evidence. And finally, the image of the concealed presence that an activity of excavation can always re-produce above ground as the foundation, that is itself grounded, of higher stratifications. It brings all this together in the structural and *internal* unity of a system, of a "region" in which all deposits, interrelated but distinct, are originally prescribed by an *archi-tectonics*.

Confronting sedimented sense, our first danger is *passivity*. In the *Origin*, Husserl dwells more on the receptive acceptance of signs—first in reading—than on the secondary technical or logical activity that is not only not contradictory to the first passivity but, on the contrary, supposes it. The synthesis which awakens the sign to signification is first, in fact, necessarily passive and associative.[16] The possibility of giving way to this first *expectation* of sense is a lasting danger. But only *freedom* can let itself be threatened in this way; we are always free to reawaken any passively received sense, to reanimate all its virtualities, and to "transform" them "back . . . into the corresponding activity." This freedom is the "capacity for reactivation that belongs originally to every human being as a speaking being" (164). By this reactivation, which, Husserl states, is not "in fact" the "norm" and without which a certain comprehension is always possible, I actively re-produce the primordial evidence; I make myself fully responsible for and conscious of the sense that I take up. *Reaktivierung* is, in the domain of ideal objectivities, the very act of all *Verantwortung* and of all *Besinnung*, in the senses defined earlier. *Reaktivierung* permits bringing to life, under the sedimentary surfaces of linguistic and cultural acquisitions, the sense arising from instituting evidence. This sense is reanimated by the fact that I restore it to its dependence on my act and reproduce it in myself such as it had been produced for the first time by another. Of course, the activity of reactivation is second. What it gives back to me is the originally presentive intuition (that of the geometrical formation, for example) which is both an activity and a passivity. If this activity is especially illuminated here, it is no doubt because the evidence considered is that of created and established ideal formations.[17]

Responsibility for reactivation is a co-responsibility. It engages the one who receives, but also and first of all the one who creates and then expresses the sense. For sedimentations obliterate sense only insofar as there are surfaces available for this. The *equivocity* of expression is the chosen field of sedimentary deposits. That is why the primally instituting geometer and those who follow after him must be concerned about "the univocity of linguistic expression and about securing, by a very careful coining of words, propositions, and complexes of propositions, the results which are to be univocally expressed" (165 [modified]).

Husserl never ceased to appeal to the imperative of univocity. Equivocity is the path of all philosophical aberration. It is all the more difficult not to be hasty here, as the sense of equivocity in general is itself equivocal. There is a *contingent* plurivocity or multisignificance and an *essential* one. These are already distinguished in the *Investigations* (*LI*, I, 1, §26, p. 314). The first depends on an objective convention; thus the word "dog" signifies both "a type of animal" and (in German) "a type of wagon (used in mines)." This plurivocity does not mislead anyone and we are always free to reduce it.[18] The second is of subjective origin, and it depends on original intentions, on always new experiences which animate the identity of objective sense and make it enter into unforeseeable configurations. This plurivocity is an "unavoidable rather than chance ambiguity [*plurivocité*], one that cannot be removed from our language by an artificial device or convention" (*LI*, p. 314).

However, this last equivocity is what science and philosophy must overcome. It is "unavoidable" only in natural language, i.e., in the factocultural phenomenon preceding the reduction. That Husserl is so anxious to reduce the equivocal sense of cultural naiveté reveals a concern that once more could be interpreted both as a refusal of history and as a deep fidelity to the pure sense of historicity. *On the one hand*, in effect, univocity removes truth out of history's reach. Univocal expression completely breaks the surface and offers no turning back [*repli*] to the more or less virtual significations that the intentions could deposit all along the advances of a language or culture. Thus Husserl's constant association of equivocal proceedings with a criticism of *profundity* is understandable.[19] Because it brings everything to view within a present act of evidence, because nothing is hidden or announced in the penumbra of potential intentions, because it has mastered all the dynamics of sense, univocal language remains *the same*. It thus keeps its ideal identity throughout all cultural development. It is the condition that allows communication among generations of investigators no matter how distant and assures the exactitude of translation and the purity of tradition.[20] In other words—*on the other hand*—the very moment univocity removes sense beyond the reach of historical modification, it alone makes pure history possible, i.e., as the transmission and recollection [*recueillement*] of sense. Univocity only indicates the limpidity of the historical ether. Once again, Husserl's demand for univocity (which he formulated before the practice of the reduction) is therefore only the reduction of empirical history toward a pure history. Such a reduction must be recommenced indefinitely, for language neither can nor should be maintained under the protection of univocity.

If a radical equivocity precludes history, in effect, by plunging it into the nocturnal and ill-transmissible riches of "bound" idealities, absolute univocity would itself have no other consequence than to sterilize or paralyze history in the indigence of an indefinite iteration. Since equivocity always evidences a certain depth of development and concealment of a past, and when one wishes to assume and *interiorize* the memory of a culture in a kind of *recollection* (*Erinnerung*) in the Hegelian sense, one has, facing this equivocity, the choice of two endeavors. One would resemble that of James Joyce: to repeat and take responsibility for all equivocation itself, utilizing a language that could equalize the greatest possible synchrony with the greatest potential for buried, accumulated, and interwoven intentions within each linguistic atom, each vocable, each word, each simple proposition, in all wordly cultures and their most ingenious forms (mythology, religion, sciences, arts, literature, politics, philosophy, and so forth). And, like Joyce, this endeavor would try to make the structural unity of all empirical culture appear in the generalized equivocation of a writing that, no longer translating one language into another on the basis of their common cores of sense, circulates throughout all languages at once, accumulates their energies, actualizes their most secret consonances, discloses their furthermost common horizons, cultivates their associative syntheses instead of avoiding them, and rediscovers the poetic value of passivity. In short, rather than put it out of play with quotation marks, rather than "reduce" it, this writing resolutely settles itself *within* the *labyrinthian* field of culture "bound" by its own equivocations, in order to travel through and explore the vastest possible historical distance that is now at all possible.

The other endeavor is Husserl's: to reduce or impoverish empirical language methodically to the point where its univocal and translatable elements are actually transparent, in order to reach back and grasp again at its pure source a historicity or traditionality that no de facto historical totality will yield of itself. This historicity or traditionality is always already presupposed by every Odyssean repetition of Joyce's type, as by all *philosophy of history* (in the current sense) and by every *phenomenology of spirit* The essences of finite totalities and the typology of figures of the spirit will always be idealities that are bound to empirical history. Only by means of historicism is it possible to remain there and confuse them with the movement of truth.[21]

But Husserl's project, as the transcendental "parallel" to Joyce's, knows the same relativity. Joyce's project, which also proceeded from a certain anti-historicism and a will "to awake" from the "nightmare" of "history,"[22] a will to master that nightmare in a total and present resumption, could only succeed by allotting its share to univocity, whether it might draw from a given univocity or try to produce another. Otherwise, the very text of its repetition would have been unintelligible; at least it would have remained so forever and for everyone. Likewise, Husserl had to admit an irreducible, enriching, and always renascent equivocity into pure historicity. In effect, absolute univocity is imaginable only in two limiting cases. *First*: suppose the designated thing is not only an absolutely singular, immutable, and natural object, but also an existent whose unity, identity, and Objectivity would in themselves be prior to all culture. Now if we suppose that such a thing or perception exists, linguistic ideality and its project of univocity—i.e., the act of language itself—intervene and from the outset place that supposition in a culture, in a network of linguistic relations and oppositions, which would load a word with intentions or with lateral and virtual reminiscences. Equivocity is the congenital mark of every culture. This first hypothesis of a univocal and natural language is, therefore, absurd and contradictory.

Second: is not the result the same if, at the other pole of language, an absolutely ideal object must be designated? This time, the chance for univocity would not be offered by a precultural, but by a transcultural object, for example, the geometrical object. In any case, univocity corresponds to the very vocation of science. Husserl writes in the *Origin*: "In accord with the essence of science, then, its functionaries maintain the constant claim, the personal certainty, that everything they put into scientific assertions has been said 'once and for all,' that it 'stands fast,' forever identically repeatable, usable in evidence and for further theoretical or practical ends—as indubitably able to be reactivated with the identity of its genuine sense" (165–66 [modified]).

But this identity of sense, the ground of univocity and the condition for reactivation, is always relative, because it is always inscribed within a mobile system of relations and takes its source in an infinitely open project of acquisition. Even if those relations are, within a science, relations of pure idealities and "truths," they do not therein give rise any less to some singular placings in perspective [*mises en perspectives*], some multiple interconnections of sense, and therefore some mediate and potential aims. If, in fact, equivocity is always irreducible, that is because words and language in general are not and can never be absolute *objects*.[23] They do not possess any resistant and permanent identity that is absolutely their own. They have their linguistic being from an intention which traverses them as mediations. The "same" word is always "other" according to the always different intentional acts which thereby make a word significative [*signifiant*]. There is a sort of *pure* equivocity here, which grows in the very rhythm of science. Consequently, Husserl specifies in a note that the scientific statement, without being questioned again as to its truth, always remains provisional, and that "Objective, absolutely firm knowledge of truth is an infinite idea" (166). Absolute univocity is inaccessible, but only as an Idea in the Kantian sense can be. If the univocity investigated by Husserl and the equivocation generalized by Joyce are in fact *relative*, they are, therefore, not so *symmetrically*. For their common *telos*, the positive value of univocity, is *immediately* revealed only within the relativity that Husserl defined. Univocity is also the absolute horizon of equivocity. In giving it the sense of an infinite task, Husserl does not make univocity, as could be feared, the value for a language impoverished and thus removed out of history's reach. Rather, univocity is both the a priori and the teleological condition for all historicity; it is that without which the very equivocations of empirical culture and history would not be possible.

The problem of univocity echoes immediately upon that of reactivation. Its schema is the same, for, without a minimal linguistic transparency, no reactivation would be imaginable. But if univocity is in fact always relative, and if it alone permits the reduction of all empirical culture and of all sedimentation, is the possibility of a pure history of sense to be doubted de jure? More particularly since, after having presented the capacity for reactivation, Husserl does not fail to ask the serious question of its *finitude*. In a science like geometry, whose potentiality for growth is extraordinary, it is impossible for every geometer, at every instant and every time he resumes his task after necessary interruptions, to perform a total and immediate reactivation of the "immense chain of foundings back to the original premises" (166 [modified]). The necessity of those interruptions is a factual one (sleep, professional breaks, and so forth), which has no sense compared with geometrical truth but is no less irreducible to it.

A *total* reactivation, even if that were possible, would paralyze the internal history of geometry just as surely as would the radical impossibility of all reactivation. Husserl is not worried about that: at this point a total recuperation of origins is still only a teleological horizon. For under the extrinsic necessity that geometrical activity be intermittent is also hidden an essential and internal necessity: since no piece of the geometrical edifice is self-sufficient, no *immediate* reactivation is possible, on any level. That is why, Husserl remarks, the "individual and even the social capacity" for reactivation is of an "obvious finitude" (168). It will always be denied immediate totality.

The obviousness [*évidence*] of that finitude and of that necessary mediacy could stamp Husserl's whole purpose as nonsense. Since that finitude is in fact irreducible, should it not furnish the true starting point for reflecting on history? Without that essential concealment of origins and within the hypothesis of an all-powerful reactivation, what would consciousness of historicity be? Also, no doubt, that consciousness would be nothing, if it was radically prohibited access to origins. But, so that history may have its proper density, must not then the darkness which engulfs the "original premises" (it can be penetrated but never dissipated) not only hide the fact but also the instituting sense? And must not the "critical" forgetfulness of origins be the faithful shadow in truth's advance rather than an accidental aberration? This distinction between fact and sense (or the de facto and the de jure) would be effaced in the sense-investigation of a primordial finitude.

But for Husserl, as we know, that finitude can *appear* precisely in its primordiality only given the Idea of an infinite history. Thus, faced with the finitude of reactivation, Husserl does not give up, as we suspect, the first direction of his investigation. He postpones the problem until later and invites us, with a slightly enigmatic brevity, to "notice" that there exists "an idealization: namely, the removal of limits from our capacity, in a certain sense its infinitization" (168). A secondary idealizing operation then comes to relieve the reactivative ability of its finitude and lets it get beyond itself. This movement is analogous to the constitution, for example, of the unity of the world's infinite horizon or (beyond the finite interconnection of retentions and protentions) to the constitution of the evidence for a total unity of the immanent flux as an Idea in the Kantian sense.[24] But above all, this movement is analogous to the production of geometry's exactitude: the passage to the infinite limit of a finite and qualitative sensible intuition. Strictly speaking, even here it is geometrical idealization which permits infinitizing the reactivative ability. Working in the diaphanousness of pure ideality, this ability easily and de jure transgresses its limits, which are then no more than the nominal limits of pure factuality. This idealization, which has for its correlate an infinite Idea, always decisively intervenes in the difficult moments of Husserl's description. The phenomenological status of its evidence remains rather mysterious. The impossibility of adequately determining the content of this Idea does not undermine, Husserl says in *Ideas I*, the rational transparency of its insightful evidence (*Einsichtigkeit*).[25] However, the certainty of what can never immediately and as such present itself in an intuition should pose some serious problems for phenomenology (problems similar to those, for example, of the constitution of the *alter ego* by an irreducibly mediate intentionality). We will come directly back to this later, when the production of geometrical exactitude by idealization will be our concern. At the present juncture, Husserl provisionally averts this difficulty. He writes: "The peculiar sort of evidence belonging to such idealizations will concern us later" (168 [modified]).

The capacity of reactivation must then be transmitted, in order that science not decay into a "tradition emptied of sense." As long as science moves away from its beginnings and its logical superstructures are accumulated, the chances for such a transmission decrease until the day when the ability happens to fail. "Unfortunately . . . this is our situation, and that of the whole modern age" (169). The advancements of science can be pursued, even when the sense of its origin has been lost. But then the very logicality of the scientific gestures, imprisoned in mediacy, breaks down into a sort of oneiric and inhuman absurdity. Did not Plato describe this situation? Was not the eternity of essences for him perhaps only another name for a nonempirical historicity? "Geometry and the studies [*sciences*] that accompany it" are exiled far from their fundamental intuitions. They are incapable of "vision" (*idein*) and riveted to the hypotheses held as their principles. Confusing symbol with truth, they seem to us to dream (*orōmen ōs oneirottousi*) (*Republic* VII, 533c).[26] The return inquiry is therefore urgent: through us and for us it will reawaken science to its primordial sense, i.e., as we know, its final sense.

Notes

1 We refer here to a comment by Jean Hyppolite during the discussion which followed the lecture of Fr. Van Breda on "La Réduction phénoménologique," in *Husserl*, Cahiers de Royaumont, p. 323.

2 This sensible embodiment has the peculiar qualities [*l'étrangeté*] of both sense's inhabitation of the word [*mot*] and the *here and now* use of the word's ideality. In the first case, embodiment is at its limit the inscription of an

absolutely *"free"* and objective ideality (that of geometrical truth, for example) within the *"bound"* ideality of the word, or in general of a *more* free ideality within a *less* free ideality. In the second case, embodiment is that of a necessarily bound ideality, that of the word's identity within language, in a real-sensible event. But this last embodiment is still done through another step of mediate ideality which Husserl does not directly describe, but which we think can be located on the basis of strictly Husserlian concepts. It is a question of ideal forms or vague morphological types (a notion that we will have occasion to specify farther on), which are proper to the corporeality of graphic and vocal signs. The forms of graphic and vocal signs must have a certain identity which is imposed and recognized each time in the empirical fact of language. Without this always intended and approximate ideal identity (that of letters and phonemes, for example), no sensible language would be possible or intelligible as language, nor could it intend higher idealities. Naturally, this morphological ideality is still more "bound" than the word's ideality. The precise place of the properly termed realizing [*réalisante*] embodiment is ultimately therefore the union of the sensible form with sensible material, a union *traversed* by the linguistic intention which always intends, explicitly or not, the highest ideality. Linguistic incarnation and the constitution of written or scriptural space suppose, then, a closer and closer "interconnection" of ideality and reality through a series of less and less ideal mediations and in the synthetic unity of an intention. This intentional synthesis is an unceasing movement of going and returning that works to bind the ideality of sense and to free the reality of the sign. Each of the two operations is always haunted by the sense of the other: each operation is already announced in the other or still retained in it. Language frees the ideality of sense, then, in the very work of its "binding" ("interconnecting" [*enchaînement*]).

3 In the *Origin*, Husserl distinguishes between literature in the broad sense, the realm of all written discourse, and literature as literary art. The literary work is often chosen by Husserl as the clue for analyzing the ideality of cultural objectivities. The ideal identity of the work will never be mistaken for its sensible embodiments. It does not derive its individual identity from the latter. The origin of identity, moreover, is the criterion which permits us to distinguish between the real and the ideal. Husserl writes in *EJ* (§65, pp. 265–66): "We call *real* in a specific sense *all that which, in real things in the broader sense, is, according to its sense, essentially individualized by its spatiotemporal position; but we call irreal every determination which, indeed, is founded with regard to spatiotemporal appearance in a specifically real thing but which can appear in different realities as identical*—not merely as similar" (Husserl's emphasis).

Thus the relation between the ideal and the real in all cultural objectivities (and first in all the arts) can be explicated. That is relatively easy for the literary work. Thus, "Goethe's *Faust* is found in any number of real books ('book' denotes here what is produced by men and intended to be read: it is already a determination which is itself not purely material, but a determination of significance!), which are termed exemplars of *Faust*. This mental sense which determines the work of art, the mental structure as such, is certainly 'embodied' in the real world, but it is not individualized by this embodiment. Or again: the same geometrical proposition can be uttered as often as desired; every real utterance has . . . identically the same sense" (ibid., p. 266).

But how can we determine the ideality of a work whose protoindividualization is tied to the work's single spatiotemporal embodiment? How can we make its ideality appear by varying factual exemplars, since the latter can only imitate a factuality and not express or "indicate" an ideal sense? Is it, in short, the same for the ideality of the plastic arts, of architecture? Or of music, whose case is even more ambiguous? Although repetition may be of a different nature here, which in each case requires an appropriate and prudent analysis, it is no less possible *in principle* and thus makes an incontestable ideality appear: "To be sure, an ideal object like Raphael's *Madonna* can in fact have only one mundane state (*Weltlichkeit*) and in fact is not repeatable in an adequate identity (of the complete ideal content). But *in principle* this ideal is indeed repeatable, as is Goethe's *Faust*"(ibid.).

From the first perception, then, of a work of plastic art as such (whose ideal value is primordially and intrinsically rooted in an *event*), there is a sort of immediate reduction of factuality which permits, next, the neutralization of the necessary imperfection of reproduction. Here is not the place to prolong these analyses of aesthetic perception and ideality. Husserl is content to situate their domain and to define preliminary, indispensable distinctions. He proposes some analogous distinctions in the cultural sphere of politics and strives to bring to light both the ideality of the constitution of the state (of the national will, for example) and the originality of its "boundness" to the factuality of a territory, a nation, etc., within which this constitution can be indefinitely repeated as its ideal validity (ibid., pp. 266–67).

4 *L'Activité rationaliste de la physique contemporaine* (Paris: Presses Universitaires de France, 1951), pp. 6–7.

5 Cf. *LI*, I, Prol., §6, p. 60: "Science exists objectively only in its literature, only in written work has it a rich relational being limited to men and their intellectual activities: in this form it is propagated down the millennia, and survives individuals, generations and nations. It therefore represents a set of *external* arrangements, which, just as they arose out of the knowledge-acts of many individuals, can again pass over into just such acts of countless individuals, in a readily understandable manner, whose exact description would require much circumlocution" (our emphasis). On this level of analysis, which above all should disengage the objective autonomy of signification, the question is clearly that of "*external* arrangements": sensible exemplars on which neither the ideality of sense nor the *clear* intention of cognition depends. But this fact neither prohibits nor contradicts at all the subsequent theme of writing as the *intrinsic possibility* and *intrinsic condition* of acts of objective cognition. The *Origin maintains* these two themes. That is the difficulty we are striving to illuminate here.

6 We take this word in the broad sense of sign-signifier or "sign-expression" (graphic or vocal), the meaning that Husserl gives this term by opposing it to the "indicative" sign (*LI*, I, 1, §§1–5, pp. 269–75). On the basis of this distinction, we could interpret the phenomenon of *crisis* (which, for Husserl, always refers to a disorder or illness of language) as a degradation of the sign-expression into a sign-indication, of a "clear" (*klar*) intention into an empty symbol.

7 In *Ideas I*; in *EJ*; but above all in *FTL* (in terms which are literally taken up again in the *Origin*), cf. in particular Appendix II, §2c, pp. 318–19.

8 On the *naiveté* of the classic problems of the Unconscious and on the question of knowing whether an intentional analysis can open a methodical access to the Unconscious, see "Fink's Appendix on the Problem of the 'Unbewussten,' " in C, pp. 385–87.

9 *Forgetfulness* is a word that Husserl rarely employs in the *Crisis*: he never uses it in the first text of the *Origin*, perhaps because habit relates it very easily to individual consciousness or to its psychological sense: perhaps also because it can suggest an annihilation of sense.

10 The opposition between intrinsic penetration and extrinsic circumspection is already announced in *Ideas I*, precisely concerning the history of geometry. There Husserl shows how psychologistic or historicist empiricism remains *"outside"* [Derrida's emphasis] "geometrical thought and intuition," whereas "we should enter vitally into these activities and . . . determine their *immanent sense*" (§25, p. 85 [modified]). Once external history is "reduced," nothing is opposed to the fact that this immanent sense may have its own particular historicity. The opposition between the two histories is an explicit theme in the *Crisis* (see, for example, §7, pp. 17–18, and §15, p. 71), in "Philosophy as Mankind's Self-Reflection" (C, pp. 338–39), and above all in the *Origin*.

11 P. 136. The movement is taken up again in CM, §7, pp. 17–18.

12 These first reductions lead us to "the very threshold of phenomenology" (*Ideas I*, §88. p. 237).

13 Already cited. [see note 7 above]. Also cf. on this *FTL*. Appendix II. §2b, pp. 316–17.

14 Already cited [see note 7 above].

15 Cf. in particular C, §9f. On "meaningless signs" [*signes dépourvus de signification*] and "games-meaning" [*signification de jeu*], cf. *LI*, I, 1, §20, pp. 304–06. On vocables and real signs as "bearers" of signified idealities, cf. *EJ*, §65, p. 268.

16 This theme of passive synthesis is copiously explicated in *EJ* and CM, but once again it is in *FTL* that it is particularly focused (as in the *Origin*) by the problem of the sign and of the sedimentation of ideal objectivities. Cf. in particular Appendix II, pp. 313–29. On the sense of activities and passivities in a phenomenology of reading as outlined in the *Origin*, also see *FTL*, §16, pp. 56–60.

Of course, the themes of passivity and sedimentation, i.e., of the potentiality of sense, derive all their seriousness from the fact that they are imposed on a philosophy of *actually present evidence* whose "principle of all principles" is the *immediate and actual* [en acte] presence of sense itself. If *reactivation* is valuable and urgent, that is because it can bring back to present and active evidence a sense which is thus retrieved out of historical virtuality. If, on the surface, phenomenology allows itself to be summoned outside of itself by history, it thus has found in *reactivation* the medium of its fidelity.

17 To try to illuminate this point, we first would have to approach directly and for itself the difficult and decisive problem in phenomenology of activity and passivity in general on the basis of texts directly devoted to this (*EJ, FTL, CM*). Such a study would perhaps have to conclude that phenomenology has only argued with the arbitrary sense [*exigence du sens*] of this couple of

concepts, or indefinitely struggled with them, namely, with the most "irreducible" heritage (and indeed thereby perhaps the most obscuring heritage) of Western philosophy. In one of the finest analyses where he works with the concepts of passivity, activity, and passivity in activity, Husserl notes that the distinction between these two notions cannot be "inflexible," and that in each case their sense must be "recreated" according to "the concrete situation of the analysis," as "for every description of intentional phenomena" (*EJ*, §23, p. 108).

18 *LI*, I, 1, §26, p. 314: "The class of ambiguous expressions illustrated by this last example are what one usually has in mind when one speaks of 'equivocation'. Ambiguity in such cases does not tend to shake our faith in the ideality and objectivity of significations. We are free, in fact, to limit our expression to *a single* signification. The ideal unity of each of the differing significations will not be affected by their attachment to a common designation" [modified].

The purpose of univocity supposes, then, a decisive rupture with spontaneous language, with the "civil language" of which Leibniz used to speak; after that, "philosophical" or "scholarly [*savant*]" language can freely be given its own particular conventions. Does not the sentence just cited sound like the faithful echo of another sentence of the *Nouveaux Essais sur l'Entendement Humain*, well known to Husserl and where Theophilus says: "it depends upon us to fix their meanings [*significations*], at least in any scholarly language, and to agree to destroy this tower of Babel" (Book II, Ch. ix, §9 [ET: *New Essays Concerning Human Understanding*, tr. Alfred Gideon Langley (Chicago: Open Court, 1916), p. 373]). This optimism is only one of the affinities between Leibniz's and Husserl's philosophies of language. More broadly speaking, Husserl also very early felt himself the heir to the Leibnizian conception of logic in general. Cf. notably *LI*, I, Prol., §60, pp. 218ff.

19 On this, cf. above all "PRS," p. 144: "Profundity [*Tiefsinn*] is a mark of the chaos that genuine science wants to transform into a cosmos, into a simple, completely clear, lucid order. Genuine science, so far as its real doctrine extends, knows no profundity." Husserl then proposes to re-strike (*umprägen*), as in the case of a currency revaluation, "the conjectures of profundity into unequivocal [German: *eindeutige*; French: *univoques*] rational forms" and thus to "constitut[e] anew the rigorous sciences." Likewise, Husserl's criticisms written in the margins of [Heidegger's] *Sein und Zeit* attribute to a *Tiefsinnigkeit* the responsibility for the Heideggerian "displacement" toward what Husserl defines as a facto-anthropological plane. Husserl prefers the value of *interiority* to that of *profundity* or depth, interiority being related to the penetration of internal, intrinsic (*inner*), i.e., essential (*wesentlich*), sense.

20 Exactitude and univocity are overlapping notions for Husserl. Moreover, the exactitude of expression will have as its condition the exactitude of sense. Geometry, the model of the sciences whose objects are exact, will therefore more easily attain univocity than will the other sciences, phenomenology in particular. We will return to this later. About the relations between exactitude and univocity in geometry, also cf. *Ideas I*, §73, pp. 189–90.

21 Husserl has always associated "Hegelianism" with "romanticism" and with "historicism," to which romanticism is led when "belief" in its "metaphysics of history" has been lost. (Cf. especially "PRS," pp. 76–77.) Was not the

expression *Weltanschauung* first Hegelian? (Cf. on this J. Hyppolite, *Genesis and Structure of Hegel's "Phenomenology of Spirit,"* tr. Samuel Cherniak and John Heckman [Evanston: Northwestern University Press, 1974], pp. 469–70.)

22 James Joyce, *Ulysses* (New York: Random, 1961), p. 34 ["History, Stephen said, is a nightmare from which I am trying to awake."]).

23 That is why, as we noted above, Husserl could not inquire as to the *absolute* ideal Objectivity concerning language itself, whose ideality is always that of a "thematic index" and not a theme. This irreducible *mediacy* thus makes illusory all the safety promised by speech or writing *themselves*.

24 Cf. *Ideas I*, especially §83, pp. 220–22.

25 Ibid., p. 221. [In his translation of the *Origin*, Derrida translates *Einsicht* by "évidence rationnelle." In this he follows, as he says, the justification and practice of S. Bachelard (see *A Study of Husserl's Logic*, p. 106). This helps elucidate the phrase "la transparence rationnelle de son évidence" as a "translation" of "Einsichtigkeit." In his *Guide for Translating Husserl*, Dorion Cairns suggests the following: insight, insightfulness, intellectual seenness, apodictic evidentness, evidentness. Note adapted by Tr.]

26 Plato, *The Collected Dialogues*, ed. Hamilton and Cairns (Princeton: Princeton University Press, 1961), p. 765. The translation is that of Paul Shorey.

8 'STRUCTURE, SIGN AND PLAY IN THE DISCOURSE OF THE HUMAN SCIENCES'

WRITING AND DIFFERENCE (DERRIDA 1978) [FIRST PUBLISHED 1967]

Translated by Alan Bass

Themes

Derrida deals with structure in knowledge as exemplified in the structuralist anthropology of Claude Lévi-Strauss. Derrida's view of structuralism, as a movement in the humanities and social sciences, is that it focuses attention on the structural aspects inherent in all knowledge. Structure is both necessary and illusory. The limitations of structure are discussed in relation to the play of the sciences. Structuralism as a movement takes the analysis of the linguistic sign as the model of structure. The irreducible play of the sign discussed by Derrida is not an appeal to irrationalism. It is really a way of expressing what Hilary Putnam calls the 'indeterminacy of reference'; and what Quine calls the 'inscrutability of reference'. Play in Derrida no more refers to an attack on logic or consistency in philosophy, than does Wittgenstein's reference to language games in *Philosophical Investigations* (Wittgenstein 2001).

In Derrida's argument, structure has always been part of ordinary language, episteme (knowledge), science, and philosophy. In that case, structuralism in Lévi-Strauss, and elsewhere, is an event of rupture and a doubling in the history of the concept of structure. 'Event' refers to the singularity of the moment, or any moment, where structure emerges as a theme in structuralism. The event is intrinsically paradoxical because structure refers to abstract relations outside time and history, but structuralism as a movement is a historical movement in time. That is why structuralism is both a rupture with structure as abstraction, and a doubling of structure which becomes an object of structure. Since structuralism is concerned with structural forms rather than objects within structures, structuralism taking itself as an object is a paradoxical event, but so is all analysis of structures in any way of thinking.

The structure must have a centre which both opens up and closes play, and which is different from structure. Without the centre, there is no structure since structure must be organised around something. The centre of the structure cannot have a full presence in any structure as a whole, and it is this that allows for a play in which signs for the centre form a claim of supplementation and substitution, which can never bring the structure itself into full presence. For Derrida this applies to the world itself in the thought of an infinite sphere with a centre that is everywhere. This labyrinthine view originates in the seventeenth century in Blaise Pascal (see 'Pascal and Derrida' (Stocker 2000)) as a reaction to the emergence of an infinite universe in early modern science. The centre is a contradiction which can be experienced as anxiety. The centre has appeared under many names which include: origin, end, *archē* (first principle), *telos* (goal), *eidos* (form), *energeia* (productivity), *ousia* (presence), essence, existence, substance, subject, *alētheia* (truth), transcendentality, consciousness, God, Man. This list contains terms central to the history of philosophy, and is a comment on the underlying structural assumptions of philosophy. Structuralism takes structure to an extreme where there is no explicit centre, but all Derrida's discussions of structuralism and phenomenology argue that they both assume pure forms that can only be explained in terms of end or *telos*. The attempt to reduce knowledge to structure is an archaeological project, which thinks of knowledge as static structural unities underlying empirical difference and heterogeneity. It must also be an eschatological project, that is a project which brings the world to an end. Without content or objects, pure structure must assume the destruction of the world. Derrida said something similar with regard to phenomenology in the previous selection. The most rational thought is also the most irrational thought, the wish for death or negation.

Structuralism both questions the metaphysics of the structure and reinforces it. Lévi-Strauss, and other structuralists, pushed the limits of structure by assuming the elimination of centre in a decentred structure where the centre has become a non-locus. The structuralist approach rests on structural linguistics focused on the system of signs. However, the system of the sign itself must be questioned if we are going to complete the questioning of metaphysics. The implicit and paradoxical centring of the structuralist system of the sign in nature, the conceptual aspect of the sign and the abstract form of structure is overcome in the play of the sign, that is its status as what can be infinitely substituted. Derrida takes empiricism as what threatens these persistent metaphysical-structural reductions. The empirical cannot be absorbed into pure form and is where the sign is constantly substituted, making any totality of the structure impossible. There is no centre which can allow the structure to be absolute, if we acknowledge that there is no point at which the centre can become present in a term which resists all, and any, substitution that could be abstracted from any contextuality and indeterminacy.

Structuralism rests on an opposition between the natural and the cultural in which it is a catastrophe. Derrida in his analyses of Saussure and Lévi-Strauss finds that while they both oppose nature to culture, they bring natural forces into the cultural system and think of 'natural' humanity as cultural. They cannot separate the natural and the cultural, but they cannot explicitly grasp this distinction, leaving a series of contradictions resulting from the rupture between natural and cultural. What underlies this according to Derrida is Jean-Jacques Rousseau's nostalgia for lost origin. When we grasp structuralism in this way, we can see in it one of two strategies of deconstruction. The way of structuralism made explicit in Rousseau and Heidegger is the search for lost origin, or Being, in the awareness that it can never be recovered. The other way is that of Nietzsche's affirmation of play, plurality and difference. Both ways are interpretations of interpretation. Interpretation always requires interpretation. There is never an absolute presence of something preceding interpretation. Knowledge is always interpretation of itself.

Context

Derrida's texts on knowledge are not directly concerned with themes of epistemology in English medium philosophy. Nevertheless issues which appear in that philosophical tradition are addressed by Derrida. Conventionally epistemology in analytic philosophy has been divided between the foundationalist and coherentist camps, with pragmatism sometimes appearing as a third option. Foundationalist epistemology refers to the idea that when we look at justifications for knowledge claims they finish at some point in a foundation which grounds all such claims. The foundational metaphor originates in Descartes, for whom the foundation is a rationalist foundation of pure ideas in consciousness. In general, foundationalism in epistemology is taken to refer to the empiricist claim that justifications for knowledge claims all originate in sensations in the mind originating in external stimulation of the senses, in a position going back to the philosophy of Locke, Berkeley and Hume. Derrida clearly attacks foundationalism even though he attacks rationalist versions in phenomenology and structuralism. Derrida's consistent adherence to empiricism undermines any attempt to think that empiricist philosophy must be foundationalist. Quine had already started down the same road in 'Two Dogmas of Empiricism' (in Quine 1980), summarised in the previous section of the present collection. The opposite of foundationalism is usually thought to be coherentism, in which knowledge claims are justified by other knowledge claims with no final ground. Knowledge obtains where beliefs justify each other. Coherentism is most obviously derived from rationalist philosophy in Descartes, Spinoza and Leibniz, and then from German idealism, particularly Hegel. It was perhaps best known to early analytic philosophers through Anglophone idealists such as F. H. Bradley. Nevertheless coherentist arguments have been taken up by empirically minded analytic philosophers, such as Donald Davidson. Davidson dropped his pure coherentism, and as with foundationalists, it is difficult to find remaining pure examples. The debate has largely been superseded by that between internalism and externalism, summarised above with regard to consciousness. In both debates, Derrida looks like someone trying to mediate between the two extremes. There is 'radical empiricism' in Derrida which refers to external causation of beliefs, but there is always context and there is always the need to transcendentalise in abstract concepts and form them into a system. Unlike other mediating figures such as Davidson and Putnam, Derrida is concerned with the necessary contradiction of the internal and the external, the criterion of groundedness and the criterion of mutual support for beliefs.

Derrida is an empiricist but one whose thought accords with Quine's criticism of the two dogmas and Sellars' criticism of the 'Given'. In *Empiricism and the Philosophy of Mind* (Sellars 1997 [first published 1956]), Sellars argues that there is no pure 'Given' in consciousness since we always see something as something as well as seeing something. It is closely related to his arguments against private language summarised above in Part II. Sellars sets up his arguments with regard to Hegel who is only mentioned briefly but strategically. Sellars resists the most circular forms of idealist philosophy in which ideas of consciousness only refer to other ideas of consciousness with no reference to anything external, but since most Hegelians would resist such a characterisation of Hegel's philosophy there is no necessary conflict. Indeed Sellars stands at the beginning of a Hegelian current in the Department of Philosophy at the University of Pittsburgh, which now comprises two major philosophers: Robert Brandom and John McDowell. McDowell represents another attempt to mediate between coherentism and foundationalism, internalism and externalism, with reference to Kant and Gadamer as well as Hegel, most notably in *Mind and World* (McDowell 1996). In general terms he is interested in the relation between concept and experience as intertwined in a way that is consistent with Derrida, but does not lend itself to detailed comparison. Brandom's Hegelianism is much more embedded in American pragmatism and Heidegger. His major work *Making It Explicit* (Brandom 1994) is concerned with the Heideggerian theme of the implicit becoming explicit, though the discussion is conducted with reference to Kant, Frege and Wittgenstein. Commitments to the reading of Hegel and Heidegger are only made explicit in *The Mighty Dead* (Brandom 2002). Brandom's connection with Sellars is confirmed by the study guide he wrote for the most recent edition of *Empiricism and the Philosophy of Mind*.

The nature of Brandom's discussion of the explicit is to show that discourse includes commitments to representation, inference, intersubjectivity and social values. Social values arise from discourse because discourse requires us to engage in the intersubjective enterprise of agreements on use of words and how to describe the world. Communication is only possible, according to Brandom, if that agreement extends to moral and social values. The interweaving of different kinds of discourse which refer to cognition and value judgements is again consistent with Derrida. The emphasis on consensus is not so consistent with Derrida, for whom contradiction is structurally necessary at every moment in which we consider thought, language and communication.

This raises the question of whether we can count Derrida as a pragmatist. It was the pragmatist William James who coined the phrase 'radical empiricist' which Derrida sometimes used. However, this is probably coincidental since Derrida's knowledge of English language philosophy, or philosophy in any language written in that tradition, was evidently extremely modest. If pragmatism means arriving at consensus through testing beliefs in experience and action, then it is rather un-Derridean. Though that clearly corresponds to a strong drive within pragmatism, there is another aspect. For example for Peirce and for Quine—who was happy to associate himself with some forms of pragmatism—scientific theories can never be completely determined by empirical evidence. There is always a choice between at least two internally consistent theories, which adequately explain the available empirical evidence. Putnam, who is also happy to identify himself with pragmatism, discusses the 'indeterminacy of reference'. Richard Rorty, though never a complete adherent of Derrida as he regards Derrida as too transcendental (Rorty 1977), believes that much of Derrida can be incorporated into his own 'neo-pragmatism', which rejects all foundationalism in philosophy and takes the contextualist aspects of pragmatism to the most radical conclusions, in which philosophy itself cannot survive as an autonomous discipline. Though Derrida always emphasised the role of 'anti-philosophy' in philosophy he would have found that last view of Rorty's to be repugnant. The view of Brandom as also having a pragmatism in some respects close to deconstruction might be justified with regard to Jürgen Habermas's criticisms in 'From Kant to Hegel' (Habermas 2000), which Brandom replied to in 'Facts, Norms and Normative Facts' (Brandom 2000). There Habermas finds Brandom too pragmatic in his generation of value commitments from discursive agreement. The problem with that is that it allows relativity and differences of values in different pragmatic contexts. Placing Derrida against the background of that debate, he would accept with Habermas that values are transcendental and with Brandom that they are contextual. It is the contradiction between these that Derrida emphasises in his own value theory, which will be explored in the following chapters.

In the questions of knowledge and truth, Derrida is sometimes compared with Davidson particularly by Samuel Wheeler. Since Davidson's thought went through some changes, including a move away from coherentism in questions of truth and knowledge, this is not necessarily a straightforward comparison. Wheeler's comparison is based on Davidson's general resistance to a completely explicit definition of truth. This can be justified with reference to an early holism, in which truth only exists in the total set of true propositions and a later 'deflationary' position in which truth serves only as a predicate of propositions, as a word that can be attached to propositions for pragmatic reasons rather than because it names a metaphysical property. The decisive moment of interest comes in Davidson's early essay of 1967 'Truth and Meaning' (in Davidson 2001a), where he suggests not only that truth is holistic but that it cannot be defined explicitly. Like Heidegger and Wittgenstein, he relies on showing over saying when he suggests that truth can only be grasped implicitly via a schema which relates a true statement in quotation marks to the same statement without quotations marks. The statement in quotation marks is true if and only if the second statement holds. This is a structure not a definition. There is nothing like this in Derrida, but it does capture Derrida's preference for the implicit over the explicit, that non-metaphysical philosophy is better written through the movement of words rather than explicit discussion of concepts which tends to reify them as abstract things. Derrida allows concepts to emerge in context, and changes the concepts according to context. Later work by Davidson, particularly the 1986 essay 'A Nice Derangement of Epitaphs' (in Davidson 2005), emphasises that words are epitaphs which belong to context, undermining any prospect of the constant conceptuality of words. Although this is a comment on language, it suggests a way to put Derrida in the context of debates about knowledge, since Davidson's essay suggests the limits of consistency and universal truths in knowledge. Attempts to put Derrida in the context of the 1973 essay 'Radical Interpretation' (in Davidson 2001a) and the 1987 essay 'What Metaphors Mean' (in Davidson 2001a) are likely to overlook strong distinctions. 'Radical Interpretation' aims to remove doubt about beliefs and interpretations in a coherentist type argument according to which, since beliefs are justified as a whole, most beliefs must be correct, particularly since Davidson derives meaning from the definition of truth. 'What Metaphors Mean' resembles Derrida in the weak sense that Derrida is also interested in metaphor. However, for Davidson, metaphor, while widespread, is purely a question of usage and adds nothing to meaning. For Derrida there is no such distinction, so that if metaphor is an essential element of usage it is an essential element of meaning. That view is expounded by Derrida in 'White Mythology' (in Derrida 1982). The most pertinent discussion of the cognitive functions of metaphor comes in the work of George Lakoff and Mark Johnson, in various texts including *Metaphors We Live By* (Lakoff and Johnson 2003 [first published 1980]). Their combination of philosophy, linguistics and cognitive science corresponds with Derrida's emphasis on the irreducibility of metaphor and the existence of consciousness in an embodied and intersubjective manner.

WRITING AND DIFFERENCE: STRUCTURE, SIGN AND PLAY IN THE DISCOURSE OF THE HUMAN SCIENCES

> We need to interpret interpretations more than to interpret things.
> (Montaigne)

Perhaps something has occurred in the history of the concept of structure that could be called an "event," if this loaded word did not entail a meaning which it is precisely the function of structural—or structuralist—thought to reduce or to suspect. Let us speak of an "event," nevertheless, and let us use quotation marks to serve as a precaution. What would this event be then? Its exterior form would be that of a *rupture* and a redoubling.

It would be easy enough to show that the concept of structure and even the word "structure" itself are as old as the *epistēmē*—that is to say, as old as Western science and Western philosophy—and that their roots thrust deep into the soil of ordinary language, into whose deepest recesses the *epistēmē* plunges in order to gather them up and to make them part of itself in a metaphorical displacement. Nevertheless, up to the event which I wish to mark out and define, structure—or rather the structurality of structure—although it has always been at work, has always been neutralized or reduced, and this by a process of giving it a center or of referring it to a point of presence, a fixed origin. The function of this center was not only to orient, balance, and organize the structure—one cannot in fact conceive of an unorganized structure—but above all to make sure that the organizing principle of the structure would limit what we might call the *play* of the structure. By orienting and organizing the coherence of the system, the center of a structure permits the play of its elements inside the total form. And even today the notion of a structure lacking any center represents the unthinkable itself.

Nevertheless, the center also closes off the play which it opens up and makes possible. As center, it is the point at which the substitution of contents, elements, or terms is no longer possible. At the center, the permutation or the transformation of elements (which may of course be structures enclosed within a structure) is forbidden. At least this permutation has always remained *interdicted* (and I am using this word deliberately). Thus it has always been thought that the center, which is by definition unique, constituted that very thing within a structure which while governing the structure, escapes structurality. This is why classical thought concerning structure could say that the center is, paradoxically, *within* the structure and *outside it*. The center is at the center of the totality, and yet, since the center does not belong to the totality (is not part of the totality), the totality *has its center elsewhere*. The center is not the center. The concept of centered structure—although it represents coherence itself, the condition of the *epistēmē* as philosophy or science is contradictorily coherent. And as always, coherence in contradiction expresses the force of a desire.[1] The concept of centered structure is in fact the concept of a play based on a fundamental ground, a play constituted on the basis of a fundamental immobility and a reassuring certitude, which itself is beyond the reach of play. And on the basis of this certitude anxiety can be mastered, for anxiety is invariably the result of a certain mode of being implicated in the game, of being caught by the game, of being as it were at stake in the game from the outset. And again on the basis of what we call the center (and which, because it can be either inside or outside, can also indifferently be called the origin or end, *archē* or *telos*), repetitions, substitutions, transformations, and permutations are always *taken* from a history of meaning [*sens*]—that is, in a word, a history—whose origin may always be reawakened or whose end may always be anticipated in the form of presence. This is why one perhaps could say that the movement of any archaeology, like that of any eschatology, is an accomplice of this reduction of the structurality of structure and always attempts to conceive of structure on the basis of a full presence which is beyond play.

If this is so, the entire history of the concept of structure, before the rupture of which we are speaking, must be thought of as a series of substitutions of center for center, as a linked chain of determinations of the center. Successively, and in a regulated fashion, the center receives different forms or names. The history of metaphysics, like the history of the West, is the history of these metaphors and metonymies. Its matrix—if you will pardon me for demonstrating so little and for being so elliptical in order to come more quickly to my principal theme—is the determination of Being as *presence* in all senses of this word. It could be shown that all the names related to fundamentals, to principles, or to the center have always designated an invariable presence—*eidos, archē, telos, energeia, ousia* (essence, existence, substance, subject) *alētheia*, transcendentality, consciousness, God, man, and so forth.

The event I called a rupture, the disruption I alluded to at the beginning of this paper, presumably would have come about when the structurality of structure had to begin to be thought, that is to say, repeated, and this is why I said that this disruption was repetition in every sense of the word. Henceforth, it became necessary to think both the law which somehow governed the desire for a center in the constitution of structure, and the process of signification which orders the displacements and substitutions for this law of central presence—but a central presence which has never been itself, has always already been exiled from itself into its own substitute. The substitute does not substitute itself for anything which has somehow existed before it. Henceforth, it was necessary to begin thinking that there was no center, that the center could not be thought in the form of a present-being, that the center had no natural site, that it was not a fixed locus but a function, a sort of nonlocus in which an infinite number of sign-substitutions came into play. This was the moment when language invaded the universal problematic, the moment when, in the absence of a center or origin, everything became discourse—provided we can agree on this word—that is to say, a system in which the central signified, the original or transcendental signified, is never absolutely present outside a system of differences. The absence of the transcendental signified extends the domain and the play of signification infinitely.

Where and how does this decentering, this thinking the structurality of structure, occur? It would be somewhat naïve to refer to an event, a doctrine, or an author in order to designate this occurrence. It is no doubt part of the totality of an era, our own, but still it has always already begun to proclaim itself and begun to *work*. Nevertheless, if we wished to choose several "names," as indications only, and to recall those authors in whose discourse this occurrence has kept most closely to its most radical formulation, we doubtless would have to cite the Nietzschean critique of metaphysics, the critique of the concepts of Being and truth, for which were substituted the concepts of play, interpretation, and sign (sign without present truth); the Freudian critique of self-presence, that is, the critique of consciousness, of the subject, of self-identity and of self-proximity or self-possession; and, more radically, the Heideggerean destruction of metaphysics, of onto-theology, of the determination of Being as presence, But all these destructive discourses and all their analogues are trapped in a kind of circle. This circle is unique. It describes the form of the relation between the history of metaphysics and the destruction of the history of metaphysics. There is no sense in doing without the concepts of metaphysics in order to shake metaphysics. We have no language—no syntax and no lexicon—which is foreign to this history; we can pronounce not a single destructive proposition which has not already had to slip into the form, the logic, and the implicit postulations of precisely what it seeks to contest. To take one example from many: the metaphysics of presence is shaken with the help of the concept of *sign*. But, as I suggested a moment ago, as soon as one seeks to demonstrate in this way that there is no transcendental or privileged signified and that the domain or play of signification henceforth has no limit, one must reject even the concept and word "sign" itself—which is precisely what cannot be done. For the signification "sign" has always been understood and determined, in its meaning, as sign-of, a signifier referring to a signified, a signifier different from its signified. If one erases the radical difference between signifier and signified, it is the word "signifier" itself which must be abandoned as a metaphysical concept. When Lévi-Strauss says in the preface to *The Raw and the Cooked* that he has "sought to transcend the opposition between the sensible and the intelligible by operating from the outset at the level of signs,"[2] the necessity, force, and legitimacy of his act cannot make us forget that the concept of the sign cannot in itself surpass this opposition between the sensible and the intelligible. The concept of the sign, in each of its aspects, has been determined by this opposition throughout the totality of its history. It has lived only on this opposition and its system. But we cannot do without the concept of the sign, for we cannot give up this metaphysical complicity without also giving up the critique we are directing against this complicity, or without the risk of erasing difference in the self-identity of a signified reducing its signifier into itself or, amounting to the same thing, simply expelling its signifier outside itself. For there are two heterogenous ways of erasing the difference between the signifier and the signified: one, the classic way, consists in reducing or deriving the signifier, that is to say, ultimately in *submitting* the sign to thought; the other, the one we are using here against the first one, consists in putting into question the system in which the preceding reduction functioned: first and foremost, the opposition between the sensible and the intelligible. For the *paradox* is that the metaphysical reduction of the sign needed the opposition it was reducing. The opposition is systematic with the reduction. And what we are saying here about the sign can be extended to all the concepts and all the sentences of metaphysics, in particular to the discourse on "structure." But there are several ways of being caught in this circle. They are all more or less naïve, more or less empirical, more or less systematic, more or less close to the formulation—that is, to the formalization—of this circle. It is these differences which explain the multiplicity of destructive discourses and the disagreement between those who elaborate them. Nietzsche, Freud, and Heidegger, for example, worked within the inherited concepts of metaphysics. Since these concepts are not elements or atoms, and since they are taken from a syntax and a system, every particular borrowing brings along with it the whole of metaphysics. This is what allows these destroyers to destroy each other reciprocally—for example, Heidegger regarding Nietzsche, with as much lucidity and rigor as bad faith and misconstruction, as the last metaphysician, the last "Platonist." One could do the same for Heidegger himself, for Freud, or for a number of others. And today no exercise is more widespread.

What is the relevance of this formal schema when we turn to what are called the "human sciences"? One of them perhaps occupies a privileged place—ethnology. In fact one can assume that ethnology could have been born as a science only at the moment when a decentering had come about: at the moment when European culture— and, in consequence, the history of metaphysics and of its concepts—had been *dislocated*, driven from its locus, and forced to stop considering itself as the culture of reference. This moment is not first and foremost a moment of philosophical or scientific discourse. It is also a moment which is political, economic, technical, and so forth. One can say with total security that there is nothing fortuitous about the fact that the critique of ethnocentrism—the very condition for ethnology—should be systematically and historically contemporaneous with the destruction of the history of metaphysics. Both belong to one and the same era. Now, ethnology—like any science—comes about within the element of discourse. And it is primarily a European science employing traditional concepts, however much it may struggle against them. Consequently, whether he wants to or not—and this does not depend on a decision on his part—the ethnologist accepts into his discourse the premises of ethnocentrism at the very moment when he denounces them. This necessity is irreducible; it is not a historical contingency. We ought to consider all its implications very carefully. But if no one can escape this necessity, and if no one is therefore responsible for giving in to it, however little he may do so, this does not mean that all the ways of giving in to it are of equal pertinence. The quality and fecundity of a discourse are perhaps measured by the critical rigor with which this relation to the history of metaphysics and to inherited concepts is thought. Here it is a question both of a critical relation to the language of the social sciences and a critical responsibility of the discourse itself. It is a question of explicitly and systematically posing the problem of the status of a discourse which borrows from a heritage the resources necessary for the deconstruction of that heritage itself. A problem of *economy* and *strategy*.

If we consider, as an example, the texts of Claude Lévi-Strauss, it is not only because of the privilege accorded to ethnology among the social sciences, nor even because the thought of Lévi-Strauss weighs heavily on the contemporary, theoretical situation. It is above all because a certain choice has been declared in the work of Lévi-Strauss and because a certain doctrine has been elaborated there, and precisely, in a *more or less explicit manner*, as concerns both this critique of language and this critical language in the social sciences.

In order to follow this movement in the text of Lévi-Strauss, let us choose as one guiding thread among others the opposition between nature and culture. Despite all its rejuvenations and disguises, this opposition is congenital to philosophy. It is even older than Plato. It is at least as old as the Sophists. Since the statement of the opposition *physis/nomos*, *physis/technē*, it has been relayed to us by means of a whole historical chain which opposes "nature" to law, to education, to art, to technics— but also to liberty, to the arbitrary, to history, to society, to the mind, and so on. Now, from the outset of his researches, and from his first book (*The Elementary Structures of Kinship*) on, Lévi-Strauss simultaneously has experienced the necessity of utilizing this opposition and the impossibility of accepting it. In the *Elementary Structures*, he begins from this axiom or definition: that which is *universal* and spontaneous, and not dependent on any particular culture or on any determinate norm, belongs to nature. Inversely, that which depends upon a system of *norms* regulating society and therefore is capable of *varying* from one social structure to another, belongs to culture. These two definitions are of the traditional type. But in the very first pages of the *Elementary Structures* Lévi-Strauss, who has begun by giving credence to these concepts, encounters what he calls a *scandal*, that is to say, something which no longer tolerates the nature/culture opposition he has accepted, something which *simultaneously* seems to require the predicates of nature and of culture. This scandal is the *incest prohibition*. The incest prohibition is universal; in this sense one could call it natural. But it is also a prohibition, a system of norms and interdicts; in this sense one could call it cultural:

> **Let us suppose then that everything universal in man relates to the natural order, and is characterized by spontaneity, and that**

everything subject to a norm is cultural and is both relative and particular. We are then confronted with a fact, or rather, a group of facts, which, in the light of previous definitions, are not far removed from a scandal: we refer to that complex group of beliefs, customs, conditions and institutions described succinctly as the prohibition of incest, which presents, without the slightest ambiguity, and inseparably combines, the two characteristics in which we recognize the conflicting features of two mutually exclusive orders. It constitutes a rule, but a rule which, alone among all the social rules, possesses at the same time a universal character.[3]

Obviously there is no scandal except within a system of concepts which accredits the difference between nature and culture. By commencing his work with the *factum* of the incest prohibition, Lévi-Strauss thus places himself at the point at which this difference, which has always been assumed to be self-evident, finds itself erased or questioned. For from the moment when the incest prohibition can no longer be conceived within the nature/culture opposition, it can no longer be said to be a scandalous fact, a nucleus of opacity within a network of transparent significations. The incest prohibition is no longer a scandal one meets with or comes up against in the domain of traditional concepts; it is something which escapes these concepts and certainly precedes them—probably as the condition of their possibility. It could perhaps be said that the whole of philosophical conceptualization, which is systematic with the nature/culture opposition designed to leave in the domain of the unthinkable the very thing that makes this conceptualization possible: the origin of the prohibition of incest.

This example, too cursorily examined, is only one among many others, but nevertheless it already shows that language bears within itself the necessity of its own critique. Now this critique may be undertaken along two paths, in two "manners." Once the limit of the nature/culture opposition makes itself felt, one might want to question systematically and rigorously the history of these concepts. This is a first action. Such a systematic and historic questioning would be neither a philological nor a philosophical action in the classic sense of these words. To concern oneself with the founding concepts of the entire history of philosophy, to deconstitute them, is not to undertake the work of the philologist or of the classic historian of philosophy. Despite appearances, it is probably the most daring way of making the beginnings of a step outside of philosophy. The step "outside philosophy" is much more difficult to conceive than is generally imagined by those who think they made it long ago with cavalier ease, and who in general are swallowed up in metaphysics in the entire body of discourse which they claim to have disengaged from it.

The other choice (which I believe corresponds more closely to Lévi-Strauss's manner), in order to avoid the possibly sterilizing effects of the first one, consists in conserving all these old concepts within the domain of empirical discovery while here and there denouncing their limits, treating them as tools which can still be used. No longer is any truth value attributed to them; there is a readiness to abandon them, if necessary, should other instruments appear more useful. In the meantime, their relative efficacy is exploited, and they are employed to destroy the old machinery to which they belong and of which they themselves are pieces. This is how the language of the social sciences criticizes *itself*. Lévi-Strauss thinks that in this way he can separate *method* from *truth*, the instruments of the method and the objective significations envisaged by it. One could almost say that this is the primary affirmation of Lévi-Strauss; in any event, the first words of the *Elementary Structures* are: "Above all, it is beginning to emerge that this distinction between nature and society ('nature' and 'culture' seem preferable to us today), while of no acceptable historical significance, does contain a logic, fully justifying its use by modern sociology as a methodological tool."[4]

Lévi-Strauss will always remain faithful to this double intention: to preserve as an instrument something whose truth value he criticizes.

On the one hand, he will continue, in effect, to contest the value of the nature/culture opposition. More than thirteen years after the *Elementary Structures*, *The Savage Mind* faithfully echoes the text I have just quoted: "The opposition between nature and culture to which I attached much importance at one time . . . now seems to be of primarily methodological importance." And this methodological value is not affected by its "ontological" nonvalue (as might be said, if this notion were not suspect here): "However, it would not be enough to reabsorb particular humanities into a general one. This first enterprise opens the way for others which . . . are incumbent on the exact natural sciences: the reintegration of culture in nature and finally of life within the whole of its physico-chemical conditions."[5]

On the other hand, still in *The Savage Mind*, he presents as what he calls *bricolage* what might be called the discourse of this method. The *bricoleur*, says Lévi-Strauss, is someone who uses "the means at hand," that is, the instruments he finds at his disposition around him, those which are already there, which had not been especially conceived with an eye to the operation for which they are to be used and to which one tries by trial and error to adapt them, not hesitating to change them whenever it appears necessary, or to try several of them at once, even if their form and their origin are heterogenous—and so forth. There is therefore a critique of language in the form of *bricolage*, and it has even been said that *bricolage* is critical language itself. I am thinking in particular of the article of G. Genette, "Structuralisme et critique littéraire," published in homage to Lévi-Strauss in a special issue of *L'Arc* (no. 26, 1965), where it is stated that the analysis of *bricolage* could "be applied almost word for word" to criticism, and especially to "literary criticism."

If one calls *bricolage* the necessity of borrowing one's concepts from the text of a heritage which is more or less coherent or ruined, it must be said that every discourse is *bricoleur*. The engineer, whom Lévi-Strauss opposes to the *bricoleur*, should be the one to construct the totality of his language, syntax, and lexicon. In this sense the engineer is a myth. A subject who supposedly would be the absolute origin of his own discourse and supposedly would construct it "out of nothing," "out of whole cloth," would be the creator of the verb, the verb itself. The notion of the engineer who supposedly breaks with all forms of *bricolage* is therefore a theological idea; and since Lévi-Strauss tells us elsewhere that *bricolage* is mythopoetic, the odds are that the engineer is a myth produced by the *bricoleur*. As soon as we cease to believe in such an engineer and in a discourse which breaks with the received historical discourse, and as soon as we admit that every finite discourse is bound by a certain *bricolage* and that the engineer and the scientist are also species of *bricoleurs*, then the very idea of *bricolage* is menaced and the difference in which it took on its meaning breaks down.

This brings us to the second thread which might guide us in what is being contrived here.

Lévi-Strauss describes *bricolage* not only as an intellectual activity but also as a mythopoetical activity. One reads in *The Savage Mind*, "Like *bricolage* on the technical plane, mythical reflection can reach brilliant unforeseen results on the intellectual plane. Conversely, attention has often been drawn to the mythopoetical nature of *bricolage*."[6]

But Lévi-Strauss's remarkable endeavor does not simply consist in proposing notably in his most recent investigations, a structural science of myths and of mythological activity. His endeavor also appears—I would say almost from outset—to have the status which he accords to his own discourse on myths, to what he calls his "mythologicals." It is here that his discourse on the myth reflects on itself and criticizes itself. And this moment, this critical period, is evidently of concern to all the languages which share the field of the human sciences. What does Lévi-Strauss say of his "mythologicals"? It is here that we rediscover the mythopoetical virtue of *bricolage*. In effect, what appears most fascinating in this critical search for a new status of discourse is the stated abandonment of all reference to a *center*, to a *subject*, to a privileged *reference*, to an origin, or to an absolute *archia*. The theme of this decentering could be followed throughout the "Overture" to his last book, *The Raw and the Cooked*. I shall simply remark on a few key points.

1. From the very start, Lévi-Strauss recognizes that the Bororo myth which he employs in the book as the "reference myth" does not merit this name and this treatment. The name is specious and the use of the myth improper. This myth deserves no more than any other its referential privilege: "In fact, the Bororo myth, which I shall refer to from now on as the key myth, is, as I shall try to show, simply a transformation, to a greater or lesser extent, of other myths originating either in the same society or in neighboring or remote societies. I could, therefore, have legitimately taken as my starting point any one representative myth of the group. From this point of view, the key myth is interesting not because it is typical, but rather because of its irregular position within the group."[7]

2. There is no unity or absolute source of the myth. The focus or the source of the myth are always shadows and virtualities which are elusive, unactualizable, and nonexistent in the first place. Everything begins with structure, configuration, or relationship. The discourse on the acentric structure that myth itself is, cannot itself have an absolute subject or an absolute center. It must avoid the violence that consists in centering a language which describes an acentric structure if it is not to shortchange the form and movement of myth. Therefore it is necessary to forego scientific or philosophical discourse, to renounce the *epistēmē* which absolutely requires, which is the absolute requirement that we go back to the source, to the center, to the founding basis, to the principle, and so on. In opposition to *epistemic* discourse, structural discourse on myths— *mythological* discourse—must itself be *mythomorphic*. It must have the form of that of which it speaks. This is what Lévi-Strauss says in *The Raw and the Cooked*, from which I would now like to quote a long and remarkable passage:

> The study of myths raises a methodological problem, in that it cannot be carried out according to the Cartesian principle of breaking down the difficulty into as many parts as may be necessary for finding the solution. There is no real end to methodological analysis, no hidden unity to be grasped once the breaking-down process has been completed. Themes can be split up *ad infinitum*. Just when you think you have disentangled and separated them, you realize that they are knitting together again in response to the operation of unexpected affinities. Consequently the unity of

the myth is never more than tendential and projective and cannot reflect a state or a particular moment of the myth. It is a phenomenon of the imagination, resulting from the attempt at interpretation; and its function is to endow the myth with synthetic form and to prevent its disintegration into a confusion of opposites. The science of myths might therefore be termed "anaclastic," if we take this old term in the broader etymological sense which includes the study of both reflected rays and broken rays. But unlike philosophical reflection, which aims to go back to its own source, the reflections we are dealing with here concern rays whose only source is hypothetical. . . . And in seeking to imitate the spontaneous movement of mythological thought, this essay, which is also both too brief and too long, has had to conform to the requirements of that thought and to respect its rhythm. It follows that this book on myths is itself a kind of myth.[8]

This statement is repeated a little farther on: "As the myths themselves are based in secondary codes (the primary codes being those that provide the substance of language), the present work is put forward as a tentative draft of a tertiary code, which is intended to ensure the reciprocal translatability of several myths. This is why it would not be wrong to consider this book itself as a myth: it is, as it were, the myth of mythology."[9] The absence of a center is here the absence of a subject and the absence of an author: "Thus the myth and the musical work are like conductors of an orchestra, whose audience becomes the silent performers. If it is now asked where the real center of the work is to be found, the answer is that this is impossible to determine. Music and mythology bring man face to face with potential objects of which only the shadows are actualized. . . . Myths are anonymous."[10] The musical model chosen by Lévi-Strauss for the composition of his book is apparently justified by this absence of any real and fixed center of the mythical or mythological discourse.

Thus it is at this point that ethnographic *bricolage* deliberately assumes its mythopoetic function. But by the same token, this function makes the philosophical or epistemological requirement of a center appear as mythological, that is to say, as a historical illusion.

Nevertheless, even if one yields to the necessity of what Lévi-Strauss has done, one cannot ignore its risks. If the mythological is mythomorphic, are all discourses on myths equivalent? Shall we have to abandon any epistemological requirement which permits us to distinguish between several qualities of discourse on the myth? A classic, but inevitable question. It cannot be answered—and I believe that Lévi-Strauss does not answer it—for as long as the problem of the relations between the philosopheme or the theorem, on the one hand, and the mytheme or the mythopoem, on the other, has not been posed explicitly, which is no small problem. For lack of explicitly posing this problem, we condemn ourselves to transforming the alleged transgression of philosophy into an unnoticed fault within the philosophical realm. Empiricism would be the genus of which these faults would always be the species. Transphilosophical concepts would be transformed into philosophical naïvetés. Many examples could be given to demonstrate this risk: the concepts of sign, history, truth, and so forth. What I want to emphasize is simply that the passage beyond philosophy does not consist in turning the page of philosophy (which usually amounts to philosophizing badly), but in continuing to read philosophers *in a certain way*. The risk I am speaking of is always assumed by Lévi-Strauss, and it is the very price of endeavor. I have said that empiricism is the matrix of all faults menacing a discourse which continues, as with Lévi-Strauss in particular, to consider itself scientific. If we wanted to pose the problem of empiricism and *bricolage* in depth, we would probably end up very quickly with a number of absolutely contradictory propositions concerning the status of discourse in structural ethnology. On the one hand, structuralism justifiably claims to be the critique of empiricism. But at the same time there is not a single book or study by Lévi-Strauss which is not proposed as an empirical essay which can always be completed or invalidated by new information. The structural schemata are always proposed as hypotheses resulting from a finite quantity of information and which are subjected to the proof of experience. Numerous texts could be used to demonstrate this double postulation. Let us turn once again to the "Overture" of *The Raw and the Cooked*, where it seems clear that if this postulation is double, it is because it is a question here of a language on language:

> If critics reproach me with not having carried out an exhaustive inventory of South American myths before analyzing them, they are making a grave mistake about the nature and function of these documents. The total body of myth belonging to a given community is comparable to its speech. Unless the population dies out physically or morally, this totality is never complete. You might as well criticize a linguist for compiling the grammar of a language without having complete records of the words pronounced since the language came into being, and without knowing what will be said in it during the future part of its existence. Experience proves that a linguist can work out the grammar of a given language from a remarkably small number of sentences. . . . And even a partial grammar or an outline grammar is a precious

acquisition when we are dealing with unknown languages. Syntax does not become evident only after a (theoretically limitless) series of events has been recorded and examined, because it is itself the body of rules governing their production. What I have tried to give is an outline of the syntax of South American mythology. Should fresh data come to hand, they will be used to check or modify the formulation of certain grammatical laws, so that some are abandoned and replaced by new ones. But in no instance would I feel constrained to accept the arbitrary demand for a total mythological pattern, since, as has been shown, such a requirement has no meaning.[11]

Totalization, therefore, is sometimes defined as *useless*, and sometimes as *impossible*. This is no doubt due to the fact that there are two ways of conceiving the limit of totalization. And I assert once more that these two determinations coexist implicitly in Lévi-Strauss's discourse. Totalization can be judged impossible in the classical style: one then refers to the empirical endeavor of either a subject or a finite richness which it can never master. There is too much, more than one can say. But nontotalization can also be determined in another way: no longer from the standpoint of a concept of finitude as relegation to the empirical, but from the standpoint of the concept of play. If totalization no longer has any meaning, it is not because the infiniteness of a field cannot be covered by a finite glance or a finite discourse, but because the nature of the field—that is, language and a finite language— excludes totalization. This field is in effect that of play, that is to say, a field of infinite finite substitutions only because it is finite, that is to say, because, instead of being an inexhaustible field, as in the classical hypothesis, instead of being too large, there is something missing from it: a center which arrests and grounds the play of substitutions. One could say—rigorously using that word whose scandalous signification is always obliterated in French—that this movement of play, permitted by the lack or absence of a center or origin, is the movement of *supplementarity*. One cannot determine the center and exhaust totalization because the sign which replaces the center, which supplements it, taking the center's place in its absence—this sign is added, occurs as a surplus, as a *supplement*.[12] The movement of signification adds something, which results in the fact that there is always more, but this addition is a floating one because it comes to perform a vicarious function, to supplement a lack on the part of the signified. Although Lévi-Strauss in his use of the word "supplementary" never emphasizes, as I do here, the two directions of meaning which are so strangely compounded within it, it is not by chance that he uses this word twice in his "Introduction to the Work of Marcel Mauss," at one point where he is speaking of the "overabundance of signifier, in relation to the signifieds to which this overabundance can refer":

> In his endeavor to understand the world, man therefore always has at his disposal a surplus of signification (which he shares out amongst things according to the laws of symbolic thought—which is the task of ethnologists and linguists to study). This distribution of a *supplementary* allowance [*ration supplémentaire*]—if it is permissible to put it that way—is absolutely necessary in order that on the whole the available signifier and the signified it aims at may remain in the relationship of complementarity which is the very condition of the use of symbolic thought.[13]

(It could no doubt be demonstrated that this *ration supplémentaire* of signification is the origin of the *ratio* itself.) The word reappears a little further on, after Lévi-Strauss has mentioned "this floating signifier, which is the servitude of all, finite thought":

> In other words—and taking as our guide Mauss's precept that all social phenomena can be assimilated to language—we see in *mana, Wakau, oranda* and other notions of the same type, the conscious expression of a semantic function, whose role it is to permit symbolic thought to operate in spite of the contradiction which is proper to it. In this way are explained the apparently insoluble antinomies attached to this notion. . . . At one and the same time force and action, quality and state, noun and verb; abstract and concrete, omnipresent and localized— *mana* is in effect all these things. But is it not precisely because it is none of these things that *mana* is a simple form, or more exactly, a symbol in the pure state, and therefore capable of becoming charged with any sort of symbolic content whatever? In the system of symbols constituted by all cosmologies, *mana* would simply be a zero symbolic value, that is to say, a sign marking the necessity of a symbolic content *supplementary* [my italics] to that with which the signified is already loaded, but which can take on any value required, provided only that this value still remains part of the available reserve and is not, as phonologists put it, a group-term.

Lévi-Strauss adds the note:

"Linguists have already been led to formulate hypotheses of this type. For example: 'A zero phoneme is opposed to all the other phonemes in French in that it entails no differential characters and no constant phonetic value. On the contrary, the proper function of the zero phoneme is to be opposed to phoneme absence.' (R. Jakobson and J. Lutz, "Notes on the French Phonemic Pattern," *Word* 5, no. 2 [August 1949]: 155). Similarly, if we schematize the conception I am proposing here, it could almost be said that the function of notions like *mana* is to be opposed to the absence of signification, without entailing by itself any particular signification."[14]

The *overabundance* of the signifier, its *supplementary* character, is thus the result of a finitude, that is to say, the result of a lack which must be *supplemented*.

It can now be understood why the concept of play is important in Lévi-Strauss. His references to all sorts of games, notably to roulette, are very frequent, especially in his *Conversations*,[15] in *Race and History*,[16] and in *The Savage Mind*. Further, the reference to play is always caught up in tension.

Tension with history, first of all. This is a classical problem, objections to which are now well worn. I shall simply indicate what seems to me the formality of the problem: by reducing history, Lévi-Strauss has treated as it deserves a concept which has always been in complicity with a teleological and eschatological metaphysics, in other words, paradoxically, in complicity with that philosophy of presence to which it was believed history could be opposed. The thematic of historicity, although it seems to be a somewhat late arrival in philosophy, has always been required by the determination of Being as presence. With or without etymology, and despite the classic antagonism which opposes these significations throughout all of classical thought, it could be shown that the concept of *epistēmē* has always called forth that of *historia*, if history is always the unity of a becoming, as the tradition of truth or the development of science or knowledge oriented toward the appropriation of truth in presence and self-presence, toward knowledge in consciousness-of-self. History has always been conceived as the movement of a resumption of history, as a detour between two presences. But if it is legitimate to suspect this concept of history, there is a risk, if it is reduced without an explicit statement of the problem I am indicating here, of falling back into an ahistoricism of a classical type, that is to say, into a determined moment of the history of metaphysics. Such is the algebraic formality of the problem as I see it. More concretely, in the

work of Lévi-Strauss it must be recognized that the respect for structurality, for the internal originality of the structure, compels a
neutralization of time and history. For example, the appearance of a new
structure, of an original system, always comes about—and this is the very
condition of its structural specificity—by a rupture with its past, its
origin, and its cause. Therefore one can describe what is peculiar to the
structural organization only by not taking into account, in the very
moment of this description, its past conditions: by omitting to posit the
problem of the transition from one structure to another, by putting
history between brackets. In this "structuralist" moment, the concepts of
chance and discontinuity are indispensable. And Lévi-Strauss does in
fact often appeal to them, for example, as concerns that structure of
structures, language, of which he says in the "Introduction to the Work
of Marcel Mauss" that it "could only have been born in one fell swoop":

> Whatever may have been the moment and the circumstances of
> its appearance on the scale of animal life, language could only
> have been born in one fell swoop. Things could not have set about
> acquiring signification progressively. Following a transformation
> the study of which is not the concern of the social sciences, but
> rather of biology and psychology, a transition came about from a
> stage where nothing had a meaning to another where everything
> possessed it.[17]

This standpoint does not prevent Lévi-Strauss from recognizing the
slowness, the process of maturing, the continuous toil of factual transformations, history (for example, *Race and History*). But, in accordance with
a gesture which was Rousseau's and Husserl's, he must "set aside all the
facts" at the moment when he wishes to recapture the specificity of a structure. Like Rousseau, he must always conceive of the origin of a new
structure on the model of catastrophe—an overturning of nature in nature,
a natural interruption of the natural sequence, a setting aside *of* nature.

Besides the tension between play and history, there is also the tension
between play and presence. Play is the disruption of presence. The presence of an element is always a signifying and substitutive reference
inscribed in a system of differences and the movement of a chain. Play is
always play of absence and presence, but if it is to be thought radically,
play must be conceived of before the alternative of presence and
absence. Being must be conceived as presence or absence on the basis of
the possibility of play and not the other way around. If Lévi-Strauss,
better than any other, has brought to light the play of repetition and the
repetition of play, one no less perceives in his work a sort of ethic of

presence, an ethic of nostalgia for origins, an ethic of archaic and natural innocence, of a purity of presence and self-presence in speech—an ethic, nostalgia, and even remorse, which he often presents as the motivation of the ethnologic project when he moves toward the archaic societies which are exemplary societies in his eyes. These texts are well known.[18]

Turned towards the lost or impossible presence of the absent origin, this structuralist thematic of broken immediacy is therefore the saddened, *negative*, nostalgic, guilty, Rousseauistic side of the thinking of play whose other side would be the Nietzschean *affirmation*, that is the joyous affirmation of the play of the world and of the innocence of becoming, the affirmation of a world of signs without fault, without truth, and without origin which is offered to an active, interpretation. *This affirmation then determines the noncenter otherwise than as loss of the center.* And it plays without security. For there is a *sure* play: that which is limited to the *substitution* of *given* and *existing*, *present*, pieces. In absolute chance, affirmation also surrenders itself to *genetic* indetermination, to the *seminal* adventure of the trace.

There are thus two interpretations of interpretation, of structure, of sign, of play. The one seeks to decipher, dreams of deciphering a truth or an origin which escapes play and the order of the sign, and which lives the necessity of interpretation as an exile. The other, which is no longer turned toward the origin, affirms play and tries to pass beyond man and humanism, the name of man being the name of that being who, throughout the history of metaphysics or of ontotheology—in other words, throughout his entire history—has dreamed of full presence, the reassuring foundation, the origin and the end of play. The second interpretation of interpretation, to which Nietzsche pointed the way, does not seek in ethnography, as Lévi-Strauss does, the "inspiration of a new humanism" (again citing the "Introduction to the Work of Marcel Mauss").

There are more than enough indications today to suggest we might perceive that these two interpretations of interpretation—which are absolutely irreconcilable even if we live them simultaneously and reconcile them in an obscure economy—together share the field which we call, in such a problematic fashion, the social sciences.

For my part, although these two interpretations must acknowledge and accentuate their difference and define their irreducibility, I do not believe that today there is any question of *choosing*—in the first place because here we are in a region (let us say, provisionally, a region of historicity) where the category of choice seems particularly trivial; and in the second, because we must first try to conceive of the common ground, and the *différance* of this irreducible difference. Here there is a kind of question, let us still call it historical, whose *conception, formation, gestation,* and *labor* we are only catching a glimpse of today. I employ these words, I admit, with a glance toward the operations of childbearing—but also with a glance toward those who, in a society from which I do not exclude myself, turn their eyes away when faced by the as yet unnamable which is proclaiming itself and which can do so, as is necessary whenever a birth is in the offing, only under the species of the non-species, in the formless, mute, infant, and terrifying form of monstrosity.

Notes

1 TN. The reference, in a restricted sense, is to the Freudian theory of neurotic symptoms and of dream interpretation in which a given symbol is understood contradictorily as both the desire to fulfil the impulse and the desire to suppress the impulse. In a general sense the reference is to Derrida's thesis that logic and coherence themselves can only be understood contradictorily, since they presuppose the suppression of *différance,* "writing" in the sense of the general economy. Cf. "La pharmacie de Platon," in *La dissémination,* pp. 125–26, where Derrida uses the Freudian model of dream interpretation in order to clarify the contradictions embedded in philosophical coherence.

2 *The Raw and the Cooked,* trans. John and Doreen Wightman (New York: Harper and Row, 1969), p. 14. [Translation somewhat modified.]

3 *The Elementary Structures of Kinship,* trans. James Bell, John von Sturmer, and Rodney Needham (Boston: Beacon Press, 1969), p.8.

4 Ibid., p.3.

5 *The Savage Mind* (London: George Weidenfeld and Nicolson, Chicago: The University of Chicago Press, 1966), p. 247.

6 Ibid., p. 17.

7 *The Raw and the Cooked,* p. 2.

8 Ibid., pp. 5–6.

9 Ibid., p. 12.

10 Ibid., pp. 17–18.

11 Ibid., pp. 7–8.

12 TN. This double sense of supplement—to supply something which is missing, or to supply something additional—is at the centre of Derrida's deconstruction of traditional linguistics in *De la grammatologie.* In a chapter entitled "The Violence of the Letter: From Lévi-Strauss to Rousseau" (pp. 149ff.), Derrida expands the analysis of Lévi-Strauss begun in this essay in order further to clarify the ways in which the contradictions of traditional logic "program" the most modern conceptual apparatuses of linguistics and the social sciences.

13 "Introduction à l' oeuvre de Marcel Mauss," in Marcel Mauss, *Sociologie et anthropologie* (Paris: P.U.F., 1950), p. xlix.

14 Ibid., pp. xlix–l.

15 George Charbonnier, *Entretiens avec Claude Lévi-Strauss* (Paris: Plon, 1961).

16 *Race and History* (Paris: Unesco Publications, 1958).

17 "Introduction à l' oeuvre de Marcel Mauss," p. xlvi.

18 TN. The reference is to *Tristes tropiques,* trans. John Russell (London: Huchinson and Co., 1961).

Part V
Ethics

9 ' HOSTIPITALITY'

Translated by Barry Stocker

This paper was presented by Derrida in 1997 in Istanbul. A previous translation undertaken by myself with the assistance of Catherine Pinguet was revised by Forbes Morlock and appeared in *Angelaki* 5 (3) (2000): 3–18. The present text is a revised version of the original translation, incorporating some of Morlock's revisions along with other changes.

Themes

The strange title is due to Derrida's concern with the way in which hostility and hospitality depend on each other. This is part of the general pattern of Derrida's exploration of paradox and contradiction in concepts. Derrida's exploration of the paradoxes of hospitality starts with another paradox. He investigates the etymology of 'host', which refers both to the guest who receives hospitality and the host who gives hospitality. There is a belonging together of opposing terms here, which exist through exclusion of the other term. As they depend on the exclusion of the other term, they also include the other term in themselves. The idea of a guest is the idea of someone who crosses the threshold of the host's home, in a crossing which denies the distinction between host and guest while confirming it. The difference between the host and the guest from the other side of the threshold is negated as the guest crosses the threshold. The guest denies another opposition in that paradoxical crossing, which is the conflict between host and enemy. The guest provides a paradoxical mediation between the host and the hostile enemy of the host. A mediation which does not end the conflict, but rather provides a violent moment of challenge to that opposition as the necessary condition of hospitality.

Derrida places his discussion of the paradoxes, aporia, and etymology, of ethical concepts in the context of the two strategies of deconstruction. The moments of aporia are the Nietzschean moments which affirm difference and plurality; the moments of etymology are the Heideggerian (or Rousseauesque) moments of a nostalgia for what can never come fully into presence.

Derrida also places the discussion of hospitality and cosmopolitanism in the context of Kant's 1795 essay, 'Perpetual Peace' (in Kant 1991). There Kant discusses hospitality and cosmopolitan right. For Kant, perpetual peace relies on cosmopolitanism. Amongst other things, that relies on a doctrine of hospitality according to which guests in foreign countries have a right to hospitality but should not demand more, as colonists do. Derrida engages in a close reading of Kant in order to both confirm the importance of hospitality and to explore its paradoxes. Paradoxes mean that we do not know what hospitality is, though we must take it as a fundamental ethical principle with political implications. In contemporary politics it is part of the right to asylum which Derrida associates with political refugees and with others who have a reason to ask for hospitality, such as AIDS sufferers seeking adequate treatment. Derrida's sympathies are evidently on the side of those seeking refuge and asylum; his discussion of the conceptual issues leaves us with both an unconditional call to hospitality and the paradox in which the host is the host in not being absolutely hospitable. The absolute hospitality would be an impossible and self-destructive state in which the host is not the host anymore, is not the master or proprietor anymore.

The not knowing of what hospitality is, is a situation in which the conceptual problem of understanding hospitality is itself an ethical question about the relation between self as host and other as guest, or potential enemy. The overlapping ethical and conceptual concerns are defined as four different 'acceptions', which itself bring the idea of hospitality under the question of the conceptual. The first acception is that the not knowing of what hospitality is allows the stranger who is what we do not know. The second acception is the otherness or absence of the stranger or guest. Derrida brings in Lévinas's ethics of the primacy of the Other here, for Lévinas I am held hostage to the Other, because I only exist in relation to the Other. There is no consciousness without transcendence of the self by what is not contained within the self, what is other than the self. The third acception is 'thinking' as discussed by Heidegger, in which thinking must contain an openness to the Other since thinking never comes to an end and is always concerned with what I cannot completely grasp. The fourth acception is itself ambiguous in its existence, as it repeats the other three in the not-yet of not-knowing which is always waiting to receive and know the other as guest. For Derrida, this is the necessary condition of our relation with concepts and with other persons. In this sense, he retains an underlying affinity with Husserlian phenomenology, according to which all that we are concerned with is intentions of consciousness. Derrida follows Lévinas's twist according to which the contents of intentionality are always other to me and therefore always contain the other person. If intentionality is infinite in content, as Husserl claims then the content always exceeds myself and faces me with responsibility and indebtedness to the Other in the constitution of myself.

Context

Two other texts by Derrida on hospitality and 'hostipitality' have been published. A dialogue on hospitality from 1996 has been published as *Hospitality* (Derrida 2000) and lecture notes from 1997 have been published as 'Hostipitality' (in Derrida 2002). The central philosophical argument is clearest in the Istanbul 'Hostipitality'; the others concentrate on texts that Derrida discussed in relation to the stranger, the enemy, the host and the guest.

The most obvious point of connection between Derrida's ethics around 'hostipitality' and analytic work is around the interest in Lévinas shown by Hilary Putnam: 'Lévinas and Judaism' (Putnam 2002) and *Ethics without Ontology* (Putnam 2004). Neither are concerned with the detail of Lévinas's ethics: the first text deals with Lévinas's writing from a religious Jewish point of view, the second text deals with Lévinas's ethics in a general way. Unlike Lévinas, Derrida was not a religious Jew but he took great interest in some aspects of Jewish religious texts. Various references appear in different texts, one of the essays more focused on this is the 1964 paper 'Edmond Jabès and the Question of the Book' in *Writing and Difference* (Derrida 1978). Putnam does not discuss Derrida much directly, though in *Ethics without Ontology* he refers to Derrida respectfully before indulging in some mockery of stereotypical Derridean positions, such as no word can be given any meaning, etc. Nevertheless, a framework is offered through which Derrida's ethics might be brought into dialogue with analytic ethics. Putnam's own encounter with Lévinas leans heavily on both Putnam's similar religious commitments and on Putnam's reading of pragmatism. Lévinas sets up his position as ethics against ontology, as the primacy of the Other against the reduction to

Being. Putnam argues that pragmatism dispenses with foundational ontology since it is not concerned with absolute external truths, but what we encounter in experience. There is no absolute ontology and therefore no foundation for absolutes of any kind. Ethics cannot be based on principles external to human experience. Just as knowledge is defined within human experience so is ethics, which must therefore be seen in very situational terms. For Putnam, this establishes a convergence between the knowledge-orientated parts of philosophy concerned with logic and the natural world (following Kant this is sometimes known as 'theoretical philosophy') and the ethically oriented parts of philosophy concerned with human action (following Kant sometimes known as 'practical philosophy'), since both aspects deal with human interests and actions in what Putnam sometimes calls 'realism with a human face' or 'internal realism'. Both knowledge and ethics are contextual and situational, and cannot be subsumed under absolute principles. The scepticism about absolute ontology and external realism (truth claims about anything external to human experience), extends to scepticism about absolute and universal principles. This is a rather different line of argument from Lévinas, but it leads Putnam towards a view of ethics as interpersonal, and as based on intuitive relations with other subjects, a view he relates to Lévinas.

There is an interesting crossing of philosophical frontiers in Putnam's use of Lévinas. As with Derrida's discussion of Austin or many analytic discussions of Derrida, there is a lack of knowledge of the intellectual context and tradition. This can lead to creative results, and the blindness to some implications of the texts concerned may open up other implications. Nevertheless, explaining Derrida's ethics in its own terms, as well as those of Lévinas – both have influenced each other and so can be taken together – does mean establishing some distance from Putnam's form of ethics without ontology. In Derrida, there is a role for absolute demands. These are not presented as external laws. 'Edmond Jabès and the Question of the Book' establishes the idea that law itself cannot be coherently a universal abstraction, because it only exists in the act of its interpretation, which can be considered poetic in potential since interpretation is always interpretation of interpretation. 'Structure, Sign and Play' confirms that interpretation is always interpretation of interpretation with reference to texts and to culture in general. The idea of universal interpretation is undermined as is that of universal ethical law, because ethics becomes an absolute obligation to the particular Other. Within 'Hostipitality' there is an absolute demand to offer hospitality, which exists in paradoxical tension with the identity of the host as proprietor, and the hostility between host and stranger. The suggestion of an absolute demand and of its necessarily contradictory status removes Derrida from the Pragmatist sphere. There might be pragmatic reasons for interpreting the ethical contradictions according to context, but the underlying ethical structure is the non-Pragmatist one of absolutes and contradiction. The absoluteness of the demand to respect the Other brings Derrida into relation with the Kantian conception of universal ethical principles as absolute, but also with the regulative ideal in Kant. The regulative ideal refers to the status of God as the highest good assumed in ethics, and which is necessary to ethics, though the existence of God can never be proven in philosophical ontology. Derrida does not follow either of the major versions of Kantian ethics: ethics grounded in universality of practical principles; the formation of a virtuous self guided by the highest good. The underlying tension between the two kinds of Kantian ethics underlies Derrida's ethics. Derrida's reading of Kierkegaard's *Fear and Trembling* (Kierkegaard 1983 [first published 1843]) in Chapter 3 of *The Gift of Death* (Derrida 1996b [first published 1992]), emphasises the conflict between the universality of ethics and absoluteness of individual obligation. As a reading of Kierkegaard, this is one of Derrida's more schematic readings. Despite an early and persisting interest in Kierkegaard, Derrrida never wrote on Kierkegaard at his highest level of philosophical argument. Nevertheless, that reading provides an important suggestion of the fundamental ethical conflict in Derrida's own thought. It is also one of the texts which established Derrida as a major figure in Philosophy of Religion, though Derrida himself seems to have been an agnostic leaning toward atheism. For Derrida, religion and God name an important space, which is the limit of naming and language, and the limit of all consciousness and experience where it strives towards the impossible presence of the absolute. Although that is a limit experience, it is a constitutive experience necessary for defining consciousness and subjectivity.

Another indication of how to place Derrida ethically comes in one of his most allusive and elusive texts, 'Envois' (always known by its French title) in *The Post Card* (Derrida 1987a [first published 1980]). Amongst other things, Derrida discusses Plato's dialogue *Philebus*, with regard to the status of hedonism. Plato advocated human flourishing in the sense of higher intellectual and moral faculties rather than promoting plea-sures. Derrida emphasises Plato's argument that a consistently hedonistic philosophy of immediate pleasures cannot be sustained intellectually because the goal of the maximisation of pleasure itself requires us to stand outside the moment in memory and in capacities for rational calculation. Derrida clearly accepts the negative argument in Plato, separating himself from the most extreme kind of hedonistic ethics, not that this is a wide-spread position, while emphasising that ethics requires calculations and that it requires subjectivity. That brings us back to the issue of universality, which rests on calculation, versus immediate obligation, which rests on subjectivity; and external law, which is rationalistic, versus virtuous will, which rests on subjectivity.

HOSTIPITALITY

Before even beginning, I will read, I will reread with you as the main epigraph, a long and celebrated passage from Kant.
I will read it to begin with almost without commentary. But in each of its words, it watches the whole of this lecture, over all the questions of hospitality, historic questions, which are at the same time ageless, archaic, modern, current or to come which magnetise the word hospitality; and the historical, ethical, juridical, political, and economical questions of hospitality.

As you have no doubt already guessed, it is found, in *Perpetual Peace*, the famous *Third Definitive Article of a Perpetual Peace* (in Kant 1991a) (*Dritter Definitivartikel zum ewigen Frieden*), the title of which is:

"*Das Weltbürgerrecht soll auf Bedingungen der allgemeinen Hospitalität eingeschränkt sein*": "Cosmopolitan Right shall be limited to Conditions of Universal Hospitality" <Therefore the question of conditionality, of conditional or unconditional hospitality is already posed.>[1]

Two words are underlined by Kant in this heading: cosmopolitan right (*Weltbürgerrecht*: the right of world citizens): we are therefore definitely in the space of right and not morality and politics or of anything else, but of a right determined in its relation to citizenship, the state, the subject of the State, if it were a world State; it is a question therefore of international law; the other underlined word, is *hospitality* (*der allgemeinen* Hospitalität, *universal hospitality*). It is a matter therefore of defining the conditions of cosmopolitan right, of a right, the terms of which would be established by a treaty between States, by a kind of UN charter before the fact, and one of the conditions would be what Kant calls universal hospitality, *die allgemeine Hospitalität*.

I am citing this heading in German to mark clearly that the word for *hospitality* is a Latin word (*Hospitalität*, word of Latin origin, of a troubled and troubling origin, a word which carries its own contradiction incorporated into itself, a Latin word which allows the parasitism on itself of its contrary, hostility, the undesirable guest,[2] which it harbours as the contradiction of itself in its own body, and of which we will speak much, later).

Kant will find for this Latin word, *Hospitalität*, a German equivalent, *Wirtbarkeit* (which he will put in parentheses as the equivalent of *Hospitalität*), from the first sentence of the article which I am going to read.

This equivalent then recalled by Kant is *Wirtbarkeit*. Kant writes: "As in the foregoing articles, we are here concerned not with philanthropy, but with *right*" (*Es ist hier . . . nicht von Philanthropie, sondern vom Recht die Rede*) [in making precise that it is a question here of right and not of philanthropy, Kant of course does not want to show that this right must be misanthropic, or even ananthropic, it is a human right, this right to hospitality—and for us it is already the announcement of a grave question, that of the anthropological dimension of hospitality or the right to hospitality: what is said and can be spoken of hospitality for the non human, the divine, for example, or the animal or vegetal; is hospitality owed, and is it the right word when it is a matter of welcoming—or to be made welcome by—the other or the stranger, as God, as animal or as plant, using these three conventional categories?][3] In underlining that it is a question here of right and not of philanthropy then, Kant does not mean that the right of hospitality is a-human or inhuman, but that in as much as it is a right it does not arise from *the love of men as a sentimental motive*. Universal hospitality concerns an obligation, a right and a duty regulated by law; elsewhere, in the *Elements of Ethics* which concludes his *Doctrine of Virtue* (Kant 1991b), Kant distinguishes philanthropy from what he calls *the friend of man* (and I permit myself to refer those whom this distinction might interest to what I said in *Politics of Friendship*, in the passage consecrated to the "black swan" (Derrida 1997).[4] I am returning therefore to this first sentence and to the German word which accompanies *Hospitalität* in parentheses: "As in the foregoing articles, we are here concerned not with philanthropy, but with *right*. In this context *hospitality* (*Hospitalität*) (*Wirtbarkeit*) means the right of a stranger (*bedeutet das Recht eines Fremdlings*) not to be treated with hostility when he arrives on someone else's territory (*seiner Ankunft auf der Boden eines andern wegen von diesem nicht feindselig behandelt zu werden*)".

You see it already, hospitality is opposed to what is nothing other than the same opposition itself, that is hostility (*Feindseligkeit*). The welcomed guest [*hôte*] is a stranger treated as a friend or as an ally, in opposition to the other stranger treated as enemy (friend/enemy [*ami/ ennemi*], hospitality/ hostility). The pair that we have not finished speaking of, hospitality/hostility, is in place. Before pursuing my simple reading or citation, I would like to underline the German word (*Wirtbarkeit*) that Kant adds in parentheses, as the equivalent of the Latin *Hospialiät*. *Wirt* (*Wirthin* feminine), then, is at the same time the *patron*[5] and the host, the host[6] who receives the *Gast*, the *Gastgeber*, the *patron* of a hotel, of a restaurant. *Wirtlich*, like *Gastlich*, signifies "hospitable", "welcoming". *Wirtshaus*, is the café, the cabaret, the inn, the place which accommodates. And *Wirt* orders the whole lexicon of *Wirtschaft*, that is to say economy, therefore *oikonomia*, the law of the household <there exactly where the *patron* of the house who defines the conditions of hospitality, welcome, he who receives, who is master in his home, in his household, in his state, in his nation, in his city, in his town, who remains the master of his home; there where consequently there can be no unconditional welcome, no unconditional passage through the door>. The *Wirt*, the *Gast* is here just as much as the host, the one who, receives, welcomes, offers hospitality in his hotel, who is, and firstly, and for a reason, is he who is the master of the household, the *patron*, the master *in his home*. At bottom, before even beginning, we could stop our reflection there, in the formalisation of a law of hospitality which violently strikes the concept of hospitality itself with a contradiction, in fixing the limit, in determining it: hospitality is very much by necessity, it is a right, a duty, an obligation, a law, it is the *welcome* of the other stranger as friend but on the condition that the host, the *hôte*, the *Wirt*, the one who receives, lodges or gives *asylum* remains the *patron*, the master of the household, on the condition that he keeps the authority of *himself in his home*, that he guards himself and guards and regards what has regard to it, and thereby affirms the law of hospitality as the law of his household, *oikonomia*, the law of his household, the law of place (household, hotel, hospital, hospice, family, city, nation, language etc.), the law of identity which de-limits the *very* place of proffered hospitality and guards authority over it, guards the truth of authority, remains the place of the guard, that is to say of truth: therefore limiting the gift offered and making of this limitation, that is the *being oneself at home with oneself*, the condition of the gift and of hospitality. It is at the same time the principle, <it could be said, the aporia,> of the constitution and of the implosion of the concept of hospitality with regard to which my hypothesis is that we will not cease in verifying the effects. This implosion or if you prefer this auto-deconstruction being already in place, we could, I was saying this, stop here <the reflection on this aporia>. Hospitality is a contradictory concept and experience in itself, which can only autode-struct <said in other words, producing itself as impossible, only possible on the condition of its impossibility> or protecting itself from itself, auto-immunising in some way, that is to say deconstructing itself—precisely—in practising itself, precisely.

But in order to not finish here before even having begun, I will go on as if we had still said nothing and we will continue for some time longer.

I will therefore continue the reading of Kant's text to the end, always with regard to the main epigraph, but this time without stopping myself. It would be possible to come to a stop before each word but as it is an epigraph, I will not do that, I will go ahead. We will have the occasion a thousand times to go back to it later.

As in the foregoing articles, we are concerned here not with philan-thropy, but with *right*. In this context, *hospitality* means the right of a stranger not to be treated with hostility when he arrives on someone else's territory. He can indeed be turned away, if this can be done without causing his death,[7] but he must not be treated with hostility so long as he behaves in a peaceable manner in the place he happens to be in. The stranger cannot claim the *right of a guest* to be entertained, for this would require a special friendly agreement whereby he might become a member of the native household for a certain time. He may only claim a *right of resort*,[8] for all men are entitled to present themselves in the society of others by virtue of their right to communal possession of the earth's surface. Since the earth is a globe, they cannot disperse over an infinite area, but must tolerate one another's company. And no one orig-inally has any greater right than anyone else to occupy any particular portion of the earth.[9] The community of man is divided by uninhabit-able parts of the earth's surface such as oceans and deserts, but even then, the *ship* or the *camel* (the ship of the desert) makes it possible for them to approach their fellows over these ownerless tracts, and to utilise as a means of social intercourse that *right to the earth's surface* which the human race shares in common. The inhospitable behaviour of coastal dwellers (as on the Barbary coast) in plundering ships on the adjoining seas or enslaving stranded seafarers, or that of inhabitants of the desert (as with the Arab Bedouins), who regard their proximity to nomadic tribes as a justification for plundering them, is contrary to natural right.[10] But this natural right of hospitality, i.e. the right of strangers, does not extend beyond those conditions which make it possible for them to *attempt* to enter into relations with the native inhabitants. In this way, continents distant from each other can enter into peaceful mutual rela-tions which may eventually be regulated by public laws, thus bringing the human race nearer and nearer to a cosmopolitan constitution.

If we compare with this ultimate end the *inhospitable* conduct of the civilised states of our continent, especially the commercial states, the injustice which they display in *visiting* foreign countries and peoples (which in their case is the same as *conquering* them) seems appallingly great. America, the negro countries, the Spice Islands, the Cape, etc. were looked upon at the time of their discovery as ownerless territories; for the native inhabitants were counted as nothing. In East India (Hindustan), foreign troops were brought in under the pretext of merely setting up trading posts. This led to oppression of the natives, incitement of the various Indian states to widespread wars, famine, insurrection, treachery and the whole litany of evils which afflict the human race.

The peoples of the earth have thus entered in varying degrees into a universal community, and it has developed to the point where a violation of rights in *one* part of the world is felt *everywhere*. The idea of a cosmopolitan right is therefore not fantastic and overstrained; it is a necessary complement to the unwritten code of political and international right, transforming it into a universal right of humanity. Only under this condition can we flatter ourselves that we are continually advancing towards a perpetual peace (Kant 1991a: 105–108).[11]

<Perpetual peace for Kant is not simply a utopian concept projected to infinity. On thinking of the concept of peace in its rigour, it is necessary to think of perpetual peace. A peace which would simply be an armistice would not be a peace. Peace implies within, its concept of peace, the promise of eternity. Otherwise there is no peace. Therefore here Kant can only orientate the structure itself of the concept of peace, which implies a promise of indefinite therefore eternal renewal.>

Now we begin or we make it seem that we are opening the door, <this impossible door, sublime or not>. We are on the threshold.

We do not know what hospitality is.

Not yet.

Not yet, but will we ever know? Is that a question of knowledge and a question of time?

In any case, here it is then, the sentence which I addressed to you and which I now place between quotation marks. "We do not know what hospitality is". It is a sentence which I address to you in my language, French, in my home, in order to begin and so as to bid you welcome <here where I am received in your home> where I take the word in my language, which seems to suppose that I am here <in my home>, master in my home, that I receive you here, invite, accept or welcome, allow to come and pass the threshold, in saying "*bienvenue*", "welcome" to you.

I repeat: "We do not know what hospitality is".

You have heard already, I utilised, I used the most used words in the code of hospitality, in which the lexicon is made up of the words "invite", "welcome", receive "at home" while one is "master at home" and of the threshold.

Addressing from now on, like a host [hôte] to a guest [hôte], the first sentence with which I began, "we do not know what hospitality is", this seems to contradict, in a self-contradiction, <an aporia, if you like,> a performative contradiction, all of what I have just recalled, that is that we understand all these words very well, and that they belong to the standard lexicon or the common semantics of hospitality, of all pre-comprehension of what it is and what "hospitality" means, that "welcoming", "accepting", "inviting", "receiving", "supporting" the welcome "at home", there where at home, one is master of the house or the master of the city, or the master of the nation, of the language or the master of the State, places from where one bids the other welcome (but what is a "welcome") and accord him a kind of *right of asylum* in authorising him to cross a threshold which was a threshold, <a door which would be a door>, a determinable threshold because identical with itself and indivisible, a threshold of which the line would be traced (the door of a house, human household of a family or a house of god, a temple or general hospital [*hotel-dieu*], hospice, hospital, or hospitalier order home, the frontier of a city, or of a country, or of a language, etc). We certainly believe that we understand all these normal words of the French language—where I am *as at home*— and in all that is translated by the French language (and translation is also a phenomenon, we were just noting this, or an enigmatic experience of hospitality, if not the condition of all hospitality in general).

And even though, I am supposing, even now that we understand each other so well, the sense or the pre-comprehension of all the vocabulary of hospitality and the said laws of hospitality, I dared to begin by saying to you, in the manner of a "welcome": "We do not know what hospitality is". A performative contradiction, in appearance, which bids welcome in avowing that we do not know what "welcome" means, and that perhaps there is no one welcomed who would be perfectly welcomed <which would not be precisely hypocritical or conditional>; a performative contradiction which is also as absolutely strange and disturbing as an apostrophe of the genre "O my friends, there are no friends" <a sentence attributed to Aristotle>, with the sense and consequences for which it is doubtless not a complete stranger, supposing that we would know what "stranger" means, and again focuses the whole question of hospitality here.

I must therefore give you, as my hosts, an explanation. This little sentence: "We do not know what hospitality is", which implicates us, which has already authoritatively implicated you, in advance, in a we which speaks French, <a sentence that we understand without understanding,> can have several acceptations. At least three and without doubt more than four.

Before beginning to unfold them, note in passing that the word "acceptation", from *accipere* or *acceptio* and which in French means the sense given to a word (and that many often make the tempting mistake of confusing with "acception"[12]), this word "acceptation' also precisely belongs to the discourse of hospitality; it's lodged at the heart of the discourse of hospitality; acceptation, in Latin, is the same as acception, the action of receiving, the welcome given, the manner in which we receive. <Evidently a reflection on hospitality is a reflection on what the word "receiving" means. What does receiving mean?> It is like a post-script to Plato's *Timaeus*, where <Khôra,> the place, is spoken of, it is that which receives (*endekhomai, endekhomenon*), the receptacle (*dekhomenon*—which can also signify "it is acceptable, permitted, possible"); in Latin, *acceptio*, is the action of receiving, reception, welcome ("reception" and "welcome" are also words that you often read at the entrance of hotels and hospitals, of what were also formerly known as hospices, places of public hospitality). *Acceptor* is the one who receives, makes welcome, who reserves, as is also said, a welcome or who approves, who accepts the other, what the other says or does. When I said that I speak here at home, my language, French, that also means that I am more welcoming to Latin, to Latin languages than to others, and you see with what violence I comport myself, at the very moment of welcoming, as master in my home. *Accepto*, the frequentative of *accipio* (that is to say the verb with the most import here, *accipio*) which signifies *taking* (*capere* or comprehending in order to make one come to oneself, to receive, welcome), *accepto*, the frequentative of which signifies "having the habit of receiving". *Accepto*: I have the habit of receiving, of making welcome, and in this measure, from this point of view, it is almost a synonym of *recipio*, which at the same time means take in return, again, and receiving, welcoming, accepting, the re often having the sense of return or repetition, the again of "again", anew, and when the re effaces itself from the sense of welcoming, accepting, as it were for the first time. You see already that besides the idea of necessary repetition and therefore of law, iterability and the law of iterability at the heart of all law of hospitality, there we have, with the semantics of acceptation or acception, the reception, the double postulation of giving and taking (*capere*), of giving and comprehending in itself and at home with itself, <in its language> not a single time but in claiming to be ready to repeat, to renew, to continue from the first time. Yes, yes, you would be welcome. Hospitality gives and takes on more than one occasion in its own home. It gives, it offers, it holds out but what it gives, offers, holds out, is the welcome which understands and makes or allows to come into its home, folding the other stranger into the interior law of the host (*Wirt*, etc.) which has a tendency to begin by dictating the law of its language and its own acceptation of the sense of the words, that is to say its own concepts as well. The acceptation of words is also the concept, the *Begriff*, the manner in which we take hold of or understand, take, apprehend the sense of the word in giving it a sense.

I said then that the phrase which I addressed to you, knowing, "we don't know what hospitality is" can have several acceptations. At least three and without doubt more than four.

1. The first acceptation, it is this which would depend on the stress put on the word "knowing": we do not *know*, we do not *know* what hospitality is. This non-knowing is not necessarily a deficiency, an infirmity, a lack. Its apparent negativity, this grammatical negativity (the non-knowing) would not signify ignorance but would signal or recall only that hospitality is not a concept which lends itself to an objective knowledge. Of course, there is a concept of hospitality, in the sense of this word *hospitality*, and we already have some pre-comprehension of it. We could not in speaking otherwise, suppose that we were speaking, knowing the meaning of speaking. But for one part, what we pre-comprehend in this way, we will verify this, rebels against an identity in itself or a consequent and stabilisable, objectifiable, conceptual determination. For another part, that for which the concept is the concept *is not*, is not a being, is not a thing which, as a being, thing or object, could arise as knowledge. Hospitality, if there is such a thing, is an experience, in the most enigmatic sense of this term, which not only calls to the act and the intention, beyond the thing, object, present being, but is an intentional experience which carries itself, beyond knowing, towards the other as absolute stranger, as unknown, there where I know that I know nothing of him (we return sooner or later to the distinction so difficult and so necessary between these two nevertheless indissociable concepts, the other and the stranger, a distinction nevertheless indispensible if we wish to delimit some specificity for hospitality). <Hospitality is due to the other as stranger. But if the other is determined as stranger, already circles of conditionality are introduced which are the family, nation, State and citizenship. But, perhaps there is an other who is yet more of a stranger than that, for which strangeness does not limit itself to strangeness through rapport with language, family, or citizenship. Therefore naturally, I am trying to determine this dimension of non-knowing which is essential in hospitality.> It is necessary then without doubt to know all that can be known of hospitality, and there is much to

know; it is certainly necessary to bring this knowledge to the highest and richest consciousness possible; but it is also necessary to know that hospitality gives itself, and gives itself in thinking beyond knowing.

2. The second acceptation of this apparently negative phrase: "we do not know what hospitality is" could perhaps seem enveloped by the first. If we do not know what hospitality is, it is what is not, it is not a present being. This intentional act, this address or this invitation,[13] this experience which calls and addresses itself to the other as stranger in order to say "welcome" to him is not in several senses of not-being, I do not speak of nothingness. First of all it is not because it often announces itself (but that will be one of the major problems), as a law, a duty or a right, an obligation, therefore a duty rather than as being or a being and without even referring to Kant's text, through which we opened this seminar, the juridical text which defines the right of the stranger, therefore, reciprocally the duty or the obligation of hospitality on the part of the host who is master in his home, which is *what he is* at home we would also be able to invoke all the texts which can be inscribed under the title "The laws of hospitality"—in particular that of Klossowski in *Roberte This Evening* (Klossowski 1997), a text which we will definitely return to and which does analyse an internal and essential contradiction of hospitality which is presented in some sort preface or protocol, entitled "Difficulties" and where the temporal contradiction of hospitality is such that the experience cannot last; it can only pre-form itself in the imminence of what is "on the point of happening" and can only last an instant, an instant precisely because a contradiction cannot last without dialectising itself (a Kierkegaardian paradox) and that the text says cannot "at the same time take and not take". I will read these "Difficulties" very quickly, underlining the temporal contradiction there and the prefatory or protocol place of these "Difficulties" in relation to the text or charter entitled "The Laws of Hospitality":

When my Uncle Octave took my Aunt Roberte in his arms, one must not suppose that in taking her he was alone. An invited guest [*un invité*] would enter while Roberte, entirely given over to my uncle's presence, was not expecting him, and while she was in fear lest the guest would arrive—for with irresistible resolution Roberte awaited the arrival of some guest—the guest would already be looming up behind her as my uncle made his entry just in time to surprise my aunt's satisfied fright at being surprised by the guest. But in my uncle's mind it would last only an instant, and once again my uncle would be on the point of taking my aunt in his arms. It would last only an instant . . . for, after all, one cannot at the same time take and not take, be there and not be there, enter a room when one is already in it. My Uncle Octave would have been asking too much had he wished to prolong the instant of the opened door, he was already doing exceedingly well in getting the guest to appear in the doorway at the precise instant he did, getting the guest to loom up behind Roberte so that he, Octave, might be able to sense that he himself was the guest as, borrowing from the guest his door-opening gesture, he could behold from the threshold and have the impression it was he, Octave, who was taking my aunt in surprise. Nothing could give a better idea of my uncle's mentality than these hand-written pages he had framed under glass and then hung on the wall of the guest room, just above the bed, a spray of fading wildflowers drooping over the old-fashioned frame.(Klossowski 1997, 11–12)

The laws of hospitality properly speaking will be marked by this contradiction inscribed in the essence of the hostess, since the interest, one of the interests of Klossowski's book is having treated the problem of hospitality in taking the most pointed and dolorous but also the most ecstatic account there of the sexual difference between the couple and in the relation of the couple to a third person (to the *terstis* who is the witness and guest at the same time here), surely, a contradiction inscribed in the essence of the hostess that Klossowski analyses, as often, in the theologico-scholastic language of essence and existence, and which must lead, according to a necessity that we will often put to the proof, into the reversal according to which the master of the abode, the master at home, the host can only accomplish his mission of host, and therefore hospitality, in becoming invited by the other into his home, in being welcomed by him whom he welcomes, in receiving the hospitality which he gives. I will content myself with reading, expecting to return here later, two passages from the *Laws of Hospitality*, one which describes the contradiction of the essence of the hostess, the other, in conclusion, which tells of the final reversal of the roles of host and guest, of the inviting host [hôte] (the master at home) and of the invited guest [hôte], of the inviting and the invited, the becoming-invited, if you like, of the inviting. The inviter became like the hostage of the invited, of his host, the hostage of him who receives and who keeps him at home. It is necessary for us, it would be necessary for us to undertake a long work on the hostage, the logic, economy and politics of the hostage. *Littré* contests that the word *hostage* [otage] in its current usage, comes from "*ostage*" resulting from *hoste*, *oste* and which could signify, in certain thirteenth-century texts, what we now call a hostage; for *Littré* "hostage" would come from the contraction *hostaticum* for *obsidaticum*, from *obsudatus*; which means "guarantee", from *obses*, *obsiditis*, hostage, war hostage (incontestable), from *obsidere*, to occupy, possess, indeed to besiege, to obsess; *Le Robert* does not make so much of a fuss in making *otage* derive from *hostage*, which means lodgings, residence, place where guests are lodged, hostages being first of all, precisely as guarantees, security, surety for the enemy, lodged with the sovereign. I have not made more serious etymological investigations but it is incontestable that *obses* means war hostage in Latin; the two etymologies ally themselves with each other easily: in both cases, the hostage is security for an occupation: the hostage is a guarantee for the other, held in a place and taking the place.

We must also pursue this terrifying and impassable strategy of the hostage in the direction of a modernity and a specific techno-politics of hostage taking (which is not now what it was only a few decades ago), in the direction (the inverse, if we can say so) of what Lévinas calls the hostage, when he says that the exercise of ethical responsibility begins there where I am and must be the hostage of the other, delivered passively to the other before being myself[14] (the theme of obsession, obsidionality, of persecution playing among other things, an essential and indissociable role from that of the hostage, in the discourse of Lévinas on responsibility before the other, which supposes that I should be, in a non-negative sense of this term, originally, as much as I am; myself, as much as I say "here I am", the subjugated substitutable subject, the hostage of the other). "It is through the condition of hostage", Lévinas says, in "La substitution", "that there can be pity, compassion, pardon and proximity in the world" or again, and here the word ipseity takes us to a higher point: *"Ipseity in its passivity without the arche of identity, is the hostage. The word 'I' would answer for all and everything"*.[15]

> The master of the house, having no greater nor more pressing concern than to shed the warmth of his joy at evening upon whomever comes to dine at his table and to rest under his roof from a day's wearying travel, waits anxiously on the threshold for the stranger he will see appear like a liberator upon the horizon. And catching a first glimpse of him in the distance, though he be still far off, the master will call out to him, "Come quickly, my happiness is at stake." (Klossowski 1997: 12)

<Therefore he waits for anyone at all, any newcomer and welcomes the newcomer in pressing him to enter as a liberator. Each word of this passage could be underlined. If there is a horizon, this is not what phenomenologists call the horizon of expectation since it is anybody at all. He waits without waiting. He waits without knowing for whom he waits. He waits for the Messiah. He waits for anyone who will be able to

come. And he will have him at his table. And he presses for him to come, he who has no means of making him come more quickly. He waits for him impatiently as a liberator. This is certainly a kind of Messiah.>

> Now it seems that the essence of the hostess, such as the host visualizes it, would in this sense be undetermined and contradictory. For either the essence of the hostess is constituted by her fidelity to the host, and in this case she eludes him the more he wishes to know her in the opposite state of betrayal, for she would be unable to betray him in order to be faithful to him; or else the essence of the hostess is really constituted by infidelity and then the host would cease to have any part in the essence of the hostess who would be susceptible of belonging, accidentally, as mistress of the house, to some one or other of the guests [*invités*]. The notion of mistress of the house reposes upon an existential basis: she is a hostess only upon an essential basis: this essence is therefore subjected to restraint by her actual existence as mistress of the house. And here the sole function of betrayal, we see, is to lift this restraint. If the essence of the hostess lies in fidelity to the host, this authorizes the host to cause the hostess, essential in the existent mistress of the house, to manifest herself before the eyes of the guest; for the host in playing host must accept the risks of the game and these include the consequences of his wife's strict application of the laws of hospitality and of the fact that she dare not be unmindful of her essence, composed of fidelity to the host, for fear that in the arms of the inactual guest come here to actualize her *qua* hostess, the mistress of the household exist only traitorously. (Klossowski 1997: 13–14)

If we do not know what hospitality is, it is therefore because this thing which is not something is not the object of knowledge nor is it in the middle of being-present but it is at least the law of what should be or of obligation, of the law of hospitality, the imperative of which seems to be moreover contradictory or paradoxical.

3. But there is still a third acceptation, or a third intonation, a third accentuation of the same phrase. This third accentuation seems also to be in a rapport with time and the achrony or essential anachrony,[16] indeed with the paradoxical instant of which we were speaking, but in truth it is a matter of another experience, of another dimension of time and space. "We do not know what hospitality is" would imply "we do not

know yet what hospitality is", in a sense of "not yet" which remains to be thought: <this is not only the "not yet" of the threshold. The threshold is the "not yet". The threshold is what has not yet been crossed>, not "not yet" because we will know better tomorrow in the future. In the present future but "not yet" for two other types of reason:

A. For one part the system of right, national or international right, the political <or State> system which determines the obligations and limits of hospitality, a system of European right of which the Kant text read at the beginning, gives us at least an idea, a regulative Idea, and a very high idea, the system of right and the concept of politics, indeed of the cosmopolitics which he inscribes and prescribes has a history, were it the history of the concept of history, of teleology and the regulative idea which it puts to work. This history and this history of history calls up questions and delimitations (of which we will be speaking, of course) that authorise the thinking in which the determination and experience of hospitality guards a future beyond this history and this thought of history—and that therefore we do not yet know what hospitality is beyond this European, universally European right.

B. And above all, the other part, the "not yet", can define the dimension itself of what remains to comes, always in the future, what comes from hospitality, what is called and called by hospitality. What we call hospitality keeps an essential rapport with the opening if what is called to come. When we say that "we do not yet know what hospitality is", we also imply that we do not yet know who and what is going to come, or furthermore what is called hospitality and what is called in hospitality, knowing that in hospitality, first of all calls itself, even if this call does not take shape in the human language. Calling the other, calling the one the other, inviting, inviting itself, making oneself and allowing to come, well coming, greeting, greeting each other as a sign of welcome, these are just as much experiences which come from the future, which come from seeing come or from allowing to come without seeing coming, no less than the "not [pas]", therefore the "not yet", the past "not yet" of the step [pas]which passes the threshold. What is called hospitality and that we do not yet know, is what is called. Although what "is called [s'appeller]" would be an untranslatable French grammatical form (and the question of translation is always the question of hospitality), although "is called" is an untranslatable privilege in French idiom, which could be thought and not thought (for one part I call myself in this way, he or she calls himself or herself by this name: for the part one calls oneself the other [l'un l'autre, l'une l'autre]), although this is all very French, I would nevertheless refer myself to a celebrated text of Heidegger, *Was heisst Denken?*

Heidegger speaks there of at least two things which matter to us here in a high degree and which I am therefore selecting too quickly.

For one part, in the opening pages that I am letting you read, he insists at length on this: "Most thought provoking is that we are still not thinking" (Heidegger 1968: 4), always 'not yet', the most disturbing, serious, grave, strange and suspicious, "*das Bedenklichste*, is that we are not yet thinking: *Das Bedenklichste ist, dass wir noch nicht denken; immer noch nicht . . .* , not even yet . . ." (Heidegger 1968: 4) and further on, after having noted that "*Das Bedenklichste in unserer bedenkliche Zeit ist, dass wir noch nicht denken* (most thought provoking [*le plus bizarre et inquiétant*] in our thought-provoking time is that we are still not thinking), he determines the noun "*das Bedenkliche*" as "*was uns zu denken gibt*" (what gives us to think) (Heidegger 1968: 6), that legitimates without doubt Granel's standard translation that rather artificially chooses to translate *das Bedenkliche* by "what gives to thinking"; *das Bedenklichste*, what gives the most to thinking.

But what I wanted above to recall from this book, still too quickly, alas, is the play there with the "is called", precisely, the "*heissen*", which means "meaning" without doubt, called, calling (*Was heisst Denken?*: what is called thinking? What does thinking mean? For *das heisst* means "it means", "that is to say"; but *heissen* also means or first calls, invites, names: *jenen willkommen heisst*, bids welcome to someone, addresses a word of welcome to someone). And when he analyses the four senses of the expression "*was heisst Denken?*" (I am taking you to the beginning of Part Two, 1952 Summer Semester, page 79 of the original), he notes in the fourth place that it also means: "what is it that calls us, as it were, commands us to think? What is it that calls us into thinking? *Was ist es, das uns heisst, uns gleichsam befiehlt, zu denken? Was ist es, das uns in das denken ruft?*" (Heidegger 1968: 114). What calls us to thought, towards the thinking of thought, in giving the order for it, the call also being the call to reply, it is me present, here I am?

It is no simple play of words here, Heidegger underlines this, and I invite you to read all these pages (I have also attempted to do it elsewhere), in particular what relates this call or this invitation of *Heissen* to the promise (*Verheissung*) here, to the alliance and the *yes* of acquiescence before the question (*Zusage, ein Zugesagtes*), to what is promised (*ein Versprochenes*). <Heidegger dedicated himself greatly later on, late enough finally in his itinerary, to this value of *Zusage*, which means acquiescence, the *yes* of some kind which would come before the question. For a long time Heidegger presented the act of questioning as the essential act of philosophy, of thought, that is to say the piety of thinking (*Frömmlichkeit des Denkens*). But before the question, if it is

possible to ask one which is neither chronologically or logically before, for there to be a question it is first of all necessary that there would be acquiescence, a "yes". In order to interrogate it, it is first of all necessary to say "yes" in a certain manner. This is what he called *Zusage* which is more originary than the question. And here, it is a question in this passage of *Zusage, ein Zusagtes*, of what is promised, of a "yes" to a promise.>

But as I come back from Freiburg-im-Breisgau where I crossed as a visitor the threshold of Heidegger's hut in the mountain, for the first time as a visitor, I have chosen to cite another passage from *Was heisst Denken?* which at the same time names Freiburg-im-Breisgau, as the village is known, Freiburg where this course was given, makes allusion to a certain hut in the mountain and says something essential regarding the call and hospitality.

Here then is what Heidegger says at the end of the Lecture, in the remainder of the *Summary and Transition*, from the first to the second lecture (I am reading directly indicating German words here and there):

> The ambiguity of the question: "What is called thinking?" lies in the ambiguity of the questioning verb "to call."
>
> The frequent idiom "what we call [*das heisst*. . .]" signifies: what we have just said is meant in substance in this or that way, is to be understood this way or that. Instead of "what we call, [*das heisst*]" we also use the idiom "that is to say [*das will sagen*]."
>
> On a day of changeable weather, someone might leave a mountain lodge, alone, to climb a peak. He soon loses his way in the fog that has suddenly descended. He has no notion of what we call [*was es heisst*] mountaineering. He does not know any of the things it calls for, all the things that must be taken into account and mastered.
>
> A voice calls us to have hope [*heisst uns hoffen*]. It beckons us to hope, invites us, commends us, directs us to hope.
>
> This town is called (*Heissen*) Freiburg. It is so named because that is what it has been called. This means: the town has been called to assume this name. Henceforth it is at the call of this name to which it has been commended. To call is not originally to name, but the other way around: naming is a kind of calling, in the original sense of demanding and commending. It is not that the call has its being in the name; every other name is a kind of call. Every call implies an approach, and thus, of course, the possibility of giving a name. We might call [*Heissen*] a guest welcome [*Geheiss*]. This does not mean that we attach to him the name

"Welcome [*Geheiss*]," but that we call him to come in and complete his arrival as a welcome friend. In that way, the welcome [*Geheiss*]—call of the invitation to come in is nonetheless also an act of naming, a calling which makes the newcomer what we call a guest whom we are glad to see.

But calling is something else than merely making a sound. Something else, again essentially different from mere sound and noise, is the cry (Heidegger 1968: 123–124).

After which Heidegger insists on the classical distinction, necessary in his view, a bit more problematic in my view, between noise, the cry and the call (*Schall und Schrei und Ruf*), but we will leave it here for the moment.

4. Finally the fourth possible acceptation of my initial address ("We do not know what hospitality is") would place us at the same time in a critical crossroads of semantic filiations (or if you prefer etymologico-institutional) and in an aporetic crossroads, that is to say in a crossroads or a sort of double postulation, contradictory double movement, double constraint or *double bind* (I prefer *double bind* because this English expression retains the link to the link and therefore to obligation, ligament and alliance). What the experience of hospitality meets in aporia, there where we think above all that the host offers to the guest passage across the threshold or the frontier in order to receive him in his home, there it is what can appear paradoxical. Is not aporia, as its name indicates, the non-road, the barred way, the non-passage? Well, my hypothesis or thesis would be above all that this necessary aporia is not negative; and that without the repeated endurance of this paralysis in the contradiction, the responsibility of a hospitality, a complete hospitality, there where we still do not know or ever know what it is, would not have any chance of coming to pass, of coming, of making or allowing to welcome.

For the moment in the name of the critical crossroads of semantics or etymology and institutions, I am passing very quickly and without transition from the welcome [*bienvenue*] to Benveniste. Welcome to the welcome which is Benveniste here.

As always, in what is a *Vocabulary of Indo-European Institutions*, Benveniste starts with an institution, that is to say what is called a "well established social fact"; and it starts with this "well established social fact", as he says, that he is going to study a lexicon, what he calls a "group of words" which he relates "to hospitality". The name of the social fact, is therefore *hospitality* here—title of Chapter 7 of Volume 1 (*Economy, Kinship, Society*). The "base term", is therefore the Latin *hospes*, in regard to which Benveniste recalls that it divides into two, two distinct elements which, he says, "finish by reuniting": hosti-pet-s. *Pet*-alternates with *pot*-which signifies "master", so clearly that *hospes* would signify "master of the host", Benveniste notes. As he finds this "designation rather singular" (these are his words) with good reason, he proposes to study these two terms separately, *potis* and *hotis* and to analyse their "etymological connections". *Hostis* is going to comport this strange passage between enemy and host, about which we will often speak. But let us begin with *potis* which assembles the semantics of power, mastery or despotic sovereignty.

Before returning in my account to this notion of mastery in regard to which we have already said much <and which conditions hospitality>, we are following Benveniste for a moment when he explains "*potis*", in the proper sense, "as proper", as he says. He goes back to Sanskrit where two significations, "master" and "spouse" (this is why I began with *Roberte ce soir* where the master is truly the master of the abode, therefore the master of the woman, the wife, the spouse) take the object in the same root of two different inflections. There is a phenomenon proper to the evolution of Sanskrit here: one inflection signifies "master" the other "spouse". When Klossowski describes the laws of hospitality in speaking of a master of the abode, a master of places like the family and as master of the spouse, spouse of the spouse who becomes as the stake and essence of hospitality, it is definitely within the domestic logic or *oikonomique* (law of the household, the domestic lineage, the family) which seems to order this Indo-European history of hospitality. Benveniste passes, from Sanskrit, to the Greek *posis*, a poetic term for spouse, husband (although Bienvensite did not note it, this also means, fiancé, lover, the secret spouse in Euripides; and this will yield *potens*, *potentis*, the master, the sovereign, the potentate in Latin). *Posis* is "distanced" from *despotes* Beveniste specifies, which only signifies power or mastery, according to Benveniste without the domestic reference to the "master of the house" (a remark which surprises me greatly, I must say, although my competence is very limited, for I definitely see references from Aeschylus elsewhere which note that *despotes* signifies master of the house, and from Plato's *Laws* or *Statesman* where *despotes* signifies master of the house, synonym of *oikonomos* (*economy* is that which makes the law in the *oikos*, the house or the family, the family master being also the master of the slaves. We are there in the passage between the family and the State). Benveniste recalls next that the Greek *despotes* and its Sanskrit equivalent *dam patih* enter into the composition of ancient expressions which relate to the social unities for which the extension can vary, the master of the house, *dam patih*, the master of the clan, *vis patih*, the master of the descent or lineage, *jas patih*. All the variables can be followed here that he cites in Iranian, Lithuanian, Hittite, etc. He does not cite, but could have, the word *hospodar*, prince, lord, which has passed into French and is used even by Voltaire, just like *l'hospodarat* (charge or dignity of the *hospodar*), a word of Slavic origin (*hospodin* in Bohemian, *gospodar* in Russian, *gospoda* in Polish, from where we have *gospodarz*, hotelier, master of the house, host, inn keeper, etc.).

We will leave Benveniste and his semantico-institutional filiations for a moment in order to underline a paradoxical trait in a very general and structural manner, that is that the host, he who offers hospitality must be the master in his home, he (masculine first of all) must be assured of his sovereignty over the space and goods which he offers or which he opens to the other as stranger. This seems to be at the same time the law of laws of hospitality and what appears to us as common sense in our culture. It does not seem to me that I can be able to open up or offer hospitality, generous as it would be, and even in order to be generous, without reaffirming: this is mine, I am in my home, would be the welcome to my home, without implying, therefore, "make yourself at home" but on the condition of observing the rules of hospitality, that is to say in respecting the being at home of my home, the being in-itself of what I am. There is something there like an axiom of auto-limitation or auto-contradiction in the law of hospitality. As reaffirmation of mastery and the being in itself in its home, hospitality limits itself from the threshold on the threshold of itself, it commands the threshold—and in this limit it even forbids what it seems to permit to pass from passing the threshold in some way. It becomes the threshold. This is why we do not know what it is, and we are not able to know. When we know of it, we do not know any more of it, what it properly is, what it's threshold of identity is.

<In order to regain the figure of the door, for there to be hospitality, there must be a door, but if there is a door there is no longer hospitality. There is no hospitable house. There is no house without doors and windows. But where there is a door and windows, that means that someone has a key for them and must consequently control the conditions of hospitality. There must be a threshold. But if there is a threshold, there is no more hospitality. This is the difference, the gap, between the hospitality if invitation and the hospitality of visitation. In visitation there is no door. Anyone who is anyone arrives at any moment and passes without needing a key for the door. The customs are not checked for the visitation. There is a customs office and a police control for the invitation. Therefore hospitality becomes the threshold or the door.>

In saying that, that is that hospitality always does in a certain manner the contrary of what it pretends to do and immobilises itself on the threshold of itself, on the threshold which it observes and constitutes, of *itself* in sum, of its phenomenon and essence at the same time, I do not claim to say that hospitality is this *double bind*[17] or this aporetic contradiction and that therefore here is where it is, that it is not there. No, I am saying that this apparent aporetic paralysis on the threshold "is" (I put "is" between inverted commas or I cross it out, if you prefer) what must be crossed, <it is the impossibility which it is necessary to cross there where it is impossible to become possible. It is necessary to do the impossible. If there is hospitality, it is necessary to do the impossible,> this "is" is in order that beyond hospitality, hospitality happens. Hospitality can only take place beyond hospitality, in deciding to let it come, crossing the hospitality which paralyses itself on the threshold that it is. It is in this sense perhaps that "we do not know (not yet, but always not yet)" what hospitality is and that it waits for its chance, that it tends towards its chance beyond what it is knowing the paralysis on the threshold of itself. In this sense it is always to come, but a to come which does not appear and never appears as such, in the present <and a future which does not even have a horizon, a future, a coming without horizon>. Thinking hospitality starting with the future, this future which does not appear, or which only appears there where it is not awaited as present or presentable, this is the thinking starting with death no less than birth. This is generally the place of birth which will always have sustained the definition of stranger in the tradition (stranger as non-autochthon, non-indigenous, we will speak much of this) and the place of death. <The stranger, first of all, is he who is born elsewhere. And the stranger is defined starting from birth rather than from death.> The "dying elsewhere" or the "dying at home". And we will perhaps read together a passage from Montaigne on this subject, on dying during a voyage, in a text where after having enumerated what he calls the "forms of dying", and notably away from home, he poses the question of what he calls with a sublime word, but perhaps only sublime, the comrades-of-death (*commourans*), those who die together, at the same time, as if this was possible, if not in the same place. With cause he does not speak of Romeo and Juliet, with cause, who illustrate in this regard an irreducible counter-time but he wonders, what I cite "Could it be made more voluptuous [death, therefore], than the comrades-of-death Anthony and Cleopatra?"[18]

While it would be necessary to pursue a bit more this analysis of the *critical* crossroads of semantic filiations (or etymologico-institutional if you prefer) and *aporetic* crossroads, that is to say of a crossroads or a sort of double bifurcation, double postulation, double contradictory movement, double constraint or double bind at the same time tetanising and cutting into hospitality, stretching out on-itself in stretching towards the other, depriving it of and gratifying it in its chance; we will see how power (despotic sovereignty and virile mastery of the master of the abode) is nothing other than *ipseity* itself, the same [*même*] as itself, in order to say nothing of the subject which is a stabilising and despotic escalation of ipseity, the being in itself or the *Selbst*. The question of hospitality is also the question of ipseity (Benveniste will also assist us, in his manner, in confirming this from language, the *ut pote* and what he calls the "mysterious "-*pse*" of ipse", we should stop at such a phrase in Benveniste and at its context, a phrase which is at the same time luminous and philosophically a bit ingenuous in the form of the question and in the astonishment that it manifests. So Benveniste writes: "While it is difficult to see how a word meaning 'the master,' could become so weakened in force as to signify 'himself,' it is easy to understand how an adjective denoting the identity of a person, signifying 'himself,' could acquire the proper meaning of 'master'" (Benveniste 1932: 72). [Benveniste greatly likes the "proper sense" and makes uses of this expression tranquilly on each page, I have already and often remarked, as if the request for the proper sense was not exactly the *same* as the request for the proper, of what is this *same* which it is, of the itself, of the essence itself, the word "same", *ipseity* will never be separate from the propriety and the identity of the self of what or who it must be]; then it would be attempting a difficult distinction, subtle but necessary between the *other* and the *stranger*; and it would be necessary to venture into what is at the same time the implication and consequence of this double bind, of this impossibility as condition of possibility, knowing the troubling analogy, in the common origin, between *hostis* as host or *hostis* as enemy, between hospitality and hostility.

Notes

1 Angle brackets indicate comments made by Derrida during the symposium and added to the text by the editors [tr.].

2 "Guest" translates "hôte" which can be translated as either "host" or "guest". "Guest" is more appropriate here. The ambivalence is of course important for Derrida [tr.].

3 Interpellations in square brackets are Derrida's, except where there are French words in brackets. These are added by the translator where it seems necessary to cite the French text [tr.].

4 *Politics of Friendship* (Derrida 1997b). The black swan appears in Derrida 1997b: 257, in the middle of a discussion of Kant on friendship. Kant's discussion can be found in the section of *The Metaphysics of Morals* discussed immediately above [tr.].

5 The French word "patron" used by Derrida does not have the same range as the English, suggesting boss or owner, not client as well. The ambiguity of the English, however, suits Derrida's point very nicely. Patron is in italics in this

translation to emphasise the French sense, which is well known to non-French speakers, while retaining the ambiguity of the English aspect [tr.].

6 English word emphasised by Derrida [tr.].

7 <Already you are seeing a large number of conditions for hospitality appear. It is possible to send someone away who arrives on the condition that returning him/her does not lead to his/her death. We now all have (in France in particular, I only permit myself to speak of France) much experience of the expulsion of foreigners where we know that this expulsion will lead to their death either for political reasons in their countries of origin or for pathological reasons. And there is the grave question of AIDS here. For example, we know that when foreigners are sent back from France, in their country of return they will be in conditions where the treatment of AIDS will not be as successful as in France. We are doing what Kant said that we must not do. That is to say we are returning someone to somewhere where the return implies their death. However, if the foreigner conducts himself well among us, we cannot send him away. But that also means that there is conditionality. Well what are the limits? What is the content of those conditions?>

8 <The foreigner can pass through but cannot stay. He is not given the rights of residence. In order for there to be a right of residence it is necessary that there is an accord between States. All of this is placed under – and this is what cosmopolitanism means – an inter-state conditionality. Therefore there is no hospitality for peoples who are not citizens. Behind this reflection there are enormous problems on which Hannah Arendt reflected with regard to what has happened in Europe. With the decline of the Nation-State we have the affair of millions of people who were not even exiles or émigrés anymore, but who were displaced persons, that is to say people who did not even have the guarantee of citizenship, the political guarantee of citizenship, and with the consequences that entails. And it is the problem of today: the one of hospitality which would be no longer cosmopolitical which went beyond the strictly cosmopolitical conditions, that is to say implying the authority of the State and State legislation. The stranger cannot claim a right of residence (this would require a particular treaty of beneficence which would make of him for a certain time the inhabitant of a home), but to a visiting right.>

9 <So what does Kant say to us here? He says that this universal right, this political right implying States, is what he calls the common possession of the surface of the earth. He insists on this common surface for two reasons which are perhaps not very much underlined by him but which are clear. One is that the earth being spherical, circular, and therefore finite, it is necessary for men to live together. And the surface is at the same time naturally space, the surface area. But it is also superficiality, that is to say that what is common, what is a priori shared by all men, is what is neither below nor above. What is above is culture, institutions, construction. That is to say, all that men construct is naturally not common property: foundation, institution, architecture and therefore culture, it is not naturally common property. What is common is the natural surface. And as will be seen further on, it is a natural right which founds this universal right hospitality.>

10 <What Kant ignores here is that the Muslim right, which was just spoken of, is exactly what is first founded on a nomadic right. The right of hospitality is first of all a nomadic right, exactly linked to a sum total of variations that is pre-Islamic right in which Islamic right and hospitality is rooted.>

11 Kant 1970: 105–108. Derrida cites *Vers le paix perpétuelle* (Paris: Flammarion, 1991): 93–95, 96–97 [tr.].

12 In English "acceptation" has the same meaning as "acception" in French, therefore "acception" in Derrida's text has been translated as "acceptation" and "acceptation" has been translated as "acception". The different evolutions of the Latin words in English and French, themselves illustrate Derrida's points about the "tempting fault" and about how these questions are always questions of translation [tr.].

13 <I say "invitation"; this permits me to mark in parenthesis the place of a development with which I will not have time to engage today. I believe that the invitation precisely defined conditional hospitality. When I invite someone to come to my home there is the condition that I receive him. All this is conditioned by the fact that I stay in my home and I expect him to come. But it would be necessary to distinguish the invitation from what would be called the invited. The visitor is someone who can come at any moment, without a horizon of expectation, who comes by surprise like the Messiah. Anyone can come at any moment. It is like this that one speaks of the visitation which is the arrival of the other. Of God where no one awaits him, in religious language, in the language of Lévinas, besides Christian language. And that no one is there is to pose the conditions of the coming. Therefore the distinction between the invitation and the visitation is perhaps the distinction betwen conditional hospitality, that is if I accept the coming of the other, the arrivance of the other who can come at any moment without asking my opinion and who can be well intentioned or who can be the worst: the visitation can also be invasion by the worst. And conditional hospitality must be open without a horizon of expectation, without anticipation, for any surprise visitation. I close this parenthesis, but evidently it should count for a lot.>

14 <I am the hostage of the other in as much as I welcome the face of the other, in as much as I welcome infinity. For Lévinas the welcome of the other is the welcome of an other who is infinitely other and who consequently overflows me infinitely and where in consequence I welcome beyond my capacity to welcome. I welcome an other greater than I am and who consequently can overwhelm the space of my home.>

15 "La substitution", in *Révue Philosophique de Louvain*, August 1968: 500, reprised in *Autrement qu' être ou au-delà de l' essence* [translated as *Otherwise than Being or Beyond Essence* (Lévinas 1998) tr.] : 142–145, where the phrase "the word 'I' answers for all and everything" becomes "The word 'I' signifies 'here I am,' answering for all and everything". Two pages before the formula resonated that we must evidently analyse in its context and the logic of what Lévinas here calls substitution, the subject as subject of substitution, therefore, the formula "The subject is the hostage" (142). And then there is the Swan of Coufontaine in Claudel's *The Hostage* which we must read together, just as we must read *The Exchange*.

16 <In Lévinas this notion of anachrony is essential to the definition of the subject as host and hostage. Therefore the anachrony of this paradoxical instant.>

17 Derrida uses the English phrase [tr.].

18 Montaigne, *Essays*, III, IX [Translation (Montaigne 1993) tr.].

10 'OLIGARCHIES: NAMING, ENUMERATING, COUNTING'

POLITICS OF FRIENDSHIP (DERRIDA 1997B [FIRST PUBLISHED 1994])

Translated by George Collins

Themes

A version of this paper was presented to the American Philosophical Association and was published in *The Journal of Philosophy* (Derrida 1988), one of a very small number of occasions in which Derrida was published in a mainstream English medium philosophy journal.

Derrida sets up his argument with reference to a paradox of friendship, 'O, my friends, there is no friend', a remark attributed to Aristotle quoted by Michel de Montaigne and Nietzsche. The contradiction between the first and second parts of the sentence is referred to by Derrida as 'counter-time', which is one way of referring to the contradictions, paradoxes and aporia which are fundamental to Derrida. He also emphasises the arithmetic of the sentence, in the paradox of counting. One side has plural friends, the other side has zero friends. The plural friends are addressed in order to tell them there are zero friends. This leads into contradictions of friendship which have moral and political aspects. The issues of friendship enter into democracy and also into sovereignty and mastery. In both cases there is friendship, but the friendship of democracy is taken as ideal by Derrida. The friendship of democracy is, however, self-contradictory guaranteeing that democracy is yet to come. The point that Derrida brings to the initial paradox is that there is less friendship the more friends there are. It is Aristotle who suggests that friendship is something that at its most meaningful is confined to a few friends of equal status. It is Cicero who suggests that the friend is the ideal double. The logic of Aristotle's position is that the fewer friends, the more friendship so that if I am my only friend that is the best friendship which is where there is no friend. The logic of Cicero's position is that I am my own best friend, because I am the best double of myself. In both cases ideal friendship is where there is no friend. Another paradox of friendship in the Ancient Greek tradition is the incommensurability of the relationship between lover and beloved, beloved and lover. That is a way of thinking about erotic relationships in which there is an object of desire and the one who desires. There may be aspects of this discussion in Ancient Greek philosophy specific to the culture of that time, but in any context erotic relationships trouble the notion of friendship because they belong to friendship but introduce physical desire along with one-sided love, absent from the ideal of friendship based on equality, reciprocity and symmetry. In Aristotle's philosophy the lover is seen as primary in the erotic form of friendship, in a context where the older, wiser and more powerful individual is the lover of a beautiful, young, less educated and less powerful beloved. The essential aspect from Derrida's point of view is the metaphysics according to which the lover as active is necessarily superior to the beloved who is passive. It is an example of the metaphysical reduction to production, which forms part of the general metaphysical tendency to place one opposite above another.

Time and death condition friendship, just as they condition inner consciousness. Friendship requires time to test it. Only the friendship tested by time is friendship. In that case friendship is not here now, it is yet to come, as we wait for results of the test over time. Friendship is caught in the paradoxical unity of the now in which we experience friendship and the eternity which tests friendship. Only death can end the test of friendship, so the test of friendship is only known after death.

The necessity for friendship to be tested is part of the selectivity of friendship. Universal friendship is necessary for democracy but friendship is contradictory. Its ultimate logic is solipsistic and narcissistic, that is the search for absolute friendship leads to a self-referring and self-regarding relationship of the self with itself. The appearance of absolute friendship with an external friend would be apocalyptic. That is because it would be the impossible becoming possible and would therefore be the abolition of reality. The apocalyptic urge intrinsic in metaphysical themes is a constant in Derrida. The structure of friendship is troubling from a democratic point of view. The universal friendship necessary to democracy would be apocalyptic. The only practical kinds of friendship have an oligarchic arithmetic. That is, since friendship can only be friendship with some people, there cannot be a democratic friendship of all. Friendship is necessarily a friendship with a selected group and so is intrinsically oligarchic. Friendship selects a group rather than universalising itself. It is not a clear support for ethics as universalist ethics. The friendship of the sovereign or master can only be a friendship with an oligarchy, undermining the idea of democratic sovereignty. Derrida's thoughts of friendship are developed in the context of readings of Aristotle's ethics, philosophical philanthropy in Kant's ethics, the friend in Nietzsche's *Thus Spoke Zarathustra*, the Other in Lévinas, the opposition of friend and enemy in Carl Schmitt's political philosophy.

Context

The presentation of this paper as 'The Politics of Friendship' at the American Philosophical Association guaranteed an immediate response from the American philosopher Thomas McCarthy – a specialist in German idealist philosophy and on the contemporary German philosopher Jürgen Habermas who is one of the more analytic of Continental European philosophers – in 'On The Margins of Philosophy' (McCarthy 1988). McCarthy thinks of the asymmetries in Derrida's theory of friendship as covering the gaps left by the universalist rationalism he defines through Kant and Habermas. Habermas was compared with Derrida through Brandom above in the discussion of epistemology. As was suggested then, Habermas has a universalism which distinguishes him both from the more resolutely contextualist forms of pragmatism and from deconstruction. McCarthy's argument adds a destabilising twist even in supporting Habermas's universalism. He suggests that deconstruction appears where universalist social theory in Habermas ends, extending social theory to the discussion of the 'generalised Other' in George Herbert Mead. This immediately raises issues that McCarthy does not seem to have considered. If there are gaps left by universalist ethics and social theory, what is the status of their universalist claims? If we accept that Derrida is filling a gap left by universalist rationalism, does that not leave the possibility that deconstruction contains universalism within itself?

Derrida himself is not anti-universalist. The point is that the Kantian norms never completely apply and for Derrida that can never be satisfactorily resolved by the kind of distinction that McCarthy makes between theory as universal and empirical bits that inevitably get left out. That gap is constitutive in a way that is at the heart of deconstruction. The universal is always both in the present and beyond the present for Derrida. The ethical is always caught between the universality of law and the particularity of the situation; general obligation and obligation to the specific Other. This is the case in every situation: we cannot divide ethical situations between those that conform to general law and those that do not. There just is no absolute applicability of universal law to particular situations in the first place. Some of the issues here, and in the preceding section, will be taken up with regard to politics in Part VI. The discussion of ethics, and the prelude to politics, will be completed with regard to equivocations about the status of ethics in the analytic tradition, and in the ways it draws upon Kant and Aristotle.

John Rawls played an enormously influential role in analytic ethics, only exceeded by his very dominant role in analytic political philosophy (often known as normative theory), which will be considered in Part VI. In his 1955 paper, 'Two Concepts of Rules' (in Rawls 1999b), Rawls brings up the very question of the limits of ethical universality. Though Rawls is associated with Kantian criticisms of utilitarian ethics, that is an ethics based on maximising pleasure or utility, he always thought that utilitarianism was a valid instrument within limits. In 'Two Concepts of Rules', he defends a particular version of utilitarianism though not with any intention of adopting it as a whole. He does so by distinguishing between justifying a practice and the justification of an action within that practice. Utilitarianism cannot work through generalising a practice from some situations. It must assume some practices, such as the practices of punishment assumed by a judge when sentencing a defendant found guilty of a crime. In considering rules we must distinguish between the immediate jump from a particular situation to universal principles, and the use of a practice to bring a situation under some generalised principle. While this is not the same as any argument in Derrida, it does bring out the general issue that appears in Derrida. The issue is that of the impossibility of abandoning universal rules together with the impossibility of knowing which rule applies to which situation without some other force intruding. For Derrida this is the 'institutional' and it is the force inherent in every speech act and every application of law. Significantly, Rawls raises the issue of promising, anticipating J. L. Austin's discussion in the context of the performative (as discussed above in 'Sense and Meaning' with regard to 'Signature Event Context'). Promising presumes a practice of promising, and does not come from an isolated act of promising. It only exists in its repetition for Rawls, as Derrida would argue. Rawls's argument is more an argument for a hierarchy of norms than an uncovering of paradoxes, as is found in Derrida, but the results are comparable.

Other issues of the duality of ethics appear in Rawls's Magnum Opus, A *Theory of Justice* (Rawls 1999a [first published 1971]): the right and the good; Aristotle and Kant; liberty and equality; utilitarianism and Kant. The distinction between the right and the good is the distinction between universal ethical law and particular ethical goals, form and substance. The distinction between Aristotle and Kant is a rather large debate, but roughly speaking it is the distinction between rules emerging from individual and social habits, and rules generated by intellectual universalisation of acts. The distinction between liberty and equality is the well-worn distinction between individual freedom and equal distribution of economic outcomes. The distinction between utilitarianism and Kant, as mentioned above, is that between principles that maximise measures of well-being and principles of universal obligation. Rawls was not concerned, as Derrida was, with necessary paradoxes. He was trying to integrate the opposing principles to form a harmonious hierarchy of principles. Nevertheless, the very basic nature of these oppositions and the recognition of their persistence means that Rawls explained those areas where Derridean investigations begin, and more will be discussed about this in Part VI on Politics. The relationship between Aristotle and Kant in Rawls is highly pertinent to Derrida's discussion of Aristotle on friendship as practically experienced, and Kant on philosophical friendship for humanity (philanthropy). The relationship is overtly paradoxical for Derrida. Reading Rawls after Derrida, we may come to see Rawls as continually dealing with paradoxes, and trying to resolve them before they become aporetic, but always returning to them. These are not just issues for Rawls. The relative status of an Aristotelian 'virtue theory' and a Kantian universality is a widespread discussion, one of the results of which has been a tendency to read Kant with an emphasis on virtuous will which seems closer to Aristotle than the abstract universalist Kant. Another recent discussion of the relation between them can be found in McDowell's *Mind and World* (McDowell 1996), which is strongly influenced by Hegel. For McDowell, virtue theory and moral universalism harmonise in the formation of a second nature of learned moral culture, added in society to biological nature, in a process which relies on the interweaving of concepts and experience close to Derrida's thoughts on the phenomenology of consciousness. According to the 1979 paper 'Virtue and Reason' (in McDowell 1988); and the overlapping 1981 paper, 'Non-Cognitivism and Rule Following' (in McDowell 1988), virtue theory and moral universalism also harmonise in 'moral cognitivism', which is part of the general process of rule-following in knowledge discussed by Wittgenstein. The emphasis on Wittgenstein connects with deconstructive approaches to the dilemmas of grounding rules and the irreducible role of pure decision in choosing to follow a general rule. As with Rawls, the emphasis is on harmonisation of apparent opposites, but the focus on oppositions brings the discussion into Derridean territory in regard to Derrida's focus on oppositions as irreducible contradictions.

POLITICS OF FRIENDSHIP: OLIGARCHIES: NAMING, ENUMERATING, COUNTING

'O my friends, there is no friend.'

I am addressing you, am I not?

How many of us are there?

—Does that count?

—Addressing you in this way, I have perhaps not said anything yet. Nothing that is *said* in this saying. Perhaps nothing sayable.

Perhaps it will have to be admitted, perhaps I have not yet even addressed myself. At least, not to you.

How many of us are there?

—How can you count?

—On each side of a comma, after the pause, 'O my friends, there is no friend' —these are the two disjoined members of the same unique sentence. An almost impossible declaration. In two times [*deux temps*]. Unjoinable, the two times seem disjoined by the very meaning of what appears to be at once both affirmed and denied: 'my friends, no friend'. In two times but at the same time, in the *contretemps* of the same sentence. If there is 'no friend', then how could I call you my friends, my friends? By what right? How could you take me seriously? If I call you my friends, my friends, if I call you, my friends, how dare I add, to you, that there is no friend?

Incompatible as they may appear, and condemned to the oblivion of contradiction, here, in a sort of desperately dialectical desire, the two

times already form two theses—two *moments*, perhaps—they concate-
nate, they appear *together*, they are summoned to appear, in the present:
they present themselves as in a single stroke, in a single breath, in the
same present, in the present itself. At the same time, and before who knows
who, before who knows whose law. The *contretemps* looks favourably on
the encounter, it responds without delay but without renunciation: no
promised encounter without the possibility of a *contretemps*. As soon as
there is more than one.

But how many of us are there?

And first of all—you already sense it—in pronouncing 'O my friends,
there is no friend', I have yet to say anything *in my name*. I have been
satisfied with quoting. The spokesman of another, I have reported his
words, which belong in the first place (a question of tone, syntax, of a
gesture in speech, and so on) to a slightly archaic language, itself unset-
tled by the memory of borrowed or translated speech. Having signed
nothing, I have assumed nothing on my own account.

' O my friends, there is no friend' —the words not only form a quotation that I am now reading in its old French spelling. They have a
different ring: already, such a very long time ago, they bore the quotation
of another reader hailing from my homeland, Montaigne: 'that saying
which', he says, 'Aristotle often repeated'. It is found in the *Essays*,[1] in
the chapter 'On Friendship'.

This, then, is a cited quotation. But the quotation of a saying
attributed, only attributed, by a sort of rumour or public opinion. 'O my
friends, there is no friend' is, then, a declaration *referred* to Aristotle.
There will be no end to the work of glossing its attribution and its very
grammar, the translation of these four words, three or four in Greek,
since the only substantive in the sentence is repeated. Like a renowned
filiation, an origin thus nicknamed seems, in truth, to lose itself in the
infinite anonymity of the mists of time. It is not, however, one of those
proverbs, one of those 'sayings' with no assignable author, whose aphoristic mode is seldom in the form of the apostrophe.

Quotation of friendship. A quotation coming from a chapter entitled
'On Friendship', after a title that repeats, already, an entire tradition of
titles. Before naming Aristotle, Montaigne had massively quoted Cicero,
his *De Amicitia* as much as the *Tusculanes*. Occasionally he had drawn the
Ciceronian treatise within the genius of his paraphrase, precisely around
this 'O my friends'. The 'sovereign and master-friendship' had then to be
distinguished from 'friendships common and customary, in relation to
which you must employ that saying which Aristotle often repeated'.

We have in memory our *Laelius de Amicitia*: we already hear the
Ciceronian echo. Let us specify, in anticipation, just that the Ciceronian

distinction between the two friendships ('true and perfect' or 'vulgar and mediocre') works only with an *arithmetical* twist. How many friends? How many of us are there? Determining a nomination and a quotation (*pauci nominantur* those who are named or whose name is quoted are few and far between when true or perfect friendship is named), the distinction expresses rarity or the small in number. We shall never forget that. Are friends rare? Must they remain rare? How many are there? What account must be taken of rarity? And what about selection or election, affinity or proximity; what about parenthood or familiarity (*oikeiótēs*, as Plato's *Lysis* already put it), what about one's *being-at-home* or *being-close-to-oneself* in regard to that which links friendship to all laws and all logics of universalization, to ethics and to law or right, to the values of equality and equity, to all the political models of the *res publica* for which this distinction remains the axiom, and especially in regard to democracy? The fact that Cicero adds democracy as an afterthought changes nothing in the force or the violence of this *oligophilial* [*oligophilique*] note:

> And I am not now speaking of the friendships of ordinary folk, or of ordinary people (*de vulgari aut de mediocri*)—although even these are a source of pleasure and profit—but of true and perfect friendship (*sed de vera et perfecta loquor*), the kind that was possessed by those few men who have gained names for themselves as friends (*qualis eorum, qui pauci nominatur, fuit*).[2]

An important nuance: the small in number does not characterize the friends themselves. It counts *those we are speaking of*, those whose legendary friendship tradition *cites*, the name and the renown, the name according to the renown. Public and political signs attest to these great and rare friendships. They take on the value of exemplary heritage.

Why *exemplary*? Why exemplary in a very strict sense? Rarity accords with the phenomenon, it vibrates with light, brilliance and glory. If one names and cites the best friends, those who have illustrated 'true and perfect friendship', it is because this friendship comes to *illuminate*. It illustrates itself, makes happy or successful things shine, gives them visibility, renders them more resplendent (*secundas res splendidiores facit amicitia*). It gives rise to a project, the anticipation, the perspective, the pro-vidence of a hope that illuminates in advance the future (*praelucet*), thereby transporting the name's renown beyond death. A narcissistic projection of the ideal image, of its own ideal image (*exemplar*), already inscribes the legend. It engraves the renown in a ray of light, and prints the citation of the friend in a convertibility of life and death, of presence and absence, and promises it to the testamental *revenance* [ghostly apparition of the *revenant*, the 'ghost', its haunting return on the scene (Translator's note)] of more [no more] life, of a *surviving* that will remain, here, one of our themes. Friendship provides numerous advantages, notes Cicero, but none is comparable to this unequalled hope, to this ecstasy towards a future which will go beyond death. Because of death, and because of this unique passage beyond life, friendship thus offers us a hope that has nothing in common, besides the name, with any other.

Why is the future thus pre-illumined, beyond life, by the hope that friendship projects and inspires in this way? What is absolute hope, if it stems from friendship? However underdeveloped it may be, the Ciceronian answer leans sharply to one side—let us say *the same* side—rather than to the other—let us say *the other*. Such a response thus sets up the given state of our discussion. In two, three or four words, is the friend the same or the other? Cicero prefers the same, and believes he is able to do so; he thinks that to prefer is also just that: if friendship projects its hope beyond life—an absolute hope, an incommensurable hope—this is because the friend is, as the translation has it, 'our own ideal image'. We envisage the friend as such. And this is how he envisages us: with a friendly look. Cicero uses the word *exemplar*, which means portrait but also, as the *exemplum*, the duplicate, the reproduction, the copy as well as the original, the type, the model. The two meanings (the single original and the multipliable copy) cohabit here; they are—or seem to be—the same, and that is the whole story, the very condition of survival. Now, according to Cicero, his *exemplar* is projected or recognized in the true friend, it is his ideal double, his other self, the same as self but improved. Since we watch him looking at us, thus watching ourselves, because we see him keeping our image in his eyes—in truth in ours— survival is then hoped for, illuminated in advance, if not assured, for this Narcissus who dreams of immortality. Beyond death, the absolute future thus receives its ecstatic light, it appears only from within this narcissism and according to this logic of the same.

(It will not suffice to claim exactly the contrary, as we will attempt to do, in order to provide a logical demonstration, in a decidable discourse; another way and another thought will be necessary for the task.)

This text by Cicero will also have been in turn, for a history (long and brief, past and to come), the glorious witness, the illustrious *exemplar*, of Ciceronian logic. This tradition is perhaps finished, even dying; it always will have been in its essence *finishing*, but its 'logic' ends up none the less, in the very consequence of the same, in a vertiginous convertibility of opposites: the absent becomes present, the dead living, the poor rich, the weak strong. And all that, acknowledges Cicero, is quite 'difficult to say', which means difficult to decide. Those who snigger at discourses on the undecidable believe they are very strong, as we know, but they should begin by attacking a certain Cicero as well. By reading him, then:

> For the man who keeps his eye on a true friend, keeps it, so to speak, on a model of himself *tamquam exemplar aliquod intuetur sui*). For this reason, friends are together when they are separated, they are rich when they are poor, strong when they are weak (*et imbecilli valent*), and—a thing even harder to explain— they live on after they have died (*mortui vivunt*), so great is the honour that follows them, so vivid the memory, so poignant the sorrow. That is why friends who have died are accounted happy (*ex quo illorum beata mors videtur*), and those who survive them are deemed worthy of praise (*vita laudabilis*).3

In this possibility of a *post mortem* discourse, a possibility that is a force as well, in this *virtue* of the funeral eulogy, everything seems, then, to have a part to play: epitaph or oration, citation of the dead person, the renown of the name after the death of what it names. A memory is engaged in advance, from the moment of what is called life, in this strange temporality opened by the anticipated citation of some funeral oration. I live in the present speaking of myself in the mouths of my friends, I already hear them speaking on the edge of my tomb. The Ciceronian variety of friendship would be the possibility of quoting myself in exemplary fashion, by signing the funeral oration in advance— the best of them, perhaps, but it is never certain that the friend will deliver it standing over my tomb when I am no longer among the living. Already, yet when I will no longer be. As though pretending to say to me, in my very own voice: rise again.

Who never dreams of such a scene? But who does not abhor this theatre? Who would not see therein the repetition of a disdainful and ridiculous staging, the putting to death of friendship itself?

This premeditation of friendship (*de amicitia, peri philías*) would also intend, then, to engage, in its very space, work on the citation, and on the citation of an apostrophe. Of an apostrophe always uttered close to the end, on the edge of life—that is to say, of death.

What transpires when an apostrophe is quoted? Does an apostrophe let itself be quoted, in its lively and singular movement, here and now, this impulse in which I turn towards the singularity of the other, towards you, the irreplaceable one who will be my witness or whom I single out? Can the transport of this unique address be not only repeated but quoted? Conversely, would the apostrophe ever take place, and the pledge it offers, without the possibility of a substitution?

We will read these themes of the apostrophic pledge and its quotation later on; they are no doubt inseparable from the theme of the name: from the name of the friend and, in the name, from the mortality of the friend, from the memories and from the testament which, using precisely the same appellation, these themes call up.

Familiarities. What is familiarity? What is familial proximity? What affinity of alliance or consanguinity (*Verwandschaft*) is concerned? To what elective familiarity could friendship be compared? In reading Montaigne, Montaigne reading Cicero, Montaigne bringing back a 'saying' 'often repeated', here we are already—another testament—back with Aristotle. Enigmatic and familiar, he survives and surveys from within ourselves (but how many of us are there?). He stands guard over the very form of our sentences on the subject of friendship. He forms our precomprehension at the very moment when we attempt, as we are about to do, to go back over it, even against it. Are we not obliged to respect at least, first of all, the authority of Aristotelian questions? The structure and the norm, the grammar of such questions? Is not Aristotle in fact the first of the maieutic tradition of *Lysis*, to be sure (*Lysis, è peri philías*), but beyond him, in giving it a directly theoretical, ontological and phenomenological form, to pose the question of friendship (*peri philías*), of knowing *what it is* (*tí esti*), *what* and *how* it is (*poîón ti*), and, above all, if it is said in one or in several senses (*monakhos légatai è pleon-akhôs*)?[4]

It is true that right in the middle of this series of questions, between the one on the being or the being-such of friendship and the one on the possible plurivocity of a saying of friendship, there is the question which is itself terribly equivocal: *kai tís o phílos*. This question asks *what* the friend is, but also asks *who* he is. This hesitation in the language between the *what* and the *who* does not seem to make Aristotle tremble, as if it were, fundamentally, one and the same interrogation, as if one enveloped the other, and as if the question 'who?' had to bend or bow in advance before the ontological question 'what?' or 'what is?'.

This implicit subjection of the *who* to the *what* will call for question on our part—in return or in appeal. The question will bring with it a protestation: in the name of the friend or in the name of the name. If this protestation takes on a political aspect, it will perhaps be less properly political than it would appear. It will signify, rather, the principle of a possible resistance to the reduction of the political, even the ethical, to the ontophenomenological. It will perhaps resist, in the name of another politics, such a reduction (a powerful reduction—powerful enough, in any case, to have perhaps constructed the dominant concept of the political). And it will accept the risk of diverting the *Lysis* tradition. It will attempt to move what is said to us in the dialogue elsewhere, from its first words, about the route and the name, the proper and the singular name, at that moment when this 'maieutic' dialogue on friendship (*è peri philías*) begins, at the crossing of who knows how many *passages*, *routes* or *aporias*, with love (*érōs*). It begins as well, let us not forget, by 'diverting'-socrates from a path leading him 'straight' (*euthu*) from the Academy to the Lyceum.

Yes, since when—whether we know it or not—have we ceased to be Aristotle's heirs? And how many of us? And turned, by him already, towards the heritage itself, towards the theme of some last will, towards the testamentary in itself? The *Eudemian Ethics*, for example, inscribes friendship, knowledge and death, but also survival, from the start, in a single, *selfsame* configuration. The same here is none other than the other. It has at least the figure of the other. The necessary *consequence* of this strange configuration is an opportunity for thought. Beyond all ulterior frontiers between love and friendship, but also between the passive and active voices, between the loving and the being-loved, what is at stake is 'lovence' [*aimance*].[5] You must know how it *can be more worthwhile* to love lovence. Aristotle recalls not only that it is more worthwhile *to love*, but that you had better love *in this way*, and *not in that way*; and that hence *it is more worthwhile to love* than *to be loved*. From then on, a singular *preference* destabilizes and renders dissymmetrical the equilibrium of all difference: an *it is more worthwhile* gives precedence to the act over potentiality. An activity carries it away, it prevails over passivity.

Ever-ready Aristotelian scholastics would tempt us confidently to take this a step further: this *it is more worthwhile* would acknowledge the pre-eminence of form over matter. And after a deduction of this sort, one would no longer be wary of a worrisome consequence. Rushing to the end, such a pre-eminence would then come, for once, with Aristotle, for a single time, not only to link lovence to dying, but to situate death on the side of act and on the side of form. For once, but irreversibly.

How does this come about? How would act, *this time*, bear itself over to death's side? How would it bear death? For it bears death in itself in this case; it contains death. Preference and reference. But it bears death in itself in bearing itself over to death. It transports itself in death by that which, in it, at the time of death, addresses its reference in a single stroke.

Let us then see death coming on the road of this argumentation. Is not death, moreover, in question—death in so far as one sees it coming, and even in so far as a knowledge knows what it knows in seeing it coming, only in seeing it coming?

Aristotle therefore declares: as for friendship, it is advisable to love rather than to be loved. Let us not forget the general horizon of this affirmation. Justice and politics are at stake. This passage from the *Eudemian Ethics* opens, in fact, with the question of what is just, *the just* (*to dikaíon*) in friendship.[6] What arises in the first place is precisely the question of the just or of justice, *dikaiosúnē*. Justice characterizes a way of behaving. It consists in behaving in a certain way: in accordance with the just, in harmony with the principle of the just. In its dignity as well as its necessity, this question is immediately equal to that of the beautiful and the desirable in friendship. It arrives, then, also in the first place, immediately following the general opening on the subject of friendship (*peri philías*): What is friendship? How or what is it? What is a friend? Is friendship said in one sense or in several?[7]

The whole task should certainly consist in determining this justice. But that seems possible only by forcing several aporias. We will begin, as always, with the implicit reference to *Lysis* (214–16), with the aporia of a friendship which seems doomed to the similar and to the dissimilar.[8] But even before this first aporia, the just will be said and the passage will be forced only by first aligning oneself on a commonly held opinion. This opinion concerns the *very work of the political*: the *properly* political act or operation amounts to creating (to producing, to making, etc.) the most friendship possible (*tês te gar politikês érgon einai dokei málista poiêsai philían*[9]).

How is this *the most possible* to be understood? How many? Can that be calculated? How can you interpret the possibility of this maximum or this optimum in friendship? How is it to be understood politically? Must the *most friendship* [*plus d'amitié*] still belong to the political?

In all good sense, what you hear above all is *loving*; you must hear loving; you cannot fail to hear it in total confidence when the word friendship resounds: friendship consists in loving, does it not; it is a way of loving, of course. Consequence, implication: it is therefore an act before being a situation; rather, the *act* of loving, before being the state of being loved. An action before a passion. The act of this activity, this intention of loving, the *phileîn*, is more proper to friendship itself (*kata ten philían*) than the situation which consists in letting oneself be loved or inducing love, in any case in being loved (*phileisthai*). Being-loved certainly speaks to something of *philía*, but only on the side of the beloved (*philéton*). It says nothing of friendship *itself* which implies *in itself*, *properly*, essentially, the act and the activity: someone must love in order to know what loving means; then, and only then, can one know what being loved means.

Friendship, the being-friend—what is that, anyway? Well, it is to love *before* being loved. Before even thinking about what *loving, love, lovence* mean, one must know that the only way to find out is by questioning first of all the act and the experience of loving rather than the state or situation of being loved. Why is that? What is its reason? Can we know? Well, precisely by reason of *knowledge*—which is accorded or allied here to the act. And here we have the obscure but invincible force of a tautology. The argument seems, in fact, simple: it is possible to be loved (passive voice) *without knowing it*, but it is impossible to love (active voice) *without knowing it*. Science or self-consciousness knows itself a priori comprehended, comprehended and *engaged* in the friendship of the *one who loves*—to wit, in the friend—but science or self-consciousness is no longer comprehended or engaged, or is not yet so on the side of *the one who is loved*. The friend is the person who loves before being the person who is loved: he who loves before being the beloved, and perhaps (but this is something else, even though the consequence follows) he who loves before being loved. *Engaged* science or consciousness here means conscripted twice over: implicated as in a condition of possibility (theoretical chain) and held in a pledge, a promise, an alliance (performative chain). This view can always fall back on the following analytic evidence: one must start with the friend-who-loves, not with the friend-who-is-loved, if one is to think friendship. This is an irreversible order. One can be loved while remaining ignorant of that very thing—that one is loved—and in this respect remain as though confined to secrecy. It could be said that such a secret is never revealed. But one cannot love, and one must not love, in such a state of ignorance of friendship itself (*ésti gar lanthánein philoúmenon, philoûnta d'oú*[10]). Axiom: the friendship I bear [*porte*] for someone, and no doubt love as well, cannot remain a secret for myself. Even before it is declared (to the other, in a loud voice), the act of love would thereby be, at its very birth, *declared*. It would be in itself declared, given over to knowledge or to consciousness. The declaration would in truth be inscribed upon its act of birth. One loves only by declaring that one loves. Let us call that, for convenience's sake, an axiom: the premiss of this entire line of reasoning seems to appeal to good sense, it is posed as unquestionable. As *incontestable*, in fact: one cannot bear witness against it without being party to it.

But there, in the dark, objections are massing up. We will abandon them to their virtuality for the moment. Being loved—what does that mean? Nothing, perhaps—nothing in any case of friendship itself in which the loved one, as such, has nothing to know, sometimes nothing to do. Being loved therefore remains—with regard to friendship itself, and therefore with regard to the friend—an accident (*to men gar phileisthai sumbebekós*[11]). Friendship, what is proper or essential to friendship, can be thought and lived without the least reference to the be-*loved*, or more generally to the *lovable*— in any case, without having to set out from there, as from a principle. If we trusted the categories of subject and object here, we would say in this logic that friendship (*philía*) is first accessible on the side of its subject, who thinks and lives it, not on the side of its object, who can be loved or lovable without in any way being assigned to a sentiment of which, precisely, he remains the object. And if we do say 'think and love', as we shall see later, life, breath, the soul, are always and necessarily found on the side of the lover or of loving, while the being-loved of the lovable can be lifeless; it can belong to the reign of the non-living, the non-psychic or the 'soulless' (*en apsúkhô*[12]). One cannot love without living and without knowing that one loves, but one can still love the deceased or the inanimate who then know nothing of it. It is indeed through the possibility of loving the deceased that the decision in favour of a certain lovence comes into being.

This incommensurability between the lover and the beloved will now unceasingly exceed all measurement and all moderation—that is, it will exceed the very principle of a calculation. It will *perhaps* introduce a virtual disorder in the organization of the Aristotelian discourse. (This 'perhaps' has already marked the hesitant gait of our reading.) Something trembles, for example, in what Aristotle calls the natural (*phúsei*) hierarchy—that is, the hierarchy inscribed from birth between those inclined to love (to kissing, to caressing), the *philetikoi*, and on the other hand, below them, the last ones, the *philótimoi*. They prefer to be loved; they thus seek honours, distinction, signs of recognition.[13] In addition, even if there were no essentially erotic dimension, no desire at work in the ever-more-dissymmetrical hierarchy of the *philía*, how will its formal structure in the relation between the sublunary world and the Prime Mover be respected?

If Eros and Philia are indeed movements, do we not have here an inverse hierarchy and an inverse dissymmetry? Prime Mover or pure Act, God sets in motion without Himself moving or being moved; He is the absolute desirable or desired, analogically and formally in the position of the beloved, therefore on the side of death, of that which can be inanimate without ceasing to be loved or desired (*apsúkhon*). Now in contrast to what takes place in friendship, no one will contest that this absolute object of desire is also found at the principle and at the summit of the natural hierarchy, whereas He does not allow himself to move or be moved by any attraction.

Let us go back down to the sublunary world. The dissymmetry risks, apparently and at first glance, complicating the egalitarian schema of the *isótēs* or—if I may use the term—the reciprocalist or *mutualist* schema of requited friendship (*antiphileîn*), such as Aristotle seems to insist on privileging them elsewhere.[14] The *phileîn* would therefore be more appropriate to the essence of friendship (*kata ten philían*); the act of loving would better suit friendship, if not the beloved (*philéton*). Aristotle, then, proposes to give proof or a sign (*semeion*) of this suitability. If a friend had to choose between knowing and being known, he would choose knowing rather than being known. Every time he evokes this alternative and determines the choice, Aristotle places himself in the hypothesis in which the two experiences (knowing and being known, loving and being-loved, the lover and the lovable) are not compatible, at the moment when they do not appear possible *at the same time*.[15] Basically it makes little difference. Even if the movement of the act and the passivity of the state were simultaneously possible, if that could take place in fact, the essential structure of the two experiences and the two relations would remain no less different. This irreducible difference is that which counts and permits counting. It is what justifies the intrinsic hierarchy: knowing will never mean, for a finite being, being known; nor loving being loved. One can love being loved, but loving will always be more, better and something other than being loved. One can love to be loved—or to be lovable—but one must first know how to love, and know what loving means by loving. The structure of the first must remain what it is, heterogeneous to that of the other; and that structure, that of loving for the lover, will always—as Aristotle tells us, in sum—be preferable to the other, to that of the being-loved as lovable. Loving will always be preferable to being-loved, as acting is preferable to suffering, act to potentiality, essence to accident, knowledge to non-knowledge. It is the reference, the preference itself.

To make this understood, the *Eudemian Ethics* stages the example of what the women do in Antiphon's *Andromache*. It is a matter of an example of adoption or of a nurse, of prosthetic maternity, of the substitution or the supposition of children, *en tais upobolais*, and here we are already in this *familiarity of election* which will everywhere remain our theme. These mothers confide their children to a nurse and love them without seeking to be loved in return. For to want to be known seems to be an 'egoistic' sentiment, as it is often translated; it is in any case a sentiment turned within oneself, in favour of oneself, for the love of self (*autou éneka*). It is passive, more in a hurry to receive or to enjoy the good than to do it, as Aristotle literally says (*tou páskhein ti agathon alla mē poiein*); but one could just as well say: ready to receive the good that one does not have rather than to give that which one possesses (or even, as Plotinus will one day say—and this is something else—ready to give that very thing that one does not have). The *Nichomachean Ethics* recalls the same example, in order to make the same point. But Aristotle insists at this point on maternal *joy* or *enjoyment* [*jouissance*], in seeing there once again a sign or a proof of the preference (*semeion d'ai metéres tô phileîn khaírousai*[16]).

How can you pass from maternal enjoyment to death? This passage is not visible in the immediacy of the text. Naming, certainly, the enjoyment of maternal love in so far as it renounces reciprocity, the *Nicomachean Ethics* associates it neither with surviving nor with dying. The *Eudemian Ethics* speaks of the renunciation of the mother, in her very love, but without naming enjoyment and in order immediately to go on [*enchaîner*] to death. We have just recalled this logical chain. To want to be known, to refer to self in view of self, to receive the good rather than to do it or to give it—this is an altogether different thing from knowing. Knowing knows in order to do and to love, for love and in view of doing and loving (*to de ginôskein tou poiein kai tou phileîn éneka*), as Aristotle then says, concluding: 'This is why we praise those who continue to love their deceased, for they know but are not known' (*dio kai tous emménontas tô phileîn pros tous tethneôtas epainoumen, ginôskousi gár, all' ou ginôskontai*[17]). Friendship for the deceased thus carries this *philía* to the limit of its possibility. But at the same time, it uncovers the ultimate spring of this possibility: I could not love friendship without projecting its impetus towards the horizon of this death. The *horizon* is the limit *and* the absence of limit, the loss of the horizon on the horizon, the ahorizontality of the horizon, the limit as absence of limit. I could not love friendship without engaging myself, *without feeling myself in advance* engaged to love the other beyond death. Therefore, beyond life. I feel myself—and in advance, before any contract—*borne* to love the dead other. I feel myself thus (borne to) love; it is thus that I *feel myself* (loving).

Autology provides food for thought, as always: I feel myself loving, borne to love the deceased, this beloved or this lovable being of whom it has already been said that he was not necessarily alive, and that therefore he was bearing death in his being-loved, smack against his being-lovable, in the range [*portée*] of the reference to his very being-loved. Let us recall it, and let us do so in the words of Aristotle. He explains to us why one can rejoice and why there is a place for rejoicing in loving (*dio to phileîn khaírein*), but one could never rejoice—or at the very least, we would say, not essentially, not intrinsically—in being loved (*all' ou to phileisthai estín*). Enjoyment, the self-rejoicing, is immanent not to the beloved but to the loving, to its act, to its proper *energeia*.[18] The criterion of this distinction follows an apparently invisible line. It passes between the living and the dead, the animate and the inanimate, the psychic and the a-psychic. A question of respiration or inspiration: loving belongs only to a being gifted with life or with breath (*en empsúkô*) . Being loved, on the other hand, always remains possible on the side of the inanimate (*en apsúkhô*), where a *psukhé* may already have expired. 'One also loves inanimate beings' (*phileitai gar kai ta ápsukha*).[19]

(We are striving to speak here in the logic of Aristotle's two *Ethics*, doing everything that seems possible to respect the conceptual veins of his argumentation. The reader who is familiar with Aristotle may find that the tone has changed, however, along with the pathos and the connotations; he may suspect some slow, discreet or secret drift. Let us ask him—let us ask ourselves—what the law of this drift is and, more precisely, if there is one, and if it be pure, the purely conceptual, logical or properly philosophical law of order. A law which would not only be of a psychological, rhetorical or poetic order. What is taking place here? And what if what is taking place were taking place precisely between the two orders that we have just distinguished, at their very juncture? Let us not forget that in the case of psychology, the question of the *psukhé*, or of animate life, is at the heart of all philosophical reflection on *philía*. For Aristotle, neither rhetoric nor poetics could ever be excluded from this reflection; and poets are quoted, more than once called up to testify, even as judges of truth.)

If *philía* lives, and if it lives at the extreme limit of its possibility, it therefore *lives*, it stirs, it becomes *psychic* from within this resource of survival. This *philía*, this *psukhé* between friends, survives. It cannot survive itself as act, but it can survive its object, it can love the inanimate. Consequently it springs forward, from the threshold of this act, towards the possibility that the beloved might be dead. There is a first and irreducible dissymmetry here. But this same dissymmetry *separates itself*, after a fashion, in an unpresentable topology; it folds, turns inside out and doubles itself at the same time in the hypothesis of *shared* friendship, the friendship tranquilly described as reciprocal. I do not survive the friend, I cannot and must not survive him, except to the extent to which he already bears my death and inherits it as the last survivor. He bears my own death and, in a certain way, he is the only one to bear it— this proper death of myself thus expropriated in advance.

(I say that using the masculine gender {the [male] friend, he, and so forth}—not in the narcissistic or fraternal violence of a distraction, but by way of announcing a question awaiting us, precisely the question of the brother, in the canonical—that is, androcentric—structure of friendship.)

In any case, *philía* begins with the possibility of survival. Surviving— that is the other name of a mourning whose possibility is never to be awaited. For one does not survive without mourning. No one alive can

get the better of this tautology, that of the stance of survival [*survivance*]—
even God would be helpless.

Here again, the difference between the effective and the virtual,
between mourning and its possibility, seems fragile and porous. The
anguished apprehension of mourning (without which the act of friendship would not spring forth in its very energy) insinuates itself a priori
and anticipates itself; it haunts and plunges the friend, before mourning,
into mourning. This apprehension weeps before the lamentation, it
weeps death before death, and this is the very respiration of friendship,
the extreme of its possibility. Hence surviving is at once the essence, the
origin and the possibility, the condition of possibility of friendship; it is
the grieved act of loving. This time of surviving thus gives the time of
friendship.

But such a time gives itself in its withdrawal. It *occurs only through self-
effacement*. [*Il n'arrive qu'à s'éffacer*, also: 'It succeeds only in effacing
itself.'] It delivers itself up and withdraws twice and according to two
modalities, as we shall see, in two times as incompatible as they are indissociable: firm and stable constancy on the one hand and, on the other,
beginning again, renewal, the indefinite repetition of the inaugural
instant, always *anew*, once again, the new in re-iteration. And this double
contretemps delivers up the truth of friendship in the eerie light of a *contre-
jour* the present presents itself there only from within a source of
phenomenal light which comes neither from the present (it is no longer
the source) nor from the place from which it arises or in which it
appears—the place of the gaze, of the self or of the 'subject', if you like.
The *contre-jour* of this *contretemps* disjoins the presence of the present. It
inscribes both intemporality and untimeliness in at least one of the figures
of what Aristotle regularly calls primary friendship (*e protè philía*). Primary
friendship: primary because it is the first to present itself according to logic
and rank, primary according to sense and hierarchy, primary because all
other friendship is determined with reference to it, if only in the gap of the
drift or the failure. Primary friendship does not work without time,
certainly, it never presents itself outside time: there is no friend without
time (*oud' áneu khrónou phílos*[20])— that is, without that which puts confidence to the test. There is no friendship without confidence (*pístis*), and
no confidence which does not measure up to some *chronology*, to the trial
of a sensible duration of time (*è de pístis ouk áneu khrónou*[21]). The fidelity,
faith, 'fidence' [*fiance*], credence, the *credit* of this engagement, could not
possibly be a-chronic. It is precisely by taking off from this *credence* [*croire*]
that something like a temporalizing synthesis or symbolicity can be appre-
hended—beyond the letter of Aristotle's text, one might say. Engagement
in friendship takes time, it gives time, for it carries beyond the present

moment and keeps memory as much as it anticipates. It gives and takes time, for it survives the living present. The paradox of the grieving survival is concentrated in the ever-so-ambiguous value of stability, constancy and firm permanence that Aristotle regularly associates with the value of credence or confidence (*pístis*). In primary friendship, such a faith must be stable, established, certain, assured (*bébaios*); it must endure the test of time. But *at the same time* if this may still be said, *áma*, it is this faith which, dominating time by eluding it, taking and giving time in *contretemps*, opens the experience of time. It opens it, however, in determining it as the stable present of a quasi-eternity, or in any case from and in view of such a present of certainty. Everything is installed at home, as it were, in this conjunction of friendship, of 'fidence' and stable certainty. There is no reliable friendship without this faith (*ouk ésti d'áneu písteōs philía bébaios*[22]), without the confirmed steadfastness of this repeated act of faith. Plato, too, associated *philía* with the same value of constancy and steadfastness. *The Symposium* recalls a few famous examples. A friendship that has become steadfast, constant or faithful (*bébaios*) can even defy or destroy tyrannical power.[23] Elsewhere, as we know—in the *Timaeus*, for example—the value of constancy is quite simply tied to that of the true or the veritable, in particular where it is a question of opinion or belief.

In its sheer stability, this assured certainty is not natural, in the late and current sense of the term; it does not characterize spontaneous behaviour because it qualifies a belief or an act of faith, a testimony and an act of responsible freedom. Only primary friendship is stable (*bébaios*), for it implies decision and reflection: that which always takes time. Only those decisions that do not spring up quickly (*me takhu*) or easily (*mēde radíōs*) result in correct judgement (*ten krísin orthén*).[24] This non-given, non-'natural', non-spontaneous stability thus amounts to a *stabilization*. This stabilization supposes the passage through an ordeal which takes time. It must be difficult to judge and to decide. A decision worthy of the name—that is, a critical and reflective decision—could not possibly be rapid or easy, as Aristotle then notes, and this remark must receive all the weight of its import. The time is the time of this decision in the ordeal of what *remains to be decided*—and hence of what has not been decided, of what there is to reflect and deliberate upon—and thus has not yet been thought through. If the *stabilized* stability of certainty is never given, if it is conquered in the course of a stabilization, then the stabilization of what *becomes* certain must cross—and therefore, in one way or another, recall or be reminded of—the suspended indecision, the undecidable *qua* the time of reflection.

Here we would find the difference between spirit (the *nous*) and the animal body, but also their analogy. The analogy is as important as the difference, for it inscribes in the living body the *habitus* of this *contretemps*. It has its place in the very movement and in the possibility of such an inscription. The contretemporal *habitus* is the acquired capacity, the cultivated aptitude, the experimented faculty against the backdrop of a predisposition; it is the *éxis* that binds together two times in the same time, a duration and an omnitemporality at the same time. Such a contretemporality is another name for this *psukhé*, it is the being-animated or the *animation* of this life uniting the human spirit (the *nous*) and animality itself. This unifying feature *conjugates* man and animal, spirit and life, soul and body. It places them under the same yoke, that of the same liability [*passibilité*], that of the same aptitude to learn in suffering, to cross, to record and to take account of the ordeal of time, to withhold its trace in the body. This conjugation will warrant the poetic figure of the analogy which we will quote in a moment and which precisely names the *yoke*, the yoke effect.

It is starting from this analogy that the difference lets itself be thought. In the *passage* of time *through* time. Time exits from time. The ordeal of stabilization, the becoming-steadfast and reliable (*bébaios*), *takes time*. For this ordeal, this experience, this crossing (*peira*), withdraws time, it removes even the time necessary to dominate time and defeat duration. *Bébaios*: the stable but also the reliable. It determines a temporal but also intemporal modality, a becoming-intemporal or omnitemporal of time, *whatever it affects* (certainty, calculability, reliability, 'fidence', truth, friendship, and so forth). But it also marks—or rather, it hides in marking—the passage between two absolutely heterogeneous orders, the passage from assured certainty, calculable reliability, to the reliability of the oath and the act of faith. This act of faith belongs—it *must* belong—to what is incalculable in decision. We know that this break with calculable reliability and with the assurance of certainty—in truth, with knowledge—is ordained by the very structure of confidence or of credence as faith.

Hence of friendship. This structure is both acknowledged and unrecognized by Aristotle. The truth of friendship, if there is one, is found there, in darkness, and with it the truth of the political, as it can be thought in Greek: not only in the word *bébaios* (for example, for we do not think it possible to load such a burden on one word, on this word), but throughout the culture, the technics, the political organization and the Greek 'world' that carry it. In a state of intense philosophical concentration, we have here the whole story of *eidos* all the way up to the Husserlian interpretation of the idealization or production of ideal objects as the production of omnitemporality, of intemporality *qua* omnitemporality. It takes time to reach a stability or a certainty which wrenches itself from time. It takes time to do without time. One must submit, one must submit oneself to time in time. One must submit it, but—and here is the history of the *subject* as the history of time—in submitting oneself to it. To conjugate it, to enslave it, to place it under the yoke, and to do so for the spirit of man or of woman as for cattle—under the yoke (*upozúgios*):

> There is no stable friendship with confidence, but confidence needs time (*áneu khrónou*). One must then make trial (*dei gar peiran labein*), as Theognis says: 'You cannot know the mind of man or woman till you have tried (*prin peiratheíes*) them as you might cattle (*ósper upozugíou*).'[25]

But—as we shall see further on, in the course of one of our sallies to and fro—if *primary* friendship is excluded among animals, excluded between man and animal, excluded between the gods, between man and God, this is because *éxis* itself does not suffice for friendship. The disposition, the aptitude, even the wish—everything that makes friendship possible and prepares it—does not suffice for friendship, for friendship *in act*. Often *éxis* alone remains a simulacrum; it simulates or dissimulates real friendship, and makes the desire for friendship a case of wishful thinking, in which the signs of friendship are mistaken for friendship itself. The nub of the Aristotelian argument, as it can be formalized through development with other examples, certainly amounts to demanding and uncovering *éxis*, to taking into account a concrete and indispensable condition of possibility and describing it not as a formal structure, but—here, in any case—as a sort of existential opening (the power-of-being-a-friend, according to primary friendship, which is given neither to the animal nor to God). Aristotle, however, insists just as much, and with faultless rigour, on the insufficiency of this *éxis*, and thus on all conditions of possibility (liability [*passibilité*], aptitude, predisposition, even desire). The analysis of conditions of possibility, even existential ones, will never suffice in giving an account of the act or the event. An analysis of that kind will never measure up to what takes place, the effectivity—actuality—of what comes to pass—for example, a friendship which will never be reduced to the desire or the potentiality of friendship. If we insist, in turn, on this necessary limitation in the analysis of conditions of possibility, in this thought of the possible, it is for at least *two reasons*.

1. First of all, beyond this singular context (Aristotle on primary friendship), the wake of such a limitation crosses an immense problematic field, that of history, of the event, of the singularity of that which

comes to pass in general. It is not enough that something *may* happen for it to happen, of course; hence an analysis of what *makes* an event *possible*— however indispensable it may continue to be, especially in Aristotle's eyes—will never tell us anything about the event itself. But this evidence would still be too simple if one merely deduced from it an *order of good sense*: one that goes from the possible to the real, and from a retrograde *analytic* of the possible to the taking into account of the event, in the novelty of its appearance and the uniqueness of its occurrence. One cannot merely analyse the conditions of possibility, even the potentiality, of what occurs 'once', and then believe—this would be so naive—that one can say something pertinent about it. That which occurs, and thereby occurs only once, for the first and last time, is always something more or less than its possibility. One can talk endlessly about its possibility without ever coming close to the thing itself in its coming. It may be, then, that the order is other—*it may well be*—and that only the coming of the event allows, after the event [*après coup*], *perhaps*, what it will previously have made possible to be thought. To stay with our example: it is the experience of primary friendship, the meeting of its presence in act, that authorizes the analysis of *éxis* and of all predisposition—as well, for that matter, as of the two other types of friendships (derived, non-primary).

Among the immense consequences of this strong logical necessity, we must reckon with those concerning nothing less than revelation, truth and the event: a thought (ontological or meta-ontological) of conditions of possibility and structures of revealability, or of the opening on to truth, may well appear legitimately and methodologically anterior to gaining access to all singular events of revelation—and the stakes of this irreducible anteriority of *good sense* or *common sense* are limitless. 'In fact', 'in truth', it would be only the event of revelation that would open—like a breaking-in, making it possible after the event—the field of the possible in which it appeared to spring forth, and for that matter actually did so. The event of revelation would reveal not only this or that—God, for example—but revealability itself. By the same token, this would forbid us saying 'God, for example'.

Is there an alternative here? Must one choose between these two orders? And is this necessary first of all in the case of the so-called 'revealed' religions, which are also religions of the social bond according to *loving* (love, friendship, *fraternity*, charity, and so forth)? Must one choose between the priority of *revelation* (*Offenbarung*) and that of *revealability* (*Offenbarkeit*), the priority of manifestation and that of manifestability, of theology and theiology, of the science of God and the science of the divine, of the divinity of God?[26] And above all, supposing there were an alternative between these two orders, what difference would it make to introduce this Aristotelian proposition according to which there could never be (primary) friendship between God and man? We shall come across this question again, but it implicitly organizes all reflection on the possibility of a politics of friendship.

2. The thought of the act or the event from which the Aristotelian argument derives its authority is also, rather than a thought of each (good sense and common sense), a thought of 'each one', of individual singularity. It is true that this thought of *each one* can take root, in order to return, in *phrónesis*, in perspicacious judgement and in the prudence of common sense. If the indispensable possibility of *éxis* does not suffice, if for that one must pass to the act and if that takes time while overcoming time, this is because one must choose and prefer: election and selection between friends and things (*prágmata*), but also between possible friends—and this will soon lead us back to the vicinity of an '*O phíloi oudeis phílos*', whose 'O' we shall not determine for the moment, and to its arithmetic lesson. Why are the mean, the malevolent, the ill-intentioned (*phauloi*) not, by definition, good friends? Why do they ignore the sharing or the community of friends (*koina ta phílōn*)? Because they prefer things (*prágmata*) to friends. They stock friends among things, they class friends at best among possessions, among good things. In the same stroke, they thus inscribe their friends in a field of relativity and calculable hypotheses, in a hierarchical multiplicity of possessions and things. Aristotle affirms the opposite: in order to accomplish the antithesis of these mean people or bad friends, I assign (*prosnémō*) relations otherwise, and distribute the priorities differently. I include good things among friends or in view of friends. Here is a preference neglected by the wicked. They invert or pervert this good hierarchy in truth by including their friends among things or in view of things, instead of treating things as things of friendship, as affairs (*prágmata*) belonging to the sphere of friends, serving the cause of friends, assigned first and foremost to friends.[27]

Recommending this preferential attribution, Aristotle speaks, then, of friends rather than of friendship. One must not only prefer friendship, but give the preference to friends. Since it is a question of singularities, this is an inevitable consequence: one must prefer *certain* friends. The choice of this preference reintroduces number and calculation into the multiplicity of incalculable singularities, where it would have been preferable not to reckon with friends as one counts and reckons with things. So the arithmetic consideration, the terrible necessity of reckoning with the plurality of friends (*phíloi*, this plural that we shall come across again later in the two possible grammars for the sentence quoted and examined by Montaigne), still depends on temporality, on the time of friendship, on the essence of *philía* that never works without time (*áneu khrónou*). One must not have too many friends, for there is not enough *time* to put them to *the test by* living with *each one*.

For one must live with each him. With each her.

Is that possible?

Living—this is understood with *with*. Whatever the modalities may later be, living is living with. But every time, it is only one person living with another: I *live*, myself, *with* (*suzao*), and with each person, every time with one person. In the passage we will quote in translation, the conjunction between the test or the experience (*peira*) of time (*khronos*) and of singularity, of each one (*ékastos*) must yet again be underlined. This bond of time and number in the principle of singularity is never separated from the hierarchical principle: if one must choose, then the best must be chosen. A certain aristocracy is analytically encompassed in the arithmetic of the choice:

> The primary friendship (*e philía e prōte*) then is not found towards *many* (*en pollois*), for it is hard to test many men (*kalepon pollôn peiram labein*), for one would have to live with each (*ekásto gar an édei suzêtai*). Nor should one choose a friend like a garment. Yet in all things it seems the mark of a sensible man (*tou noun ékhontos*) to choose the *better* of two alternatives; and if one has used the worse garment for a long time and not the *better*, the better is to be chosen, but not in place of an old friend (*anti tou pálai philou*), one of whom you do not know whether he is *better*. For a friend is not to be had *without trial* (*áneu peíras*) nor in a single day (*mias ēméras*), *but there is need of time* (*alla khrónou dei*) and so 'the bushel of salt' has become proverbial.[28]

The bushel-of-salt proverb recalls simultaneously the test and the parcelling-out, the experience and the part taken: one must have eaten *the whole* bushel of salt *with someone* before one is able to trust him, in a stable, sure, time-tested way, but the time of renewed 'fidence' eludes time, it conquers time in yet another way. Previously, the stable steadfastness of the reliable (*bébaios*) appeared to us in the form of continuity, duration or permanence: the omnitemporality that in time overcomes time. But to pass to the act beyond *éxis*, to be renewed and reaffirmed at every instant, the reliable in friendship supposes a re-invention, a reengagement of freedom, a virtue (*areté*) that interrupts the animal analogy we were discussing above. This is another way of negating time in time, this time in the form of discontinuity, through the reinvention of the event. But here again the economy of time, even of the 'at the same time' (*áma*), commands that the instant of the act and the plenitude of *energeia* be linked to the calculation of number. The test of friendship remains, for a finite being, an endurance of arithmetic. Indeed, the friend must not only be good in himself, in a simple or absolute (*aplôs*) manner, he must be good for you, in relation to you who are his friend. The friend is absolutely good *and* absolutely or simply the friend when these two qualities are in harmony, when they are 'symphonious' with one another. All the more so, no doubt, when the friend is useful to his friend even if he is not absolutely virtuous or good (*spoudaios*). This last passage[29] is famous for its reputed obscurity, but the conclusion seems clear: it is not possible to love while one is simultaneously, at the same time (*áma*), the friend of numerous others (*to de pollois áma einai phílon kai to phileîn kōlúei*); the numerous ones, the numerous others—this means neither number nor multiplicity in general but *too great a number* a certain determined excess of units. It is possible to love more than one person, Aristotle seems to concede; to love in number, but not too much so—not too many. It is not the number that is forbidden, nor the more than one, but the numerous, if not the crowd. The measure is given by the act, by the capacity of loving *in act*: for it is not possible to be in act (*energein*), effectively, actively, presently at the heart of this 'numerous' (*pros pollous*) which is more than simple number (*ou gar oión te áma pros pollous energein*). A finite being could not possibly be present *in act* to too great a number. There is no belonging or friendly community that is *present*, and first present *to itself*, *in act*, without election and without selection.

This will have been understood in a flash: if the question of arithmetic seems grave and irreducible here, the word 'arithmetic' remains inadequate. The units in question are neither things, these *prágmata* to which the friend must always be preferred, nor numbers. This restrained multiplicity calls for an account, certainly, and one must not have too many friends, but it nevertheless resists enumeration, counting-off, or even pure and simple quantification.

Why do we insist on this difficulty here and now? First of all, because it announces one of the possible secrets—thus hiding it still—in the cryptic tradition of the apostrophe brought up by Montaigne and so many others. One of the secrets which has remained a secret for the reporters themselves, as if it had to reserve itself for a few people. We will come back to this later. Next, because this secret merges with virtue's (*areté*). We should not pretend to know what this word means without having thought the enigma of *phileîn*. No doubt they are one and the same. And finally, because the quantification of singularities will always have been one of the political dimensions of friendship, of a becoming-political of a friendship which may not be political through and through—not originarily, necessarily or intrinsically. With this becoming-political, and with all the schemata that we will recognize therein—beginning with the most problematic of all, that of fraternity— the question of democracy thus opens, the question of the citizen or the subject as a countable singularity. And that of a 'universal fraternity'. There is no democracy without respect for irreducible singularity or alterity, but there is no democracy without the 'community of friends' (*koína ta philōn*), without the calculation of majorities, without identifiable, stabilizable, representable subjects, all equal. These two laws are irreducible one to the other. Tragically irreconcilable and forever wounding. The wound itself opens with the necessity of having to *count* one's friends, to count the others, in the economy of one's own, there where every other is altogether other.

But where every other is *equally* altogether other. More serious than a contradiction, political desire is forever borne by the disjunction of these two laws. It also bears the chance and the future of a democracy whose ruin it constantly threatens but whose life, however, it sustains, like life itself, at the heart of its *divided virtue*, the inadequacy to itself. Would virtue ever have existed without the chaos opening in silence, like the ravenous mouth of an immeasurable abyss, between one or the other of these laws of the other? There is no virtue without this tragedy of number without number. This is perhaps even more unthinkable than a tragedy. The unthinkable filters through Aristotle's staid treatise, under his worldly-wise counsel, under the wisdom of his precepts: my friends, if you want to have friends, do not have too many.

Note that the counsellor never says *how many*, nor at what number virtue becomes impossible. What knowledge could ever measure up to the injunction to choose between those whom one loves, whom one must love, whom one can love? Between themselves? Between them and the others? All of them?

At stake is virtue, which is no longer in nature, this virtue whose name will remain suspended, without an assured concept, as long as these two laws of friendship will not have been thought. For the reliability of the stable (*bébaios*), that on which virtue depends—therefore of liberty, decision and reflection—can no longer be only natural. No more so than time, which does not belong to nature when it puts primary friendship to the test. In the history of the concept of nature—and already in its Greek history—the virtue of friendship will have dug the trench of an opposition. For it obliges Aristotle himself to restrain the concept of nature: he must oppose it to its other—here to virtue—when he classes friendship among stable things (*tôn bebaíōn*), in the same way as happiness belongs to self-sufficient and autarkic things (*tôn autárkōn*). It is the same immanence that provides shelter from external or random causalities. And constancy is virtuous only by reason of its autonomy, of the autarky of decisions which renew themselves, freely and according to a spontaneous repetition of their own movement, always new but anew and newly the same, 'samely' new. This is not possible without some naturality, but that is not in nature: it does not come down to nature. Having quoted and approved Euripides' *Electra* (*e gar phúsis bébaios, ou ta khremata*: for nature is stable, not wealth), Aristotle adds that it is much more beautiful (*polu de kállion*) to say virtue (*areté*) in this case rather than nature (*polu de kállion eipein oti ē areté tés phúseōs*).[30] Since friendship does not—and above all must not—have the reliability of a natural thing or a machine; since its stability is not given by nature but is won, like constancy and 'fidence', through the endurance of a virtue, primary friendship, 'that which allows all the others to be named' (*di'ēn ai állai légontai*), we must say that it is founded on virtue (*é kat'aretēn estí*).[31] The pleasure it gives, the pleasure that is necessary—this is the immanent pleasure of virtue. There may well be other forms of friendship, those whose name is thereby derived from primary friendship (for example, says Aristotle, with children, animals, and the wicked), but they never imply virtue, nor equality in virtue. For if all the species of friendship (the three principal ones, according to virtue, to usefulness or to pleasure) imply equality or equity (*isótēs*), only primary friendship demands an equality of virtue between friends, in what assigns them reciprocally to one another.

What can such equality in virtue be? What can it be measured against? How do you calculate a non-natural equality whose evaluation remains both immanent, as we have just seen, but at the same time obliged to reciprocity—that is, to a certain symmetry? One wonders what is left of a friendship which makes the virtue of the other its own condition (be virtuous if you want me to love you), but one wonders, too, what would be left of friendship without this condition, and when the number without number intervenes, when virtue is not dispensed in excess. And how can we reconcile this first imperative, that of primary friendship, with what we have begun to uncover: the necessary unilaterality of a dissymmetrical *phileîn* (you are better off loving than being loved) and the terrible but so righteous law of *contretemps*?

Is there a conflict here in the philosophy of *phileîn*, in the Aristotelian philosophy of friendship? For other Aristotelian axioms, which we shall consider, seem to forbid or contradict the call of dissymmetry and this law of *contretemps*. For example, the axiom which holds that the friend is

another self who must have the feeling of his own existence—an inseparable axiom which makes friendship proceed from self-love, from
philautía, which is not always egoism or *amour-propre*.

Unless one would find the other in oneself, already: the same dissymmetry and tension of *surviving* in self, in the 'oneself' thus out of joint
with its own existence. To be able or to have to be the friend of
oneself—this would change nothing in the testamentary structure we are
discussing. It would break all ipseity apart in advance, it would ruin in
advance that which it makes possible: narcissism and self-exemplarity.
We are speaking about anything but narcissism as it is commonly understood: Echo, the possible Echo, she who speaks from, and steals, the
words of the other [*celle qui prend la parole aux mots de l'autre*], she who
takes the other at his or her word, her very freedom preceding the first
syllables of Narcissus, his mourning and his grief. We are speaking of
anything but the exemplarity of the Ciceronian *exemplar*. An arche-
friendship would inscribe itself on the surface of the testament's seal. It
would call for the last word of the last will and testament. But in
advance it would carry it away as well.

It would be extraneous neither to the other justice nor to the other
politics whose possibility we would like, perhaps, to see announced here.

Through, perhaps, another experience of the possible.

Notes

1 Michel de Montaigne, *The Essays* [trans. M. A. Screech, Allen Lane, Penguin
  Press, London 1991].
2 Cicero, *Laelius de Amicitia* [trans. F. O. Copley, *On Friendship*, Ann Arbor
  Paperbacks, University of Michigan Press 1971], p. 56. For the numerous
  translations we will henceforth be quoting, the following rule will be
  followed: no revision or modification (one always says: 'slightly' modified) of
  any kind, nor additions in parentheses from the original text except when
  we deem them indispensable for the clarity of our argument.
3 Ibid.
4 *Eudemian Ethics*, 1234b, 18 ff. [Revised Oxford trans.]
5 A fortunate coincidence: in the seminar that I am following here, I believed
  the word *aimance* indispensable for the naming of a third or first voice, the
  so-called middle voice, on the near or far side of loving (friendship or love),
  of activity or passivity, decision or passion. Now, luckily, I come across this
  word, invented by a friend, a poet-thinker I admire: Abdelkebir Khatibi,
  who sings this new word in *Dédicace à l' année qui vient* [*Dedication to the
  Upcoming Year*], Fata Morgana 1986: 'I will have desired only aimance,
  lovence', 'our law of lovence', 'on the frontiers of lovence', 'Go and come in
  the cycle of lovence', 'Lovence. Lovence. . . . The only word I ever invented/
  In the sentence of my life?'. He recalls the word at the beginning of *Par-
  dessus l'épaule* [*Over the Shoulder*], Aubier 1988, which presents 'lovence in
  two sequences, one addressed to women, and the other to men'.

6 *Eudemian Ethics*, 1234b 21.
7 1234b 18–20.
8 1235a 5.
9 1234b 22–3.
10 1239a 33–4.
11 Ibid.
12 1237a 35–40.
13 1239a 27–30.
14 For example, *Eudemian Ethics*, 1239a 4, 20; *Nicomachean Ethics*, 1159b [revised Oxford trans.].
15 *Eudemian Ethics*, 1239a 36; *Nicomachean Ethics*, 1159a 30.
16 *Eudemian Ethics*, 1159a 29.
17 1239a 40; 1239b 1–2.
18 1237a 40, 1239b 1–2.
19 Ibid.
20 1237b 17.
21 1237b 13.
22 1237b 10–15
23 Plato, *The Banquet*, 182c.
24 Plato, *Timaeus*, 37b.
25 *Eudemian Ethics*, 1237b 15.
26 For these distinctions marked notably by Heidegger, and for the questions they bring up, allow me to refer to 'Comment ne pas parler' in *Psyché, Inventions de l'autre*, Galilée 1987, pp. 586 ff. ['How to Avoid Speaking', in *Languages of the Unsayable*, ed. Sanford Budick and Wolfgang Iser, trans. Ken Frieden, Columbia University Press, New York.] What I called elsewhere *iterability* might not dissolve this alternative but might at least give access to a structure of experience in which the two poles of the alternative cease to oppose one another to form another node, another 'logic', another 'chronology', another history, another relation to the order of orders.
27 *Eudemian Ethics*, 1237b 30–34.
28 1237b 34, 1238a 3.
29 1238a 5–10.
30 1238a 10–15.
31 1238a 30.

Part VI
Politics

11 'ONTO-THEOLOGY OF NATIONAL-HUMANISM (PROLEGOMENA TO A HYPOTHESIS)'

ORIGINALLY PUBLISHED IN 1992 IN *OXFORD LITERARY REVIEW* 14: 1–23

Translated by Geoffrey Bennington

Themes

Philosophy is both necessarily universal in its claims and is necessarily idiomatic. That is, all philosophy is written in a particular language and that language is just one idiom. The use of the word 'idiom' emphasises something local and limited, which is the condition of all languages in relation to the assumed universality of philosophy. This is a constitutive contradiction of philosophy, which may appear to be a scandal of philosophy. There is no possibility of philosophy which is not a scandal since contradiction can never be eliminated. The question of idiom in philosophy is not just a linguistic question, and in general no question of language could be just a linguistic question for Derrida. The question of idiom is also the question of property and propriety. Property refers to the way that an idiom lays claim to be the owner of philosophy, and propriety refers to the way that an idiom claims that it is the proper idiom for philosophy.

Derrida refers to the ways in which philosophers have explicitly claimed that their language is the philosophical language, a claim most associated with German philosophers. The argument is also concerned with the implicit claim to be using the right language for philosophy whenever writing about language. This goes beyond deliberate nationalism, or accusations of nationalism. It is the unavoidable claim we are making when philosophising. We must be claiming that what we have said is right, so we are implicitly claiming that the words of a particular idiom are the words appropriate to that philosophical truth. Questions of nationality are therefore not accidental and make up a 'philosopheme', that is a necessary theme of philosophy. The self-positing of a nation is a philosophical moment including the questions of language and proper language, with regard to the language of that nation. Another Derridean concern here is the paradox of self-constitution and origin which will be discussed in the next chapter.

Derrida ties the question of nationalism in philosophy to the emergence of political nationalism as a theme in philosophy in J.G. Fichte's *Addresses to the German Nation* (Fichte 1979 [originally published 1808]), written as a response to Napoleon Bonaparte's invasion of France and generally regarded as a key moment in the emergence of modern nationalism in Germany and in general. Derrida points out that Fichte does not just argue for nationalism, he is also arguing for cosmopolitanism. Cosmopolitanism is an issue Derrida addresses in 'Hostipitality' (Chapter 9). Nationalism and cosmopolitanism can co-exist and even reinforce each other, where 'the Nation' is taken as a uniquely universal nation, bearing the ends of humanity as a whole. Philosophical nationalism and cosmopolitanism connect with the humanist issues Derrida discusses in his 1968 paper 'The Ends of Man' (in Derrida 1982). In accordance with this, German nationality becomes a philosophical *telos* in Fichte, and he is able to offer a cosmopolitan basis for annexationist politics.

Derrida refers to Marx in the diagnosis of nationalism in philosophical essentialism. The text is *The German Ideology* (Marx 1998 [written 1845]), the one Althusser thought marked the emergence of a 'mature Marx' in the 'epistemological break' that marks the emergence of a science of social formations (For Marx, Althusser 1996 [first published 1965]). It is only after the 1989 fall of the Berlin Wall, and the Soviet socialist bloc, that Derrida starts to put much emphasis on Marx. The most notable example is *Spectres of Marx* (Derrida 1994 [first published 1993]). The overall effect is not a return to Marxism, but rather an absorption of Marx into a politics of social justice and globalist ethics, which is more left-liberal than Marxist revolutionary. Some Derrideans find support for more radical left politics in his texts, but many radical left writers find Derrida to be too integrated into an individualistic and abstract legalistic way of thinking. If Derrida is a Marxist, it is only at the extreme liberal frontier of revisionist thinking, though that is a position with notable precedents. It has even become a crowded territory that includes notable social and political thinkers like Jürgen Habermas and Slavoj Žižek. Occasional references to Tran Duc Thao, a Vietnamese

Marxist and phenomenologist, who studied with Merleau-Ponty, in *Speech and Phenomena* were expanded when Derrida published his graduate thesis on phenomenology, *The Problem of Genesis in Husserl's Philosophy* (Derrida 2003 [written 1954]). Tran's *Phenomenology and Dialectical Materialism* (Tran 1986 [first published 1951]) brings a Marxist inspired materialist reading to phenomenology, which Derrida found of considerable interest. The relevant history is covered in a paper by Tim Herrick (Herrick 2005). Derrida finds a double nationalism analysed in Marx in which first there is national identity and second there is the superiority of one nation. This is something evidently present in Fichte and Hegel, and as Derrida points out later, in Heidegger and Adorno. The issue arises for all discussions of national philosophical tradition and translation between traditions.

Context

In the context of analytic philosophy, tradition and nationhood is subordinated to the neutrality of pure concepts. Nevertheless considerations of philosophical nationalism do enter into analytic philosophy, as with Fichte in claiming a cosmopolitan status. Analytic philosophy can claim to be multi-national and multi-lingual in origin. Apart from the English language founders, like Bertrand Russell and Charles Peirce, there are Germans such as Frege and Reichenbach; the Austrians Wittgenstein and Carnap; the Pole Tarski. Nevertheless, the distinction between analytic and Continental philosophy goes back to J. S. Mill's suggestion of a distinction between British empiricism and German Romanticism, though Mill himself combined both influences. Many American philosophers, including W. V. O. Quine, Donald Davidson, Hilary Putnam and Richard Rorty, associate themselves with pragmatism. Pragmatism is a distinctly American school of philosophy, strongly associated with a spirit of American democracy, moral equality and practical hard-headedness. This is not what Quine, Davidson and Putnam emphasise, but that is certainly what is suggested in the classic texts of Charles Peirce, William James and John Dewey. Bertrand Russell condemned pragmatism in *A History of Western Philosophy* (Russell 1993 [first published 1946]). He also condemned Marx, Bergson and Nietzsche in terms which clearly suggest that he found them to represent the less empirical and logical spirit of Continental culture, which had political consequences in Stalinism, Nazism and collaborationist regimes in Nazi occupied Europe. Russell's book was published just after the Second World War, and clearly has cultural-political motivation. He condemns political totalitarianism and its presumed roots in Continental European philosophy, while suggesting that American pragmatism is a justification for opportunism which sacrifices truth to convenience. There are clear echoes of traditional British and Continental European assumptions that the USA has a culture of acquisitiveness and money-making unconcerned with deeper principles. In Russell's time British analytic philosophy seemed to be at least the equal of American work. That has changed, partly because the Second World War pushed many German-speaking analytic philosophers into the USA, and it would be hard now to separate British and American philosophy because of the huge amount of cross influence which is inevitably weighted towards the USA.

Russell's assumptions were clearly shared by other analytic critics of Continental European philosophy, even those of European origins such as Karl Popper who moved from Vienna to London. Analytic philosophy is often surrounded by the assumption that it expresses an Anglo-American realistic and empirical outlook, and pragmatism is often surrounded by the assumption that American culture is uniquely democratic and practical. German philosophers like the Marxist Adorno and the ultra-conservative, sometime Nazi, Heidegger, assumed that German culture and philosophy were superior to American consumerism, liberalism and empiricism. These distinctions were never absolute (for example Putnam was a Maoist and Nietzsche, though difficult to tie down politically, was clearly more liberal, in a way partly inspired by the American transcendentalist Ralph Waldo Emerson, than nationalist or communist) and look less and less relevant as Continental European countries have become increasingly liberal democratic in politics, and market liberal in economics. The increasing influence of analytic philosophy in Continental Europe and the increasing study of Continental European philosophy in the Anglophone world is surely weakening the old philosophical oppositions. Nevertheless, the study of philosophy must include the study of these nationalist-cosmopolitan equivocations.

These issues enter into political philosophy both in the sense that normative theory (analytic political philosophy) includes national assumptions in its universalist claims and that nationalism has become an object of philosophical discussion. Political philosophy is heavily influenced by the work of John Rawls, which is itself constructed around notions of legality and justice that clearly reflect the role of legalism, constitutionalism and the institutional role of the Supreme Court in American politics (A *Theory of Justice*, Rawls 1999a [first published 1971]). Another major source of American political philosophy is found in Ronald Dworkin (*Law's Empire*, Dworkin 1998) who brings philosophy of law and political philosophy together. The major alternatives still have markedly American traces. The libertarianism of Robert Nozick

(*Anarchy, State and Utopia*, Nozick 1977) is established in terms of absolutism about property rights and the devolution of power to basic communities, held together only by pure legalism, which has very evident precedents in American traditions of property-owning free market individuals and decentralised federalism. The communitarianism of Michael Sandel (*Liberalism and the Limits of Justice*, Sandel 1998 [first published 1982]) has very evident precedents in American traditions of moralistic community and voluntary social solidarity promoted by a morally inspired state. There are different positions and even opposing positions within American political philosophy. Rawls and Nozick, for example, have opposed views on the redistribution of wealth by the state. Nevertheless there are clear, shared presuppositions. American Marxism exists but is weak generally and is not central to political philosophy. The limited role of the state; the strong role of law and of moral cohesion as substitutes for state coercion are important in all these thinkers.

Recent additions to these currents do not entirely originate in the USA but have filtered out to the world philosophical community via the USA and reflect American assumptions. Republicanism, which has its most influential philosophical representative in the Australian Philip Pettit, particularly in his book *Republicanism* (Pettit 1997), tends to emphasise social solidarity within the context of a state constituted by principles of consent, citizenship as an expression of human life, and the sovereignty of law. The Republican tradition in political philosophy is partly up with the emergence of the American Republic, though it does have other sources.

Nationalism and sub-national communities have been established as major philosophical themes by the Canadian Will Kymlicka. The thrust of his work, and related work, is simultaneously sub-national and cosmopolitan. The state is regarded as a member of a cosmopolitan community in which it is constrained by human rights standards, which include respect for minorities within the state (*Multicultural Citizenship*, Kymlicka 1995). The assumption is that federalism, interpreted as strong measures of political decentralisation weakening national state sovereignty, is the best way of protecting human rights in general, and sub-national communities in particular, from an over-mighty, homogenising, top-heavy central state. The central national state is weakened from the other side by the increasing importance of international law and international institutions. Minority rights extend to the treatment of migrants and refugees, in a general structure of thought which makes the protection of minorities a paramount concern of politics and of political philosophy. It is a rather Anglophone view of the issues, since it reflects an emphasis on multi-culturalism and ethnicity rather than the integrationism and less ethnic-difference-oriented politics of other political cultures. That is to use an extremely simplified opposition, but nevertheless a very recognisable one. The issues in Kymlicka include those Derrida is concerned with of immigration, refugees, international law and ethics, and pluralism of identity within a nation. Much of this is discussed in *On Cosmopolitanism and Forgiveness* (Derrida 2001 [first published 1997]). The last issue is given a linguistic context in *Monolingualism of the Other* (Derrida 1998a [first published 1996]).

In 'The Ends of Man', Derrida considers humanist metaphysics, a philosophy of the essence of man, as an expression of Western philosophy. Suggestions that Western metaphysics is ethnocentric also appear in 'Structure, Sign and Play', the 1971 paper 'White Mythology' (in Derrida 1982) and *Of Grammatology*. In the latter text, the suggestion is that Western metaphysics, with reference to Hegel, places the alphabetic languages of the West, which seem phonocentric, above the non-alphabetic characters of Chinese, which might seem to exclude the voiced word. Though these remarks have been taken up by some in the direction of post-colonial theory, there is very little of this kind of analysis in Derrida's own texts. What we have is Derrida looking at the supposed limits of Western metaphysics in vague reference to its supposed Other. The internal discussion is certainly the more substantial part of his philosophy.

ONTO-THEOLOGY OF NATIONAL-HUMANISM (PROLEGOMENA TO A HYPOTHESIS)

Under this title, my purpose is not, or at least not in the first place or, if you prefer, the last instance, to proceed to the historical, social, linguistic analysis of what would be called a philosophical nation or nationality. Such an analysis (in the terms of the social or human sciences) is of course not excluded from the seminar, and will even be necessary in it; I hope we shall undertake such an analysis in more than one way and above all that we shall interrogate its possibility—but it is not my first concern.

My principal concern, here, would, rather, move towards the aporias of the philosophical translation of philosophical idioms. In a slightly abrupt way, as with any beginning, I shall say that there are—this is our experience and I shall speak of this experience and its rights in a moment—there are and we experience the fact that there are *several* philosophical idioms and that this experience alone cannot not be lived by a philosopher, by a self-styled philosopher, by whoever claims to be a philosopher, as both a *scandal* and as the very *chance* of philosophy.

A scandal: i.e. what makes philosophy trip and fall, what stops it in its tracks if the self-styled philosopher considers that philosophy is essentially universal and cosmopolitan, that national, social, idiomatic difference in general should only befall it as a provisional and non-essential accident that could be overcome. Philosophy ought not to *suffer* difference of idiom: it ought not to tolerate it, and ought not to suffer from it. So any affirmation of the idiom or of the irreducibility of the idiom would be an aggression or a profanation with regard to the philosophical as such.

A scandal, but also a chance, in so far as the only possibility for a philosophy, for philosophy itself to speak itself, to be discussed, to get (itself) across, to go from the one to the other, is to pass through idioms, to transport the idiom and transport itself, translate itself via or rather in the body of idioms which are not closures or enclosings of self but allocutions, passages to the other. For the question, obviously, is: what is an idiom?

I do not want to overhasten the elaboration of this question. For a long time to come it will form the very horizon, that is, if we speak Greek, if we say the horizon in Greek, both the opening and the *limit* of this seminar.

I shall say simply of this word 'idiom', that I have just very rapidly thrust forward, that for the moment I am not restricting it to its linguistic, discursive circumscription, although, as you know, usage generally folds it back towards that limit—idiom as linguistic idiom. For the moment, while keeping my eye fixed especially on this linguistic determination which is not all there is to idiom, but which is not just one determination of it among others, I shall be taking 'idiom' in a much more indeterminate sense, that of prop(ri)e(r)ty, singular feature, in principle inimitable and inexpropriable. The *idion* is the proper. And given this, if I say that my most proper concern in this seminar is idiomatic difference in philosophy, it is nonetheless not entirely in an accessory or absent-minded manner that I chose for its title, 'Philosophical nationality and nationalism'. So the question would be, if you would be so kind as to take this title seriously: what is a national idiom in philosophy? How does a philosophical idiom pose itself, claim its rights, appear to itself, attempt to impose itself as a national idiom? Which comes down to wondering, naturally, 1. What is a nation?—and the question, as you well imagine, is not a simple one, it has a history that's as hard as can be to delimit, it is to be confused neither with the question of people, nor that of race, nor that of State, although at every step it crosses these questions and gives rise to the most serious equivocations. We shall return to this at great length. *And* this comes down to wondering, 2. Even supposing that we have a clear concept, secured by a consensus (the question of the consensus being itself implied in that of the so-called national feeling, consciousness or reality), even supposing that a consensus take place as to the concept of nationality, the second question comes down to wondering what a national idiom, a philosophical nationality can be. In order to wonder what that can be, we have all the same to begin by recognising that there have been *at least* pretensions to philosophical nationality, discourses which claim to recognise national philosophical characteristics, in oneself or in others, sometimes to praise them, sometimes to discredit them. This national idiom may or may not be linked, by those who speak of it, to a given language. We shall have to talk about this a lot more.

When I say that my principal *concern*, at least in this seminar, is primarily that of philosophical idiom or translatability, and immediately afterwards the link of that idiom to a national characteristic, what does this mean, and why do I call it a concern?

I call it a concern—I could have used a different word—to mark the fact that this is not for me, nor, I imagine, for anyone involved with philosophy, an *object* of study, meaning by that a theme or a problem that one has before one and in which one is not really and gravely situated, circumvented, precomprehended, in what is precisely a historical and philosophical situation with respect to which no overarching view is possible—and in the first instance for the obvious reason that the question is set out in a language, in an idiom, and with certain features of the national idiom. I believe that the question of philosophical nationality and nationalism, which, in a variety of ways has always occupied all philosophers, concerns us today in a particular way. Let's say in an unavoidable way, if that means that the destiny of philosophy is played out here in a way permitting of no distraction on this subject. We are today in a phase of the history of this problem which I believe to be extremely acute and paradoxical. Paradoxical because never as much as today has what is called by the confused and problematical word 'communication' between territories, institutions, groups, schools, national idioms been apparently, quantitatively, technically, statistically more manifest, more intense or important. Statistical evaluation here goes via the number of colloquia, translations, exchanges of teachers and researchers, instruments of storage and archivisation, etc. Yet at the same moment, it seems to me, the effects of opacity, national limits or even nationalistic claims have never been as marked as they are today. These two facts—one could give many illustrations and a great deal of evidence for them, but allow me for the moment to leave that to one side—are only apparently contradictory and what I've been calling a paradox is at the same time a very intelligible phenomenon, let's even say a normal one. It is at the very moment at which there is an intensification of what takes the form of exchanges, meetings, so-called philosophical communication, at which this exposes the at least supposed national differences to influences, grafts, deformations, hybridisations, etc., at this very moment that national consciousness, search for identity, affirmation or even national demands show up more clearly, or even become exasperated and tense up into nationalism. The intensification of exchanges is also a sort of state of war, a war in the course of which, as in all wars, you see the enemy everywhere, and the collaborator, the enemy within, the one who in France likes German philosophy too much, who in the USA is over-impressed by French philosophy, or in Britain by Continental philosophy, etc. And then, as always in such cases, there are in each national territory those who want to revive the national philosophical fibre, reconstitute the right tradition, reevaluate the corpus and the national heritage (there are examples of this everywhere, here and there, especially in France or the USA, and even in Japan where there is a flurry of articles trying to demonstrate that for example post-structuralism or what is called deconstruction is very like what Zen thinking, and especially that of Master Dogen, developed centuries ago. There has been an analogous phenomenon in China over the last few years, since a certain opening to the West is producing exactly the same effects there. I do not read Chinese, and I don't know what is being published there, but if I am to judge by what I've been given to read in English (in itself a significant fact which we shall return to), written by young Chinese philosophers gone to study in the USA, the same phenomenon is being reproduced: an insistence on the analogy of French post-structuralism, for example, and the deconstruction of phono-logocentrism, with this or that Chinese national tradition.) And these demonstrations—I won't go into the detail of them, at least not today—are simultaneously convincing and irrelevant, plausible and blind to their own presupposition. What I'm saying about post-structuralism or deconstruction (I get more signs of it because I get sent the texts, or because there's a higher probability I'll come across them) is obviously also taking place with other currents of thought, as they say. It would be interesting, or at least amusing, to draw up today a map, or more precisely a national and international table of different philosophical situations, not by sticking little flags in, as some philosophical warmongers sometimes do, but by analysing the paths of influence, the implantations, the transplant rejections, the fronts, with all the institutional phenomena (academic or not), and all the political stakes that meet up here. The theory and category of reception is no doubt inadequate to measure up to these phenomena, but let's say for the moment, for convenience, that a table of this sort, which I certainly shan't sketch out now, would bring out for example the reception of Anglo-American analytical philosophy in West Germany over the last 20 years, its old and new premises, its philosophical and extra-philosophical conditions, its development, its transformation, what essentially distinguishes it from the reception of the same tradition in France; or again the difference between the reception of French philosophy, or at least a certain French theoretical discourse from the '60s and '70s, in Britain or the

USA, i.e. in a milieu which, at least from the linguistic point of view, is, if not homogeneous, then at least extremely permeable. Why are things happening in radically different ways in Britain and the USA? This fact would suffice, to a large extent, to dissociate the national phenomenon in philosophy from the narrowly, strictly linguistic one.

Of course, this intensification of so-called international exchanges, and this exasperation of national identities and identifications, which for now I am merely pointing out in their most obvious manifestations, call for a great many vigilant precautions in the approach one might make to them. For now, I shall simply situate three of four of them.

1. We cannot yet trust what I' ve been calling 'national identity'. We shall have to ask ourselves . . . and this will be one of the objects of the seminar—not only what is the essence of a nation, if there is such a thing, but what is the history of the concept or of national identity as such. For the moment, I am making or reproducing a 'doxical', common, trivial but not insignificant use of the word 'nationality'. And when I say 'doxical', this does not only mean that it is used outside strictly philosophical discourse, but that it is also in use, most often, among many philosophers.

2. This determination of a current situation—for the moment it is no more than approximative . . . cannot be purely external, outside the philosophical as such: sociological, linguistic, techno-economic, historico-political, etc. All these knowledges, indispensible here, are nonetheless situated in the same field and situated with respect to the philosophical as such, in relation with it—however this relation be determined. The inter-national situation I am talking about is also a situation of the philosophical as such. Call it a historical situation, or an epoch in the history of Being, the fact remains that each of the names and concepts used to define and name this situation corresponds to a gesture which is either philosophical or meta-philosophical but cannot in any case correspond to a region of knowledge, to a given social or human science (sociology, linguistics, history, political science, techo-economics, political economy) as such—again, whatever the interest and the necessity of such a 'scientific' or supposedly scientific procedure in this case. I do not say this to reconstitute the fundamental or funda-mentalist problematic that institutes philosophy as general or fundamental ontology, as Greater Logic from which all determinate knowledge, all sciences, would occupy a regional and dependent position. For a long time now, I have tried to show how in apparently regional scientific practices, in ontologies that philosophy says are regional, one can find general deconstructive movements, where the ground falls away or shifts, disorganising or calling into question the beautiful order of

dependence between a fundamental ontology and regional ontologies. This 'rhetoric' —let's call it that—of the region, which was explicitly used by Husserl and after him, is, moreover, not without its links with a thinking of territory ruled by a law, subordinated in its regional circumscriptions to a central juridico-political authority, to a philosophical capital—and, given this, in this rhetoric which is more that a rhetoric, the schema of the relations between State and nation is not far off.

So if I insist on this problem—on this fact that the situation of the philosophical international I'm talking about is not determinable on the basis of a social or human science—this is not in order to reconstitute a higher critical, transcendental or ontological authority over the human or social sciences, but also in order to problematise a certain authority of the same type that a given social science might claim over the treatment of this problem, and as to its competence to deal with it.

[I insist on this fact so as not to evade reflecting on the situation of this seminar and the initiative I'm taking in it, the slightly odd place marked here. Officially, legally, symbolically, this is a seminar given in the premises of the Ecole normale supérieure in the rue d' Ulm, in a room, on a day and time at which I am supposed to have been teaching philosophy for 20 years, but this time a seminar given under the aegis of the Ecole des Hautes Etudes en Sciences Sociales, an institution to which I henceforth belong, having been elected to it last year. Does this mean that *de jure* or *ipso facto* the discourse I shall be producing or the teaching I shall be giving here will fall under the social sciences, social sciences talking about philosophy or 'philosophical institutions' (since this is the title of the post I chose to occupy)? This seminar will also be a philosophical seminar talking philosophically about philosophy, even if it is not limited to this self-questioning or reflexive dimension of philosophy. It is not insignificant that this post should be the first to involve the name 'philosophy' in its title—and this fact, which is no doubt very overdetermined, cannot be insignificant and would be worth interrogating as such. What has to happen for a social sciences institution to receive into itself—*de jure*—someone or some discourse statutarily defined by an essential relation to the philosophical, there's a question I leave hanging for the moment but which I did not want to evade in this opening session. The reply is doubtless not all ready in some already given state, in a situation already past, but is waiting, can come only from the future, at least for a large part.]

3. Third preliminary precaution. This situation that I was just describing as paradoxical (intensification, acceleration of exchanges and so-called communication going along with an exasperation of identities, or claims to national identity), is one which it is very difficult to pick

out in its scansion or historical periodisation. When did this start? What is specific to our present today? What difference is there between what is happening today in this regard and what happened in the Seventeenth Century (and even before the Seventeenth Century), then in the Eighteenth and Nineteenth Centuries, in the Twentieth Century before and after the two World Wars, etc? These are questions that will lay siege to this seminar for a long time—for years, for I want the seminar to continue under this title for several years. What is certain is that today all the so-called professional philosophers feel this question to be inseparable from the stakes of philosophy itself, from the fate, destiny or destination of the philosphical as such, in its heart or its centre. I say that they 'feel' this, for it is often a sort of feeling, a sort of motivation which is more or less linked to a discursive elaboration as such, but which is one of those motivations that make things shift even if they are not taken up by a philosophical project as such, in the form of philosophy.

This depends, among other things, on the fact that, whatever its momentary indeterminacy and equivocality for us, the value of nation, nationality or nationalism—which we shall have to analyse incessantly—cannot have, with respect to the philosophical, to the philosophical project or decision, to philosophical affirmation as such, an extrinsic, accidental or contingent relation. The national problem, as we shall have ceaselessly to verify, is not one problem among others, nor one philosophical dimension among others. Even before any elaboration of the concept of nation and of philosophical nationality, of idiom as national philosophical idiom, we know at least this much—it's a minimal but indubitable predicate—namely that the affirmation of a nationality or even the claim of nationalism does not happen to philosophy by chance or from the outside, it is essentially and thoroughly philosophical, *it is a philosopheme*.

What does this mean? It means at least that a national identity is never posited as an empirical, natural character, of the type: such and such a people or such and such a race has black hair or is of the dolicephalic type, or else we recognise ourselves by the presence of such and such a characteristic. The self-positing or self-identification of the nation always has the form of a *philosophy* which, although better represented by such and such a nation, is none the less a certain relation to the universality of the philosophical. This philosophy, as structure of nationality, does not necessarily take the form or the representation of a system stated by professional philosophers in philosophical institutions; it can show up as spontaneous philosophy, an implicit philosophy but one that is very constitutive of a non empirical relationship with the world and a sort of potentially universal discourse, 'embodied', 'represented', 'localised' (all problematic words) by a particular nation. What I am saying is not limited to a reminder—although this is also true and I expect that we shall verify this—that the concept and word 'nation' are philosophical, and could not have been constituted, historically, outside a philosophical-type milieu and a discourse marked by a certain history of the philosophical as such. (A genealogy of the concept 'nation' would be more necessary than ever.) No, what I am saying is not limited to that. What I am saying concerns the structure of national consciousness, feeling and demand which means that a nation posits itself not only a bearer of a philosophy but of an exemplary philosophy, i.e. one that is both particular and potentially universal—and which is philosophical by that very fact. Not only does nationalism not happen like an accident or evil to a philosophy supposedly a stranger to it and which would, by essential vocation, be cosmopolitan and universalist, it is a philosophy, a discourse which is, structurally, philosophical. And it is universalist or cosmopolitan. Fichte's famous *Discourses to the German Nation*, to which we shall return often and at length, wants to be both nationalistic, patriotic and cosmopolitan, universalistic. It essentialises Germanity to the point of making it an entity bearing the universal and the philosophical as such. Nationalism never presents itself as a particularism but as a universal philosophical model, a philosophical *telos*, is why it is always philosophical in essence, even in its worst and most sinister manifestations, those that are the most imperialistic and the most vulgarly violent. In anticipation (for we shall come back to this attentively and systematically), listen to this passage from Fichte's 7th Discourse:

> In the nation (*In der Nation*) which to this day calls itself *the* people, or Germans (*sich nennt das Volk schlezchtweg oder deutsch*), originality (*ürsprungliches*) has broken forth into the light of day in modern times, at any rate up to now, and the power of creating new things (*Schöpferkraft des Neuen*) has shown itself. Now, at last, by a philosophy that has become clear in itself, the mirror [the mirror the clarity of which the philosophy has achieved] is being held up to this nation, in which it may recognise and form a clear conception of that which it has hitherto become by nature without being distinctly conscious of it (*ohne deutliches Bewusstsein*), and to which it is called by nature [*wozu sie von derselben bestimmt ist*: to which it is destined, according to its destinal determination]; and a proposal is being made to this nation to make itself wholly and completely what it ought to be (*sich selbst zu dem zu machen, was sie seyn soll*), to do this according to that clear conception and with free and deliberate

art, to renew this alliance (*den Bund zu erneuern*), and to close the circle (*ihren Kreis zu schliessen*).[1]

I interrupt for a moment my translation and quotation to emphasise certain points. 1. The German national principle is an essentially philosophical principle and it is to a philosophical discourse as such, i.e. one which is systematic and insofar as it is a thought of principles, a thought of the originary—here as we shall see of life and creativity—it is to such a discourse that it falls to bring to the clarity of the concept what was already there, as unconscious philosophy, but as philosophy nonetheless, in the German people. German nationality is essentially philosophical, it is philosophy, philosophical in essence; and in this sense, its idiom will be destined to universality. 2. The relation between the national principle (originary principle of originarity and creativity) as unconscious philosophical principle and its becoming-conscious in the philosophy of today, this relation between unconscious philosophy and conscious philosophy is a *circular* relation, of course. The figure of the circle imposes itself since the point for thematic philosophy is to return to an origin which, moreover, itself consists only in a principle of originarity and creativity. Creativity is circular, the creation of the new [*Schöpferkraft des Neuen*] is only a recourse, a ressource, a circular return to the source. But, 3. The figure of this circle is not of the order of geometry or of abstract movement, of mechanics, this circle is that of an alliance, of a bond [*Bund*] that must thus be reaffirmed, the alliance with its own origin and therefore its own destination, its own provenance which enjoins the German people to become what it is or what it must be. Whence the appeal to the liberty presupposed by every commitment, every alliance, even an alliance with oneself, with one's own unconscious, with one's originary past. One must contract and renew the alliance which thus shows up as much as a promise or an injunction as it does as a fact. This is an affirmation. In it the nationality affirmed immediately becomes a nationalism. This is why, as you will see, there is not, as it were, a German *fact*, a national fact in this discourse of nationalistic philosophy. The essence of the German is not to be confused with empirical factuality, with empirical belonging to the factual German nation, any more than empirical non-belonging to that German nation excludes the non-Germans from participation in some originary Germanity. All of this has an essential relation with a feature of Fichtean nationalism to which we shall return at length later, i.e. its (apparently) essentially linguistic, language-based essence, its rootedness in an interpretation of the German language—and nowhere else. Whence this paradoxical consequence, which one can consider either as an expansion of generosity, or as the imperialist expansionism of a people sure of itself, and dominant: whoever shares in this originary philosophy—of originarity, of life, of creative freedom—is German, even if they apparently belong to another people. They participate in the telological German identity, whereas on the contrary a *de facto* German is foreign to it if he is not a philosopher of that philosophy. I continue my quotation-translation:

> The principle (*Grundsatz*) according to which it has to close its circle is laid before it: whoever (*was*) believes in spirituality and in the freedom of this spirituality [the national principle: spiritual and non-natural, biological, or innate], who wills the eternal development (*ewige Fortbildung*) of this spirituality by freedom, wherever he may have been born and whatever language he speaks, is of our blood [*ist unser Geslecht*: is with us, is of our race, family, genealogy, filiation, almost 'sex'?: later, with regard to a text of Heidegger's, we really shall have to talk about this word, *Geschlecht*, so hard to translate], *es gehört uns an und es wird sich uns zu thun*, he is one of us, and will come over to our side. Whoever believes in stagnation (*Stillstand*), retrogression (*Rückgang*), and the round dance [*Cirkeltanz*: another circle, the circle of the dance and not of the alliance, the *Bund*] of which we spoke, or who sets a dead nature at the helm of the world's government (*an das Ruder der Weltregierung*), wherever he may have been born and whatever language he speaks, *ist undeutsch und fremd für uns*, is non-German and a stranger to us; and it is to be wished that he would separate himself from us completely [so even if he is born German and appears to speak German—in truth he does not speak German, not true German]. (pp. 107–8)

You see here—this is the only thing I wanted to illustrate for now by quoting Fichte, whom we shall study systematically later—that this nationalism is essentialist and archeo-teleological enough not to concern any German naturality or factuality—at least not in principle, and philosophically speaking, and that by that very fact, on the other hand, nationalist affirmation is thoroughly philosophical, it becomes merged with the evaluating, hierarchising evaluation of the best, true philosophy, with the philosophical principle and the philosophical *telos* as such. This nationalism does not even present itself as *a* philosophy, but as philosophy *itself*, philosophy par excellence. It will remain to find out whether in this way, its exemplary and exemplarist character warrants our saying that every nationalism in turn has the same destiny, i.e. that of presenting itself as philosophical and, better, as the universal *telos* of philosophy. Philosophy which is foreign (to German philosophy) is, in truth, so Fichte will say a little further on, a philosophy of death and therefore a non-philosophy:

> On the basis of what we said above about freedom, we can reveal at last and unmistakably to all those who have ears to hear what that philosophy, which with good reason calls itself German philosophy (*wer noch Ohren hat zu hören, der höre, was diejenige Philosophie, die mit gutem Fuge sich die deutsche nennt*) really wants, and wherein it is strictly, earnestly, and inexorably opposed to any foreign (*ausländischen*) philosophy that believes in death (*todtgläubigen Philosophie*). Let it appear before you, not in the least with the intention of making the dead understand it, which is impossible, but so that it may be harder for the dead to twist its words, and to make out that they themselves want more or less the same thing and at bottom are of the same kind (*dasselbe wolle und im Grunde meine*). (p. 108)

The logic of this last series of propositions is a little odd: a philosophy is foreign (understood as foreign to the German nation represented or rather identified with German philosophy) in so far as it is dead philosophy, philosophy as belief in death rather than in the living originarity, in so far as it is a philosophy of death—i.e. in so far as it is that of a dead people. As a dead people (be it composed factually of Germans, of so-called or self-styled Germans or not matters little) this dead one has no chance of understanding the truth of living philosophy, of philosophy as life, of the philosophy of life. So it is useless to proclaim this truth for him, at least with a view to convincing him—one cannot convince a dead man of life, of the force or necessity of life. But one must—and here is what is odd, but this is an oddness on which nonetheless rests the whole justification of a philosophical discourse or pedagogy (for there is no sense either in convincing the living of life), the dead man has nonetheless to be diverted, prevented from causing harm, we must prevent the doleful return of the dead who can still—for the dead have some power— *verdrehen die Worte*, falsify words, divert them from their meaning, twist them, pervert them, corrupt them in the shadow, in the shadow of death, which is shadow of nothing, the shadow of the shadow of a shadow, as Fichte calls it a little further on, still in the 7th Discourse:

> *In diesen Schatten von den Schatten der Schatten bleibt nun jene todtgläubige Seynsphilosophie ... behangen, die wohl gar*

Naturphilosophie wird, in these shadows of shadows of shadows that philosophy of beings which believes in death and becomes a mere philosophy of nature, the deadest of all philosophies (*die erterbenste von allen Philosophies*), remains a captive, and dreads and worships its own creature (*und fürchtet und betet an ihr eigenes Geschöpf*). (p. 109)

The philosophy of Being as philosophy of nature (in opposition to the philosophy of spirit and therefore life) is a philosophy of death, and therefore, as philosophy of nature, a denaturation of life. Between life and death, nationalism has as its own proper space the experience of haunting. There is no nationalism without some ghost.

But what must be saved above all, and this is the point I was keen to emphasize here, is language, the language, the true destination of words, their living destination which is still exposed to the return of the dead one, the malfeasant haunting of the foreigner who can still corrupt the language—which is, as we shall see later, the sole true foundation of German nationality as German philosophy. And yet belonging to the German nation, although it does not depend on birth, nor citizenship, nor geography, nor race, but only a certain relation to the language, is not, however, linguistic in the current and strict sense of the term . . . One may speak this essential German, this philosophical, philosophy-of-life German without speaking what is commonly called the German language; and conversely a German linguistic subject may not speak this essential German and speak, in German, a philosophy of death that is essentially foreign to the essential German. In that case, one would be speaking a German of the shades, a shade of the living tongue, of German as living tongue. Which means that, paradoxically, one can justifiably say that the foundation of essential Germanity is not even linguistic for Fichte—although it has an essential relation with a certain experience of language, for this essence of the national language is defined by philosophy, as philosophy of spirit and life, of originary creativity, and not by what is called the fact of natural language. In this sense Guéroult was correct to write this, for example: 'The word "German" takes on . . . an entirely cosmopolitan meaning . . . independently of any reference to ethnic, linguistic or geographical characteristics'.

You see how huge are the stakes, you see the extreme and threatening, worrying, murky equivocality of the signs—signs which are also pre—I will not say premonitory but preparatory, in the shadow of the shadows— of the most sinister and unavoidable modernity. In saying 'modernity', I am using a word which is very obscure and no doubt quite inappropriate, since I am not only using this word to refer to yesterday's modernity

(Nazism or other forms of nationalism) but to today's and tomorrow's, and since on the other hand, that so-called modernity begins the day before yesterday, not only with the age (we shall study others) for which Fichte is merely one of the heralds, but no doubt well before then too.

The equivocality of the signs, the heritages, the historical junctions, depends, among other things, on the following fact, which has not escaped you: this essentially philosophical nationalism (as I believe every nationalism is philosophical, and this is the main point I wanted to emphasise at the outset) claims to be totally foreign to any naturalism, biologism, racism, or even ethnocentrism—it does not even want to be a political nationalism, a doctrine of the Nation-State. It is, further, a cosmopolitanism, often associated with a democratic and republican politics, a progressivism, etc. But you can see quite clearly that everything that ought thus to withdraw it from reappropriation into a Nazi heritage (which is biologising, racist, etc.) remains in essence equivocal. It is in the name of a philosophy of life (even if it is spiritual life) that it sets itself apart from naturalising biologism. And it is perhaps of the essence of every nationalism to be philosophical, to present itself as a universal philosophy, to sublimate or *aufheben*, to sublate its philosophy of life into a philosophy of the life of the spirit—and as for cosmopolitanism, this is a fearfully ambiguous value: it can be annexionist and expansionist, and combat in the name of nationalism the enemies within, the false Germans who, even though they speak German, are Germans living on the German soil, are essentially less authentically German than certain 'foreigners' who, etc.

Nationalism *par excellence* is thus not foreign to philosophy, like an accident come along to pervert an essentially universalist, cosmopolitan, essentialist destination of philosophy. It always presents itself as a philosophy, or better, as philosophy *itself*, in the name of philosophy, and it claims *a priori* a certain essentialist universalism—showing thus that philosophy, by virtue of a structural paradox that will dominate this seminar, always has in some way the potential or the yearning, as you wish, for nationality and nationalism. To remain with the historical sequence that for the moment serves as my simple introductive index, as a sort of exergue, a sequence we shall study for itself and in a different way later—the sequence of German national-philosophism before and after the nineteenth century, I shall situate further, as exergues again, two further indices that can scan this story. I shall not speak of Nietzsche to whom we shall also devote long developments, for he was inexhaustible on this subject. I shall speak of Marx and Adorno.

Marx was no doubt one of the first, perhaps *the* first, to suspect lucidly what I have just called national-philosophism: i.e. the claim laid by one country or nation to the privilege of 'representing', 'embodying', 'ident-ifiying with' the universal essence of man, the thought of which is supposedly produced in some way in the philosophy of that people or that nation. In the *German Ideology*,[2] in the text on Karl Grün, entitled 'The Social Movement in France and Belgium (Darmstadt, 1845), or the Historiography of True Socialism', Marx ironises with some verve at the expense of Karl Grün, through whom he is obviously aiming at Feuerbach, praised by Grün in the name of 'pure, essential man':

> To *speak* of Feuerbach, is to speak of all philosophic labours from Bacon of Verulam up to the present; one defines at the same time the ultimate purpose and meaning of philosophy, one sees *man* as the final result of world history . . . We have gained *Man*, man who has divested himself of religion, of moribund thoughts, of all that is foreign to him, with all their counterparts in the prac-tical world: we have gained *pure, essential man*. (quoted p. 536)

Marx denounces the alliance between this humanism, this humanist teleology and a philosophical nationalism which confers on German philosophy a mission in which it cannot be replaced, the mission of thinking and realising this essence of man: 'The powerful trumpetings of Herr Grün in praise of true socialism and of German science exceed anything his fellow-believers have achieved in this respect' (Ibid.). And after having accused him of merely reproducing all the socialists who preceded him, and of plagiarising Hess (Moses Hess, *Socialism and Communism*), he defines and denounces exactly this national-essentialism, this national philosophism which is also a national-humanism:

> German philosophy must be deeply indebted to him for his praise of it, seeing how little he knows of it. The national pride of the true socialist, their pride in Germany as the land of 'Man', of 'human essence', as opposed to the other profane nationalities, reaches its climax in him. We give below a few samples of it: 'But I should like to know whether they won't all have to learn from us, these French and English, Belgians and North Americans'. (p. 28)

He now enlarges upon this.

> 'The *North Americans* appear to me thoroughly prosaic and, des-pite their legal freedom, it is from us that they will probably have to learn their socialism' (p. 101). (p. 537)

Before pursuing this quotation, let me stress this reference to the North Americans because, as we shall see progressively, the United States of America have played a quite odd and revealing role in this question of philosophical nationalisms since the beginning of the nineteenth century. Today, it is the market or the *Kampfplatz*, as you wish, which is the most open to the greatest intensity of exchanges, debates, evaluations of the Philosophical International (it would be easy to show that the USA is the major place, the obligatory passage for all philosophical circulation, with all the problems that that poses (we shall return to this)), among other things the place today of the Anglo-American idiom in the socially and economically most powerful legitimating discourse; taking account also of the fact—to which we shall also return—that today there seems to be developing, because of but also against the grain of this concentration of the Philosophical International in the USA, a sort of American nationalist renewal or reaction which claims to defend or restore, against the European invasion, be it Continental or British, a more properly American tradition. What is happening [*se passe*] today in the USA, what passes and does not pass via the USA is a central or unavoidable symptom for what is of interest to us in this seminar. Now this situation which is current and has a very current originality (it is not the same as only ten years ago!) was announcing itself, through dissociated, disordered, erratic but definite precursors right back in the nineteenth century, and was beginning to fascinate from afar a few lucid minds, not always professional philosophers (next week we shall be taking an interest from this point of view in some intuitions or analyses of Toqueville).

After attacking American liberalism (combatted by Cooper) which was developing from 1829, and even a certain American socialism, as philosophical blindness—i.e. blindness to German socialism—Grün has a go at the Belgian democrats, but what is interesting in this case, and this is exactly what Marx emphasises, is that what the Belgians are reproached with is not so much not being as far advanced as 'we Germans', as not believing in man himself, in the realisation and accomplishment of human being, the essence of man. In other words, it is the same thing not to be as advanced as the Germans and not to understand or believe in the humanity of man, his liberty, the history of his liberty, the *telos* of the accomplishment of his essence as liberty. Nationalism, once more, does not present itself as a retrenchment onto an empirical particularity, but as the assigning to a nation of a universalistic, essentialist representation. In shorthand, we could say that the German is Man, to be German or attuned to German, i.e. to German philosophy, is up to the measure of man, of human essence as liberty. The German man is the measure of all mankind. And that is what the nearest neighbours, Belgians or French, are the last to understand. First the Belgians:

> 'The *Belgian* democrats! Do you really think that they are *half so far advanced* as the Germans? Why, I have just had a tussle with one of them who considered the *realisation of free humanity* to be a chimera!' (p. 28) (p. 537)

And Marx comments: 'This is the nationality of "man" [This is a very fine expression which in its apparent paradox says something essential, precisely, about every modern nationalism assuming (the question awaits us) that nationalism *stricto sensu* is not *par excellence* a modern phenomenon—namely that it always presents itself as a nationalism not of a nation, of a nationality, as one would naturally be tempted to think, taking its word for it, but as the discours of man on man himself], of "human essence", of the freedom of human being, showing itself off as vastly superior to Belgian nationality'. (p. 537)

Marx thus situates with the greatest rigour the *doubling* of the concept of nationality which sustains both national identification and nationalistic hierarchisation. In truth, the word 'hierarchisation' which has just imposed itself on me out of convenience is not appropriate, or at least it translates from outside, in a denunciatory way, an operation that does not appear to itself as a hierarchisation, a doubling that claims to dissociate without subordinating. What does this consist in? In distinguishing an essential nationality, which is philosophical nationality—in this case, the one which thinks and accomplishes the essence of human freedom (an accomplishment that in the case under consideration passes through socialism), the essence of man as the being of philosophical liberty-nationality which *comes to* be confused with German nationality (and this 'coming to', which I leave to its indetermination, is the whole of *history* that cannot even be called a history—and you understand why I say *comes to* to avoid saying too soon has itself or lets itself be *represented* by German nationality (we're dealing here with something other than a representation), or to avoid saying lets itself be *embodied* (the word embodiment would make the German nation into the body of a spiritual nationality and to all appearances in neither Fichte nor Grün, whatever the differences that separate them, is the relationship of this type)), a doubling, then, that consists in distinguishing between an essential nationality—a philosophical one—and another one which comes into the category of empirical accident, no doubt, but which nonetheless cannot be dominated by this opposition of the essence and the accident.

One of the most interesting traits for us of this historical sequence is that this philosophical nationalism, in its essential essentialism, if I can say that, is linked, in the case of Grün, to Socialism, to an affirmation of true Socialism and not its contrary, as one often, very often tends to think. All the second volume of *The German Ideology* (manuscript in Engels's hand) aims at those who lay claim to what they call 'true Socialism'. These theoreticians are presented by Marx and Engels as 'writers' who have 'adopted' certain French and English communist ideas and 'amalgamated' them to their 'philosophico-German' premises, by considering the French or English texts as texts, precisely, or as purely theoretical writings come from 'pure thought', as they imagine is the case for the German philosophical systems. The accusations issued by Marx against Grün, as I have said, are in fact aimed at Moses Hess (whom we shall have to study here), whose 'obvious blunders' Grün is supposed to have transcribed and paraphrased. The relationship with France is naturally privileged in this debate. Grün has a go first at the French socialists and apostrophises them in these terms (I must quote at length):

> '*Frenchmen!* Leave Hegel in peace until you understand him.' (We believe that *Lerminier's* criticism of the *Philosophy of Right*, however weak it may be, shows more insight into Hegel than anything which Herr Grün has written either under his own name or that of 'Ernst von der Haide'.) 'Try drinking no coffee, no wine for a year; don't give way to passionate excitement; let Guizot rule and let Algeria come under the sway of Morocco' (how is Algeria ever to come under the rule of Morocco, even if the French were to relinquish it?); 'sit in a garret and study the *Logik* and the *Phäno-menologie*. And when you come down after a year, lean in frame and red of eye, and go into the street and stumble over some dandy or town crier, don't be abashed. For you will have become in the interval great and mighty men, your mind will be like an oak that is nourished by miraculous' (!) 'sap; whatever you see will yield up to you its most secret weaknesses; though you are created spirits, you will nevertheless penetrate to the heart of nature; your glance will be fatal, your word will move mountains, your dialectic will be keener than the keenest guillotine. You will present yourself at the Hotel de Ville—and the bourgeoisie is a thing of the past. You will step up to the Palais Bourbon—and it collapses. The whole Chamber of Deputies will disappear into the void. Guizot will vanish, Louis Philippe will fade into an historical

ghost and out of all these forces which you have annihilated there will rise victorious the absolute idea of free society. Seriously, you can only subdue Hegel by first of all becoming Hegel yourselves. As I have already remarked—Moor's beloved can only die at the hands of Moor.' (pp. 115–6) (p. 538)

Grün judges the French mind to be 'disappointing and superficial', and affirms that German socialism is 'the critique of French socialism'. 'Far from taking the French to be the inventors of the new Social Contract', he invites them in his book to 'perfect themselves at the school of German science'. And there follows an assertion which appears to me to be inspired, lucidly or not, I mean by an intuition which, theorised or not by Grün, says something which may be essential as to the advent of this German nationalism as essence of philosophical nationalism and as a thing of our modernity, i.e. that if Germany has been, alone in this perhaps, the place (in what sense of place, that's what remains to be determined) of emergence of this nationalism, this is perhaps because in a certain way, at the centre of Europe (this is a theme which will return), it will have marked a curious national void, a strange a-nationality. We shall come across this motif later, right up to Heidegger, that of an empty milieu, a central void, a between that, against the background of abyss and non-nationality, calls up the most powerful national-philosophical affirmation in the course of this unique sequence that goes from the eighteenth to the twentieth centuries. Without going any further down this path today, listen to what Grün, quoted by Marx, says in this context:

'At this moment, an edition of a translation of Feuerbach's *Wesen des Christenthums* is being prepared here in Paris. May their German schooling do the French much good! Whatever may arise from the economic position of the country or the constellation of present-day politics, only the humanistic outlook will ensure a *human* existence for the future. The Germans, unpolitical and despised as they are, this people which is no people, will have laid the cornerstone of the building of the future.' (p. 353) (p. 538)

It is thus in the name of a socialism doubled by a humanism, in the name of an apolitical people which is not a people that the national-philosophical assertion as cosmopolitanism states its paradoxes which are also, as we shall see, paradigms for the future, in spite of the basically rather caricatural character they take on here. We shall find the recurrent effects of this on the most opposite sides, in Heidegger as well as in

Adorno. At the very moment that the latter opposes all German philosophical nationalisms, Heidegger's *Jargon der Eigentlichkeit*, he nonetheless reiterates, in his 'Reply to the question: "What is German?"' (which we shall be studying shortly), the affirmation of a 'metaphysical character of the German language', a 'metaphysical excess of the language' (cf. Fichte), and even if this metaphysical character, which Adorno says is a 'specific and objective property of the German language' does not guarantee the truth nor constitute a privilege, it is nonetheless posited as the essence of Germanity. An essence that in this text, Adorno, explaining why he had to leave the USA and return home after the war, opposes to something American, to English. It was because he was unable to say in English what he had to say that he returned. So we must therefore ask the question of America, and we shall sketch it out during the next session or one soon, expecially via a text of Toqueville's.

If, in conclusion, I have insisted so much on language today, this is also to recognise a paradox, a paradigm and an aporia. 1) Final recourse of a universalistic philosophical nationalism, language is not language (Fichte). 2) One can denounce, suspect, devalorise, combat philosophical nationalism only by taking the risk of reducing or effacing linguistic difference or the force of the idiom, thus in making that metaphysico-technical gesture which consists in instrumentalising language (but is there a language which is purely non-instrumental?), making it a medium which is neutral, indifferent and external to the philosophical act of thought. Is there a thought of the idiom that escapes this alternative? That is one of our questions. It does not belong to the past, but is a question of the future. And here I am not just talking about the future of this seminar.

Notes

1. All quotations from Fichte are taken, with a few minor modifications, from J. G. Fichte, *Addresses to the German Nation*, ed. G. A. Kelley, tr. R. F. Jones and G. H. Turnbull (New York: Harper and Row, 1968). Here, p. 107.
2. All quotations from Marx are taken (with minor alterations) from the translation of *The German Ideology* by S. Ryanzanskaya (London: Lawrence and Wishart, 1965), Vol. II.

12 'THE LAWS OF REFLECTION: NELSON MANDELA, IN ADMIRATION' (1986)

FOR NELSON MANDELA (DERRIDA 1987C)

Translated by Mary Ann Caws and Isabelle Lorenz

Themes

This text was written before Nelson Mandela was released from prison and the South African Apartheid system was replaced by non-racial democracy. It was part of a collection, which included contributions from Nadine Gordimer, Susan Sontag, Hélène Cixous, Edmond Jabès and Maurice Blanchot. The last three were all important to Derrida in his own work. The intention of the collection was to form part of the campaign to draw attention to Mandela's imprisonment and the injustice of Apartheid.

There is an undertone of the cult of Mandela's personality in the title, which is both to be taken literally, and is undercut in the text. The point is that Mandela's struggle and personality are exemplary and admirable, but what is most admirable and exemplary is that Mandela served law; and law is what is to be respected over individuals, although only in the understanding of its contradictory constitution. The contradictory aspects of law arise when dealing with the struggle against an unjust constitution and unjust laws. Even in the face of such injustice, Mandela was a lawyer and argued respect for the law. Mandela's defence speech at the trial, which led to his imprisonment, itself is an example of legal argument in the service of justice. What Mandela did was to argue that even in terms of the legal and constitutional tradition that the Apartheid governments claimed to uphold, they had failed to follow universal principles of law.

For Derrida, the name 'Mandela' cannot be separated from theoretical reflection on history, culture and jurisprudence. What comes out of Mandela's struggles with, and for, law are the paradoxes of law. These are specular paradoxes, that is paradoxes of reflection inherent in the reversible structure of law.

'Admiration' is not an accidental or trivial word in Derrida's title. It is the first of the passions identified by Descartes in his treatise on *The Passions of the Soul*. The question of 'admiration' is identified as a classical philosophical problem, so that the 'admiration for Nelson Mandela' is an inquiry into 'admiration' rather than the pretext for an uncritical eulogy of Mandela. Mandela is admired and he is admirable because he admires law.

Mandela expressed admiration for Western democracy and law at his trial, leading Derrida to ask if the struggle against Apartheid is a mirror of Western history. Derrida does not provide an answer himself, suggesting ambiguities about how far he interprets Mandela as following Western liberal democracy, and how much Derrida himself supports that tradition. Derrida's discussion of Mandela brings out the tensions between Mandela's admiration for British-style parliamentary democracy and his admiration for Marxism and traditional African forms of communal justice and equality. As Derrida points out, Mandela could feel connected with the latter tradition because he was a hereditary traditional Chief even if he renounced use of his title.

Derrida considers the paradoxes which are necessary in instituting a constitution. The constitution of a nation presumes the unity of the nation for which the constitution is established. The institution of a constitution is itself a performative act, an act of force, which creates a nation in the moment that it describes the nation under law. Law gives both itself and the nation in its performative foundation, in the paradox of force to establish legality. Derrida refers this to the paradox of the 'general will' in Jean-Jacques Rousseau's *The Social Contract*. The general will is the legitimate source of law for Rousseau that rises above particular wills and sectional interests. It is not the same as the 'will of all' for Rousseau, it is the will of those who rise above private interests. The general will is assumed to be the will of the community but can only be the will of those who have accepted that there should be a general will rising above a mere majority of individual wills.

The reflection on law has a phenomenological aspect of making the invisible visible. Law as it existed in South Africa only makes the visible in presenting a reality defined by white South Africans for white South Africans. It excludes the invisible injustice and violence against blacks behind the forms of legal universalism. Reflection must make the invisible visible by reflecting on the violence of law, which always conceals violence behind its universalist form. Here Derrida is using the language of Merleau-Ponty in *The Visible and the Invisible* (Merleau-Ponty 1969 [written 1960]), which Merleau-Ponty had used for describing the invisibility to consciousness of its chiasmic origin in flesh. Derrida also uses the language of Kant and Hegel, when he says that we must go beyond understanding to reason in reflection. Derrida runs together Kant's distinction between understanding as knowledge of objects, and reason as the regulation of understanding; Kant's discussion of reflective judgements which underlie determinate judgements of knowledge and morality; Hegel's discussion of reason as consciousness aware of itself beyond the limits of the grasp of objects of consciousness in understanding which is merely reflective.

Mandela's speech at his trial justifies himself and his nation before the law, and in a double reflection on the violence of law, which both promotes a political programme of liberation and demonstrates the paradoxes of all law. Mandela also makes a Kantian kind of appeal to an imperative beyond existing law, what Kant calls the 'categorical imperative', which provides the form for moral principles with the principles that a moral maxim should only be willed if you can will it universally for all humanity. Mandela needs to do that to separate the limitations of Apartheid law, which strongly hampered his own professional work as a lawyer, from what law should be. The figure of Mandela also has a resemblance to Christ, as Mandela is a martyr for pure principles. The point of contradiction in the constitution of law is where we arrive at what is often represented through religion, God and prophets.

Context

In his 'admiration' for Mandela, Derrida brings out ambiguities in Mandela's discourse, which are also ambiguities in the anti-Apartheid struggle, reflected in the Freedom Charter of the African National Congress (ANC). These issues have come to be at the heart of South African politics since the fall of Apartheid, in the interpretation of the constitution, the relation of the constitution to the Freedom Charter, and the relation of Mandela's legacy as a hero – to all those who welcome the passing of Apartheid – to the governmental policies of the ANC. They were anticipated during the Apartheid period in debates within the opposition between African nationalists, Black consciousness activists, traditional Black African leaders, communists, the non-communist left, liberals.

Ambiguities in Mandela's legacy may also be ambiguities in Derrida's own political thought between a universalist liberalism, advocating something similar to Western liberal traditions and institutions internationally; and a radical opposition to Western metaphysics which extends to opposition to Western liberalism in the hope of new communities based on social equality and communal spirit. In the end, once in power, Mandela advocated liberal institutions and legalism, and so does Derrida. The urge toward socialism rooted in traditional African communalism is apparent in Mandela and in Derrida's reading, but it never takes over from the liberal universalism. Of course it is possible to seek harmonisation between these currents, but where there is a conflict it is hard to read Derrida as coming down against a liberalism, which may seem abstracted from communal justice within a communalist point of view. This conflict is also a conflict within Western liberalism, and a conflict between liberal and non-liberal thinking, as can be seen in the communitarian ethical and political philosophy of Alasdair McIntyre (*After Virtue*, MacIntyre 1997 [first published 1984]) and Michael Sandel (*Liberalism and the Limits of Justice*, Sandel 1998 [first published 1982]). MacIntyre is more critical of the liberal tradition than Sandel, as he seeks alternatives in ancient and medieval ethical practice and thought, as well as Marxist thought. Sandel is more seeking a communitarian version of liberalism. The questions of liberalism versus communalism can appear within liberalism or as questioning liberalism itself. Any questioning of liberalism in Derrida seems closer to Sandel than MacIntyre. Derrida's interest in the inevitable idiolects of law and philosophy, that is their variation according to language, and all other forms of context, brings him to the point of questioning universalism, but his end position is always that of cosmopolitanism and 'cosmopolitics' which were major concerns towards the end of his career.

The question of law as force provides the topic for his long 1990 paper 'Force of Law: The "Mystical Foundation of Authority"' (in Derrida 2002). There Derrida argues, with reference to Walter Benjamin and Blaise Pascal, that law is a violence against what it applies to, that undermines the claims of law to be pure law. The violence of law means that sovereignty, and legal authority, lack foundations in pure law. That leaves the foundation as paradoxical, and the paradoxical can also be referred to as the mystical. The tendency of authority to justify itself with reference to religion, ancient tradition and mystical origins is a reaction to the violence that undermines any claim to purely legal foundation. These paradoxes themselves repeat the paradoxes of transcendence in all concepts. A concept necessarily claims to be abstract and therefore what transcends empirical force, but can only be conceived as the negation of empirical force by empirical force.

The sense of paradox in the origins of law and authority can be found in the social contract theories of Thomas Hobbes, John Locke and

Jean-Jacques Rousseau in the seventeenth and eighteenth centuries. They were faced with the difficulty of explaining how obligations to follow law can emerge from a natural state of lawless liberty, particularly as they wanted to use 'natural liberty' as the basis of law and sovereignty, which can only exist legitimately in order to preserve liberty. In the late twentieth century, the problematic moment of institution was revived by John Rawls in *A Theory of Justice* (Rawls 1999a [first published 1971]). Rawls was concerned with the 'initial position' in which the best possible principles of justice are designed. Rawls thought the best way to work out the principles of justice would be a thought experiment in which we imagine a fictional moment in which individuals establish basic principles. Rawls's thought experiment requires a 'veil of ignorance' in which individuals establish principles of justice for a society which they will live in, but at the moment of the 'initial position' they would not know what status they would have in that society.

The way Rawls develops the argument from there is very influential but not obviously connected with Derrida's concerns. What is important is that Rawls thought it possible to arrive at a state of 'reflective equilibrium' in which we find harmony between our moral and political intuitions and the results of the moral and political principles we adopt. Consistently following an initially attractive principle may undermine a deeply held moral intuition, so we need to find those principles that will lead to results consistent with our intuitions. Equally we need to test our intuitions to see if there is any rationally consistent set of principles which will enable us to keep our intuitions. If not we must modify them.

The harmonisation and hierarchy of norms Rawls seeks is in conflict with Derrida's emphasis on paradox and contradiction but Rawls's own emphasis on conflict is important from the Derridean point of view. For Derrida, the fiction of the 'veil of ignorance' in the 'initial position' must demonstrate the contradictions in the origin of justice. The indeterminacy of initial assumptions is covered over in a fictional assumption that rational people will arrive at certain conclusions under specially designed circumstances. There is no guarantee of this. Indeed there must be a heterogeneous set of differing principles emerging in such circumstances, however constrained. The emphasis on the absence of the real social world follows the logic of phenomenology and structuralism. Both rely on the assumption that we can conceive of forms without empirical content. This means that they need to assume an apocalypse in which the empirical world has been destroyed. Rawls has done something similar. He can only start his political philosophy by assuming the destruction of any real political world. The formalism is consistent in Rawls though not always the same in form. The 'initial position' aims to reformulate Kant.

Other aspects of A *Theory of Justice* aim to incorporate the arithmetic of utilitarian judgements, though within Kantian limits. He also follows the method of economic model building that necessarily establishes mathematical models, which abstract from reality in order to clarify it. Derrida does not deal with mathematical economics or even with utilitarian attempts to derive moral conclusions from measuring benefits and costs of certain acts or rules. There is certainly no quarrel with such methods. For Derrida as for Rawls they require a place in abstract philosophical reasoning. Derrida always advocates that metaphysics be challenged by the empirical, but never in a way that would lead to reductionist empiricist philosophy in politics or anywhere else. As Rorty notes, there is a transcendental element in Derrida's philosophy in which we grasp the limit of abstraction in the contradictions of transcendental claims. The contradiction of the transcendental with the empirical can never be eliminated. That contradiction structures the speech act and the principles of justice. Rawls is not directly concerned with jurisprudence in A *Theory of Justice*, but he is seeking a broad understanding of justice which will underpin a legal system. His way of establishing general principles of justice already assumes legal reasoning about hierarchies of norms and institutions. Ronald Dworkin's *Empire of Laws* (Dworkin 1998) provides an example of analytic political philosophy from the more explicitly legal aspect which makes it particularly clear how we can contextualise Derrida in normative theory. Dworkin's paper 'Law as Interpretation' (Dworkin 1982) provides further context with regard to models of interpretation of law, including politics and literature, matching Derrida's own suggestions that law requires interpretation and that is poetics, and that law is never pure law so it involves political decisions.

THE LAWS OF REFLECTION: NELSON MANDELA, IN ADMIRATION

1

Admirable Mandela.

Period, no exclamation point. I am not using this punctuation to temper any enthusiasm or to be a killjoy. Instead of speaking only in honor of Nelson Mandela, I shall say something about his honor without succumbing, if possible, to loftiness, without proclaiming or acclaiming.

The homage will perhaps be more exact, as will its tone, if it seems to surrender its impatience, without which there would be no question of admiring, to the coldness of an analysis. Admiration reasons, whatever is said of it, it works things out with reason, it astonishes and interrogates: how can one be Mandela? Why does he seem exemplary and admirable in what he thinks and says, in what he does or in what he suffers? Admirable in himself, as well as in what he conveys as a witness, another word for martyrdom, that is to say the experience of his people?

"My people and I," he always says, without speaking like a king.

Why does he also *force* admiration in this manner? This word presupposes some resistance, for his enemies admire him without admitting it. Unlike those who love him among his people and together with his inseparable Winnie, from whom these enemies have always futilely kept him separated, these enemies fear him. If his most hateful persecutors secretly admire him, this proves that, as one might say, he forces such admiration.

So, this is the question: where does that force come from? Where does it lead? It is used or is applied, but for what? Or rather: what *folds* under it? What form is to be recognized in this fold? What line?

First of all we will see in it, and let's say it without any other premise, *the line of a reflection*. This is first of all a force of reflection. What is obvious right away is that Mandela's political experience or passion can never be separated from a theoretical reflection: about history, culture, and above all jurisprudence. An unremitting analysis enlightens the rationality of his acts, his demonstrations, his speeches, his strategy. Even before being constrained to withdraw from the world into prison, and during a quarter of a century of incarceration, he has been acting endlessly and giving a direction to the struggle. Mandela has always been, like all the greatest politicians, a man of reflection.

But by force of reflection, something else can be understood, beckoning toward the literality of the mirror and the scene of specularity/ speculation. Not so much toward the physical laws of reflection as toward specular paradoxes in the experience of the law. There is no law without a mirror. And in this properly reversible structure, we shall never avoid the moment of admiration.

Admiration, as its name indicates, it will be said, etc. No, no matter what its name or that it always enables us to *see*, admiration does not just belong to sight. It translates emotion, astonishment, surprise, interrogation in the face of that which oversteps the mark: in the face of the "extraordinary," says Descartes, and he considers it a passion, the first of the six primitive passions, before love, hate, desire, joy, and sadness. It enables understanding. Outside of it there is only ignorance, he adds, and in it resides "a great deal of force" of "surprise" or of "sudden arrival." The admiring look is astonished, it questions its intuition, it opens upon the light of a question but of a question received no less than asked. This experience lets the light of a question pass through it, which in no way prevents it from reflecting it. The light has as focus the very thing which forces admiration, it partitions it then into a specular movement which seems strangely fascinating.

Mandela becomes admirable for having known how to admire. And what he has discovered, he has found through admiration. He fascinates too, as we shall see, for having been fascinated.

That, in a certain way which we will have to understand, is what *he says*. He states what he does and what has happened to him. Such a light, its reflected passage, as experience of the give-and-take of a question would thus also be the burst of a voice.

Nelson Mandela's voice—what does it remind us of, ask from us, demand of us? I mean to say what do the dynamics of that voice have to do with sight, reflection, admiration, but also what sings in his name? (Listen to the clamor of his people when they demonstrate in his name: Man-de-la!)

Admiration of Nelson Mandela, as we might say Nelson Mandela's passion. Admiration of Mandela, a double genitive: the one he inspires and the one he feels. The two have the same focus, they reflect upon each other. I have already stated my hypothesis: he becomes admirable for having, with all his force, admired, and for having made a force of his admiration, a combative, untreatable, and irreducible power. The law itself, law above other laws.

For in fact what has he admired? In one word: the Law. And what inscribes it in discourse, in history, in the institution is jurisprudence.

A first quotation—a lawyer is speaking, during a trial, his trial, the one where he is also prosecuting, the one in which he prosecutes those who accuse him, in the name of the law:

> The basic task at the present moment is the removal of race discrimination and the attainment of democratic rights on the basis of the Freedom Charter. . . . From my reading of Marxist literature and from conversations with Marxists, I have gained the impression that communists regard the parliamentary system of the West as undemocratic and reactionary. But, on the contrary, *I am an admirer* of such a system. The *Magna Charta*, the Petition of Rights, and the Bill of Rights are documents which are held in veneration by democrats throughout the world. *I have great respect* for British political institutions, and for the country's system of justice. I regard the British Parliament as the most democratic institution in the world, and the independence and impartiality of its judiciary never fail to arouse my admiration.[1]

He admires the law, he says it clearly, but is this law, which gives orders to constitutions and declarations, essentially a thing of the West? Does its formal universality retain some irreducible link with European history, even with an Anglo-American one? If it were so, we would of course still have to meditate upon this strange possibility: that its formal character would be as essential to the universality of the law as its presentation in a determined moment and place in history. How could we conceive of such a history? The struggle against apartheid, wherever it takes place and such as Mandela carries it on and reflects it, would this remain a sort of specular opposition, a domestic war that the West carried on with itself, in its own name? An internal contradiction which would not put up with either a radical otherness or a true dissymmetry?

In this form, such a hypothesis still implies too many indistinct presuppositions. We shall try to recognize them later. For the moment, let's retain an obvious, more limited but also more certain fact: what Mandela admires and says he admires is the tradition inaugurated by the Magna Charta, the Universal Declaration of the Rights of Man under their diverse forms (he frequently calls upon "human dignity," upon what is human and "worthy of that name"); it's also parliamentary democracy and, still more precisely, the doctrine of the separation of powers, the independence of justice.

But if he admires this tradition, does it mean that he is its inheritor, its simple inheritor? Yes and no, depending on what is meant here by inheritance. You can recognize an authentic inheritor in the one who conserves and reproduces, but also in the one who respects the *logic* of the legacy enough to turn it upon occasion against those who claim to be its guardians, enough to reveal, despite and against the usurpers, what has never yet been seen in the inheritance: enough to give birth, by the unheard-of *act* of a reflection, to what had never seen the light of day.

2

This inflexible logic of reflection was also Mandela's practice. Here are at least two signs of it.

1. *First sign.* The African National Congress, of which he was one of the leaders after having joined it in 1944, succeeded the South African National Congress. Now the structure of the latter already reflected that of the American Congress and the House of Lords. It included in particular a High Chamber. The paradigm was then already this parliamentary democracy Mandela admired. The Charter of Freedom, which he promulgated in 1955, also enunciates those democratic principles inspired by the Universal Declaration of the Rights of Man. And yet, with an exemplary rigor, Mandela nonetheless refuses pure and simple alliance with the liberal whites who wanted to maintain the struggle within the constitutional framework, such at least as it was then established. Mandela reminds us, in fact, of the truth: the establishment of this constitutional law had not only, both in fact and in practice, taken the form of a singular coup de force, but this violent act *at once* produced *and* presupposed the unity of a nation. In this case, the coup de force *remained* a coup de force, thus, as a bad coup—a bad blow—and the failure of a law that never managed to establish itself. It always had, in fact, for its authors and benefactors, only a particular will, that of a part of the population, a limited sum of private interests, those of the white minority. The latter becomes the privileged subject, the only subject in truth of this anticonstitutional constitution. It is probable, as it might be said, that such a coup de force always marks the founding of a nation, state, or nation-state. In the event of such a founding or institution, the properly *performative* act must produce (proclaim) what in the form of a *constative* act it merely claims, declares, assures it is describing. The simulacrum or

fiction then consists in bringing to daylight, in *giving birth to*, that which one claims to reflect so as to take note of it, as though it were a matter of recording *what will have been there*, the unity of a nation, the founding of a state, while one is in the act of producing that event. But legitimacy, indeed legality, becomes permanently installed, it recovers its originating violence, and is forgotten only under certain conditions. Not all performatives, a theoretician of *speech acts* would say, are "happy." That depends on a great number of conditions and conventions that form the context of such events. In the case of South Africa, certain "conventions" were not respected, the violence was too great, *visibly too great*, at a moment when this visibility extended to a new international scene, and so on. The white community was *too* much in the minority, the disproportion of wealth *too* flagrant. From then on this violence remains at once excessive and powerless, insufficient in its result, lost in its own contradiction. It cannot manage to have itself forgotten, as in the case of states founded on a genocide or a quasi-extermination. Here, the violence of the origin must repeat itself indefinitely and act out its rightfulness in a legislative apparatus whose monstrosity fails to pay back: a pathological proliferation of juridical prostheses (laws, acts, amendments) destined to legalize to the slightest detail the effects of fundamental racism, of a state racism, the unique and the last in the world.

The constitution of such a state cannot then, even with a sufficient verisimilitude, refer back to the popular will. As the Charter of Liberty reminds us: "South Africa belongs to all its inhabitants, black and white. No government can prevail over an authority which isn't founded on the will of the entire nation." Referring to the general will, which cannot be reduced to the sum of the wills of the "entire nation," Mandela often reminds us of Rousseau even if he never quotes him. And he thus contests the authority, the legality, the constitutionality of the Constitution. He thus refuses the proposal of—and the alliance with—the white liberals who would struggle against apartheid even as they claim to respect the legal framework:

> The credo of the liberals consists in "the use of democratic and constitutional means, rejecting the several forms of totalitarianism: fascism and communism." Only a people already enjoying democratic and constitutional rights has any grounds for speaking of democratic and constitutional rights. This does not have any meaning for those who do not benefit from them.[2]

What does Mandela oppose to the coup de force of the white minority which has instituted a supposedly democratic law, but a law which in fact benefits only a single ethnonational entity? The "entire nation," that is to say another ethnonational entity, another collectivity formed of all the groups, including the white minority, inhabiting the territory named South Africa. This other entity could not have instituted, nor in the future will be able to institute, itself as the subject of the State of the Constitution of South Africa except by a performative act. And the perforrnative will not appear to refer to any fundamental preexisting law, only to the "convention" of geographic and demographic delimitation effected, in large measure, by white colonization. This fact remains ineffaceable. No doubt the will of the "entire nation," in any case the general will, should erase itself from all empirical determination. Such is at least its regulating ideal. It seems no more accessible here than anywhere else. The definition of the "entire nation" registers—and thus seems to reflect—the event of the coup de force that white occupation, followed by the founding of the South African Republic, was. Without this event, how could we recognize the slightest relationship between a general will and what the Charter of Freedom calls the "will of the entire nation"? The latter finds itself paradoxically united by the violence done to it, which tends to disintegrate or to destructure it forever, in its more virtual identity. This phenomenon marks the establishment of almost all states after a decolonization. Mandela knows that no matter how democratic it is, and even if it seems to conform to the principle of the equality of all before the law, the absolute inauguration of a state cannot presuppose the previously *legitimized* existence of a national entity. The same is true for a first constitution. The total unity of a nation is not identified for the first time except by a contract—formal or not, written or not—which institutes some fundamental law. Now this contract is never actually signed, except by supposed representatives of the nation which is supposed to be "entire." This fundamental law cannot, either in law or in fact, simply precede that which at once institutes it and nevertheless supposes it: projecting and reflecting it! It can in no way precede this extraordinary performative by which a signature authorizes itself to sign, in a word, legalizes itself on its own without the guarantee of a preexisting law. This violence and this autographic fiction are found at work just as surely in what we call individual autobiography as in the "historical" origin of states. In the case of South Africa, the fiction lies in this—and it is a fiction against a fiction: the unity of the "entire nation" could not correspond to the delimitation effected by the white minority. It should now constitute a whole (the white minority plus all the inhabitants of South Africa) whose configuration was only able to be established, in any case to be identified, by beginning with a minority violence. That it can from then on oppose this violence alters nothing about this terrifying contradiction. The "entire nation," a unity of "all the national groups," will grant itself existence and legal force only by the very same act to which the Charter of Freedom appeals. This Charter speaks in the present, a present supposed to be founded on the *description* of a historical fact, which, in turn, should be recognized in the future. It also speaks in the future, a future which has *presciptive* value:

> South Africa belongs to all its inhabitants, black and white. No government can claim an authority which is not founded on the will of the entire people.
> –The people will govern.
> –All the national groups will enjoy equal rights—
> –All will be equal before the law.[3]

The Charter does not annul the founding act of the law, this act necessarily alegal in itself, which finally institutes South Africa and can only become legal after the fact, notably if it is ratified by the right of the international community. No, the Charter refounds it, or in any case intends to refound it, by *reflecting* against the white minority the principles from which it was claiming to be inspired, whereas *actually* it never ceased to betray them. A democracy, yes, South Africa yes, but this time, says the Charter, the "entire nation" must include all the national groups, such is the very logic of the law to which the white minority was pretending to appeal. Upon this territory so marked out, all human beings, all the people "worthy of this name," will thus become effectively the subjects of the law.

2. *Second sign*. The "admiration" declared for the model of parliamentary democracy of the Anglo-American type and for the separation of powers, the faithfulness of the Charter to all the principles of such a democracy, the logic of a radicalization which opposes these very principles to the Western defenders of apartheid, all of this could be seen to resemble the coup de force of a simple specular inversion: the struggle of the black community (or non-"white" communities) would be undertaken in the name of an imported law and model, which were betrayed, in the first place, by the first to import them. A terrifying dissymmetry. But it seems to reduce itself, or rather, to reflect itself to the point of withdrawing from every objective representation: neither symmetry nor dissymmetry. And this because there would be no importation, no simply assignable origin for the history of law, only a reflecting apparatus, with projections of images, inversions of paths, interior duplications, and effects of history for a law whose structure and whose "history" consist in taking away the origin. Such an apparatus, and by this word I only mean

that this x is not natural (which does not necessarily define it as an arti-
fact brought forth from human hands), cannot be represented in
objective space. For at least *two reasons* that I shall here relate to the
case that occupies us.

The first reason concerns the structure of the law, of the principle or
model being considered. Whatever the historical place of its formation or
formulation, of its revelation or presentation, a structure of this kind
tends toward universality. Here we have, as it were, its intentional
content; its meaning requires that in its immediacy it must extend
beyond the historical, national, geographical, linguistic, and cultural
limits of its phenomenal origin. Everything should begin by uprooting.
The limits would then appear to be empirical contingencies. They could
even dissimulate what they seem to show. Thus one might think that the
"white minority" of South Africa is hiding the essence of the principles
to which it claims to be appealing, it is privatizing them, particularizing
them, appropriating them, and in that way taking them over against
their very reason for being, against reason itself. Whereas, in the struggle
against apartheid, the "reflection" of which we are speaking here would
make visible what was not even visible any longer in the political
phenomenality dominated by the whites. It would oblige us to see what
was no longer seen or was not yet to be seen. It tries to open the eyes of
the whites; it does not reproduce the visible, it produces it. This reflection
makes visible a law that in truth it does more than reflect, because this
law, in its phenomenon, was invisible—had become or continued to be
invisible. Transporting the invisible into the visible, this reflection does
not proceed from the visible, rather it passes through understanding.
More exactly, it reveals to understanding what goes past understanding
and relates only to reason. It was a first reason, reason itself.

The second reason seems more problematic. It specifically concerns
this phenomenal apparition, the historical constitution of the law, of
democratic principles and the democratic model. Here again, the experience of declared admiration—this time of an admiration that is said to
be *fascinated*—follows the line of a reflection. Still a reflection upon the
law: Mandela perceives, he *sees*, others might say that he *projects and
reflects without seeing it*, the very presence of this law in the interior of
African society. Even before "the arrival of the white man."

In what he himself says about this subject, I will underline three themes:

1.   that of *fascination*: the attentiveness of the long stare, petrified, by
     something that, without being simply a visible object, looks at you,
     already concerns you, understands you, and orders you to continue
     observing, responding, making you responsible for the look that

looks at you and beckons you beyond the visible: neither perception nor hallucination.

2. that of the *seed*: it furnishes an indispensable scheme for interpretation. It is by its virtuality that the democratic model would have been present in the society of ancestors, even if it was not to be revealed, *developed* as such for reflection, until afterward, after the violent eruption of the "white man," the bearer of the same model.

3. that of the South African "homeland," the birthplace of all the national groups called upon to live under the law of the new South African Republic. This country is not to be confused either with the state or with the nation:

Many years ago, when I was a boy brought up in my village in the Transkei, I listened to the elders of the tribe telling stories about the good old days, *before the arrival of the white man*. Then our people lived peacefully, under the democractic rule of their kings and their *amapakati*, and moved freely and confidently up and down the country without let or hindrance. Then the country was ours. . . . I hoped and vowed then that, among the treasures that life might offer me, would be the opportunity to serve my people and make my own humble contribution to their freedom struggles.

The structure and organization of early African societies in this country *fascinated* me very much and greatly influenced the evolution of my political outlook. The land, then the main means of production, belonged to the whole tribe, and there was no individual ownership whatsoever. There were no classes, no rich or poor, and no exploitation of man by man. All men were free and equal and this was the foundation of government. Recognition of this general principle found expression in the constitution of the council . . .

There was much in such a society that was primitive and insecure and it certainly could never measure up to the demands of the present epoch. But in such a society are contained *the seeds of a revolutionary democracy* in which none will be held in slavery or servitude, and in which poverty, want, and insecurity shall be no more . . .

It is common knowledge that the conference decided that, in place of the unilateral proclamation of a Republic by the White minority of South Africans only, it would demand in the name of the African people the calling of a truly national convention representative of all South Africans, irrespective of their color, black and white, to sit amicably round a table, to debate a new constitution for South Africa, which was in essence what the Government was doing by the proclamation of a Republic, and furthermore, to press on behalf of the African people, that such a new constitution should differ from the constitution of the proposed South African Republic by guaranteeing democratic rights on a basis of full equality to all South Africans of adult age. (p. 141)

What fascination seems to bring into view here, what mobilizes and immobilizes Mandela's attention, is not only parliamentary democracy, whose principle would be presented in the West *as an example but not exemplarily*. It is also the *already virtually* accomplished passage, if one can say this, from parliamentary democracy to revolutionary democracy: a society without class and without private property. We have just recognized, then, this supplementary paradox: the *effective* accomplishment, the filling out of the democratic form, the *real* determination of the formality, *will only have taken place* in the past of this non-Western society, under the species of virtuality, in other words, those "seeds." Mandela lets himself be *fascinated* by what he sees being reflected in advance, what is not yet to be seen, what he fore-sees: the really revolutionary democracy of which the Anglo-American West would, in sum, have only given an image at once incomplete, formal, *and thus also potential*. Potentiality against potentiality, power against power. For if he "admires" the parliamentary systems of the most Western West, he also declares his "admiration," and it is still his word, still the same one, for the "structure and organization of early African societies in this country." It is a question of "seed" and of preformation, according to the same logic or the same rhetoric, a sort of genoptics. The figures of African society prefigure, they make visible ahead of time, what still remains invisible in its historical phenomenon, that is to say, the "classless" society and the end of the "exploitation of man by man":

Today I am attracted by the idea of a classless society, an attraction which springs in part from Marxist reading and, in part, from my *admiration* of the structure and organization of early African societies in this country. The land, then the main means of production, belonged to the tribe. There were no rich or poor, and there was no exploitation of man by man. (p. 170)

3

In all the senses of this term, Mandela remains, then, *a man of the law*. He has always appealed to the law even if, in appearance, he has to oppose himself to such-and-such specific legality, and even if certain judges have made of him, at certain moments, an outlaw.

A man of the law, he was this first *by vocation*. On the one hand, he always appeals to law. On the other hand, he has always felt himself attracted by, appealed to by the law before which people have wanted him to appear. He has moreover accepted to appear before it, even if he was also constrained to do so. He seizes the occasion, we don't dare to say, the good opportunity. Why the good opportunity? Let us reread his "defense" which is in truth an indictment. We will find there a political autobiography, his and that of his people, indissociable. The "I" of this autobiography establishes himself and justifies himself, reasons and signs in the name of "we." He always says "my people," as we have already noted, especially when he asks the question of the subject responsible *before the law*:

> I am charged with inciting people to commit an offence by way of protest against the law, a law which neither I nor any of my people had any say in preparing. The law against which the protest was directed is the law which established a Republic in the Union of South Africa. . . . But in weighing up the decision as to the sentence which is to be imposed for such an offence, the Court must take into account the question of responsibility, whether it is I who is responsible or whether, in fact, a large measure of the responsibility does not lie on the shoulders of the Government which promulgated that law, knowing that my people, who consti-tute the majority of the population of this country, were opposed to that law, and knowing further that every legal means of demon-strating that opposition had been closed to them by prior legislation, and by Government administrative action. (pp. 139–140)

So he presents himself in this way. He presents himself in his people, before the law. Before a law he rejects, beyond any doubt, but which he rejects in the name of a superior law, the very one he declares to admire and before which he agrees *to appear*. In such a presentation of the self, he justifies himself in resuming his history, which he reflects in a single center, a single and double center, his history and that of his people. Appearance: they appear together, he becomes himself again appearing before the law that he summons as much as he is summoned by it. But he does not present himself in view of a justification which would follow his appearance. The presentation of the self is not *in the service* of the law, it is not a means. The unfolding of this history is a *justification*, it is possible and has meaning only before the law. He is only what he is, he,

Nelson Mandela, he and his people, he has presence only in this movement of justice.

Memories and confessions of a lawyer. The latter "confesses" in fact, even as he justifies it, even to the point of claiming it proudly, a fault in the eyes of legality. Taking as his witness humanity as a whole, he addresses himself to the universal justice above his judges of one day only. Whence this paradox: we can perceive a sort of joyous quivering throughout the tale of this martyrdom. And sometimes we think we hear Rousseau's accent in these confessions, hearing a voice which never ceases to appeal to *the voice of conscience*, to the immediate and unfailing sentiment of justice, to this law of laws that speaks in us before us, because it is inscribed within our heart. In the same tradition, it is also the place of a categorical imperative, of a morality incommensurate with the conditional hypotheses and strategies of self-interest, as it is with the figures of such-and-such civil law:

I do not believe, Your Worship, that this Court, in inflicting penalties on me for the crimes for which I am convicted, should be moved by the belief that penalties deter men from the course that they believe is right. History shows that penalties do not deter men when their *conscience* is aroused . . . (p. 150)

Whatever sentence Your Worship sees fit to impose upon me for the crime for which I have been convicted before this Court, may it rest assured that when my sentence has been completed, I will still be moved, as men are always moved, by their *consciences*; I will still be moved by my dislike of the race discrimination against my people when I come out from serving my sentence, to take up again, as best I can, the struggle for the removal of those injustices until they are finally abolished once and for all. (p. 151)

It was an act of defiance of the law. We were aware that it was, but, nevertheless, that act had been forced on us against our wishes, and we could do no other than to choose between compliance with the law and compliance with our *consciences*. (p. 143)

[We] were faced with this *conflict between the law and our conscience*. In the face of the complete failure of the Government to heed, to consider, or even to respond to our seriously proposed objections and our solutions to the forthcoming Republic, what were we to do? Were we to allow the law, which states that you shall not commit an offence by way of protest, to take its course and thus betray our *conscience*? . . . In such a dilemma, men of honesty, men of purpose, and men of public morality and of conscience can only have one answer. They must *follow the dictate of their conscience* irrespective of the consequences which might overtake them for it. We of the Action Council, and I particularly, as secretary, *followed our conscience*. (p. 145)

Conscience and conscience of the law, these two make only one. Presentation of oneself and presentation of one's people, these two make only a single history in a single reflection, in both cases, as we have said, a single and double focus. And it is that of admiration, since this conscience presents itself, resumes itself, gathers in reflecting upon itself before the law. That is to say, let's not forget, before what is admirable.

The experience of admiration is also *doubly interior*. It reflects reflection and draws from it all the strength it uses against its Western judges. For it proceeds dramatically, from a double interiorization. Mandela interiorizes also, at the same time, the *principles of interiority* in the figure that the Christian West has given it. All its traits are to be found in the philosophy, the politics, the jurisprudence, and the morality which dominate in Europe: the law of laws resides in the most intimate conscience, we must in the final instance judge intentions and goodwill, and so on. Before any juridical or political discourse, before the texts of positive law, the law speaks by the voice of conscience or is inscribed in the depths of the heart.

A man of law *by vocation*, then, Mandela was that also by profession. It is known that he first studied jurisprudence on the advice of Walter Sisulu, then the Secretary of the National African Council. It was in particular a question of mastering Western law, this weapon to turn against the oppressors. These do not finally realize, in spite of all their legal ruses, the true force of a law that they manipulate, violate, and betray.

To be able to inscribe himself in the system, and above all in the faculty of law, Mandela takes courses by *correspondence*.

He wants to obtain first a degree in letters. Let's stress this episode. Since he cannot have immediate access to direct personal conversation, he has to begin by correspondence. Mandela will complain about this later. The context, no doubt, will be different, but there will always be a politics of voice and writing, of the difference between what is said "aloud" and what is written, between the "live voice" and "correspondence."

We have been conditioned by the history of White governments in this country to accept the fact that Africans, when they make their demands strongly and powerfully enough to have some chance of success, will be met by force and terror on the part of the Government. This is not something we have taught the African people; this is something the African people have learned from their own bitter experience. . . . Already there are indications in this country that people, my people, Africans, are turning to deliberate acts of violence and of force against the Government, in order to persuade the Government, in the only language which this Government shows, by its behavior, that it understands.

Elsewhere in the world, a court would say to me, "You should have made representations to the Government." This Court, I am confident, will not say so. Representations have been made, by people who have gone before me, time and time again. Representations were made in this case by me; I do not want again to repeat the experience of those representations. The Court cannot expect a respect for the process of representation and negotiation to grow amongst the African people, when the Government shows every day, by its conduct, that it despises such processes and frowns upon them and will not indulge in them. Nor will the Court, I believe, say that, under the circumstances, my people are condemned forever to say nothing and to do nothing. (pp. 147–148)

In order not to hear, not to understand, the white Government requires that one writes to it. But it also means thus not to answer and first of all not to read. Mandela reminds us of the letter that Albert Luthuli, then the president of the ANC, had addressed to the first minister Strijdom. It was a lengthy analysis of the situation, accompanied by a request for a consultation. Not the slightest response.

The standard of behavior of the South African Government towards my people, and its aspirations, has not always been what it should have been, and is not always the standard which is to be expected in serious high-level dealings between *civilized* peoples. Chief Luthuli's letter was not even favored with the courtesy of an acknowledgment from the Prime Minister's office. (p. 144)

The white power does not believe itself required to respond, does not hold itself responsible before the black people. The blacks cannot assure themselves, by return mail, by verbal exchange, by any look or sign, that any image of them has been formed on the other side, which might afterward return to it in some way. For the white power does not content itself with not answering. It does worse: it does not even acknowledge receipt. After Luthuli, Mandela experiences it himself. He has just written to Verwoerd to inform him of a resolution voted on by the action committee of which he is then the secretary. He requests also that a national convention be convoked before the deadline determined by the resolution. Neither an answer nor acknowledgment of receipt:

> In a *civilized* country one would be outraged by *the failure* of the head of Government even *to acknowledge receipt of a letter*, or to consider such a reasonable request put to him by a broadly representative collection of important personalities and leaders of the most important community of the country. Once again, Government standards in dealing with my people fell below what the *civilized* world would expect. No reply, response whatsoever, was received to our letter, no indication was even given that it had received any consideration whatsoever. Here we, the African people, and especially we of the National Action Council, who had been entrusted with the tremendous *responsibility* of safeguarding the interests of the African people, were faced with this *conflict between the law and our conscience.* (p. 145)

Not to acknowledge receipt is to betray the laws of civility but first of all those of civilization: a primitive behavior, a return to the state of nature, a presocial phase, *before the establishment of the law*. Why does the Government return to this noncivilized practice? Because it considers the majority of the people, the "most numerous community," as noncivilized, before or outside the law. Acting in this way, interrupting the correspondence thus in a unilateral fashion, the white man no longer respects his own law. He is blinded by this evidence: a letter received means that the other is appealing to the law of the community. In scorning his own law, the white man gives the law over to being scorned:

> Perhaps the court will say that despite our human rights to protest, to object, to make ourselves heard, we should stay within the letter of the law. I would say, Sir, that it is the Government, its administration of the law, which brings the law into such contempt and disrepute that one is no longer concerned in this country to stay within the letter of the law. I will illustrate this from my own experience. The Government has used the process of law to handicap me, in my personal life, in my career, and in my political work, in a way which is calculated, in my opinion, to bring about *contempt of the law.* (p. 148)

This scorn for the law (the symmetrical inverse of the respect for the moral law, as Kant would say: *Achtung/Verachtung*) is not then his, is not Mandela's. He reflects somehow, by accusing, by answering, by acknowledging receipt, the scorn of the whites for their own law. It is still and always a reflection. Those who one day made him an outlaw just did not have that right: they had already placed themselves outside the law. By describing his own outlawed condition, Mandela analyzes and reflects the outlawed being of the law in the name of which he will have been not judged but persecuted, prejudged, judged a criminal beforehand, as if, in this endless trial, the trial had *already* taken place, before the investigation, whereas it has been endlessly adjourned:

> I was made, by the law, a criminal, not because of what I had done, but because of what I stood for, because of what I thought, because of my conscience. Can it be any wonder to anybody that such conditions make a man an outlaw of society? Can it be wondered that such a man, having been outlawed by the Government, should be prepared to lead the life of an outlaw, as I have led for some months, according to the evidence before this Court? . . . But there comes a time, as it came in my life, when a man is denied the right to live a normal life, when he can only live the life of an outlaw because the Government has so decreed to use the law to impose a state of outlawry upon him. (pp. 148-149)

Mandela is thus accusing the white governments of never *answering* even as they demand that the blacks be quiet and use correspondence: resign yourself to correspondence and to corresponding all alone.

Sinister irony of a counterpoint: after his condemnation, Mandela is isolated twenty-three hours a day in a house in the center of Pretoria. He has to sew together postal bags.

4

A man of the law by vocation, Mandela submits the laws of his métier to the same reflection, professional deontology, its essence and its contradictions. This lawyer, enjoined by the "code of deontology to observe the laws of this country and to respect its traditions," how could he have conducted a campaign and incited others to strike against the politics of this same country? He asks this question himself in front of his judges. To answer it requires nothing less than the story of his life. The decision to conform or not to a code of deontology does not depend on deontology *as such*. The question "what to do about professional deontology, should one respect it or not?" is not of a professional order. It takes as a response a decision that engages one's whole existence in its moral, political, historical dimensions. In a way, one has to recount one's life in order to explain or rather to justify the transgression of a professional rule:

> In order that the Court shall understand the frame of mind which leads me to action such as this, it is necessary for me to explain the background to my own political development and to try to make this Court aware of the factors which influenced me in deciding to act as I did.
> Many years ago, when I was a boy brought up in my village in the Transkei . . . (p. 141)

Is Mandela treating professional obligations lightly? No, he is trying to think through his profession, which is not just an ordinary profession. He is reflecting the deontology of deontology, the deep meaning and the spirit of the deontological laws. And once again by admiring respect, he decides to adopt uncompromising measures in the name of a deontology of deontology that is just as clearly a deontology beyond itself, a law beyond legality. But the paradox of this reflection (the deontology *of* deontology), which carries *beyond* what it reflects, is that responsibility takes on once again its meaning *in the inside* of the professional apparatus. It is reinscribed therein, for Mandela decides, to all appearances against the legal code, to exercise his profession just where they wanted to keep him from doing so. As a "lawyer worthy of that name," he sets himself *against the code in the code*, reflects the code, but making visible thereby just what the code in action rendered unreadable. His reflection, once more, shows what phenomenality still kept in hiding. It does not re-produce, it produces the visible. This production of light is justice— moral or political. For the phenomenal dissimulation must not be confused with some natural process; it has nothing neutral about it, either innocent or fatal. It translates here the political violence of the whites, it holds to their interpretation of the laws, to that proliferation of legal apparatuses and purviews whose letter is destined to contradict the spirit of the law. For example, because of the color of his skin and his belonging to the Council for National Action, Mandela cannot occupy any professional premises in town. He must therefore, unlike any white lawyer, have a special authorization from the Government, conforming to the Urban Areas Act. Authorization refused. Then a waiver that is not renewed. Mandela must from then on practice in an indigenous reservation, accessible only with difficulty to those who need his counsel in town:

This was tantamount to asking us to abandon our legal practice, to give up the legal service of our people, for which we had spent many years training. No attorney worth his salt will agree easily to do so. For some years, therefore, we continued to occupy premises in the city, illegally. The threat of prosecution and ejection hung menacingly over us throughout that period. It was an act of *defiance of the law*. We were aware that it was, but, nevertheless, that act had been forced on us against our wishes, and we could do no other than to choose between compliance with the law and compliance with our consciences. . . . I regarded it as a duty which I owed, not just to my people, but also to my profession, to the practice of law, and to justice for all mankind, to cry out against this discrimination which is essentially unjust and opposed to the whole basis of the attitude towards justice which is part of the tradition of legal training in this country. (pp. 142–43)

A man of the law by vocation: it would be greatly simplifying things to say that he places respect for the law and a certain categorical imperative above professional deontology. The "profession of jurist" is not a métier like any other. It professes, we could say, what we are all bound to, even outside the profession. A jurist is an expert of respect or admiration, he judges or delivers himself to judgment with an increased rigor, or in any case he should. Mandela must then find, *inside* professional deontology, the best reason for failing in a legislative code which already betrayed the principles of every *good* professional deontology. As if, upon reflection, he were also to repair, supplement, reconstruct, add on to a deontology where the whites were finally showing themselves deficient.

Twice, then, he confesses a certain "scorn for the law" (still his expression) in order to hold out to his adversaries the mirror in which they should recognize and see their own contempt for the law being reflected. But with this *supplementary inversion*: on the side of Mandela, the apparent contempt signifies an increase of respect for the law.

However, he does not accuse his judges, not immediately, at least not in the moment when he appears before them. Doubtless he will first have objected to them: on one hand, the Court had as yet no black in its composition and thus offered no guarantees of the necessary impartiality ("The South African Government affirms that the Universal Declaration of the Rights of Man is applied in this country but, in truth, equality before the law in no way exists in relation to the concerns of our people"); on the other hand, the president happens to remain, between sessions, in contact with the political police. But once in front of his judges, these objections having of course not been sustained, Mandela no longer accuses the tribunal. First, he still maintains inside him this respectful admiration for those who exercise a function exemplary in his eyes and for the dignity of a tribunal. Then the respect of rules permits him to confirm the ideal legitimacy of an instance before which he also needs to *appear*. He wants to seize the occasion, I don't dare repeat the chance once more, of this trial in order to *speak*, to give to his word a space of *public* resonance, virtually universal. His judges must represent a universal instance. He will thus be able to speak to them, while speaking over their heads. This double opportunity permits him to gather together the meaning of his history, his and that of his people, in order to articulate it into a coherent account. The image of what allies his story to that of his people must form itself in this double focus, which at once welcomes it, gathers it up by drawing it together, and keeps it, yes, keeps it above all: the judges here present who are listening to Mandela, and behind them, rising high and far above them, the universal court. And in a while we find the man and the philosopher of this tribunal again. For once, then, there will have been a discourse aloud *and* correspondence, the written text of his pleading, which is also an indictment: it has come over to us, here it is, we are reading it at this very moment.

5

This text is at once unique and exemplary. Is it a *testament*? What has become of it over the past twenty years? What has history done, what will it do with it? What will become of the example? And Nelson Mandela himself? His jailers dare speak of exchanging him, negotiating for his freedom, bargaining for his freedom and that of Sakharov.

There are two ways, at least, to receive a testament and two senses of the word—two ways, in short, to acknowledge receipt. One can inflect it toward what *bears witness* only to a past and knows itself condemned to reflecting on what will not return: a sort of West in general, the end of a trip which is also the trajectory from a luminous source, the end of an epoch, for example that of the Christian West (Mandela speaks its language, he is also an English Christian). But, another inflection, if the testament is always made in front of witnesses, a witness in front of witnesses, it is also to open and enjoin, it is to confide in others the responsibility of a future. To bear witness, to test, to attest, to contest, to present oneself before witnesses. For Mandela, it was not only to show himself, to give himself to be known, him and his people, it was also to reinstitute the law for the future, as if, finally, it had never taken place. As if, having never been respected, it were to remain, this arch-ancient thing that had never been present, as the future even—still now invisible.

These two inflections of the testament are not opposed: they meet in the exemplarity of the example when it concerns, respect for the law. Respect for a person, Kant tells us, is first addressed to the law of which this person only gives us the example. Properly, respect is due only to the law, which is its sole cause. And yet—it's the law—we must respect the other for himself, in his irreplaceable singularity. It is true that, as a person or a reasonable being, the other always bears witness, in his very singularity, to the respect for the law. He is exemplary in this sense. And still reflecting, according to the same optics, that of admiration and respect, these figures of the gaze. Some will be tempted to see in Mandela the witness or the martyr of the past. According to them, he let himself be captured (literally, imprisoned) in the view of the West, as in the machination of his reflecting apparatus; he has not only interiorized the law, we were saying, he has interiorized the principle of interiority in its testamentary tradition (Christian, Rousseauist, Kantian, and so on).

But one could say the opposite: his reflection lets us see, in the most singular geopolitical conjunction, in this extreme concentration of all human history that are the places or the stakes today called, for example, "South Africa," or "Israel," the promise of what has not yet ever been seen or heard, in a law that has not yet presented itself in the West, at the Western border, except briefly, before immediately disappearing. What will be decided in these so-called places—these are also formidable metonymies—would decide everything, if there were still that—everything.

So the exemplary witnesses are often those who distinguish between the law and laws, between respect for the law which speaks immediately to the conscience and submission to positive law (historical, national, institutional). Conscience is not only memory but promise. The exemplary witnesses, those who make us think about the law they reflect, are those who, in certain situations, *do not respect* laws. They are sometimes torn between conscience and law, they are sometimes condemned by the tribunals of their country. And there are some in *every country*, which proves that the place where these things occur is also for the law the place of the first uprooting. For example, in England a peer of the Realm (still this admiration for the most elevated forms of parliamentary democracy), a philosopher who is the "most respected in the Western world," knew how, in certain situations, not to respect the law, how to put "conscience," "duty," "faith in the justice of the cause" before the "respect for the law." It is out of respect that he did not show respect: no more respect. Respect for the sake of respect. Can we regulate some optical model on what such a possibility promises? Admiration of Mandela—for Bertrand Russell:

Your Worship, I would say that the whole life of any thinking African in this country drives him continuously to a conflict between his conscience on the one hand and the law on the other. This is not a conflict peculiar to this country. The conflict arises for men of conscience, for men who think and who feel deeply in every country. Recently in Britain, a peer of the realm, Earl Russell, probably *the most respected* philosopher of the Western world, was sentenced, convicted for precisely the type of activities for which I stand before you today, for following his conscience in defiance of the law, as a protest against a nuclear-weapons policy being followed by his own government. For him, his duty to the public, his belief in the morality of the essential rightness of the cause for which he stood, rose superior to his *high respect for the law*. He could not do other than to oppose the law and to suffer the consequences for it. Nor can I. Nor can many Africans in this country. The law as it is applied, the law as it has been developed over a long period of history, and especially the law as it is written and designed by the Nationalist Government is a law which, in our view, is immoral, unjust, and intolerable. Our consciences dictate that we must protest against it, that we must oppose it, and that we must attempt to alter it. (pp. 143–144)

To oppose the law, to then try and transform it: once the decision is made, the recourse to violence should not take place without measure and without rule. Mandela explains in minute detail the strategy, the limits, the progress reflected upon and observed. First there was a phase in the course of which, all legal opposition being forbidden, the infraction had nevertheless to remain nonviolent:

All lawful modes of expressing opposition to this principle had been closed by legislation, and we were placed in a position in which we had either to accept a permanent state of inferiority or to defy the Government. We chose to defy the law. We first broke the law in a way which avoided any recourse to violence. (p. 156)

The infraction still manifests the absolute respect of the supposed spirit of the law. But it was impossible to stop there. For the Government invented new legal devices to repress nonviolent challenges. To this violent response, which was also a nonresponse, the passage to violence was in its turn the only possible response. Response to the nonresponse:

> When this form was legislated against, and then the Government resorted to a show of force to crush opposition to its policies, only then did we decide to answer violence with violence. (Ibid)

But there again, the violence remains subject to a rigorous law, "a strictly controlled violence." Mandela insists, he underlines these words at the moment when he explains the genesis of the *Umkonto we Sizwe* (the Nation's Spear) in November 1961. In founding that combative organization, he means to submit it to the political directives of the Council for National Action, whose statutes prescribe nonviolence. In front of his judges, Mandela describes in detail the rules of action, the strategy, the tactics, and above all the limits imposed on the militants charged with sabotage: to wound or kill no one, either in the preparation or the execution of the operations. The militants must not bear arms. If he recognizes "having prepared a plan of sabotage," it was neither through "adventurism" nor through any "love of violence in itself." On the contrary, he wanted to interrupt what is so oddly called the cycle of violence, one implying the other because first of all it answers, reflects, sends it back its image. Mandela meant to limit the risks of explosion in controlling the actions of the militants, in constantly devoting himself to what he calls a "reflective" analysis of the situation.

He is arrested four months after the creation of the *Umkonto*, in August 1962. In May 1964, at the end of the trial of Rivonia, he is condemned to permanent criminal detention.

P.S. The postscript is for the future—for that part of the future most undecided today. I wanted to speak, of course, of Nelson Mandela's future, of what does not allow itself to be anticipated, caught, captured by any mirror. Who is Nelson Mandela?

We will never cease to admire him, himself and his admiration. But we don't yet know whom to admire in him, the one who, in the past, will have been the captive of his admiration or the one who, in a future anterior, will always have been free (the freest man in the world, let us not say that lightly) for having had the patience of his admiration and having known, passionately, what he had to admire. The one refusing as early as yesterday a conditioned freedom.

Would they have also imprisoned him, almost a quarter of a century ago, in his admiration itself? Was that not the *objective*—I mean that in the sense of photography and of the optic machine—the right to look? Did he *let* himself be imprisoned ? Did he *have* himself imprisoned? Was that an accident? Perhaps we should place ourselves at a point where these alternatives lose their meaning and become the justification and the starting point for new questions. Then leave these questions still open, like doors. And what remains to be seen in these questions, which are not only theoretical or philosophical, is also the figure of Mandela. Who is he?

We have looked at him through words which are sometimes the devices for observation, which can in any case become that if we are not careful. What we have described, in trying precisely to escape speculation, was a sort of great historical watchtower or observation post. But nothing permits us to imagine this unity as assured, still less the legitimacy of this optic of reflection, of its singular laws, of the law, of its place of institution, of presentation or of revelation, for example of what we assemble too quickly under the name of the West. But doesn't this presumption of unity produce something like an effect (I don't hold to this word) that so many forces, always, try to appropriate for themselves? An effect visible and invisible, like a mirror, also hard, like the walls of a prison.

All that still hides Nelson Mandela from our sight

Translated from the French by Mary Ann Caws and Isabelle Lorenz

Notes
1. Nelson Mandela, *The Struggle Is My Life* (London: International Defence and Aid for Southern Africa, 1978), p. 170. All the following quotes are taken from this publication and the italicized words are Jacques Derrida's.
2. Translators' note: The translation of this quote is ours; Jacques Derrida takes it from the French introduction and its source is unclear; Nelson Mandela, *L'Apartheid*, préface de Breyten Breytenbach (Paris, Les Editions de Minuit, 1985), p. 19. A comparative reading can be obtained for all the following Mandela quotes from the French mentioned above.
3. Translators' note: Translation is ours; pp. 19–20 in the French publication.

Part VII
Literature and aesthetics

13 'FORCE AND SIGNIFICATION' (1963)

WRITING AND DIFFERENCE (DERRIDA 1978
[FIRST PUBLISHED 1967])

Translated by Alan Bass

Themes

Derrida is concerned with literary aesthetics in this text, with regard to a
structuralist analysis of literary texts. He sees structuralist literary criticism both in terms of the history of metaphysics, and metaphysics in the
literary, particularly Aristotle's Poetics; the symbolist aesthetic which
emerged in nineteenth-century literature that emphasises the aesthetics
of the pure word and of pure form over representation in literature.

Structuralism is concerned with language as the origin of history. Its
approach is to place language over history in the triumph of form over
force. Structuralism is therefore concerned with the weakening of force.
The result is empty forms, like the post-apocalyptic city haunted by
meaning and culture.

The history of philosophical aesthetics provides an alternative to the
reduction to static forms in Kant's emphasis on non-schematic judgement
in the *Critique of the Power of Judgement* (Kant 2000 [first published
1790]). More recently Maurice Blanchot has discussed the inspiration of
pure absence as the source of literature. Both Kant and Blanchot refer us
to the anguish of writing as what emerges from indeterminacy. Nothing
precedes writing because the structuralists are correct to say that the
origin of history is tied up with writing even if they are wrong to turn
that into the triumph of pure empty forms. As writing is writing in
general, there is no book that contains the origin of writing and meaning

within itself. No book can exist as a self-contained internally unified thing, in any case. These are issues discussed in the extract from *Of Grammatology*, the first chapter of this book.

Structuralism claims to be neutral with regard to metaphysics, but it is full of metaphysical assumptions. It places space above time, because it presumes that literary texts can be analysed in terms of atemporal patterns rather than in the unfolding of narrative over time. That basic assumption is tied up with broader metaphysical assumptions. It is preformationist, that is it assumes that the final product, the text as a whole, is present from the very beginning, because the opening of the text is already part of the structure as a whole which places it in an atemporal relation that logically precedes its status as opening. Preformationism refers to biological theories according to which the organism as a whole is already present in the earliest stages of the embryo or even in the sperm. The theory is given metaphysical shape by Leibniz, and on some readings also in Kant. Structuralism is also teleological because it assumes that all parts of the text are devoted to the final goal, the text as a whole. Teleologism is a general metaphysical and physical position, particularly associated with Aristotle. In embryology it appears as epigenesis, the belief that the embryo is internally guided towards the goal of its final state, so that the goal is present from the beginning, but not the complete organism. Structuralism is teleological because it assumes that the inner development of the text guides itself to a final goal of the complete unity of the text, which is present formally from the beginning. Epigenesis and preformationism both exist as respectable hypotheses in biology, to be tested by the experimental procedures of biological science. What Derrida is concerned with is the way they have been turned into absolute metaphysical positions. They represent opposing positions in the history of biology, and they are metaphysically complicit in structuralist aesthetics because metaphysics is constituted by contradictions that it represses. Structuralism conceals the contradiction between the basic assumption that the text exists as a whole from its beginning and the basic assumption that text has an inner development towards its goal. Literary texts themselves play on these ambiguities in conceiving the text, as can be seen in Marcel Proust's *In Search of Lost Time* (1913–27) where preoccupation with structural unity (preformationism) gives the multi-volume novel a strong teleology. Though Proust is never discussed at length by Derrida, his emphasis on time, memory, death, and writing are all rather Derridean themes, and there is something rather phenomenological about Proust's writing. It may or may not be significant that Proust was related by marriage to the philosopher Henri Bergson, in any case his major novel has been deeply appreciated by many philosophers.

Proust's literature and aesthetic sensibility were formed by symbolism and Derrida refers in this paper to one of the major symbolist poets, Stéphane Mallarmé. Derrida addresses Mallarmé at length in *Dissemination* (Derrida 2004 [first published 1972]). He addresses another major symbolist figure Paul Valéry in the 1971 paper 'Qual Quelle' (in Derrida 1982). The issues of symbolism are present in all the modern and earlier literature which Derrida discusses in many places. The significance of symbolism is that it both emphasises the aesthetic purity of the literary object, and also draws attention to the material forces of the words that escape reduction to general form. Structuralism picks up on symbolist formalism but in a reduction of force which denies the nature of literature, and aesthetic objects in general.

Context

Literature is a persistent concern of Derrida's. One large book *Glas* (Derrida 1986 [first published 1974]) is divided into two parallel columns on each page. One column deals with the poet and dramatist Jean Genet. Two papers in *Writing and Difference* (Derrida 1978) deal with the dramatist Antonin Artaud: 'La parole soufflée' and 'The Theatre of Cruelty and the Closure of Representation'. Various other papers are collected in the volume *Acts of Literature* (Derrida 1992), which is only a small sample of Derrida's writing on literature. Literary texts are important even where Derrida is not writing specifically on literary aesthetics. A key passage in Edmund Husserl's *Origin of Geometry: An Introduction*, reproduced in Chapter 7, establishes a distinction between two approaches to history with reference to James Joyce's novel *Ulysses*. Derrida's whole approach to writing philosophy is an attempt to bring literary style into philosophy. Questions of style are the central theme of *Spurs: Nietzsche's Styles* (Derrida 1979 [first published 1976]).

It is Derrida's style that has separated him most from analytic philosophy. Accusations that Derrida is an extreme relativist and sceptic, even if they were true, would not be enough to separate Derrida from analytic philosophy, since such positions appear in analytic philosophy. Derrida's style aims to make the limits of abstract conceptuality and metaphysics through use of the material aspects of language, in emphasising style, which is part of the communicative act but cannot be reduced to abstract concepts. The reader is left to draw conclusions from the interplay between linguistic patterns, themes and explicit arguments, just as Derrida concentrates on these aspects in his readings of philosophical texts. Metaphors and patterns of unity of words across a text, which may or may not be accidental, communicate just as much as the explicit arguments.

However odd analytic readers might find these aspects of Derrida, they are not absent from analytic philosophy. Not all analytic philosophers devote much attention to Wittgenstein, but all analytic philosophy has been conditioned and affected by Wittgenstein, who uses the resources of language in ways that are close to Derrida's strategies.

Literature, and literary language, do not play the role in analytic philosophy, that they do in Derrida or in Continental European philosophy before Derrida. Analytic aesthetics has tended to concentrate on aesthetics as a branch of philosophy of mind so that pictorial art is taken as the aesthetic paradigm. Discussion of literature in analytic philosophy, often takes the form of ethics of literature, in which a literary text is examined for ethical points of view, which are analysed independently of questions of literary form and style. Nevertheless there are important moments in which analytic philosophers have considered literary language.

Amongst the central figures in analytic philosophy, it is Donald Davidson who has had the most to say about literary language. This perspective is developed in the 1978 paper 'What Metaphors Mean' and the 1982 paper 'Communication and Convention', joined in the section on 'The Limits of the Literal' in *Inquiries into Truth and Interpretation* (Davidson 2001a). In 'What Metaphors Mean' Davidson rejects any view according to which metaphor refers to some secondary aspect of meaning. Metaphor tells us nothing about meaning as it belongs to use rather than meaning. Any metaphor has a meaning, which is the literal meaning of the words concerned. This is rather distinct from Derrida as a view of metaphor, since Derrida denies that there is any non-metaphorical meaning. Nevertheless, since for Derrida there is no determinate boundary between meaning and use, as that would be a boundary between meaning and context, a theory of use is a theory of meaning. In that case we can extend Davidson's view of use as metaphorical to meaning. Meaning always occurs in the context of use, and use always introduces the possibility of metaphor, of the non-literal use of the word. In 'Communication and Convention', Davidson claims that language is not conventional, that is words are not connected to the world by conventions, because convention itself depends on language. Because language is what establishes conventional relations it cannot be just a convention itself. According to Davidson, we can define meaning through truth, without resort to any metaphysical theories of truth but just through the structure of language. Truth is a relation between words and objects, or the world, so that is a non-conventional relationship between language and the world. The emphasis on the non-conventional nature of language is rather un-Derridean. However, there are at least two points of contact with Derrida. For Derrida, language is never purely conventional or institutional, it always contains, and is conditioned by 'natural' empirical forces. There is still no equivalent to Davidson's interest in finding the truth conditions of propositions. The second point of contact is that, for Derrida, questions of language are always questions of the whole of knowledge and thought, and questions of all institutions. Like Davidson, he finds that language institutes, or founds, all conventional relations.

Davidson develops these reflections on the non-literal aspects of language in the papers collected in the section on 'Language' in *Truth, Language, and History* (Davidson 2005). The 1986 paper 'A Nice Derangement of Epitaphs', considers the difficulties of establishing general meanings for words, which all become epitaphs for particular occasions. The 1989 paper 'James Joyce and Humpty Dumpty' and the 1993 paper 'Locating Literary Language' are specifically concerned with literary texts. The approach is based on the issue of intentionality. Davidson regards literature, and other aesthetic forms as expressions of the author's intentions. That seems far from Derrida's claim that we do not know what our own intentions are in any absolute sense, and we certainly have no way of determining the intention behind someone else's language use. Nevertheless, Davidson's concern with the external influences on internal mental states along with the very variable ways in which intentions show themselves in the literary work, which can never be given a final determinate meaning, at least puts us in contact with what Derrida does. It must also be noted that in his remarks on literature, Derrida is often concerned with the appearance of the signature of the author in disguised references to the author's names in literary texts. It would therefore be wrong to believe that Derrida denies that the author is present in a text, and wrong to say that all the issues of intentionality are eliminated.

The other major figure who provides context for Derrida's work on literary aesthetics is Martha Nussbaum. Her definitive work in this field is the large-scale study *Fragility of Goodness* (Nussbaum 2001 [first published 1986]). *Love's Knowledge* (Nussbaum 1990) connects more with Derrrida's interests in literature and literary thought since the symbolists, but is a more schematic work than *Fragility of Goodness*. In some respects, *Fragility of Goodness* is very far from Derrida's approach. Nussbaum develops the tradition of ethics in literature while Derrida is concerned with the movement of language and style in literature at the limits of expression. However, ethics does appear in literature for Derrida, as it appears in all language in the uneliminable presence of the Other. In Derrida's literary reflections, literature is a form of language particularly concerned with the presence of the Other in contrast to more technical uses of language. Nussbaum looks at themes of Platonic and Aristotelian ethics in Ancient Greek literature as ways of testing very specific moral theories, while Derrida never discusses literature in that way. The perspective Nussbaum adopts is still not so far from Derrida's thought. She questions Platonic moral absolutism based on an abstract conception of moral personality. She looks at the ambiguities in Plato and the preferable model in Aristotle of the empirical and fallible nature of moral personality. Moral luck means that we might always fall from reliable moral personality because of the force of events, particularly personal disaster which are rooted in chance or accidental decisions rather than deep moral faults. For Nussbaum, literary style makes this clear and makes manifest the fluid, changeable nature of moral personality and personal identity, existing in the context of intersubjective communication. She deploys formidable classical scholarship in emphasising the material qualities of literary language, and its sensual qualities, in ways that strongly parallel Derrida's approach.

WRITING AND DIFFERENCE: FORCE AND SIGNIFICATION

> It might be that we are all tattooed savages since Sophocles. But
> there is more to Art than the straightness of lines and the perfec-
> tion of surfaces. Plasticity of style is not as large as the entire
> idea. . . . We have too many things and not enough forms.
>
> (Flaubert, *Préface à la vie d'écrivain*)

If it recedes one day, leaving behind its works and signs on the shores of
our civilization, the structuralist invasion might become a question for
the historian of ideas, or perhaps even an object. But the historian would
be deceived if he came to this pass: by the very act of considering the
structuralist invasion as an object he would forget its meaning and would
forget that what is at stake, first of all, is an adventure of vision, a
conversion of the way of putting questions to any object posed before us,
to historical objects—his own—in particular. And, unexpectedly among
these, the literary object.

By way of analogy: the fact that universal thought, in all its domains,
by all its pathways and despite all differences, should be receiving a
formidable impulse from an anxiety about language—which can only be
an anxiety of language, within language itself—is a strangely concerted
development; and it is the nature of this development not to be able to
display itself in its entirety as a spectacle for the historian, if, by chance,
he were to attempt to recognize in it the sign of an epoch, the fashion of
a season, or the symptom of a crisis. Whatever the poverty of our knowledge in this respect, it is certain that the question of the sign is itself
more or less, or in any event something other, than a sign of the times.

To dream of reducing it to a sign of the times is to dream of violence. Especially when this question, an unexpectedly historical one, approaches the point at which the simple significative nature of language appears rather uncertain, partial, or inessential. It will be granted readily that the analogy between the structuralist obsession and the anxiety of language is not a chance one. Therefore, it will never be possible, through some second- or third-hand reflection, to make the structuralism of the twentieth century (and particularly the structuralism of literary criticism, which has eagerly joined the trend) undertake the mission that a structuralist critic has assigned to himself for the nineteenth century: to contribute to a "future history of imagination and affectivity."[1] Nor will it be possible to reduce the fascination inherent in the notion of structure to a phenomenon of fashion,[2] except by reconsidering and taking seriously the meanings of imagination, affectivity, and fashion—doubtless the more urgent task. In any event, if some aspect of structuralism belongs to the domains of imagination, affectivity, or fashion, in the popular sense of these words, this aspect will never be the essential one. The structuralist stance, as well as our own attitudes assumed before or within language, are not only moments of history. They are an astonishment rather, by language as the origin of history. By historicity itself. And also, when confronted by the possibility of speech and always already within it, the finally acknowledged repetition of a surprise finally extended to the dimensions of world culture—a surprise incomparable to any other, a surprise responsible for the activation of what is called Western thought, the thought whose destiny is to extend its domains while the boundaries of the West are drawn back. By virtue of its innermost intention, and like all questions about language, structuralism escapes the classical history of ideas which already supposes structuralism's possibility, for the latter naively belongs to the province of language and propounds itself within it.

Nevertheless, by virtue of an irreducible region of irreflection and spontaneity within it, by virtue of the essential shadow of the undeclared, the structuralist phenomenon will deserve examination by the historian of ideas. For better or for worse. Everything within this phenomenon that does not in itself transparently belong to the question of the sign will merit this scrutiny; as will everything within it that is methodologically effective, thereby possessing the kind of infallibility now ascribed to sleepwalkers and formerly attributed to instinct, which was said to be as certain as it was blind. It is not a lesser province of the social science called history to have a privileged concern, in the acts and institutions of man, with the immense region of somnambulism, the *almost-everything* which is not the pure waking state, the sterile and silent acidity of the question itself, the *almost-nothing*.[3]

Since we take nourishment from the fecundity of structuralism, it is too soon to dispel our dream. We must muse upon what it *might* signify from within it. In the future it will be interpreted, perhaps, as a relaxation, if not a lapse, of the attention given to *force*, which is the tension of force itself. *Form* fascinates when one no longer has the force to understand force from within itself. That is, to create. This is why criticism is structuralist in every age, in its essence and destiny. Criticism has not always known this, but understands it now, and thus is in the process of thinking itself in its own concept, system and method. Criticism henceforth knows itself separated from force, occasionally avenging itself on force by gravely and profoundly proving that separation is the condition of the work, and not only of the discourse on the work.[4] Thus is explained the low note, the melancholy pathos that can be perceived behind the triumphant cries of technical ingenuity or mathematical subtlety that sometimes accompany certain so-called "structural" analyses. Like melancholy for Gide, these analyses are possible only after a certain defeat of force and within the movement of diminished ardor. Which makes the structural consciousness consciousness in general, as a conceptualization of the past, I mean of facts in general. A reflection of the accomplished; the constituted, the *constructed*. Historical, eschatalogical, and crepuscular by its very situation.

But within structure there is not only form, relation, and configuration. There is also interdependency and a totality which is always concrete. In literary criticism, the structural "perspective" is, according to Jean-Pierre Richard's expression, "interrogative and totalitarian."[5] The force of our weakness is that impotence separates, disengages, and emancipates. Henceforth, the totality is more clearly perceived, the panorama and the panoramagram are possible. The panoramagram, the very image of the structuralist instrument, was invented in 1824, as Littré states, in order "to obtain immediately, on a flat surface, the development of depth vision of objects on the horizon." Thanks to a more or less openly acknowledged schematization and spatialization, one can glance over the field divested of its forces more freely or diagrammatically. Or one can glance over the totality divested of its forces, even if it is the totality of form and meaning, for what is in question, in this case, is meaning rethought as form; and structure is the *formal* unity of form and meaning. It will be said that this neutralization of meaning by form is the author's responsibility before being the critic's, and to a certain extent—but it is just this extent which is in question—this is correct. In any event, the project of a conceptualization of totality is more easily stated today, and such a project in and of itself escapes the *determined* totalities of classical history. For it is the project of exceeding them. Thus, the relief and design of structures appears more clearly when content, which is the living energy of meaning, is neutralized. Somewhat like the architecture of an uninhabited or deserted city, reduced to its skeleton by some catastrophe of nature or art. A city no longer inhabited, not simply left behind, but haunted by meaning and culture. This state of being haunted, which keeps the city from returning to nature, is perhaps the general mode of the presence or absence of the thing itself in pure language. The pure language that would be housed in pure literature, the object of pure literary criticism. Thus it is in no way paradoxical that the structuralist consciousness is a catastrophic consciousness, simultaneously destroyed and destructive, *destructuring*, as is all consciousness, or at least the moment of decadence, which is the period proper to all movement of consciousness. Structure is perceived through the incidence of menace, at the moment when imminent danger concentrates our vision on the keystone of an institution, the stone which encapsulates both the possibility and the fragility of its existence. Structure then can be *methodically* threatened in order to be comprehended more clearly and to reveal not only its supports but also that secret place in which it is neither construction nor ruin but lability. This operation is called (from the Latin) *soliciting*. In other words, *shaking* in a way related to the *whole* (from *sollus*, in archaic Latin "the whole," and from *citare*, "to put in motion"). The structuralist solicitude and solicitation give themselves only the illusion of technical liberty when they become methodical. In truth, they reproduce, in the register of method, a solicitude and solicitation of Being, a historico-metaphysical threatening of foundations. It is during the epochs of historical dislocation, when we are expelled from the *site*, that this structuralist passion, which is simultaneously a frenzy of experimentation and a proliferation of schematizations, develops for itself. The baroque would only be one example of it. Has not a "structural poetics" "founded on a rhetoric"[6] been mentioned in relation to the baroque? But has not a "burst structure" also been spoken of, a "rent poem whose structure appears as it bursts apart"?[7]

The liberty that this critical (in all the senses of this word)[8] disengagement assures us of, therefore, is a solicitude for and an opening into totality. But what does this opening hide? And hide, not by virtue of what it leaves aside and out of sight, but by virtue of its very power to illuminate. One continually asks oneself this question in reading Jean Rousset's fine book: *Forme et Signification: Essais sur les structures littéraires de Corneille à Claudel.*[9] Our question is not a reaction against what others have called "ingenuity" and what seems to us, except in a few instances, to be something more and something better. Confronted by this series of brilliant and penetrating exercises intended to illustrate a method, it is rather a question of unburdening ourselves of a mute anxiety, and of doing so at the point at which this anxiety is not only ours, the reader's, but also seems to conform, beneath the language, operations, and greatest achievements of this book, to the anxiety of the author himself.

Rousset certainly acknowledges kinships and affiliations: Bachelard, Poulet, Raymond, Picon, Starobinski, Richard, etc. However, despite the familial air, the many borrowings and numerous respectful acknowledgments, *Forme et Signification* seems to us, in many respects, a solitary attempt.

In the first place, this is due to a *deliberate* difference. Rousset does not isolate himself within this difference, keeping his distance; rather, he scrupulously examines a community of intentions by bringing to the surface enigmas hidden beneath values that are today accepted and respected—modern values they may be, but values already traditional enough to have become the commonplaces of criticism, making them, therefore, open to reflection and suspicion. Rousset presents his theses in a remarkable methodological introduction that, along with the introduction to *l'Univers imaginaire de Mallarmé*, should become an important part of the discourse on method in literary criticism. In multiplying his introductory references Rousset does not muddle his discourse but, on the contrary, weaves a net that tightens its originality.

For example: that in the literary fact language is one with meaning, that form belongs to the content of the work; that, according to the expression of Gaeton Picon, "for modern art, the work is not expression but creation"[10]—these are propositions that gain unanimous acceptance only by means of a highly equivocal notion of form or expression. The same goes for the notion of *imagination*, the power of mediation or synthesis between meaning and literality, the common root of the universal and the particular—as of all other similarly dissociated couples—the obscure origin of these structural frameworks and of the empathy between "form and content" which makes possible both the work and the access to its unity. For Kant, the imagination was already in itself an "art," was art itself, which originally did not distinguish between truth and beauty; and despite all the differences, Kant speaks of the same imagination in the *Critique of Pure Reason* and the *Critique of Judgment* as does Rousset. It is art, certainly, but a "hidden art"[11] that cannot be "revealed to the eyes."[12] "Now since the reduction of a representation of the imagination to concepts is equivalent to giving its exponents, the aesthetic idea may be called an *inexponible* representation of the imagination (in its free play)."[13] Imagination is the freedom that reveals itself only in its works. These works do not exist *within* nature, but neither do they inhabit a world *other* than ours. "The imagination (as a productive faculty of cognition) is a powerful agent for creating, as it were, a second nature out of the material supplied to it by actual nature.[14] This is why intelligence is not necessarily the essential faculty of the critic when he sets out to encounter imagination and beauty; "in what we call beautiful, intelligence is at the service of the imagination, and the latter is not at the service of intelligence."[15] For "the freedom of the imagination consists precisely in the fact that it schematizes without a concept."[16] This enigmatic origin of the work as a structure and indissociable unity—and as an object for structuralist criticism—is, according to Kant, "the first thing to which we must pay attention."[17] According to Rousset also. From his first page on, he links "the nature of the literary fact," always insufficiently examined, to the "role in art of imagination, that fundamental activity" about which "uncertainties and oppositions abound." This notion of an imagination that produces metaphor—that is, everything in language except the verb *to be*—remains for critics what certain philosophers today call a naively utilized *operative concept*. To surmount this technical ingenuousness is to reflect the operative concept as a *thematic concept*. This seems to be one of Rousset's projects.

To grasp the operation of creative imagination at the greatest possible proximity to it, one must turn oneself toward the invisible interior of poetic freedom. One must be separated from oneself in order to be reunited with the blind origin of the work in its darkness. This experience of conversion, which founds the literary act (writing or reading), is such that the very words "separation" and "exile," which always designate the interiority of a breaking-off with the world and a making of one's way within it, cannot directly manifest the experience; they can only indicate it through a metaphor whose genealogy itself would deserve all of our efforts.[18] For in question here is a departure from the world toward a place which is neither a *non-place* nor an *other* world, neither a utopia nor an alibi, the creation of "a universe to be added to the universe," according to an expression of Focillon's cited by Rousset (*Forme et Signification*, p. 11). This universe articulates only that which is in excess of everything, the essential nothing on whose basis everything can appear and be produced within language; and the voice of Maurice Blanchot reminds us, with the *insistence* of profundity, that this excess is the very possibility of writing and of literary *inspiration* in general. Only *pure absence*—not the absence of this or that, but the absence of everything in which all presence is announced—can *inspire*, in other words, can *work*, and then make one work. The pure book naturally turns toward the eastern edge of this absence which, beyond or within the prodigiousness of all wealth, is its first and proper content. The pure book, the book itself, by virtue of what is most irreplaceable within it, must be the "book about nothing" that Flaubert dreamed of—a gray, negative dream, the origin of the total Book that haunted other imaginations. This emptiness as the situation of literature must be acknowledged by the critic as that which constitutes the specificity of his object, as that *around which* he always speaks. Or rather, his proper object—since nothing is not an object—is the way in which this nothing *itself* is determined by disappearing, It is the transition to the determination of the work as the disguising of its origin. But the origin is possible and conceivable only in disguise. Rousset shows us the extent to which spirits as diverse as Delacroix, Balzac, Flaubert, Valéry, Proust, T. S. Eliot, Virginia Woolf, and many others had a sure consciousness of this. A sure and certain consciousness, although in principle not a clear and distinct one, as there is not intuition of a thing involved.[19] To these voices should be added that of Antonin Artaud, who was less roundabout: "I made my debut in literature by writing books in order to say that I could write nothing at all. My thoughts, when I had something to say or write, were that which was furthest from me. I never had any ideas, and two short books, each seventy pages long, are about this profound, inveterate, endemic absence of any idea. These books are *l'Ombilic des limbes* and *le Pèse-nerfs*."[20] The consciousness of having something to say as the consciousness of nothing: this is not the poorest, but the most oppressed of consciousnesses. It is the consciousness of nothing, upon which all consciousness of something enriches itself, takes on meaning and shape. And upon whose basis all speech can be brought forth. For the thought of the thing as *what* it *is* has already been confused with the experience of pure speech; and this experience has been confused with experience *itself*. Now, does not pure speech require inscription[21] somewhat in the manner that the Leibnizian essence requires existence and pushes on toward the world, like power toward the act? If the anguish of writing is not and must not be a *determined* pathos, it is because this anguish is not an empirical modification or state of the writer, but is the responsibility of *angustia*:[22] the necessarily restricted passageway of speech against which all possible meanings push each other, preventing each other's emergence. Preventing, but calling upon each other, provoking each other too, unforeseeably and as if despite oneself, in a kind of autonomous overassemblage of meanings, a power of pure equivocality that makes the creativity of the classical God appear all too poor. Speaking frightens me because, by never saying enough, I also say too much. And if the necessity of becoming breath or speech restricts meaning—and our responsibility for it—writing restricts and constrains speech further still.[23] Writing is the anguish of the Hebraic *ruah*,[24] experienced in solitude by human responsibility; experienced by

Jeremiah subjected to God's dictation ("Take thee a roll of a book, and write therein all the words that I have spoken unto thee"), or by Baruch transcribing Jeremiah's dictation (Jeremiah 36:2,4); or further, within the properly human moment of *pneumatology*, the science of *pneuma*, *spiritus*, or *logos* which was divided into three parts: the divine, the angelical and the human. It is the moment at which we must *decide* whether we will engrave what we hear. And whether engraving preserves or betrays speech. God, the God of Leibniz, since we have just spoken of him, did not know the anguish of the choice between various possibilities: he conceived possible choices in action and disposed of them as such in his Understanding or Logos; and, in any event, the narrowness of a passageway that is *Will* favors the "best" choice. And each existence continues to "express" the totality of the Universe. There is, therefore, no tragedy of the book. There is only one Book, and this same Book is distributed throughout all books. In the *Theodicy*, Theodorus, who "had become able to confront the divine radiancy of the daughter of Jupiter," is led by her to the "palace of the fates;" in this palace "Jupiter, having surveyed them before the beginning of the existing world, classified the possibilities into worlds, and chose the best of all. He comes sometimes to visit these places, to enjoy the pleasure of recapitulating things and of renewing his own choice, which cannot fail to please him." After being told all this by Pallas, Theodorus is led into a hall which "was a world." "There was a great volume of writings in this hall: Theodorus could not refrain from asking what that meant. It is the history of this world which we are now visiting, the Goddess told him; it is the book of its fates. You have seen a number on the forehead of Sextus. Look in this book for the place which it indicates. Theodorus looked for it, and found there the history of Sextus in a form more ample than the outline he had seen. Put your finger on any line you please, Pallas said to him, and you will see represented actually in all its detail that which the line broadly indicates. He obeyed, and he saw coming into view all the characteristics of a portion of the life of that Sextus."[25]

To write is not only to conceive the Leibnizian book as an impossible possibility. Impossible possibility, the limit explicitly named by Mallarmé. To Verlaine: "I will go even further and say: the Book, for I am convinced that there is only One, and that it has [unwittingly] been attempted by every writer, even by Geniuses."[26] " . . . revealing that, in general, all books contain the amalgamation of a certain number of age-old truths; that actually there is only one book on earth, that it is the law of the earth, the earth's true Bible. The difference between individual works is simply the difference between individual interpretations of one true and established text, which are proposed in a mighty gathering of those ages we call civilized or literary."[27] To write is not only to know that the Book does not exist and that forever there are books, against which the meaning of a world not conceived by an absolute subject is shattered, before it has even become a unique meaning; nor is it only to know that the non-written and the non-read cannot be relegated to the status of having no basis by the obliging negativity of some dialectic, making us deplore the absence of the Book from under the burden of "too many texts!" It is not only to have lost the theological certainty of seeing every page bind itself into the unique text of the truth, the "book of reason" as the journal in which accounts (*rationes*) and experiences consigned for Memory was formerly called,[28] the genealogical anthology, the Book of Reason this time, the infinite manuscript read by a God who, in a more or less deferred way, is said to have given us use of his pen. This lost certainty, this absence of divine writing, that is to say, first of all, the absence of the Jewish God (who himself writes, when necessary), does not solely and vaguely define something like "modernity." As the absence and haunting of the divine sign, it regulates all modern criticism and aesthetics. There is nothing astonishing about this. "Consciously or not," says Georges Canguilhem, "the idea that man has of his poetic power corresponds to the idea he has about the creation of the world, and to the solution he gives to the problem of the radical origin of things. If the notion of creation is equivocal, ontological and aesthetic, it is not so by chance or confusion."[29] To write is not only to know that through writing, through the extremities of style, the best will not necessarily transpire, as Leibniz thought it did in divine creation, nor will the transition to what transpires always be *willful*, nor will that which is noted down always infinitely *express* the universe, resembling and reassembling it.[30] It is also to be incapable of making meaning absolutely precede writing: it is thus to lower meaning while simultaneously elevating inscription. The eternal fraternity of theological optimism and of pessimism: nothing is more reassuring, but nothing is more despairing, more destructive of our books than the Leibnizian Book. On what could books in general live, what would they be if they were not alone, so alone, infinite, isolated worlds? To write is to know that what has not yet been produced within literality has no other dwelling place, does not await us as prescription in some *topos ouranios*, or some divine understanding. Meaning must await being said or written in order to inhabit itself, and in order to become, by differing from itself, what it is: meaning. This is what Husserl teaches us to think in *The Origin of Geometry*. The literary act thus recovers its true power at its source. In a fragment of a book he intended to devote to *The Origin of Truth*, Merleau-Ponty wrote: "Communication in literature is not the simple appeal on the part of the writer to meanings which would be part of an a priori of the mind; rather, communication arouses these meanings in the mind through enticement and a kind of oblique action. The writer's thought does not control his language from without; the writer is himself a kind of new idiom, constructing itself."[31] "My own words take me by surprise and teach me what I think,"[32]—he said elsewhere.

It is because writing is *inaugural*, in the fresh sense of the word, that it is dangerous and anguishing. It does not know where it is going, no knowledge can keep it from the essential precipitation toward the meaning that it constitutes and that is, primarily, its future. However, it is capricious only through cowardice. There is thus no insurance against the risk of writing. Writing is an initial and graceless recourse for the writer, even if he is not an atheist but, rather, a writer. Did Saint John Chrysostom speak of the writer? "It were indeed meet for us not at all to require the aid of the written Word, but to exhibit a life so pure, that the grace of the spirit should be instead of books to our souls, and that as these are inscribed with ink, even so should our hearts be with the Spirit. But, since we have utterly put away from us this grace, come let us at any rate embrace the second best course."[33] But, all faith or theological assurance aside, is not the experience of *secondarity* tied to the strange redoubling by means of which constituted—written—meaning presents itself as prerequisitely and simultaneously *read*: and does not meaning present itself as such at the point at which the other is found, the other who maintains both the vigil and the back-and-forth motion, the work, that comes between writing and reading, making this work irreducible? Meaning is neither before nor after the act. Is not that which is called God, that which imprints every human course and recourse with its secondarity, the passageway of deferred reciprocity between reading and writing? or the absolute witness to the dialogue in which what one sets out to write has already been read, and what one sets out to say is already a response, the third party as the transparency of meaning? Simultaneously part of creation and the Father of Logos. The circularity and traditionality of Logos. The strange labor of conversion and adventure in which grace can only be that which is missing.

Thus, the notion of an Idea or "interior design" as simply anterior to a work which would supposedly be the expression of it, is a prejudice: a prejudice of the traditional criticism called *idealist*. It is not by chance that this theory—or, one could now say, this theology—flowered during the Renaissance. Rousset, like so many others past or present, certainly speaks out against this "Platonism" or "Neo-Platonism." But he does not forget that if creation by means of "the form rich in ideas" (Valéry) is not the purely transparent expression of this form, it is nevertheless, simultaneously, revelation. If creation were not revelation, what would happen to the finitude of the writer and to the solitude of his hand abandoned by God? Divine creativity, in this case, would be reappropriated by a hypocritical humanism. If writing is *inaugural* it is not so because it creates, but because of a certain absolute freedom of speech, because of the freedom to bring forth the already there as a sign of the freedom to augur. A freedom of response which acknowledges as its only horizon the world as history and the speech which can only say: Being has always already begun. To create is to reveal; says Rousset, who does not turn his back on classical criticism. He comprehends it, rather, and enters into dialogue with it: "Prerequisite secret and unmasking of this secret by the work: a reconciliation of ancient and modern aesthetics can be observed, in a certain way, in the possible correspondence of the preexisting secret to the Idea of the Renaissance thinkers stripped of all Neo-Platonism."

This revelatory power of true literary language as poetry is indeed the access to free speech, speech unburdened of its signalizing functions by the word "Being" (and this, perhaps, is what is aimed at beneath the notion of the "primitive word" or the "theme-word," *Leitwort*, of Buber).[34] It is when that which is written is *deceased* as a sign-signal that it is born as language; for then it says what is, thereby referring only to itself, a sign without signification, a game or pure functioning, since it ceased to be *utilized* as natural, biological, or technical information, or as the transition from one existent to another, from a signifier to a signified. And, paradoxically, inscription alone—although it is far from always doing so—has the power of poetry; in other words has the power to arouse speech from its slumber as sign. By enregistering speech, inscription has as its essential objective, and indeed takes this fatal risk, the emancipation of meaning—as concerns any actual field of perception—from the natural predicament in which everything refers to the disposition of a contingent situation. This is why writing will never be simple "voice-painting" (Voltaire). It creates meaning by enregistering it, by entrusting it to an engraving, a groove, a relief, to a surface whose essential characteristic is to be infinitely transmissible. Not that this characteristic is always desired, nor has it always been; and writing as the origin of pure historicity, pure traditionality, is only the *telos* of a history of writing whose philosophy is always to come. Whether this project of an infinite tradition is realized or not, it must be acknowledged and respected in its sense as a project. That it can always fail is the mark of its pure finitude and its pure historicity. If the play of meaning can overflow signification (signalization), which is always enveloped within the regional limits of nature, life and the soul, this overflow is the moment of the attempt-to-write. The attempt-to-write cannot be understood on the basis of voluntarism. The will to write is not an ulterior determination of a primal will. On the contrary, the will to write reawakens the willful sense of the will: freedom, break with the domain of empirical history, a break whose aim is reconciliation with the hidden essence of the empirical, with pure historicity. The will and the attempt to write are not the desire to write, for it is a question here not of affectivity but of freedom and duty. In its relationship to Being, the attempt-to-write poses itself as the only way out of affectivity. A way out that can only be aimed at, and without the certainty that deliverance is or that it is outside affectivity. To be a affected is to be finite: to write could still be to deceive finitude, and to reach Being—a kind of Being which could neither be, nor affect me by *itself*—from without existence. To write would be to attempt to forget difference: to forget writing in the presence of so-called living and pure speech.[35]

In the extent to which the literary act proceeds from this attempt-to-write, it is indeed the acknowledgment of pure language, the responsibility confronting the vocation of "pure" speech which, once understood, constitutes the writer as such. Heidegger says of pure speech that it cannot "be conceived in the rigor of its essence" on the basis of its "character-as-sign" (*Zeichencharakter*), "nor even perhaps of its character-as-signification" (*Bedeutungscharakter*).[36]

Does not one thus run the risk of identifying the work with original writing in general? Of dissolving the notion of art and the value of "beauty" by which literature is currently distinguished from the letter in general? But perhaps by removing the specificity of beauty from aesthetic values, beauty is, on the contrary, liberated? Is there a specificity of beauty, and would beauty gain from this effort?

Rousset believes so. And the structuralism proper to Jean Rousset is defined, at least theoretically, against the temptation to overlook this specificity (the temptation that would be Poulet's, for example, since he "has little interest in art"),[37] putting Rousset close to Leo Spitzer and Marcel Raymond in his scrupulousness about the formal autonomy of the work an "independent, absolute organism that is self-sufficient" (*Forme et Signification* p. xx). "The work is a totality and always gains from being experienced as such" (p. xxi). But here again, Rousset's position depends upon a delicate balance. Always attentive to the unified foundations of dissociation, he circumvents the "objectivist" danger denounced by Poulet by giving a definition of structure that is not purely objective or formal; or circumvents it by at least not in principle dissociating form from intention, or from the very act of the writer: "I will call 'structures' these formal constants, these liaisons that betray a mental universe reinvented by each artist according to his needs" (p. xii).

Structure is then the unity of a form and a meaning. It is true that in some places the form of the work, or the form as the work, is treated *as if* it had no origin, as if, again, in the masterpiece—and Rousset is interested only in masterpieces—the wellbeing of the work was without history. Without an intrinsic history. It is here that structuralism seems quite vulnerable, and it is here that, by virtue of one whole aspect of his attempt—which is far from covering it entirely—Rousset too runs the risk of conventional Platonism. By keeping to the legitimate intention of protecting the *internal* truth and meaning of the work from historicism, biographism or psychologism (which, moreover, always lurk near the expression "mental universe"), one risks losing any attentiveness to the internal historicity of the work itself, in its relationship to a subjective origin that is not simply psychological or mental. If one takes care to confine classical literary history to its role as an "indispensable" "auxiliary," as "prologomenon and restraint" (p. xii, n. 16), one risks overlooking another history, more difficult to conceive: the history of the meaning of the work itself, of its *operation*. This history of the work is not only its *past*, the eve or the sleep in which it precedes itself in an author's intentions, but is also the impossibility of its ever being *present*, of its ever being summarized by some absolute simultaneity or instantaneousness. This is why, as we will verify, there is no *space* of the work, if by space we mean *presence* and *synopsis*. And, further on, we will see what the consequences of this can be for the tasks of criticism. It seems, for the moment, that if "literary history" (even when its techniques and its "philosophy" are renewed by "Marxism," "Freudianism," etc.) is only a restraint on the internal criticism of the work, then the structuralist moment of this criticism has the counterpart role of being the restraint on an internal geneticism, in which value and meaning are reconstituted and reawakened in their proper historicity and temporality. These latter can no longer be *objects* without becoming absurdities, and the structure proper to them must escape all classical categories.

Certainly, Rousset's avowed plan is to avoid this stasis of form, the stasis of a form whose completion appears to liberate it from work, from imagination and from the origin through which alone it can continue to signify. Thus, when he distinguishes his task from that of Jean-Pierre Richard,[38] Rousset aims directly at this totality of thing and act, form and intention, entelechy and becoming, the totality that is the literary fact as a concrete form: "Is it possible to embrace simultaneously imagination and morphology, to experience and to comprehend them in a simultaneous act? This is what I would like to attempt, although well persuaded that this undertaking, before being unitary, will often have to make itself *alternative* [my italics]. But the end in sight is indeed the simultaneous comprehension of a homogenous reality in a unifying operation" (p. xxii).

But condemned or resigned to alternation, the critic, in acknowledging it, is also liberated and acquitted by it. And it is here that Rousset's difference is no longer *deliberate*. His personality, his *style* will affirm themselves not through a methodological decision but through the play of the critic's spontaneity within the freedom of the "alternative." This spontaneity will, in fact, unbalance an alternation construed by Rousset as a theoretical norm. A practiced inflection that also provides the style of criticism—here Rousset's—with its structural form. This latter, Claude Lévi-Strauss remarks about social models and Rousset about structural motifs in a literary work, "escapes creative will and clear consciousness" (p. xv). What then is the imbalance of this preference? What is the preponderance that is more actualized than acknowledged? It seems to be *double*.

II

> There are lines which are monsters. . . . A line by itself has no meaning; a second one is necessary to give expression to meaning. Important law. (Delacroix)

> Valley is a common female dream symbol. (Freud)

On the one hand, structure becomes the object itself, the literary thing itself. It is no longer what it almost universally was before: either a heuristic instrument, a method of reading, a characteristic particularly revelatory of content, or a system of objective relations, independent of content and terminology; or, most often, both at once, for the fecundity of structure did not exclude, but, on the contrary, rather implied that relational configuration exists within the literary object. A structural realism has always been practiced, more or less explicitly. But never has structure been the exclusive *term*—in the double sense of the word—of critical description. It was always a *means* or relationship for reading or writing, for assembling significations, recognizing themes, ordering constants and correspondences.

Here, structure, the framework of construction, morphological correlation, becomes *in fact and despite his theoretical intention* the critic's sole preoccupation. His sole or almost sole preoccupation. No longer a method within the *ordo cognescendi*, no longer a relationship in the *ordo essendi* but the very being of the work. We are concerned with an ultra-structuralism.

On the other hand (and consequently), structure as the literary thing is this time taken, or at least practiced, *literally*. Now, stricto sensu, the notion of structure refers only to space, geometric or morphological space, the order of forms and sites. Structure is first the structure of an organic or artificial work, the internal unity of an assemblage, a *construction*; a work is governed by a unifying principle, the *architecture* that is built and made visible in a location. "Superbes monuments de l'orgueil des humains, / Pyramides, tombeaux, dont la noble structure / a temoigné que l'art, par l'adresse des mains / Et l'assidu travail peut vaincre la nature" ("Splendid monuments of human pride, pyramids, tombs, whose noble structure Bears witness that art, through the skill of hands and hard work, can vanquish nature"—Scarron). Only metaphorically was this *topographical* literality displaced in the direction of its Aristotelean and *topical* signification (the theory of commonplaces in language and the manipulation of motifs or arguments.) In the seventeenth century they spoke of "the choice and arrangement of words, the structure and harmony of the composition, the modest grandeur of the thoughts."[39] Or further: "In bad *structure* there is always something to be added, or diminished, or changed, not simply as concerns the topic, but also the words."[40]

How is this history of metaphor possible? Does the fact that language can determine things only by spatializing them suffice to explain that, in return, language must spatialize itself as soon as it designates and reflects upon itself? This question can be asked in general about all language and all metaphors. But here it takes on a particular urgency.

Hence, for as long as the metaphorical sense of the notion of structure is not acknowledged *as such*, that is to say interrogated and even destroyed as concerns its figurative quality so that the nonspatiality or original spatiality designated by it may be revived, one runs the risk, through a kind of sliding as unnoticed as it is *efficacious*, of confusing meaning with its geometric, morphological, or, in the best of cases, cinematic model. One risks being interested in the figure itself to the detriment of the play going on within it metaphorically. (Here, we are taking the word "figure" in its geometric as well as rhetorical sense. In Rousset's style, figures of rhetoric are always the figures of a geometry distinguished by its suppleness.)

Now, despite his stated propositions, and although he calls structure the union of formal structure and intention, Rousset, in his analyses, grants an absolute privilege to spatial models, mathematical functions, lines, and forms. Many examples could be cited in which the essence of his descriptions is reduced to this. Doubtless, he acknowledges the inter-dependency of space and time (*Forme et Signification*, p. xiv.). But, in fact, time itself is always reduced. To a *dimension* in the best of cases. It is only the element in which a form or a curve can be displayed. It is always in league with a line or design, always extended in space, level. It calls for measurement. Now, even if one does not follow Claude Lévi-Strauss when he asserts that there "is no necessary connection between measure and *structure*,"[41] one must acknowledge that for certain kinds of structures—those of literary ideality in particular—this connection is excluded in principle. The geometric or morphological elements of *Forme et Signification* are corrected only by a kind of mechanism, never by energetics. Mutatis mutandis, one might be tempted to make the same reproach to Rousset, and through him to the best literary formalism, as Leibniz made to Descartes: that of having explained everything in nature with figures and movements, and of ignoring force by confusing it with the quantity of movement. Now, in the sphere of language and writing, which, more than the body, "corresponds to the soul," "the ideas of size, figure and motion are not so distinctive as is imagined, and . . . stand for something imaginary relative to our perceptions."[42]

This geometry is only metaphorical, it will be said. Certainly. But metaphor is never innocent. It orients research and fixes results. When the spatial model is hit upon, when it functions, critical reflection rests within it. In fact, and even if criticism does not admit this to be so.

One example among many others.

At the beginning of the essay entitled "*Polyeucte*, or the Ring and the Helix," the author prudently warns us that if he insists upon "schemas that might appear excessively geometrical, it is because Corneille, more than any other, practiced symmetry." Moreover, "this geometry is not cultivated for itself," for "in the great plays it is a means subordinated to the ends of passion" (p. 7).

But what, in fact, does this essay yield? Only the geometry of a theater which is, however, one of "mad passion, heroic enthusiasm" (p. 7). Not only does the geometric structure of *Polyeucte* mobilize all the resources and attention of the author, but an entire teleology of Corneille's progress is coordinated to it. Everything transpires as if, until 1643, Corneille had only gotten a glimpse of, or anticipated the design of, *Polyeucte*, which was still in the shadows and which would eventually coincide with the Corneillean design itself, thereby taking on the dignity of an entelechy toward which everything would be in motion. Corneille's work and development are put into perspective and inter-preted teleologically on the basis of what is considered its destination, its final structure. *Before Polyeucte*, everything is but a sketch in which only what is missing is due consideration, those elements which are still shapeless and lacking as concerns the perfection to come, or which only foretell this perfection. "There were several years between *La galerie du palais* and *Polyeucte*. Corneille looks for and finds himself. I will not here trace the details of his progress, in which *Le Cid* and *Cinna* show him inventing his own structure" (p. 9). After *Polyeucte*? It is never mentioned. Similarly, among the works prior to it, only *La galerie du palais* and *Le Cid* are taken into account, and these plays are examined, in the style of preformationism, only as structural prefigurations of *Polyeucte*.

Thus, in *La galerie du palais* the inconstancy of Célidée separates her from her lover. Tired of her inconstancy (but why?), she draws near him again, while he, in turn, feigns inconstancy. They thus separate, to be united at the end of the play, which is outlined as follows: "Initial accord, separation, median reunification that falls, second separation symmetrical to the first, final conjunction. The destination is a return to the point of departure after a circuit in the form of a crossed ring" (p. 8). What is singular is the crossed ring, for the destination as return to the point of departure is of the commonest devices. Proust himself . . . (cf. p. 144).

The framework is analogous in *Le Cid*: "The ring-like movement with a median crossing is maintained" (p. 9). But here a new signification intervenes, one that panorography immediately transcribes in a new dimension. In effect, "at each step along the way, the lovers develop and grow, not only each one for himself, but through the other and for the other, according to a *very Corneillean* [my italics] law of progressively discovered interdependence; their union is made stronger and deeper by the very ruptures that should have destroyed it. Here, the phases of distanciation are no longer phases of separation and inconstancy, but tests of fidelity" (p. 9). The difference between *La galerie du palais* and *Le Cid*, one could be led to believe, is no longer in the design and movement of presences (distance–proximity), but in the *quality* and inner intensity of the experiences (tests of fidelity, manner of being for the other, force of rupture, etc.). And it could be thought that by virtue of the very enrichment of the play, the structural metaphor will now be incapable of grasping the play's quality and intensity, and that the work of forces will no longer be translated into a difference of form.

In believing so one would underestimate the resources of the critic. The dimension of *height* will now complete the analogical equipment. What is gained in the tension of sentiments (quality of fidelity, way of being-for-the-other, etc.) is gained in terms of *elevation*; for values, as we know, mount scalewise, and the Good is most high. The union of the lovers is deepened by an "aspiration toward the highest" (p. 9). *Altus*: the deep is the high. The ring, which remains, has become an "ascending spiral" and "helical ascent." And the horizontal flatness of *La galerie* was only an appearance still hiding the essential: the ascending movement. *Le Cid* only begins to reveal it: "Also the destination (in *Le Cid*), even if it apparently leads back to the initial conjunction, is not at all a return to the point of departure; the situation has changed, for the characters have been elevated. *This is the essential* my italics]: the Corneillean movement is a movement of violent elevation..." (but where has this violence and the force of movement, which is more than its quantity or direction, been spoken of?) "... of aspiration toward the highest; joined to the crossing of two rings, it now traces an ascending spiral, helical ascent. This formal combination will receive all the richness of its signification in *Polyeucte*" (p. 9). The structure thus was a receptive one, waiting, like a girl in love, ready for its future meaning to marry and fecundate it.

We would be convinced if beauty, which is value and force, were subject to regulation and schematization. Must it be shown once more that this is without sense? Thus, if *Le Cid* is beautiful, it is so by virtue of, that within it which surpasses schemes and understanding. Thus, one does not speak of *Le Cid* itself, if it is beautiful, in terms of rings, spirals, and helices. If the movement of these lines is not *Le Cid*, neither will it become *Polyeucte* as it perfects itself still further. It is not the *truth of Le Cid* or *of Polyeucte*. Nor is it the psychological truth of passion, faith, duty, etc., but, it will be said, it is this truth according to Corneille; not according to Pierre Corneille, whose biography and psychology do not interest us here: the "movement toward the highest," the greatest specificity of the schema, is none other than the Corneillean movement (p. 1). The progress indicated by *Le Cid*, which also aspires to the heights of *Polyeucte* is a "progress in the Corneillean meaning" (ibid.). It would be helpful here to reproduce the analysis of *Polyeucte*, "in which the schema reaches its greatest perfection and greatest internal complication; and does so with a mastery such that one wonders whether the credit is due Corneille or Rousset. We said above that the latter was too Cartesian and not Leibnizian enough. Let us be more precise. He is also Leibnizian: he seems to think that, confronted with a literary work, one should always be able to find a line, no matter how complex, that accounts for the unity, the totality of its movement, and all the points it must traverse.

In the *Discourse on Metaphysics*, Leibniz writes, in effect: "Because, let us suppose for example that someone jots down a quantity of points upon a sheet of paper helter skelter, as do those who exercise the ridiculous art of Geomancy; now I say that it is possible to find a geometrical line whose concept shall be uniform and constant, that is, in accordance with a certain formula, and which line at the same time shall pass through all of those points, and in the same order in which the hand jotted them down; also if a continuous line be traced, which is now straight, now circular, and now of any other description, it is possible to find a mental equivalent, a formula or an equation common to all the points of this line by virtue of which formula the changes in the direction of the line must occur. There is no instance of a fact whose contour does not form part of a geometric line and which can not be traced entire by a certain mathematical motion."[44]

But Leibniz was speaking of divine creation and intelligence: "I use these comparisons to picture a certain imperfect resemblance to the divine wisdom. . . . I do not pretend at all to explain thus the great mystery upon which depends the whole universe."[45] As concerns qualities, forces and values, and also as concerns nondivine works read by finite minds, this confidence in mathematical-spatial *representation* seems to be (on the scale of an entire civilization, for we are no longer dealing with the question of Rousset's language, but with the totality of our language and its credence) *analogous* to the confidence placed by Canaque artists[46] in the level representation of depth. A confidence that the structural ethnographer analyzes, moreover, with more prudence and less abandon than formerly.

Our intention here is not, through the simple motions of balancing, equilibration or overturning, to oppose duration to space, quality to quantity, force to form, the depth of meaning or value to the surface of figures. Quite to the contrary. To counter this simple alternative, to counter the simple choice of one of the terms or one of the series against the other, we maintain that it is necessary to seek new concepts and new models, an *economy* escaping this system of metaphysical oppositions. This economy would not be an energetics of pure, shapeless force. The differences examined *simultaneously* would be differences of site[47] and differences of force. If we appear to oppose one series to the other, it is because from within the classical system we wish to make apparent the noncritical privilege naively granted to the other series by a certain structuralism. Our discourse irreducibly belongs to the system of metaphysical oppositions. The break with this structure of belonging can be announced only through a *certain* organization, a certain *strategic* arrangement which, within the field of metaphysical opposition, uses the strengths of the field to turn its own stratagems against it, producing a force of dislocation that spreads itself throughout the entire system, fissuring it in every direction and thoroughly *delimiting* it.[48]

Assuming that, in order to avoid "abstractionism," one fixes upon—as Rousset does at least theoretically—the union of form and meaning, one then would have to say that the aspiration toward the highest, in the "final leap which will unite them . . . in God," etc., the passionate, qualitative, intensive, etc., aspiration, finds its form in the spiraling movement. But to say further that this union—which, moreover authorizes *every* metaphor of elevation—is *difference itself*, Corneille's own idiom—is this to say much? And if this were the essential aspect of "Corneillean movement," where would Corneille be? Why is there more beauty in *Polyeucte* than in "an ascending movement of two rings"? The force of the work, the force of genius, the force, too, of that which engenders in general is precisely that which resists geometrical metaphorization and is the proper object of literary criticism. In another sense than Poulet's, Rousset sometimes seems to have "little interest in art."

Unless Rousset considers every line, every spatial form (but every form is spatial) beautiful a priori, unless he deems, as did a certain medieval theology (Considérans in particular), that form is transcendentally beautiful, since it is and makes things be, and that Being is Beautiful; these were truths for this theology to the extent that monsters themselves, as it was said, were beautiful, in that they exist through line or form, which bear witness to the order of the created universe and reflect divine light. *Formosus* means beautiful.

Will Buffon not say too, in his *Supplement to Natural History* (vol. XI, p. 417): "Most monsters are such with symmetry, the disarray of the parts seeming to have been arranged in orderly fashion?"

Now, Rousset does not seem to posit, in his theoretical Introduction, that every form is beautiful, but only the form that is aligned with meaning, the form that can be understood because it is, above all, in league with meaning. Why then, once more, this geometer's privilege? Assuming, in the last analysis, that beauty lets itself be espoused or exhausted by the geometer, is he not, in the case of the sublime—and Corneille is said to be sublime—forced to commit an act of violence?

Further, for the sake of determining an essential "Corneillean movement," does one not lose what counts? Everything that defies a geometrical-mechanical framework—and not only the pieces which cannot be constrained by curves and helices, not only force and quality, which are meaning itself, but also *duration*, that which is pure qualitative heterogeneity within movement—is reduced to the appearance of the inessential for the sake of this essentialism or teleological structuralism. Rousset understands theatrical or novelistic movement as Aristotle understood movement in general: transition to the act, which itself is the repose of the desired form. Everything transpires as if everything within the dynamics of Corneillean meaning, and within each of Corneille's plays, came to life with the aim of final peace, the peace of the structural *energeia: Polyeucte*. Outside this peace, before and after it, movement, in its pure duration, in the labor of its organization, can itself be only sketch or debris. Or even debauch, a fault or sin as compared to *Polyeucte*, the "first impeccable success." Under the word "impeccable," Rousset notes: "*Cinna* still sins in this respect" (p. 12).

Preformationism, teleologism, reduction of force, value and duration—these are as one with geometrism, creating structure. This is the *actual* structure which governs, to one degree or another, all the essays in this book. Everything which, in the first Marivaux, does not announce the schema of the "double register" (narration and look at the narration) is "a series of youthful novelistic exercises" by which "he prepares not only the novels of maturity, but also his dramatic works" (p. 47). "The *true* Marivaux is still *almost* absent from it" (my italics). "From our perspective, there is only one fact to retain . . ." (ibid.). There follows an analysis and a citation upon which is concluded: "This outline of a dialogue above the heads of the characters, through a broken-off narration in which the presence and the absence of the author alternate, is the outline of the veritable Marivaux. . . . Thus is sketched, in a first and rudimentary form, the properly Marivauldian combination of spectacle and spectator, perceived and perceiver. We will see it perfect itself" (p. 48).

The difficulties accumulate, as do our reservations, when Rousset specifies that this "permanent structure of Marivaux's,"[49] although invisible or latent in the works of his youth, "belongs," as the "willful dissolution of novelistic illusion," to the "burlesque tradition" (p. 50; cf. also p. 60). Marivaux's originality, which "retains" from this tradition only "the free construction of a narration which simultaneously shows the work of the author and the author's reflection on his work," is then "critical consciousness" (p. 51). Marivaux's idiom is not to be found in the structure described but in the intention that animates a traditional form and creates a new structure. The truth of the general structure thus restored does not *describe* the Marivauldian organism along its own lines. And less so its force.

Yet: "The structural fact thus described—the double register—appears as a constant. . . . At *the same time* [my italics] it corresponds to the knowledge that Marivauldian man has of himself: a 'heart' without vision, caught in the field of a consciousness which itself is only vision" (p. 64). But how can a "structural fact," traditional during this era (assuming that as it is defined, it is determined and original enough to belong to an era) "correspond" to the consciousness of "Marivauldian man"? Does the structure correspond to Marivaux's most singular intention? Is Marivaux not, rather, a *good example*—and it would have to be demonstrated why he is a *good* example—of a literary structure of the times and, through it, an example of a structure of the era itself? Are there not here a thousand unresolved methodological problems that are the prerequisites for a *single* structural study, a monograph on an author or a work?

If *geometrism* is especially apparent in the essays on Corneille and Marivaux, preformationism triumphs à propos of Proust and Claudel. And this time in a form that is more organicist than topographical. It is here too, that preformationism is most fruitful and convincing. First, because it permits the mastering of a richer subject matter, penetrated more from within. (May we be permitted to remark that we feel that what is best about this book is not due to its method, but to the quality of the attention given to its objects?) Further, because Proust's and Claudel's aesthetics are profoundly aligned with Rousset's.

For Proust himself—and the demonstration given leaves no doubt, on this subject, if one still had any—the demands of structure were constant and conscious, manifesting themselves through marvels of (neither true nor false) symmetry, recurrence, circularity, light thrown backward, superimposition (without adequation) of the first and the last, etc. Teleology here is not a product of the critic's projection, but is the author's own theme. The implication of the end in the beginning, the strange relationships between the subject who writes the book and the subject of this book, between the consciousness of the narrator and that of the hero—all this recalls the style of becoming and the dialectic of the "we" in the *Phenomenology of the Mind*.[50] We are indeed concerned with the phenomenology of a mind here: "One can discern still more reasons for the importance attached by Proust to this circular form of a novel whose end returns to its beginning. In the final pages one sees the hero and the narrator unite too, after a long march during which each sought after the other, sometimes very close to each other, sometimes very far apart; they coincide at the moment of resolution, which is the instant when the hero becomes the narrator, that is, the author of his own history. The narrator is the hero revealed to himself, is the person that the hero, throughout his history, desires to be but never can be; he now takes the place of this hero and will be able to set himself to the task of edifying the work which has ended, and first to the task of writing *Combray*, which is the origin of the narrator as well as of the hero. The end of the book makes its existence possible and comprehensible. The novel is conceived such that its end engenders its beginning" (p. 144). Proust's aesthetics and critical method are, ultimately, not outside his work but are the very heart of his creation: "Proust will make this aesthetic into the real subject of his work" (p. 135). As in Hegel, the philosophical, critical, reflective consciousness is not only contained in the scrutiny given to the operations and works of history. What is first in question is the history of this consciousness *itself*. It would not be deceptive to say that this aesthetic, as a concept of the work in general, exactly overlaps Rousset's. And this aesthetic is indeed, if I may say so, a practiced preformationism: "The *last chapter* of the last volume," Proust notes, "was written immediately after the *first chapter* of the first volume. Everything in between was written afterward."

By preformationism we indeed mean preformationism: the well-known biological doctrine, opposed to epigenesis, according to which the totality of hereditary characteristics is enveloped in the germ, and is already in action in reduced dimensions that nevertheless respect the forms and proportions of the future adult. A theory of *encasement* was at the center of preformationism which today makes us smile. But what are we smiling at? At the adult in miniature, doubtless, but also at the attributing of something more than finality to natural life—providence in action and art conscious of its works. But when one is concerned with an art that does not imitate nature, when the artist is a man, and when it is consciousness that engenders, preformationism no longer makes us smile. *Logos spermatikos* is in its proper element, is no longer an export, for it is an anthropomorphic concept. For example: after having brought to light the necessity of *repetition* in Proustian composition, Rousset writes: "Whatever one thinks of the device which introduces *Un amour de Swann*, it is quickly forgotten, so tight and organic is the liaison that connects the part to the whole. Once one has finished reading the *Recherche*, one perceives that the episode is not at all isolable; without it, the ensemble would be unintelligible. *Un amour de Swann* is a novel within a novel, a painting within a painting . . . , it brings to mind, not the stories within stories that so many seventeenth- or eighteenth-century novelists encase in their narratives, but rather the inner stories that can be read the *Vie de Marianne*, in Balzac or Gide. At one of the entryways to his novel, Proust places a small convex mirror which reflects the novel in abbreviated form" (p. 146). The metaphor and operation of encasement impose themselves, even if they are finally replaced by a finer, more adequate image which, at bottom, signifies the same relationship of implication. A reflecting and representative kind of implication, this time.

It is for these same reasons that Rousset's aesthetic is aligned with Claudel's. Moreover, Proust's aesthetic is defined at the beginning of the essay on Claudel. And the affinities are evident, above and beyond all the differences. These affinities are assembled in the theme of "structural monotony": "' . . . And thinking once more about the monotony of Vinteuil's works, I explained to Albertine that great writers have created only a single work, or rather have refracted the same beauty that they bring to the world through diverse elements'" (p. 171). Claudel: "' *Le Soulier de satin* is *Tête d'or* in another form. It summarizes both *Tête d'or* and *Partage de midi*. It is even the conclusion of *Partage de midi* . . .'" "'A poet does hardly anything but develop a preestablished plan'" (p. 172).

This aesthetic which neutralizes duration and force as the *difference* between the acorn and the oak, is not autonomously Proust's or Claudel's. It translates a metaphysics. Proust also calls "time in its pure state" the "atemporal" or the "eternal." The truth of time is not temporal. Analogously (analogously only), time as irreversible succession, is, according to Claudel, only the phenomenon, the epidermis, the surface image of the essential truth of the universe as it is conceived and created by God. This truth is absolute *simultaneity*. Like God, Claudel, the creator and composer, "has a taste for things that exist together" (*Art poétique*).[51]

This metaphysical intention, in the last resort, validates, through a series of mediations, the entire essay on Proust and all the analyses devoted to the "fundamental scene of Claudel's theater" (p. 183), the "pure state of the Claudelian structure" (p. 177) found in *Partage de midi*, and to the totality of this theater in which, as Claudel himself says, "time is manipulated like an accordion, for our pleasure" such that "hours last and days are passed over" (p. 181).

We will not, of course, examine in and of themselves this metaphysics or theology of temporality. That the aesthetics they govern can be legitimately and fruitfully applied to the reading of Proust or Claudel is evident, for these are *their* aesthetics, daughter (or mother) of *their* metaphysics. It is also readily demonstrable that what is in question is the metaphysics implicit in all structuralism, or in every structuralist proposition. In particular, a structuralist reading, by its own activity, always presupposes and appeals to the theological simultaneity of the book, and considers itself deprived of the essential when this simultaneity is not accessible. Rousset: "In any event, reading, which is developed in duration, will have to make the work simultaneously present in all its parts in order to be global. . . . Similar to a 'painting in movement,' the book is revealed only in successive fragments. The task of the demanding reader consists in overturning this natural tendency of the book, so that it may present itself in its entirety to the mind's scrutiny. The only complete reading is the one which transforms the book into a simultaneous network of reciprocal relationships: it is then that surprises emerge" (p. xiii). (What surprises? How can simultaneity hold surprises in store? Rather, it neutralizes the surprises of nonsimultaneity. Surprises emerge from the dialogue between the simultaneous and the nonsimultaneous. Which suffices to say that structural simultaneity *itself* serves to reassure.) Jean-Pierre Richard: "The difficulty of every structural account resides in that it must describe sequentially, successively, that which in fact exists all at once, simultaneously" (*L'univers imaginaire de Mallarmé*, p. 28). Thus, Rousset invokes the difficulty of gaining access to the simultaneity which is truth within reading, and Richard the difficulty of accounting for it within writing. In both cases, simultaneity is the myth of a total reading or description, promoted to the status of a regulatory ideal. The search for the simultaneous explains the capacity to be fascinated by the spatial image: is space not "the order of coexistences" (Leibniz)? But by saying "simultaneity" instead of space, one attempts to *concentrate* time instead of *forgetting* it. "Duration thus takes on the illusory form of a homogenous milieu, and the union between these two terms, space and duration, is simultaneity, which could be defined as the intersection of time with space."[52] In this demand for the flat and the horizontal, what is intolerable for structuralism is indeed the richness implied by the volume, every element of signification that cannot be spread out into the simultaneity of a form. But is it by chance that the book is, first and foremost, volume?[53] And that the meaning of meaning (in the general sense of meaning and not in the sense of signalization) is infinite implication, the indefinite referral of signifier to signifier? And that its force is a certain pure and infinite equivocality which gives signified meaning no respite, no rest, but engages it in its own *economy* so that it always signifies again and differs? Except in the *Livre irréalisé* by Mallarmé, that which is written is never identical to itself.

Unrealized: this does not mean that Mallarmé did not succeed in realizing a Book which would be at one with itself—he simply did not want to. He unrealized the unity of the Book by making the categories in which it was supposed to be securely conceptualized tremble: while speaking of an "identification with itself" of the Book, he underlines that the Book is at once "the same and other," as it is "made up of itself." It lends itself not only to a "double interpretation," but through it, says Mallarmé, "I sow, so to speak, this entire double volume here and there ten times."[54]

Does one have the right to constitute this metaphysics or aesthetics so well adapted to Proust and Claudel as the general method of structuralism?[55] This, however, is precisely what Rousset does, in the extent to which, as we have at least tried to demonstrate, he decides that everything not intelligible in the light of a "preestablished" teleological framework, and not visible in its simultaneity, is reducible to the inconsequentiality of accident or dross. Even in the essays devoted to Proust and Claudel, the essays guided by the most comprehensive structure, Rousset must decide to consider as "genetic accidents" "each episode, each character" whose "eventual independence" from the "central theme" or "general organization of the work" is noticeable (p. 164); he must accept the confrontation of the "true Proust" with the "Novelist" to whom, moreover, he can sometimes "do wrong," just as the true Proust, according to Rousset, is also capable of missing the "truth" of love, etc. (p. 166). In the same way that "the true Baudelaire is perhaps only in the *Balcon*, and all of Flaubert is in *Madame Bovary*" (p. xix), the true Proust is not simultaneously everywhere. Rousset must also conclude that the characters of *l'Otage* are severed not by " circumstance," but, "to express it better," by the "demands of the Claudelian framework" (p.179); he must deploy marvels of subtlety to demonstrate that in *Le Soulier de satin* Claudel does not "repudiate himself" and does not "renounce" his "constant framework" (p. 183).

What is most serious is that this "ultrastructuralist" method, as we have called it, seems to contradict, in certain respects, the most precious and original intention of structuralism. In the biological and linguistic fields where it first appeared, structuralism above all insists upon preserving the coherence and completion of each totality at its own level. In a given configuration, it first prohibits the consideration of that which is incomplete or missing, everything that would make the configuration appear to be a blind anticipation of, or mysterious deviation from, an orthogenesis whose own conceptual basis would have to be a *telos* or an ideal norm. To be a structuralist is first to concentrate on the organization of meaning, on the autonomy and idiosyncratic balance, the completion of each moment, each form; and it is to refuse to relegate everything that is not comprehensible as an ideal type to the status of aberrational accident. The pathological itself is not the simple absence of structure. It is organized. It cannot be understood as the deficiency, defect, or decomposition of a beautiful, ideal totality. It is not the simple undoing of *telos*.

It is true that the rejection of finalism is a rule, a methodological norm, that structuralism can apply only with difficulty. The rejection of finalism is a vow of infidelity to *telos* which the actual effort can never adhere to. Structuralism lives within and on the difference between its promise and its practice. Whether biology, linguistics, or literature is in question, how can an organized totality be perceived without reference to its end, or without presuming to know its end, at least? And if meaning is meaningful only within a totality, could it come forth if the totality were not animated by the anticipation of an end, or by an intentionality which, moreover, does not necessarily and primarily belong to a consciousness? If there are structures, they are possible only on the basis of the fundamental structure which permits totality to open and over-flow itself such that it *takes on meaning* by anticipating a *telos* which here must be understood in its most indeterminate form. This opening is certainly that which liberates time and genesis (even coincides with them), but it is also that which risks enclosing progression toward the future—becoming—by giving it form. That which risks stifling force under form.

It may be acknowledged, then, that in the rereading to which we are invited by Rousset, light is menaced from within by that which also metaphysically menaces every structuralism: the possibility of concealing meaning through the very act of uncovering it. *To comprehend* the structure of a becoming, the form of a force, is to lose meaning by finding it. The meaning of becoming and of force, by virtue of their pure, intrinsic characteristics, is the repose of the beginning and the end, the peaceful-ness of a spectacle, horizon or face.[56] Within this peace and repose the character of becoming and of force is disturbed by meaning itself. The meaning of meaning is Apollonian by virtue of everything within it that can be seen.[57]

To say that force is the origin of the phenomenon is to say nothing. By its very articulation force becomes a phenomenon. Hegel demon-strated convincingly that the explication of a phenomenon by a force is a tautology.[58] But in saying this, one must refer to language's peculiar inability to emerge from itself in order to articulate its origin, and not to the *thought* of force. Force is the other of language without which language would not be what it is.

In order to respect this strange movement within language, in order not to reduce it in turn, we would have to attempt a return to the metaphor of darkness and light (of self-revelation and self-concealment), the founding metaphor of Western philosophy as metaphysics. The founding metaphor not only because it is a photological one—and in this respect the entire history of our philosophy is a photology, the name given to a history of, or treatise on, light—but because it is a metaphor. Metaphor in general, the passage from one existent to another, or from one signified meaning to another, authorized by the initial *submission* of Being to the existent, the *analogical* displacement of Being, is the essen-tial weight which anchors discourse in metaphysics, irremediably repressing discourse into its metaphysical state.[59] This is a fate which it would be foolish to term a regrettable and provisional accident of "history"—a slip, a mistake of thought occurring *within* history (*in historia*). *In historiam*, it is the fall of thought into philosophy which gets history under way. Which suffices to say that the metaphor of the "fall" deserves its quotation marks. In this heliocentric metaphysics, force, ceding its place to *eidos* (i.e., the form which is visible for the metaphorical eye), has already been separated from itself in acoustics.[60] How can force or weakness be understood in terms of light and dark?

That modern structuralism has grown and developed within a more or less direct and avowed dependence upon phenomenology suffices to make it a tributary of the most purely traditional stream of Western philosophy, which, above and beyond its anti-Platonism, leads Husserl back to Plato. Now, one would seek in vain a concept in phenomenology which would permit the conceptualization of intensity or force. The conceptualization not only of direction but of power, not only the *in* but the *tension* of intentionality. All value is first constituted by a theoretical subject. Nothing is gained or lost except in terms of clarity and nonclarity, obviousness, presence or absence for a consciousness, coming to awareness or loss of consciousness. Diaphanousness is the supreme value; as is univocity. Hence the difficulties in thinking the genesis and pure temporality of the transcendental ego, of accounting for the successful or unsuccessful incarnation of *telos*, and the mysterious failures called crises. And when, in certain places, Husserl ceases to consider the phenomena of crisis and the failure of *telos* as "accidents of genesis," or as the *inessential* (*Unwesen*), it is in order to demonstrate that forgetting is eidetically dictated, and is necessary, under the rubric of "sedimentation," for the development of truth. For the revealing and illumination of truth. But why these forces and failures of consciousness? And why the force of weakness which dissimulates in the very act by which it reveals? If this "dialectic" of force and weakness is the finitude of thought itself in its relationship to Being, it can only be articulated in the language of form, through images of shadow and light. For force is not darkness, and it is not hidden under a form for which it would serve as substance, matter, or crypt. Force cannot be conceived on the basis of an oppositional couple, that is, on the basis of the complicity between phenomenology and occultism. Nor can it be conceived, from within phenomenology, as the *fact* opposed to *meaning*.

Emancipation from this language must be attempted. But not as an *attempt* at emancipation from it, for this is impossible unless we forget *our* history. Rather, as the dream of emancipation. Nor as emancipation from it, which would be meaningless and would deprive us of the light of meaning. Rather, as resistance to it, as far as is possible. In any event, we must not abandon ourselves to this language with the abandon which today characterizes the worst exhilaration of the most nuanced structural formalism.

Criticism, if it is called upon to enter into explication and exchange with literary writing, some day will not have to wait for this resistance first to be organized into a "philosophy" which would govern some methodology of aesthetics whose principles criticism would receive. For philosophy, during its history, has been determined as the reflection of poetic inauguration. Conceived apart, it is the twilight of forces, that is, the sun-splashed morning in which images, forms, and phenomena speak; it is the morning of ideas and idols in which the relief of forces becomes repose, its depth flattened in the light as it stretches itself into horizontality. But the enterprise is hopeless if one muses on the fact that literary criticism has already been determined, knowingly or not, voluntarily or not, as the philosophy of literature. As such—that is to say, until it has purposely opened the strategic operation we spoke of above, which cannot simply be conceived under the authority of structuralism—criticism will have neither the means nor, more particularly, the motive for renouncing eurythmics, geometry, the privilege given to vision, the Apollonian ecstasy which "acts above all as a force stimulating the eye, so that it acquires the power of vision."[61] It will not be able to exceed itself to the point of embracing both force and the movement which displaces lines, nor to the point of embracing force as movement, as desire, for itself, and not as the accident or epiphany of lines. To the point of embracing it as writing.

Hence the nostalgia, the melancholy, the fallen Dionysianism of which we spoke at the outset. Are we mistaken in perceiving it beneath the praise of structural and Claudelian "monotony" which closes *Forme et Signification?*

We should conclude, but the debate is interminable. The divergence, the *difference* between Dionysus and Apollo, between ardor and structure, cannot be erased in history, for it is not *in* history. It too, in an unexpected sense, is an original structure: the opening of history, historicity itself. *Difference* does not simply belong either to history or to structure. If we must say, along with Schelling, that "all is but Dionysus," we must know—and this is to write—that, like pure force, Dionysus is worked by difference. He sees and lets himself be seen. And tears out (his) eyes. For all eternity, he has had a relationship to his exterior, to visible form, to structure, as he does to his death. This is how he appears (to himself).

"Not enough forms . . . ," said Flaubert. How is he to be understood? Does he wish to celebrate the other of form? the "too many things" which exceed and resist form? In praise of Dionysus? One is certain that this is not so. Flaubert, on the contrary, is sighing, "Alas! not enough forms." A religion of the work as form. Moreover, the things for which we do not have enough forms are already phantoms of energy, "ideas" "larger than the plasticity of style." In question is a point against Leconte de Lisle, an affectionate point, for Flaubert "likes that fellow a lot."[62]

Nietzsche was not fooled: "Flaubert, a new edition of Pascal, but as an artist with this instinctive belief at heart: 'Flaubert est toujours haïssable, l'homme n'est rien, l'oeuvre est tout.'"[63]

We would have to choose then, between writing and dance.

Nietzsche recommends a dance of the pen in vain: " . . . dancing with the feet, with ideas, with words, and need I add that one must also be able to dance with the pen—that one must learn how to write?"[64] Flaubert was aware, and he was right, that writing cannot be thoroughly Dionysiac. "One can only think and write sitting down," he said. Joyous anger of Nietzsche: "Here I have got you, you nihilist! A sedentary life is the real sin against the Holy Spirit. Only those thoughts that come when you are walking have any value."[65]

But Nietzsche was certain that the writer would never be upright; that writing is first and always something over which one bends. Better still when letters are no longer figures of fire in the heavens.

Nietzsche was certain, but Zarathustra was positive: "Here do I sit and wait, old broken tables around me and also new half tables. When cometh mine hour? The hour of my descent, of my down-going."[66] "Die Stunde meines Niederganges, Unterganges." It will be necessary to descend, to work, to bend in order to engrave and carry the new Tables to the valleys, in order to read them and have them read. Writing is the outlet as the descent of meaning outside itself within itself: metaphor-for-others-aimed-at-others-here-and-now, metaphor as the possibility of others here-and-now, metaphor as metaphysics in which Being must hide itself if the other is to appear. *Excavation within the other toward the other in which the same seeks its vein and the true gold of its phenomenon.* Submission in which the same can always lose (itself). *Niedergang, Untergang.* But the same is nothing, is not (it)self before taking the risk of losing (itself). For the fraternal other is not first in the peace of what is called intersubjectivity, but in the work and the peril of inter-rogation; the other is not certain within the peace of the *response* in which two affirmations *espouse each other*, but is called up in the night by the excavating work of interrogation. Writing is the moment of this original Valley of the other within Being. The moment of depth as decay. Incidence and insistence of inscription.

"Behold, here is a new table; but where are my brethren who will carry it with me to the valley and into hearts of flesh?"[67]

Notes

1 In *L'univers imaginaire de Mallarmé* (Paris: Editions du Seuil, 1961, p. 30, n.27), Jean-Pierre Richard writes: "We would be content if our work could provide some new materials for a future history of imagination and affectivity,

this history, not yet written for the nineteenth century, would probably be an extension of the works of Jean Rousset on the baroque, Paul Hazard on the eighteenth century, André Monglond on preromanticism."

2 In his *Anthropology* (New York: Harcourt, Brace and World, 1948, p. 325) A. L. Krober notes "'structure' appears to be just a yielding to a word that has a perfectly good meaning but suddenly becomes fashionably attractive for a decade or so—like 'streamlining' —and during its vogue tends to be applied indiscriminately because of the pleasurable connotations of its sound."

To grasp the profound necessity hidden beneath the incontestable phenomenon of fashion, it is first necessary to operate negatively: the choice of a word is first an ensemble—a structural ensemble, of course—of exclusions. To know why one says "structure" is to know why one no longer wishes to say "*eidos*," "essence," "form," "*Gestalt*," "ensemble," "composition," "complex," "construction," "correlation," "totality," "Idea," "organism," "state," "system," etc. One must understand not only why each of these words showed itself to be insufficient but also why the notion of structure continues to borrow some implicit signification from them and to be inhabited by them.

3 TN. The most consistently difficult sections of Derrida's texts are his "prefatory" remarks, for reasons that he has explained in "Hors-livre," the preface to *La dissémination* (Paris: Seuil, 1972). The question hinges upon the classical difference between a philosophical text and its preface, the preface usually being a recapitulation of the truth presented by the text. Since Derrida challenges the notion that *a text* can *present a truth*, his prefaces—in which this challenge is anticipated—must especially mark that which makes a text explode the classical ideas of truth and presence. And they must do so without letting the preface anticipate this "conclusion" as a single, clear, luminous truth. Thus the *complication* of these prefaces. One way of complicating a preface is to leave as a knot that which will later become several strands. Here, the relationship between history, somnambulism, the "question" and the difference between almost-everything and almost-nothing is not explained, for the unraveling of this question touches at least on the topics of the relationship between history and philosophy (cf. "Violence and Metaphysics" in *Writing and Difference*), and the relation of both of these, as writing or texts, to Freud's analysis of the "text of somnambulism," i.e., *The Intepretation of Dreams* (cf. "Freud and the Scene of Writing" in *Writing and Difference*).

4 On the theme of the *separation* of the writer, cf. particularly chapter 3 of Jean Rousset's introduction of his *Forme et Signification*. Delacroix, Diderot, Balzac, Baudelaire, Mallarmé, Proust, Valéry, Henry James, T.S. Eliot, Virginia Woolf are called upon to bear witness to the fact that separation is diametrically opposed to critical impotency. By insisting upon this separation between the critical act and creative force, we are only designating the most banally essential—others might say, structural—necessity attached to these two actions and moments. Impotence, here, is a property not of the critic but of criticism. The two are sometimes confused. Flaubert does not deny himself this confusion. This is brought to light in the admirable collection of letters edited by Geneviève Bollème and entitled *Preface à la vie d'écrivain* (Paris: Seuil, 1963). Attentive to the fact that the critic takes his material from the work rather than bringing anything to it, Flaubert writes: "One writes criticism when one cannot create art, just as one becomes a spy when one cannot be a soldier . . . Plautus would have laughed at Aristotle

had he known him! Corneille resisted him all he could! Voltaire himself was belittled by Boileau! We would have been spared much evil in modern drama without Schlegel. And when the translation of Hegel is finished, Lord knows where we will end up!" (Bollème, p. 42). The translation of Hegel hasn't been finished, thank the Lord, thus explaining Proust, Joyce, Faulkner and several others. The difference between Mallarmé and these authors is perhaps the reading of Hegel. Or that Mallarmé chose, at least to approach Hegel. In any even, genius has some respite, and translations can be left unread. But Flaubert was right to fear Hegel: "One may well hope that art will continue to advance and perfect itself, but its form has ceased to be the highest need of the spirit. In all these relationships art is and remains for us, on the side of its highest vocation, something past" ("Vorlesungen über die Aesthetik," in Martin Heidegger: *Poetry, Language, Thought*, trans. Albert Hofstadter [New York: Harper and Row, 1971]). The citation continues: "It [art] has lost, for us, its truth and its life. It invites us to a philosophical reflection which does not ensure it any renewal, but rigorously recognizes its essence."

5 Richard, *L'univers imaginaire de Mallarmé*, p. 14.

6 Cf. Gérard Genette, "Une poétique structurale," *Tel Quel*, no 7, Autumn 1961, p. 13.

7 Cf. Jean Rousset, *La littérature de l'âge baroque en France*, vol. 1: *Circe et le paon* (Paris: José Corti, 1954). In particular, the following passage à propos of a German example, can be read: "Hell is a world in pieces, a pillage that the poem imitates closely through its disordered shouts, bristling with scattered tortures in a torrent of exclamations. The sentence is reduced to its disordered elements, the framework of the sonnet is broken: the lines are too short or too long, the quatrains unbalanced; the poem burst" (ibid, p. 194).

8 TN. The play is on the etymology of the word *critic*, which comes from the Greek verb *krinein*, meaning both "to separate, to cut into" and "to discern, to judge."

9 Jean Rousset, *Forme et Signification: Essais sur les structures littéraires de Corneille à Claudel* (Paris: José Corti, 1962).

10 After citing (ibid. p. vii) this passage of Picon: "Before modern art, the work seems to be the expression of a previous experience . . . the work says what has been conceived or seen; so much so that from the experience to the work there is only the transition to the techniques of execution. For modern art the work is not expression but creation: it makes visible that which was not visible before it, it forms instead of reflecting," Rousset makes this idea more specific with this distinction: "An important difference and, in our eyes, an important conquest of modern art, *or rather of the consciousness of the creative process achieved by this art* . . . " (my italics; according to Rousset, we are becoming conscious *today* of the *creative process in general*). For Picon, the mutation affects art and not only the modern consciousness of art. He wrote elsewhere: "The history of modern poetry is entirely that of the substitution of a language of creation for a language of expression . . . . Language must now produce the world it can no longer express" (*Introduction à une esthétique de la littérature*, vol. 1: *L'écrivain et son ombre* [Paris: Gallimard, 1953], p. 195).

11 *Critique of Pure Reason*, translated by Norman Kemp Smith (London: Macmillan and Co., 1929). The texts of Kant to which we will refer—and numerous other texts which we will call upon later—are not utilized by

Rousset. It will be our rule to refer directly to the page numbers of *Forme et Signification* each time that a citation presented by Rousset is in question.

12 Ibid.

13 *The Critique of Judgment*, trans. James Creed Meredith (London: Oxford University Press, 1952), p. 212.

14 Ibid., p. 176.

15 Ibid., p. 88.

16 Ibid., p. 43.

17 *Critique of Pure Reason.*

18 TN. On the nonmetaphoricity of the verb *to be* and the philosophical implications of tracing a word's genealogy through its etymology, cf. "Violence and Metaphysics," III, 1, B, and "Of Ontological Violence." In question is the notion of metaphor, which implies the transfer of the name of a thing to another thing with a different name. In a sense, any application of a name to a thing is always metaphorical, and for many philosophies (e.g. those of Rousseau and Condillac) metaphor is the origin of language. The question, then, is whether there is an *origin* of metaphor, an absolutely nonmetaphorical concept, as, for example, the verb *to be*, or the notion of breathing, for which Nietzsche says the notion of being is a metaphor (in *Greek Philosophy during the Tragic Age*). If it could be shown that there is no absolute origin of metaphor, the separation or space implied in metaphor as transfer would become problematical, as it would then be nonreducible.

19 TN. The reference is to Descartes, for whom everything perceived clearly and distinctly had to be something understandable, could not be nothing. Cf. *Meditations.*

20 Cited by Maurice Blanchot in *L'Arche*, nos. 27–28 (August–September 1948), p. 133. Is not the same situation described by in *l'Introduction à la méthode de Léonard de Vinci?*

21 Is it not constituted by this requirement? Is it not a kind of privileged representation of inscription?

22 TN. The play is on the etymology of *anguish*, from the Latin *angustia*, meaning narrowness or distress.

23 Also, the anguish of a breath that cuts itself off in order to reenter itself, to aspirate itself and return to its original source. Because to speak is to know that thought *must* become alien to itself in order to be pronounced and to appear. It wishes, then, to take itself back by offering itself. This is why one senses the gesture of withdrawal, of retaking possession of the exhaled word, beneath the language of the authentic writer, the writer who wishes to maintain the greatest proximity to the origin of his act. This too is inspiration. One can say of original language what Feuerbach says of philosophical language: "Philosophy emerges from mouth or pen only in order to return immediately to its proper *source*; it does not speak for the pleasure of speaking—whence its antipathy for fine phrases—but in order not to speak, in order *to think* . . . . To demonstrate is simply to show that what I *say* is *true*; simply to grasp once more the alienation (*Entäusserung*) of thought at the *original source* of thought. Thus the signification of the demonstration cannot be conceived without reference to the signification of language. Language is nothing other than the *realization of the species*, the mediation between the I and the Thou which is to represent the unity of the species by means of the suppression (*Aufhebung*) of their individual isolation. This is

why the element of speech is air, the most spiritual and most universal vital medium" (*Zur Kritk der Hegelschen Philosophie*, 1839, in L. Feuerbach, *Sämtliche Werke*, vol. 2 [Stuttgart-Bad Canstatt, 1959], pp. 169–70).

But did Feuerbach muse upon the fact that *vaporized* language forgets itself? That air is not the element in which history develops if it does not rest (itself) on earth? Heavy, serious, solid earth. The earth that is worked upon, scratched, written upon. The no less universal element in which meaning is engraved so that it will last.

Hegel would be of more assistance here. For even though he too, in a spiritual metaphorization of natural elements, thinks that "earth is the tightly compact knot of this articulated whole, the subject in which these realities *are*, where their processes take effect, that which they start from and to which they return" (*Phenomenology of the Mind*, trans. J. B. Baillie [London: George Allen & Unwin, 1931], p. 518.

The problem of the relation between writing and the earth is also that of the possibility of such a metaphorization of the elements. Of its origin and meaning.

24 TN. The Hebrew *ruah*, like the Greek *pneuma*, means both wind or breath and soul or soul or spirit. Only in God are breath and spirit, speech and thought, absolutely identical; man can always be duplicitous, his speech can be other than his thought.

25 G. W. Leibniz, *Theodicy: Essays on the Goodness of God, the Freedom of Man, and the Origin of Evil*, trans. E.M. Huggard (New Haven: Yale University Press, 1952), pp. 370–72. [At issue again is the distinction between the divine and the human, the Book and books. For Leibniz, God's thought is his action and he is not in the world; but for man, whose action is limited but whose thoughts are not, being in the world means that he must always choose between alternatives. Man's will, the power to choose between alternatives as a function of their merits, implies that he is finite, that his actions do not always equal his thought. God is infinite *because* his thought and his action are coextensive, because he is extraworldly, transcendent.—Trans.]

26 Stéphane Mallarmé, *Selected Poems, Essays and Letters*, trans, Bradford Cook (Baltimore: Johns Hopkins University Press, 1956), p. 15.

27 " . . . à illuminer ceci—que, plus ou moins, tous les livres contiennent la fusion des quelques redites complètes: même il n' en serait qu' un—au monde sa loi—bible comme la simulent les nations. La différence, d' un ouvrage à l' autre, offrant autant de leçons proposées dans un immense concours pour le texte véridique, entre les âges dits civilisés—ou lettrés." Ibid., pp. 41–42.

28 TN. The *Livre de raison* was the journal kept by the head of a family during the Middle Ages.

29 "Réflexions sur la creation artistique selon Alain," *Revue de métaphysique et de morale*, April–June 1952, p. 171. This analysis makes evident that the *Système des beaux-arts*, written during the First World War, does more than foretell the most apparently original themes of "modern" aesthetics. Particularly through a certain anti-Platonism which does not exclude, as Canguilhem demonstrates, a profound alliance with Plato, beyond Platonism "understood without malice."

30 TN. According to Leibniz, each monad—the spiritual (nonmaterial) building blocks of the universe—is the representation of the entire universe as ordained by God. Cf. *Monadology*.

31 Maurice Merleau-Ponty, "An Unpublished Text," trans. Arleen B. Ballery, in *The Primacy of Perception*, ed. James M. Edie (Evanston: Northwestern University Press, 1964), pp. 8–9. The text was first published in the *Revue de métaphysique et de morale*, October–December, 1962.

32 "Problèmes actuels de la phénoménologie," in *Actes du colloque internationale de phénoménologie* (Paris: 1952), p. 97.

33 Saint John Chrysostom, *Homilies on the Gospel of Saint Matthew*, vol. 10 of the *Select Library of the Nicene and Post-Nicene Fathers of the Christian Church*, ed. Philipo Schaff (Grand Rapids: William B. Eerdman, 1956), p. 1.

34 TN. In his translation of the Old Testament, Buber attempted to restore as much as possible the polysemantic structure of certain key words upon which he based his interpretations. Derrida here is attempting to examine the presupposition of construing certain words or ideas as the source of the play of difference implied in linguistic multivalence. The idea that seems to support the next few sentences (in the text) is that if there is no source of "Being," "Being" must then be understood like a game, that is, only in function of itself. Language would then most accurately "approximate" Being when it, too, functions only in relation to itself—"poetry"—without attempting to adequate itself to any particular existent. One could then be led to speak of language as having no reference to signified meanings but rather as creating these meanings through the play of signifiers. The signifier is always that which is inscribed or written.

35 TN. Finitude: empiricity and historicity. Derrida's vocabulary here is Heideggerean—which is not to say that he is simply adopting Heidegger's ideas, but is rather gradually putting Heidegger into question. To suggest that the hidden essence of the empirical is historicity, to deal with affectivity as the index of finitude—these are all Heideggerean themes related to the problem of transcendence as discussed at length, and unreproduceably in Heidegger's *Kant and the Question of Metaphysics*, trans. James S. Churchill (Bloomington: Indiana University Press, 1962).

36 "Brief über den 'Humanismus,'" in *Wegmarken* (Frankfurt, 1967), p. 158.

37 Rousset, *Forme et Signification*, p. xviii, "For this very reason Georges Poulet has little interest in *art*, in the work as a reality incarnated in a language and in formal structures; he suspects them of 'objectivity': the critic runs the risk of grasping them from without.".

38 "Jean-Pierre Richard's analyses are so intelligent, his results so new and so convincing that one must agree with him, regarding his own questions. But in conformity with his own perspectives, he is primarily interested in the imaginary world of the poet, in the latent work, rather than in the work's morphology and style."

39 Guez de Balzac, book 8, letter 15.

40 Vaugelas, *Rem.*, vol. 2, p. 101.

41 Claude Lévi-Strauss, *Structural Anthropology*, trans. C. Jacobson and B. G. Schoepf (New York: Basic Books, 1963), p. 283.

42 G. W. Leibniz, *Discourse on Metaphysics, Correspondence with Arnauld and Monadology*, trans. George R. Montgomery (LaSalle Ill.: Open Court Publishing Co., 1968), pp. 18–19.

43 Let us at least reproduce the synthesizing conclusion, the resumé of the essay: "An itinerary and a metamorphosis, we said after the analysis of the first and fifth acts, as concerns their symmetry and variants. We must now affix to this another essential characteristic of Corneillean drama: the movement it describes is an ascending movement towards a centre situated in infinity." (In this spatial schema, what happens to infinity, which is here the essential, that is, is not only the irreducible *specificity* of the "movement," but also its *qualitative* specificity?) "Its nature can be further specified. An upward movement of two rings is a helical ascent; two ascending lines separate, cross, move away from and rejoin each other in a common profile beyond the play itself . . . " (the structural meaning of the expression "beyond the play itself?") "Pauline and Polyeucte meet and separate in the first act; they meet again, closer to each other and on a higher plane, in the third act, only to separate again; they climb up another level and reunite in the fifth act, the culminating phase of the ascension, from which they jump forth in a final leap which will unite them definitively, at the supreme point of freedom and triumph, in God" (Rousset, *Forme et Signification*, p. 6).

44 Leibniz, *Discourse on Metaphysics*, p. 10.

45 Ibid.

46 Cf., for example, Maurice Leenhardt, *L'art océanien: Gens de la grande terre*, p. 99; *Do kamo*, pp. 19–21.

47 TN. I.e. of structure as a metaphor for locality, site.

48 TN. This is the question of the closure of metaphysics, for metaphysics contains every discourse that attempts to emerge from it. According to Derrida, metaphysics can only be destroyed from within, by making its own language—which is the only language we have—work against it.

49 Here are several formulations of this "permanent structure": "where is the true play? It is in the superimposing and interweaving of the two levels, in the separation and exchanges established between them, offering us the subtle pleasure of binocular viewing and double reading" (Rousset, *Forme et Signification*, p. 56) "From this point of view, all of Marivaux's plays could be defined as an organism existing on two levels whose designs gradually approach until they are completely joined. The play is over when the two levels are indistinguishable, that is, when the group of heroes watched by the spectator sees itself as the spectator-characters saw them. The real resolution is not the marriage promised to us in the fall of the curtain but the encounter of heart and vision" (ibid., p. 58) "We are invited to follow the development of the play in two registers, which offer us two parallel curves that are separated, however, different in their importance, in their language, and their function: the one rapidly sketched, the other fully drawn in all its complexity, the first letting us guess the direction that the second will take, the second deeply echoing the first, providing its definitive meaning. This play of interior reflections contributes to the imparting of a rigorous and supple geometry to Marivaux's play, while at the same time closely linking the two registers, even up to the movements of love" (ibid., p. 59)

50 TN. In the *Phenomenology* Hegel takes the reader on a "voyage of discovery" that Hegel himself has already made. The dialectical turning points of the *Phenomenology* are always marked by the reader's being brought to a point where he can grasp what Hegel has already grasped, the concept in question

becoming true "for us," the distance between subject and object having been annihilated. Hegel defines the structure of the *Phenomenology* as circular, a return to its point of departure.

51 Cited in *Forme et Signification*, p. 189. And Rousset, in fact, comments: "Not isolated, such a declaration is valid for all orders of reality. Everything obeys the law of *composition*, which is the law of the artist as it is of the Creator. For the universe is simultaneity, by virtue of which things at a remove from each other lead a concerted existence and form a harmonic solidarity; to the metaphor that unites them corresponds, in the relations between beings, love, the link between separated souls. It is thus natural for Claudel's thought to admit that two beings severed from each other by distance can be conjoined in their simultaneity, henceforth resonating like two notes of chord, like Prouhèze and Rodrique in their inextinguishable relationship."

52 Bergson, *Essai sur les données immédiates de la conscience*.

53 For the man of literary structuralism (and perhaps of structuralism in general), the letter of books—movement, infinity, lability, and instability of meaning rolled up in itself in the wrapping, the volume—has not yet replaced (but can it ever?) the letter of the flattened, established Law: the commandment on the Tables.

54 On this "identification with itself" of the Mallarmean book, cf. Jacques Scherer, *le 'Livre' de Mallarmé*, p. 95 and leaf 94, and p. 77 and leaves 129–30.

55 We will not insist upon this type of question, banal but difficult to get round, and posing itself, moreover, at each step of Rousset's work, whether he is concerned with an author taken by himself or with an isolated work. Is there only one fundamental structure each time? How is it to be recognized and given its privilege? The criterion can be neither an empirical-statistical accumulation, nor an intuition of an essence. It is the problem of induction which presents itself to a Structuralist science concerned with works, that is to say, with things whose structure is not apriorical. Is there a material a priori of the work? But the intuition of a material a priori poses formidable preliminary problems.

56 TN. This is a reference to Lévinas and his attempted pacification of philosophy through the notion of the Other as face. For Derrida, philosophy, metaphysics, is irreducibly violent, practices an economy of violence. Cf. "Violence and Metaphysics."

57 TN. This reference is to Nietzsche's opposition of the Apollonian and the Dionysian (sculpture/music, individuation/unification of the many with the one, tranquillity/bacchanal) in *The Birth of Tragedy*.

58 TN. This explication is to be found in the chapter of the *Phenomenology* entitled "Force and Understanding." The title of that chapter alone demonstrates its relationship to this essay.

59 TN. Cf. above, note 18.

60 TN. Derrida here is specifying several characteristics of metaphysics without demonstrating their interrelatedness. 1. "Heliocentric metaphysics" refers to the philosophical language founded on metaphors of light and dark, e,g. truth as light, error as dark, etc. 2. This language always implies a privileged position of "acoustic," i.e. a privilege accorded to a phonological, spoken model of the *presence* of truth in living, spoken discourse, and a concomitant abasement of the silent work of the "force" of differentiation. This abasement is typically revealed in the philosophical treatment of writing. 3. This

system is set in motion by Platonism, whose doctrine of the *eidos* implies both points just mentioned.

61 Friedrich Nietzsche, *The Twilight of the Idols*, translated by Anthony M. Ludovici (New York: Russell and Russell, 1964), p. 67.
62 Flaubert, *Préface à la vie d'écrivain*, p. 111.
63 Friedrich Nietzsche, "Nietzsche contra Wagner," in *The Case of Wagner*, trans. Anthony M. Ludovici (New York: Russell and Russell, 1964), p. 116 [In Nietzsche's text the French is left untranslated: "Flaubert is always despicable, the man is nothing, the work is everything."] It is not without interest, perhaps, to juxtapose this barb of Nietzsche's with the following passage from *Forme et Signification*: "Flaubert's correspondence is precious, but in Flaubert the letter writer cannot find Flaubert the novelist; when Gide states that he prefers the former I have the feeling that he chooses the lesser Flaubert or, at least, the Flaubert that the novelist did everything to eliminate" (Rousset, p. xx).
64 Nietzsche, *The Twilight of the Idols*, p. 59.
65 Ibid., p. 6.
66 Friedrich Nietzsche, *Thus Spake Zarathustra*, trans. Thomas Common (New York: Russell and Russell, 1964), p. 239.
67 Ibid., p. 242, slightly modified.

THE TRUTH IN PAINTING (DERRIDA 1987B [FIRST PUBLISHED 1978])

Translated by Geoffrey Bennington and Ian McLeod

Themes

This text is concerned with views of the aesthetic in Kant; Hegel and Heidegger. It can be seen as situating Derrida in relation to those thinkers in general philosophical terms, as well as with regard to aesthetics. He is concerned with deconstruction in general as well as with aesthetic deconstruction. Derrida emphasises that deconstruction is concerned with social structures and material institutions, which are the necessary context for philosophy including aesthetics.

Philosophy of art engages with questions of relations between philosophy and history that always interested Derrida. The specific way in which this issue arises for art is that art tends to be regarded as historical rather than natural. It is one of the things that might be taken to distinguish historical existence from natural existence. The identification of art with history leads to the view that art is history and that is an issue for philosophy of art. Hegel thought of art as historical in a way which historicises art but also turns into the expression of ahistorical philosophical concepts that unfold in history but are not in themselves historical.

The definition of art often looks for a content behind form, so that art is given an inner meaning which is an inner intention expressing itself in the form of art. This structure of outer form and inner meaning is disturbed by abyssal relations emphasised by Derrida. The abyssal is another way of referring to the paradoxical, the contradictory and the aporetic. The abyss emerges where the opposing concepts necessarily contain each other and depend on each other. If the inner meaning relies on outer form and the outer form relies on inner meaning, then there is an infinite regress, or spiral, in which one term refers to the other term, that term refers back to the first and so on. The opposition of outer form and inner meaning rests on the primary metaphysical distinction between outside and inside, in which the inside is assumed to be primary in metaphysics. That opposition is repeated in the distinctions between frame and work, interpretation and object. The work dominates the frame and the object dominates interpretation in metaphysical aesthetics.

Circularity and the abyssal emerge in the relation between object and interpretation because art is conceived in metaphysics as the product of the mind and the mind produces a discourse on what it produces as interpretation. The interpretation is the mind commenting on its own creation; the object is the product of the mind which interprets it. The metaphysics of art produced by the mind reaches a culmination in Hegel, for whom the mind is just as much universal thought as the individual mind. For Hegel, beauty is the product of the mind as is art. Art is art because it is beautiful. The beauty comes from the mind as does art. Art is a product of mind because it is beautiful. Beauty is a product of mind because it belongs to beauty. In this case, the beautiful is in the place of interpretation. Derrida considers the continuation of that discussion in Heidegger who makes the circularity inherent in Hegel's account circular and suggests entering the circle in an affirmative way as the structure of Being and the origin of history. That leaves an enclosed circle which Derrida wishes to break in the emphasis on contradiction and force in aesthetics.

The consideration of abyssal structure in aesthetics leads Derrida to Kant's aesthetics in the *Critique of the Power of Judgement* (Kant 2000 [first published 1790]). He concentrates on the analogy of aesthetic judgement as a bridge across the abyss. In Kant there is a gap between the two forms of determinate judgement: theoretical judgements of knowledge and practical judgements of morality. Reflective judgements of aesthetics are a bridge over the abyss. Reflective judgements in Kant are themselves abyssal, because lacking in determinacy, but also provide the bridge. Derrida advocates an aesthetics referring to the contradictions of the abyss and the bridge; and the need for philosophy to use analogies to complete itself. The bridge is an analogy for the analogies which make up aesthetic judgements.

Context

Derrida's work on aesthetics is very tied in with the reading of Kant. This means that the context for Derrida's aesthetics in analytic philosophy exists in part through readings of Kant's aesthetics. Two of the leading Kant commentators, Henry Allison and Paul Guyer, perhaps the leading current close readers of, and commentators on, Kant's texts have produced substantial readings of Kant's aesthetics in the *Critique of the Power of Judgement*. Guyer has written on this in *Kant and the Experience of Freedom* (Guyer 1993) and *Kant and the Claims of Taste* (Guyer 1997); Allison in *Kant's Theory of Taste* (Allison 2001). Neither Allison nor Guyer have much knowledge of recent French philosophy, including Derrida, but it is clear their work on Kant's aesthetics derives great impetus from Derrida's focus on this aspect of Kant, along with work by other French philosophers, particularly Jean-François Lyotard. Although Kant's aesthetics is evidently a major source for aesthetic theory, Kant scholars have not previously given it a great deal of attention; and clearly the realisation that French commentators were ahead of them made a difference to how much work they did on Kant's aesthetic. The work of Guyer and Allison is more concerned with proving that Kant's work on the beautiful and the sublime reinforces the theoretical and practical philosophy, rather than changing our view of them. For Derrida, the aesthetic forces us to see Kant's philosophy as a whole as grounded on the aesthetic.

Derrida also approached issues of painting in *Memoirs of the Blind* (Derrida 1993), where he is not so concerned with Kant, though the issues of reflection are continued in the idea of blindness in painting. The act of painting is concerned with vision. At the limits of vision there is blindness, a blindness which must be at the origin of vision. Painting is concerned with limits of representation in vision and so is concerned with blindness which parallels the paradox of reflection at the origin of judgement. In this context, Derrida deals with Merleau-Ponty's phenomenological concern with the limits of vision and consciousness in *The Visible and the Invisible* (Merleau-Ponty 1969).

The best context for Derrida on painting, and other branches of aesthetics, in recent analytic aesthetics, rather than works of Kant commentary, is to be found in Nelson Goodman. Goodman, whose work is rooted in logic and logical method, does not look the most obvious philosopher to bring into relation with Derrida, but his philosophical approach does have strong connections. Of all the major figures in analytic philosophy, Goodman has had the most to say about aesthetics. Davidson might come second, but his contribution is a long way behind Goodman. Goodman published a major work of aesthetics, *Languages of*

Art (Goodman 1976) along with many papers, some of them in literature journals. He owned an art gallery and put aesthetics at the centre of
his work in many ways. He is also famous for his 'new' riddle of induction
and his nominalist ontology. In his work on induction he questioned the
possibility of attaching properties to objects with certainty into the
future. In his nominalism, be denied the existence of all abstract objects.
The discussion of properties connects with nominalism since nominalism denies that properties have any abstract reality. This work is at
least compatible with Derrida's adherence to 'radical empiricism' and
denial of ideal reality for concepts.

The framework of Goodman's philosophy establishes themes in his
aesthetics, which connect with Derrida. Goodman argues that art works
are never primarily representations of anything. They are always denotations, that is they may refer to some object but they do not depict it. A
picture is not essentially something that resembles an object: it is what
depicts an object. Art may denote a fictional object and the reality of
the object is not an issue for art. Fakes and forgeries are an essential issue
for art. He distinguished between autographic works, which can be
faked, like a picture, or the original manuscript for a musical score or a
novel, and allographic works that cannot be faked. For a work that is
allographic, the printed book or the performance of a musical score there
is no substantial aesthetic issue of forgery. The book could be a forgery in
the sense of being an unauthorised copy but that would not affect its
aesthetic status as long as it is a book derived from the autographic
manuscript. The forgery can never be perfect, since there is always a
physical difference between a copy and the original, however minute.
Even the most minute differences affect our perceptual system. The
artwork only exists as a set of concrete symbols, not as an abstract object
transcending empirical objects. Any difference however minute in
versions of an artwork producers a different art work.

All these points in Goodman open up ways of thinking which
Derrida shares. An artwork is never mimetic (imitative) for Derrida.
Mimesis itself rests on a metaphysical notion of an object ontologically
prior to its representation. Part of Derrida's point is that objects which
are different in any way cannot be said to be identical because that
would be to deny difference. He has an underlying commitment to
nominalism. The insistence in Goodman that a forgery is never perfect
is in line with Derrida's insistence on the difference between every individual. The lack of authenticity for allographic objects which already
exist as multiple objects is also in line with Derrida's views on irreducible
difference. The same applies to Goodman's emphasis on purely individual existence of every instance of a set of symbols in art. Goodman's

position is extreme. He insists that the slightest difference between two versions of a Shakespeare play leaves us with two plays. He is not, however, willing to go so far as to say that any two copies are distinctive artworks. Since all instantiations of a work are different in some physical aspect, this does leave the question of why we should regard any two instantiations as the same work. On the other hand, Derrida never deals with the question of individuating artworks if every instance is different, as he must say. In this case there is no artwork in general unless we group instances together, which leaves the problem of how we can group instances together.

Goodman certainly gets into Derrida's territory when he suggests that there is no clear distinction between style and content in art; and there is no clear distinction between representation and what is represented. For Goodman a world is no more than a series of representations, so we can make no distinction between aesthetic representations and the world to which they refer. We certainly cannot abstract content from the stylistic features of aesthetic objects. The content of an object is its stylistic features. From the nominalist point of view the object is no more than the sum of its features. So there is no point in abstracting content from style. There is no way that stylistic features or content features exist in abstraction from the object we are interpreting. That object cannot exist separately from our act of interpretation. There is no clear distinction between the object as interpreted and the object of my interpretation. There is no clear origin for aesthetic denotations in any real object. The denotating aesthetic object is just as real as any object it may denote, if it denotes any real object. All objects are equally part of the world so there is nothing to be gained by regarding the aesthetic object as a secondary form of existence, as a copy of real existence.

TRUTH IN PAINTING: PARERGON I LEMMATA

it's enough

to say: abyss and satire of the abyss

‾

|

|‾ begin and end with a "that's enough" which would have *nothing to do with* the sufficing or self-sufficing of sufficiency, *nothing to do* with satisfaction. Reconsider, further on, the whole syntax of these untranslatable locutions, the *with* of the *nothing to do* [*rien à voir avec, rien à faire avec*]. Write, if possible, finally, without *with*, not *without*[1] but without *with*, finally, *not even oneself.*

Opening with the *satis*, the *enough* (inside and outside, above and below, to left and right), satire, farce on the edge of excess

‾

|

|‾ displacement of the "pivot" [*cheville*, also "ankle"] ("avec," "cum," "ama," "simul," etc.) *since* "Ousia et grammē."[2] Seek as always the lock and the "little key." Lure of writing *with oneself.* "With resources which would lead into the

404 Literature and aesthetics

interior of the system of painting, importing *into* the theory of painting all the questions and all the question-codes developed here, around the effects of the 'proper name' and the 'signature,' stealing, in the course of this break-in, all the rigorous criteria of a framing—between the inside and the outside—carrying off the frame (or rather its joints, its angles of assembly) no less than the inside or the outside, the painting or the thing (imagine the damage caused by a theft which robbed you only, of your frames, or rather of their joints, and of any possibility of reframing your valuables or your art-objects')." (*Glas*)

‎‎
what is a title?
And what if *parergon* were the title?

Here the false title is art. A seminar would treat *of art*. Of art and the fine arts. It would thus answer to a program and to one of its great questions. These questions are all taken from a determinate set. Determined according to history and system. The history would be that of philosophy within which the history of the philosophy of art would be marked off, insofar as it treats of art and of the history of art: its models, its concepts, its problems have not fallen from the skies, they have been constituted according to determinate modes at determinate moments. This set forms a system, a greater logic and an encyclopedia within which the fine arts would stand out as a particular region. The *Agrégation de philosophie* also forms a history and a system

how a question of this type—art—becomes inscribed in a program. We must not only turn to the history of philosophy, for example to the Greater Logic or the Encyclopedia of Hegel, to his *Lectures on Aesthetics* which sketch out, precisely, one part of the encyclopedia, system of training for teaching and cycle of knowledge. We must take account of certain specific relays, for example those of so-called philosophy teaching in France, in the institution of its programs, its forms of examinations and competitions, its scenes and its rhetoric.

Whoever undertook such an inquiry—and I do no more here than point out its stakes and its necessity—would no doubt have to direct herself, via a very overdetermined political history, toward the network indicated by the proper name of Victor Cousin, that very French philosopher and politician who thought himself very Hegelian and never stopped wanting to *transplant* (that is just about his word for it) Hegel into France, after having insistently asked him, in writing at least, to impregnate him, Cousin, and through him French philosophy (letters quoted in *Glas*, pp. 207ff). Strengthened, among other things, by this more or less hysterical pregnancy, he played a determinant role, or at least represented one, in the construction of the French University and its philosophical institution—all the teaching structures that we still inhabit. Here I do no more than name, with a proper name as one of the guiding threads, the necessity of a deconstruction. Following the consistency of its logic, it attacks not only the internal edifice, both semantic and formal, of philosophemes, but also what one would be wrong to assign to it as its external housing, its extrinsic conditions of practice: the historical forms of its pedagogy, the social, economic or political structures of this pedagogical institution. It is because deconstruction interferes with solid structures, "material" institutions; and not only with discourses or signifying representations, that it is always distinct from an analysis or a "critique." And in order to be pertinent, deconstruction works as strictly as possible in that place where the supposedly "internal" order of the philosophical is articulated by (internal *and* external) necessity with the institutional conditions and forms of teaching. To the point where the concept of institution itself would be subjected to the same deconstructive treatment. But I am already leading into next year's seminar (1974–5)

___

|

to delimit now a narrower entry into what I shall try to expound this year in the course. Traditionally, a course begins by the semantic analysis of its title, of the word or concept which entitles it and which can legitimate its discourse only by receiving its own legitimation from that discourse. Thus one would begin by asking oneself: What is *art*? Then: Where does it come from? What is the origin of art? This assumes that we reach agreement about what we understand by the word *art*. Hence: What is the origin of the *meaning* of "art"? For these questions, the *guiding thread* (but it is precisely toward the notion of the *thread* and the *interlacing* that I should like to lead you, from afar) will always have been the existence of "works," of "works of art." Hegel says so at the beginning of the *Lectures on Aesthetics*: we have before us but a single representation, namely, that there are works of art. This representation can furnish us with an appropriate point of departure. So the question then becomes: What is "the origin of the work of art"? And it is not without significance that this question gives its title to one of the last great discourses on art, that of Heidegger.

This protocol of the question installs us in a fundamental presupposition, and massively predetermines the system and combinatory possibilities of answers. What it begins by implying is that art—the word, the concept, the thing—has a unity and, what is more, an originary meaning, an *etymon*, a truth that is *one* and *naked* [*une vérité une et nue*], and that it would be sufficient to unveil it *through* history. It implies first of all that "art" can be reached following the three ways of word, concept, and thing, or again of signifier, signified, and referent, or even by some opposition between presence and representation.

Through history: the crossing can in this case just as well denote historicism, the determining character of the historicity of meaning, as it can denote ahistoricity, history crossed, transfixed in the direction of meaning, in the sense of a meaning [*le sens d'un sens*] in itself ahistorical. The syntagm "through history" could entitle all our questions without constraining them in advance. By presupposing the *etymon*— one and naked [*un et nu*]—a presupposition without which one would perhaps never open one's mouth, by beginning with a meditation on the apparent polysemy of *tekhnē* in order to lay bare the simple kernel which supposedly lies hidden behind the multiplicity, one gives oneself to thinking that art has a meaning, one meaning. Better, that its history is not a history or that it is *one* history only in that it is governed by this one and naked meaning, under the regime of its internal meaning, as history of the meaning of art. If one were to consider the *physis/tekhnē* opposition to be irreducible, if one were to accredit so hastily its translation as *nature/art or nature/technique*, one would easily commit oneself to thinking that art, being no longer nature, is history. The opposition nature/history would be the analogical relay of *physis/tekhnē*. One can thus already say: as for history, we shall have to deal with the contradiction or the oscillation between two apparently incompatible motifs. They both ultimately come under one and the same logical formality: namely, that if the philosophy of art always has the greatest difficulty in dominating the history of art, a certain concept of the historicity of art, this is, paradoxically, because it too easily thinks of art as historical. What I am putting forward here obviously assumes the transformation of the concept of history, from one statement to the other. That will be the work of this seminar.

                                                                              |

|‾‾

      If, therefore, one were to broach lessons on art or aesthetics by a question of this type ("What is art?" "What is the origin of art or of works of art?" "What is the meaning of art?" "What does art mean?" etc.), the form of the question would already provide an answer. Art would be predetermined or precomprehended in it. A conceptual opposition which has traditionally served to comprehend art would already, always, be at work there: for example the opposition between meaning, as inner content, and form. Under the apparent diversity of the historical forms of art, the concepts of art or the words which seem to translate "art" in Greek, Latin, the Germanic languages, etc. (but the closure of this list is already problematic), one would be seeking a one-and-naked meaning [*un sens un et nu*] which would inform from the inside, like a content, while distinguishing itself from the forms which it informs. In order to think art in general, one thus accredits a series of oppositions (meaning/form, inside/outside, content/container, signified/signifier, represented/representer, etc.) which, precisely, structure the traditional interpretation of works of art. One makes of art in general an object in which one claims to distinguish an inner meaning, the invariant, and a multiplicity of external variations *through* which, as through so many veils, one would try to see or restore the true, full, originary meaning: one, naked. Or again, in an analogous gesture, by asking what art *means* (to say), one submits the mark "art" to a very determined regime of interpretation which has supervened in history: it consists, in its *tautology* without reserve, in interrogating the *vouloir-dire* of every work of so-called art, even if its form is not that of saying. In this way one wonders what a plastic or musical work means (to say), submitting all productions to the authority of speech and the "discursive" arts   ‾‾

                                                                              |

|‾‾

---

such that by accelerating
the rhythm a little one would go on to this collusion: between the question
("What is art?" "What is the origin of the work of art?" "What is the
meaning of art or of the history of art?") and the hierarchical classification
of the arts. When a philosopher repeats this question without transforming
it, without destroying it in its form, its question-form, its onto-interrogative
structure, he has already subjected the whole of *space* to the discursive
arts, to voice and to the *logos*. This can be verified: teleology and hierarchy
are prescribed in the envelope of the question   ___

|

|___
                                              the philosophical encloses
art in its circle but its discourse on art is at once, by the same token,
caught in a circle.

Like the figure of the third term, the figure of the circle asserts itself
at the beginning of the *Lectures on Aesthetics* and the *Origin of the Work
of Art*. So very different in their aim, their procedure, their style, these
two discourses have in common, as a common interest, that they exclude
(that) which then comes to form, close and bound them from inside and
outside alike.

And if it were a frame   ___

|

|___
                                one of them, Hegel's, gives classical teleology its
greatest deployment. He finishes off, as people say a little too easily, onto-
theology. The other, Heidegger's, attempts, by taking a step backwards,
to go back behind all the oppositions that have commanded the history of
aesthetics. For example, in passing, that of form and matter, with all its
derivatives. Two discourses, then, as different as could be, on either side of
a line whose tracing we imagine to be simple and nondecomposable. Yet
how can it be that they have in common this: the subordination of all the
arts to speech, and, if not to poetry, at least to the poem, the said, language,
speech, nomination (*Sage, Dichtung, Sprache, Nennen*)? (Reread here the
third and final part of the *Origin* . . . , "Truth and Art.")

not go any further, for the moment, in the reading of these two discourses. Keeping provisionally to their introductions, I notice the following: they both start out from a figure of the circle. And they stay there. They stand in it even if their residence in the circle apparently does not have the same status in each case. For the moment I do not ask myself: What is a circle? I leave to one side the figure of the circle, its place, its privilege or its decadence in the history of art. Since the treatment of the circle is part of the history of art and is delimited in it as much as it delimits it, it is perhaps not a neutral gesture to apply to it something that is also nothing other than one of its figures. It is still a circle, which redoubles, re-marks, and places *en abyme* the singularity of this figure. Circle of circles, circle in the encircled circle. How could a circle place itself *en abyme*?

The circle and the abyss, that would be the title. On the way we will no doubt encounter the question of the title. What happens when one entitles a "work of art"? What is the *topos* of the title? Does it take place (and where?) in relation to the work? On the edge? Over the edge? On the internal border? In an overboard that is re-marked and reapplied, by invagination, within, between the presumed center and the circumference? Or between that which is framed and that which is framing in the frame? Does the *topos* of the title, like that of a *cartouche*, command the "work" from the discursive and juridical instance of an *hors d'oeuvre*, a place outside the work, from the exergue of a more or less directly definitional statement, and even if the definition operates in the manner of a performative? Or else does the title play *inside* the space of the "work," inscribing the legend, with its definitional pretension, in an ensemble that it no longer commands and which constitutes it—the title—as a localized effect? If I say for example that the circle and the abyss will be the title of the play that I am performing today, as an introduction, what am I doing and what is happening? Will the circle and the abyss be the object of my discourse and defined by it? Or else do they describe the form which constrains my discourse, its scene rather than its object, and moreover a scene stolen away by the abyss from present representation? As if a discourse on the circle also had to *describe* a circle, and perhaps the very one that it describes, describe a circular movement at the very moment that it describes a circular movement, describe it displacing itself in its meaning [*sens*]; or else as if a discourse on the abyss had to know the abyss, in the sense that one knows something that happens to or affects one, as in "to know failure" or "to know success" rather than to know an object. The circle and the abyss, then, the circle *en abyme*.

      |

| beginning of the *Lectures on Aesthetics*. From the first pages of the introduction, Hegel poses, as always, the question of the point of departure. How is one to begin a philosophical discourse on aesthetics? Hegel had already linked the essence of the beautiful to the essence of art. According to the determinate opposition of nature and mind, and *thus* of nature and art, he had already posited that a philosophical work devoted to aesthetics, the philosophy or science of the beautiful, must exclude natural beauty. It is in everyday life that one speaks of a beautiful sky. But there is no natural beauty. More precisely, artistic beauty is superior to natural beauty, as the mind that produces it is superior to nature. One must therefore say that absolute beauty, the *telos* or final essence of the beautiful, appears in art and not in nature as such. Now the problem of the introduction causes no difficulty in the case of the natural or mathematical sciences: their object is given or determined in advance, and with it the method that it requires. When, on the contrary, the sciences bear on the products of the mind, the "need for an introduction or preface makes itself felt." Since the object of such sciences is produced by the mind, by that which knows, the mind will have to have engaged in a self-knowledge, in the knowledge of what it produces, of the product of its own production. This autodetermination poses singular problems of priority. The mind must put itself into its own product, produce a discourse on what it produces, introduce itself of itself into itself. This circular duction, this intro-reduction to oneself, calls for what Hegel names a "presupposition" (*Voraussetzung*). In the science of the beautiful, the mind presupposes itself, anticipates itself, precipitates itself. *Head first.* Everything with which it commences is already a result, a *work*, an effect of a projection of the mind, a *resultare*. Every foundation, every justification (*Begründung*) will have been a result—this is, as you know, the mainspring of the speculative dialectic. Presuppositions must proceed from a "proven and demonstrated necessity," explains Hegel. "In philosophy, nothing must be accepted which does not possess the character of

necessity, which means that everything in philosophy must have the value of a result."

We are, right from the introduction, encircled.

No doubt art figures one of those productions of mind thanks to which the latter returns to itself, comes back to consciousness and cognizance and comes to its proper place by *returning* to it, in a circle. What is *called* [*s'appelle*: lit. "calls itself"] mind is that which says to itself "come" only to hear *itself* already saying "come back." The mind is what it is, says what it means, only *by returning*. Retracing its steps, in a circle. But art forms only one of the circles in the great circle of the *Geist* or the revenant (this visitor can be called *Gast*, or *ghost*, *guest* or *Gespenst*). The end of art, and its truth, is religion, that other circle of which the end, the truth, will have been philosophy, and so on. And you know—we shall have to get the most out of this later on—the function of the ternary rhythm in this circulation. The fact remains that here art is studied from the point of view of its end. Its pastness is its truth. The philosophy of art is thus a circle in a circle of circles: a "ring" says Hegel, in the totality of philosophy. It turns upon itself and in annulling itself it links onto other rings. This annular concatenation forms the circle of circles of the philosophical encyclopedia. Art cuts out a circumscription or takes away a circumvolution from it. It encircles itself

           |

|‾‾‾   the inscription of a circle in the circle does not necessarily *give* the abyss, onto the abyss, *en abyme*. In order to be abyssal, the smallest circle must inscribe in itself the figure of the largest. *Is there* any abyss in the Hegelian circulation? To the question posed in this form there is no decidable answer. What does the "there is" mean in these statements? Wherein does the "there is" differ from a "there exists," or "X is," "X presents itself," "X is present," etc.? Skirting round a necessary protocol here (it would proceed via the gift or the giving of the abyss, onto the abyss, *en abyme*, via the problematic of the *es gibt*, *il y a*, it gives [*ça donne*], and of the *es gibt Sein*, opened by Heidegger), I note only this: the answer arrests the abyss, unless it be already dragged down into it in advance. And can be in it without knowing it, at the very moment that a proposition of the type "this is an abyss or a *mise en abyme*" appears to destroy the instability of the relations of whole to part, the indecision of the structures of

inclusion which throws *en abyme*. The statement itself can *form part of the whole*

|

metaphor of the circle of circles, of training (*Bildung*) as philosophical encyclopedia. Organic metaphor, finalized as a whole whose parts conspire. Biological metaphor too. But it is also a metaphor, if it is a metaphor, for art and for the work of art. The totality of philosophy, the encyclopedic corpus is described *as* a living organism *or as* a work of art. It is represented on the model of one of its parts which thus becomes greater than the whole of which it forms part, which it makes into a part. As always, and Kant formalized this in an essential way, the communication between the problem of aesthetic judgment and that of organic finality is internal. At the moment of describing *lemmatic* precipitation, the need to treat the concept of *philosophy of art* in an anticipatory way, Hegel has to have recourse, certainly, to the metaphor of the circle and of the circle of circles which he says, moreover, is only a representation. But also to the metaphor of the organic whole. Only philosophy in its entirety (*gesammte Philosophie*) gives us knowledge of the universe as a unique organic totality in itself, which develops "from its own concept." Without losing anything of what makes it a whole "which returns to itself," this "sole world of truth" is contained, retained, and gathered together in itself. In the "circlet" of this scientific necessity, each part represents a "circle returning into itself" and keeping a tie of solidarity with the others, a necessary and simultaneous interlacing. It is animated by a "backward movement" (*ein Rückwärts*) and by a "forward movement" (*Vorwärts*) by which it develops and reproduces itself in another in a fecund way (*fruchtbar*). Thus it is that, for us, the concept of the beautiful and of art is "a presupposition given by the system of philosophy." Philosophy alone can pose the question "What is the beautiful?" and answer it: the beautiful is a production of art, i.e., of the mind. The idea of beauty is given to us by art, that circle inside the circle of the mind and of the philosophical encyclopedia, etc.

Before beginning to speak of the beautiful and of the fine arts, one ought therefore, by right, to develop the whole of the *Encyclopedia* and the *Greater Logic*. But since it is necessary, in fact, to begin "lemmatically, so to speak" (*sozusagen lemmatisch*) by anticipation or precipitation of the circlet, Hegel recognizes that his point of departure is vulgar, and its philosophical justification insufficient. He will have begun by the "representation" (*Vorstellung*) of art and of the beautiful for the "common consciousness" (*im gewöhnlichen Bewusstsein*). The price to be paid may seem very heavy: it will be said for example that the whole aesthetics develops, explicates, and lays out the representations of naïve consciousness. But does not this negative cancel itself at once? On the immediately following page, Hegel explains that on a circle of circles, one is justified in starting from any point. "There is no absolute beginning in science."

The chosen point of departure, in everyday *representation: there are works of art, we have them in front of us* in representation (*Vorstellung*). But how are they to be recognized? This is not an abstract and juridical question. At each step, at each example, in the absence of enormous theoretical, juridical, political, etc. protocols, there is a trembling of the limit between the "there is" and the "there is not" "work of art," between a "thing" and a "'work," a "work" in general and a "work of art." Let's leave it. What does "leave" [*laisser*] mean ((*laisser*) *voir* [allow to see (or be seen)], (*laisser*) *faire* [allow to do (or be done)], *voir faire*, *faire voir*, *faire faire* [cause (something) to be done], leave as a remainder, leave in one's will), what does "leave" do? etc.

               certainly not insignificant that more than a century later, a meditation on art begins by turning in an analogous circle while pretending to take a step beyond or back behind the whole of metaphysics or western ontotheology. *The Origin of the Work of Art* will have taken a running start for an incommensurable leap. Certainly, and here are some dry indications of it, pending a more patient reading.

1. All the oppositions which support the metaphysics of art find themselves questioned, in particular that of form and matter, with all its derivatives. This is done in the course of a questioning on the being-work of the work and the being-thing of a thing in all the determinations of the thing that more or less implicitly support any philosophy of art (*hypokeimenon, aistheton, hylē*).

2. As the *Postface* indicates, it is from the possibility of its death that art can here be interrogated. It is possible that art is in its death throes, but "it will take a good few centuries" until it dies and is mourned (Heidegger does not mention mourning). The *Origin* is situated in the

zone of resonance of Hegel's *Lectures on Aesthetics* in as much as they think of art as a "past": "In the most comprehensive (*umfassendsten*) meditation which the West possesses on the essence of art—comprehensive because thought out from metaphysics—in Hegel's *Lectures on Aesthetics* stands the following proposition: 'But we no longer have an absolute need to bring a content to presentation (*zur Darstellung*) in the form of art. Art, from the aspect of its highest destination, is for us something past (*ein Vergangenes*).'" After recalling that it would be laughable to elude this proposition under the pretext that works have survived this verdict—a possibility which, one can be sure, did not escape its author—Heidegger continues: "But the question remains: is art still, or is it no longer, an essential and necessary mode (*Weise*) according to which the decisive [deciding] truth happens (*geschieht*) for our historical (*geschichtliches*) Dasein? But if it is no longer that, then the question remains: why? The decision about Hegel's proposition has not yet been reached." So Heidegger interrogates art and more precisely the work of art as the advent or as the history of truth, but of a truth which he proposes to think beyond or behind metaphysics, beyond or behind Hegel. Let's leave it for the moment.

3. Third indication, again recalled in the *Postface*: the beautiful is not relative to pleasure or the "pleasing" (*Gefallen*) as one would, according to Heidegger, always have presupposed, notably with Kant. Let us not be too hasty about translating this as: the beautiful beyond the pleasure principle. Some mediations will be necessary, but they will not be lacking.

4. The beautiful beyond pleasure, certainly, but also art beyond the beautiful, beyond aesthetics as beyond callistics (Hegel says he prefers the "common word" aesthetics to this word). Like Hegel, who saw in it the destination of universal art, Heidegger places Western art at the center of his meditation. But he does so in order to repeat otherwise the history of its essence in relation to the transformation of an essence of truth: the history of the essence of Western art "is just as little to be conceived on the basis of beauty taken for itself as on the basis of lived experience (*Erlebnis*)." Even supposing, concludes Heidegger, that it could ever be a question of a "metaphysical concept" acceding to this essence. Thus nothing rules out the possibility that this concept is even constructed so as not to accede to it, so as not to get around to what happens [*advient*] under the name of art. And which Heidegger already calls "truth," even if it means seeking that truth *beneath* or *behind* the metaphysical determination of truth. For the moment I leave this "beneath" or this "behind" hanging vertically.

Keeping to these preliminary indications, one receives Heidegger's text as the nonidentical, staggered, discrepant "repetition" of the Hegelian "repetition" in the *Lectures on Aesthetics*. It works to untie what still keeps Hegel's aesthetics on the unperceived ground of metaphysics. And yet, what if this "repetition" did no more than make explicit, by repeating it more profoundly, the Hegelian "repetition"? (I am merely defining a risk, I am not yet saying that Heidegger runs it, simply, nor above all that one must in no circumstances run it: in wanting to avoid it at all costs, one can also be rushing toward the false exit, empirical chit-chat, spring-green impulsive avant-gardism. And who said it was necessary to avoid all these risks? And risk in general?) And yet, what if Heidegger, too, once again under the lemmatic constraint, went no further than the "common representation" [*représentation courante*] of art, accepting it as the guiding thread (saying for example also "works of art are before us," this one, that one, the well-known shoes of Van Gogh, etc.) of his powerful meditation ⎯

|

| ⎯ deposits here the "famous painting by Van Gogh who often painted such shoes." I leave them. They are, moreover, abandoned, unlaced, take them or leave them. Much later, interlacing this discourse with another, I shall return to them, as to everything I leave here, in so apparently disconcerted a way. And I shall come back to what comes down to leaving, lacing, interlacing. For example more than one shoe. And further on still, much later, to what Heidegger says of the trait of the "interlacing" (*Geflecht*), of the "tie which unties" (or frees, delivers) (*entbindende Band*) and of the "road" in *Der Weg zur Sprache*. Accept here, concerning the truth in painting or in *effigy*, that interlacing causes a lace to disappear periodically: over under, inside outside, left right, etc. Effigy and fiction ⎯

| ⎯ and in this discrepant repetition, it is less astonishing to see this meditation, closed upon a reference to Hegel, open up by a *circular* revolution whose rhetoric, at least, greatly resembles that which we followed in the introduction to the *Lectures on Aesthetics*.

Why a circle? Here is the schema of the argument: to look for the origin of a thing is to look for that from which it starts out and whereby it is what it is, it is to look for its essential provenance, which is not its empirical origin. The work of art stems from the artist, so they say. But what is an artist? The one who produces works of art. The origin of the artist is the work of art, the origin of the work of art is the artist, "neither is without the other." Given this, "artist and work *are* in themselves and in their reciprocity (*Wechselbezug*) by virtue of a third term (*durch ein Drittes*) which is indeed the first, namely that from which artist and work of art also get their name, art." What is art? As long as one refuses to give an answer in advance to this question, "art" is only a word. And if one wants to interrogate art, one is indeed obliged to give oneself the guiding thread of a representation. And this thread is the work, the fact that *there are* works of art. Repetition of the Hegelian gesture in the necessity of its lemma: there are works which common opinion [*l'opinion courante*] designates as works of art and they are what one must interrogate in order to decipher in them the essence of art. But by what does one recognize, commonly [*couramment*], that these are works of art if one does not have in advance a sort of precomprehension of the essence of art? This hermeneutic circle has only the (logical, formal, derived) appearance of a vicious circle. It is not a question of escaping from it but on the contrary of engaging in it and going all round it: "We must therefore complete the circle (*den Kreisgang vollziehen*). It is neither a stopgap measure (*Notbehelf*) nor a lack (*Mangel*). To engage upon such a road is the force of thought and to remain on it is the feast of thought, it being admitted that thinking is a craft (*Handwerk*)." Engaging on the circular path appeals on the one hand to an artisanal, almost a manual, value of the thinker's trade, on the other hand to an experience of the feast [*fête*] as experience of the limit, of closure, of resistance, of humility. The "it is necessary" [*il faut*] of this engagement is on its way toward what, in *Unterwegs zur Sprache*, gathers together, between propriation and dispropriation (*Ereignis/Enteignis*), the step [*pas*], the road to be opened up (*einen Weg bahnen, bewegen*), the trait which opens (*Aufriss*), and language (speech-language: *Sprache*), etc. That which, later in the text, joins the whole play of the trait (*Riss, Grundriss, Umriss, Aufriss, Gezüge*) to that of the stela, of stature or installation (*thesis, Setzen, Besetzen, Gesetz, Einrichten, Gestalt, Gestell*, so many words I will not attempt to translate here) belongs to that law of the *pas* [not/step] which urges the circle to the lemmatic opening of the Origin: "it being admitted that thinking is a craft. Not only the chief step (*Hauptschritt*) of the work toward art, *qua* step of the work toward art, is a circle, but each of the steps we attempt to take here circles in that circle (*kreist in diesem Kreise*)."

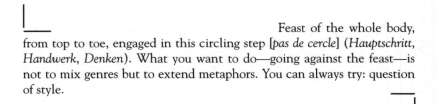

⎿ Feast of the whole body, from top to toe, engaged in this circling step [*pas de cercle*] (*Hauptschritt, Handwerk, Denken*). What you want to do—going against the feast—is not to mix genres but to extend metaphors. You can always try: question of style.

⎿ not break the circle violently (it would avenge itself), assume it resolutely, authentically (*Entschlossenheit, Eigentlichkeit*). The experience of the circular closure does not close anything, it suffers neither lack nor negativity. Affirmative experience without voluntarism, without a compulsion to transgression: not to transgress the law of circle and *pas de cercle* but *trust in them*. Of this trust would thought consist. The desire to accede, by this faithful repetition of the circle, to the not-yet-crossed, is not absent. The desire for a new step, albeit a backward one (*Schritt zurück*), *ties and unties* this procedure [*démarche*]. Tie without tie, get across [*franchir*] the circle without getting free [*s'affranchir*] of its law. *Pas sans pas* [step without step/step without not/not without step/not without not]

⎿ so I break off here, provisionally, the reading of *The Origin*.

The encirclement of the circle was dragging us to the abyss. But like all *production*, that of the abyss came to saturate what it hollows out.

It's enough to say: abyss and satire of the abyss.

The feast, the "feast of thought" (*Fest des Denkens*) which engages upon the *Kreisgang*, in the *pas de cercle*: what does it feed on [*de quoi jouit-*

---

elle]? Opening and simultaneously filling the abyss. Accomplishing: *den Kreisgang vollziehen.*

Interrogate the comic effect of this. One never misses it if the abyss is never sufficient, if it must remain—undecided—between the bottom-less and the bottom of the bottom. The *operation* of the *mise en abyme* always occupies itself (activity, busy positing, mastery of the subject) with somewhere filling up, full of abyss, filling up the abyss   —

      |

|

—   "a third party" (*ein Drittes*) ensures the circulation, regulates the encirclement. The *Mitte*, third, element and milieu, watches over the entrance to the hermeneutic circle or the circle of speculative dialectic. Art plays this role. Every time philosophy determines art, masters it and encloses it in the history of meaning or in the ontological encyclopedia, it assigns it a job as medium.

Now this is not ambiguous, it is more or less than ambiguous. Between two opposites, the third can participate, it can touch the two edges. But the ambiguity of participation does not exhaust it. The very thing that makes—the believers—believe in its mediacy can also give up to neither of the two terms, nor even to the structure of opposition, nor perhaps to dialectic insofar as it needs a mediation.

Index of a discrepancy: in relation to all the machinery of the *pose* (position/opposition, *Setzung/Entgegensetzung*). By giving it the philosophical name *art*, one has, it would seem, domesticated it in onto-encyclopedic economy and the history of truth   —

      |

|

—   and the place which *The Origin of the Work of Art* accords to the *Lectures on Aesthetics* ("the West's most comprehensive meditation on the essence of art") can only be determined, in a certain historical topography, on the basis of the *Critique of the Faculty of Judgment.* Heidegger does not name it here, but he defends it elsewhere against Nietzsche's reading. What holds of speculative dialectic in general is made rigorously clear in the *Lectures*: an essential affinity with the *Critique*, the only book—third book—which it can reflect and reappropriate almost at once. The first two critiques of pure (speculative and practical) reason had opened an apparently infinite gulf. The third could, should, should have, could have thought it: that is, filled it, fulfilled it in infinite reconciliation. "Already the Kantian philosophy not only felt the need for this junction-point (*Vereinigungspunkt*) but recognized it with precision and furnished a representation of it." The third *Critique* had the merit of identifying in art (in general) one of the middle terms (*Mitten*) for resolving (*auflösen*) the "opposition" between mind and nature, internal and external phenomena, the inside and the outside, etc. But it still suffered, according to Hegel, from a lacuna, a "lack" (*Mangel*), it remained a theory of subjectivity and of judgment (an analogous reservation of principle is expressed in *The Origin*). Confined, unilateral, the reconciliation is not yet effective. The *Lectures* must supplement this lack, the structure of which has, as always, the form of a representative anticipation. The reconciliation is only announced, represented in the third *Critique* in the form of a duty, a *Sollen* projected to infinity.

And so it indeed appears.

On the one hand, Kant declares that he "neither wants nor is able" (§ 22) to examine whether "common sense" (here reinterpreted as a nondetermined, nonconceptual, and nonintellectual norm) exists as a constitutive principle of the possibility of aesthetic experience or else whether, in a regulative capacity, reason commands us to produce it (*hervorbringen*) for more elevated purposes. This common sense is constantly presupposed by the *Critique*, which nevertheless holds back the analysis of it. It could be shown that this suspension ensures the complicity of a moral discourse and an empirical culturalism. This is a permanent necessity.

On the other hand, recalling the division of philosophy and all the irreducible oppositions which the first two *Critiques* had determined, Kant does indeed project the plan of a work which could reduce the "enigma" of aesthetic judgment and fill a crack, a cleavage, an abyss (*Kluft*): "If thus an abyss stretching out of sight (*unübersehbare Kluft*) is established between the domain of the concept of nature, that is, the sensible, and the domain of the concept of freedom, that is, the suprasensible, such that no passage (*Übergang*) is possible from the one to the other (by means, therefore, of the theoretical use of reason), as between worlds so different that the first can have no influence (*Einfluss*) on the second, the second *must* yet (*soll doch*) have an influence on the former [. . .]. Consequently it must be (*muss es*) that there is a foundation of unity (*Grund der Einheit*) . . ." Further on, we find related metaphors or analogies: it is again a question of the immense "abyss" which separates the two worlds and of the apparent impossibility of throwing a bridge (*Brücke*) from one shore to the other. To call this an *analogy* does not yet say anything. The bridge is not an analogy. The recourse to analogy, the concept and effect of analogy are or make *the bridge* itself—both in the *Critique* and in the whole powerful tradition to which it still belongs. The analogy of the abyss and of the bridge over the abyss is an analogy which says that there must surely be an analogy between two absolutely heterogeneous worlds, a third term to cross the abyss, to heal over the gaping wound and think the gap. In a word, a *symbol*. The bridge is a symbol, it passes from one bank to the other, and the symbol is a bridge.

The abyss calls for analogy—the active recourse of the whole *Critique*—but analogy plunges endlessly into the abyss as soon as a certain art is needed to describe analogically the play of analogy

Notes

NOTE—Unless followed by the author's initials, all notes to "Parergon" have been added by the translators. The longer passages from Kant are quoted from the English translation, *Kant's Critique of Aesthetic Judgement* by James Creed Meredith (Oxford: Clarendon Press, 1911), and page references to this work are given in brackets in the text.

1 In English in the text.
2 "Ousia et grammē: note sur une note de *Sein und Zeit*," in *Marges de la philosophie* (Paris: Minuit, 1972), 31–78; translated by Alan Bass as *Margins of Philosophy* (Chicago: University of Chicago Press, 1982), 29–67.

BIBLIOGRAPHY

Jacques Derrida

(1973) *Speech and Phenomena*; and *Other Essays on Husserl's* Theory of Signs, trans. David B. Allison and Newton B. Garver, Evanston IL: Northwestern University Press.

(1977) *Limited Inc*, trans. Samuel Weber and Jeffrey Mehlman, Evanston IL: Northwestern University Press.

(1978) *Writing and Difference*, trans. Alan Bass, London: Routledge.

(1979) *Spurs: Nietzsche's Styles*, trans. Barbara Harlow, Chicago IL: University of Chicago Press.

(1982) *Margins of Philosophy*, trans. Alan Bass, Chicago IL: University of Chicago Press.

(1986) *Glas*, trans. John P. Leavey and Richard Rand, Lincoln NE: University of Nebraska Press.

(1987a) *The Post Card: From Socrates to Freud and Beyond*, trans. Alan Bass, Chicago IL: University of Chicago Press.

(1987b) *The Truth in Painting*, trans. Geoffrey Bennington and Ian McLeod, Chicago IL: University of Chicago Press.

(1987c) *For Nelson Mandela*, eds Jacques Derrida and Mustapha Tlili, New York NY: Seaver Books/Henry Holt and Company.

(1988) 'The Politics of Friendship', *The Journal of Philosophy* 85(11): 632–644.

(1989 [reprint of 1979 edn]) *Edmund Husserl's* Origin of Geometry: An *Introduction*, trans. John P. Leavey, Lincoln NE: University of Nebraska Press.

(1992) *Acts of Literature*, ed. Derek Attridge, London: Routledge.

(1993) *Memoirs of the Blind: The Self-Portrait and other Ruins*, trans. Pascale-Anne Brault and Michael Naas, Chicago IL: University of Chicago Press.

(1994) *Spectres of Marx: The State of the Debt, the Work of Mourning and the New International*, trans. Peggy Kamuf, London: Routledge.

(1996a) '"Il courait mort": salut, salut. Notes pour un courrier aux Temps Modernes', *Les Temps Modernes*, 587: 7–54.

(1996b) *The Gift of Death*, trans. David Wills, Chicago IL: University of Chicago Press.

(1997a) *Of Grammatology* (revised edn) trans. Gayatri Chakravorty Spivak, Baltimore MD: Johns Hopkins University Press.

(1997b) *The Politics of Friendship*, trans. George Collins, London: Verso.

(1998a) *Monolingualism of the Other; Or, the Prosthesis of the Other*, trans. Patrick Mensah, Stanford CA: Stanford University Press.

(1998b) 'The Retrait of Metaphor', trans. F, Gardner et al., in *The Derrida Reader: Writing Performances*, ed. Julian Wolfreys, Edinburgh: University of Edinburgh Press.

(1999) 'Hostipitalité', trans. Barry Stocker in *Pera Peras Poros*, (Cogito 85) ed. Ferda Keskin and Önay Sözer, Istanbul, Yapi Kredi Yayinlari: 17–44; revised by Forbes Morlock in *Angelaki: Journal of Theoretical Humanities* 5 (3) (2000): 3–18.

(2000) *Of Hospitality: Anne Dufourmantelle Invites Jacques Derrida to Respond*, trans. Rachel Bowlby, Stanford CA: Stanford University Press.

(2001) *On Cosmopolitanism and Forgiveness*, trans. unknown, London: Routledge.

(2002) *Acts of Religion*, ed. Gil Anidjar, London: Routledge.

(2003) *The Problem of Genesis in Husserl's Philosophy*, trans. Marian Hobson, Chicago IL: University of Chicago Press.

(2004 [reprint of 1981 edn]) *Dissemination*, trans. Barbara Johnson, London: Continuum.

(2005a) 'Fors' as foreword in Nicholas Abraham and Maria Torok, *The Wolfman's Magic Word: A Cryptonymy*, trans. Richard Rand, Minneapolis MN:University of Minnesota Press.

(2005b) *Touching——Jean-Luc Nancy*, trans. Christine Irigarry, Stanford CA: Stanford University Press.

FURTHER READING

Allison, Henry E. (2001) *Kant's Theory of Taste: A Reading of the Critique of Aesthetic Judgment*, Cambridge: Cambridge University Press.

Althusser, Louis (1996) *For Marx*, trans. Ben Brewster, London: Verso Books.

Austin, J.L. (1975) *How to do Things with Words*, Oxford: Oxford University Press.

Bennington, Geoffrey with Jacques Derrida (1993) *Jacques Derrida*, Chicago IL: University of Chicago Press.

Benveniste, Émile (1973) *Indo-European Language and Society*, trans. Elizabeth Palmer, London: Faber.

Blanchot, Maurice (1986) *The Writing of the Disaster*, trans. Anne Smock, Lincoln NE: University of Nebraska Press.

Brandom, Robert B. (1994) *Making It Explicit: Reasoning, Representing, and Discursive Commitment*, Cambridge MA: Harvard University Press.

——(2000) 'Facts, Norms and Normative Facts: A Reply to Habermas', *European Journal of Philosophy* 8(3): 356–374.

——(2002) *Tales of the Mighty Dead: Historical Essays in the Metaphysics of Intentionality*, Cambridge MA: Harvard University Press.

Canguilhem, Georges (1988) *Ideology and Rationality in the History of the Life Sciences*, trans. Arthur Goldhammer, Cambridge MA: MIT Press.

Carnap, Rudolf (1966) 'The Elimination of Metaphysics Through Logical Analysis of Language', in *Logical Positivism*, ed. A.J. Ayer, New NY: Free Press.

——(1988) *Meaning and Necessity: A Study in Semantics and Modal Logic*, Chicago IL: Midway/University of Chicago Press.

Cavell, Stanley (1995) *Philosophical Passages: Wittgenstein, Emerson, Austin, Derrida*, Cambridge: Harvard University Press.

Chomsky, Noam (2003) *Cartesian Linguistics: A Chapter in the History of Rationalist Thought* (2nd edn) Christchurch: Cybereditions.

Clark, Andy (1997) *Being There: Putting Brain, Body, and World Together Again*, Cambridge MA: MIT Press.

Davidson, Donald (2001a) *Inquiries into Truth and Interpretation: Philosophical Essays Volume 2*, Oxford: Oxford University Press.

——(2001b) *Subjective, Objective, Intersubjective: Philosophical Essays Volume 3*, Oxford: Oxford University Press.

——(2005). *Truth, Language, and History: Philosophical Essays Volume 5*, Oxford: Oxford University Press.

Dreyfus, Hubert L. (1991) *Being-in-the-World: A Commentary on Heidegger's Being and Time*, Cambridge MA: MIT Press.

Dworkin, Ronald (1982) 'Law as Interpretation', *Critical Inquiry* 9(1): 179–200.

——(1998) *Law's Empire*, Cambridge MA: Belknap/Harvard University Press.

Farrell, Frank (1988) 'Iterability and Meaning: The Searle–Derrida Debate', *Metaphilosophy* 19(1): 53–61.

Feyerabend, Paul (1993) *Against Method* (revised edn) London: Verso.

Fichte, J.G. (1979 [reprint of 1922 edn]) *Addresses to the German Nation*, trans. R.F. Jones and G.H. Jones, Westport CT: Greenwood Press.

Foucault, Michel (2000) 'My Body, This Paper, This Fire', trans. Geoffrey Bennington in *The Essential Works of Foucault, 1954–1984: Vol. 2 Aesthetics, Method, and Epistemology*, ed. Paul Rabinow, Harmondsworth, Middlesex: Penguin.

——(2001) *Madness and Civilisation*, trans. Richard Howard, London: Routledge.

Frege, Gottlob (1997) 'On Sinn and Bedeutung' in *The Frege Reader*, ed. Michael Beaney, Oxford: Blackwell.

Gallagher, Shaun (2005) *How the Body Shapes the Mind*, Oxford: Oxford University Press.

Gallagher, Shaun and Dan Zahavi (forthcoming) *The Phenomenological Mind*, London: Routledge.

Golumba, David (1999) 'Quine, Derrida, and the Question of Philosophy', *The Philosophical Forum* 30(3): 163–186.

Goodman, Nelson (1976) *Languages of Art: An Approach to a Theory of Symbols*, Indianapolis IN: Hackett Publishing.

Guyer, Paul (1993) *Kant and the Experience of Freedom: Essays on Aesthetics and Morality*, Cambridge: Cambridge University Press.

——(1997) *Kant and the Claims of Taste*, Cambridge: Cambridge University Press.

Grice, H. Paul (1989) *Studies in the Way of Words*, Cambridge MA: Harvard University Press.

Habermas, Jürgen (2000) 'From Kant to Hegel: On Robert Brandom's Philosophy of Language', *European Journal of Philosophy* 8(3): 322–355.

Herrick, Tim (2005) '"A book which is no longer discussed today", Tran Duc Thao, Jacques Derrida, and Maurice Merleau-Ponty', *Journal of the History of Ideas* 66(1): 113–131.

Hegel, G.W.F. (1977) *Hegel's Phenomenology of Spirit*, trans. A.V. Miller, Oxfrod: Oxford University Press.

Heidegger, Martin (1962) *Being and Time*, trans. John Macquarrie and Edward Robinson, Oxford: Blackwell.

——(1968) *What is Called Thinking?*, trans. J. Glenn Gray, New York NY: Harper and Row.

Husserl, Edmund (1962) *Ideas: General Introduction to Pure Phenomenology*, trans, W.R. Boyce Gibson, New York NY: Collier Books.

——(2001) *Logical Investigations*, 2 vols, ed. Dermot Moran, trans. J.N. Findlay, London: Routledge.

Irzik, Gurol and Teo Grunberg (1995) 'Carnap and Kuhn: Arch Enemies or Close Allies?', *The British Journal for the Philosophy of Science* 46(3): 285–307.

Kant, Immanuel (1991a) *Political Writings*, ed. H.S. Reiss, trans. H.B. Nisbet, Cambridge: Cambridge University Press.

——(1991b) *The Metaphysics of Morals*, trans. Mary Gregor, Cambridge: Cambridge University Press.

——(1996) *Practical Philosophy*, ed. Mary J. Gregor, Cambridge: Cambridge University Press.

——(1998) *The Critique of Pure Reason*, trans. Paul Guyer and Allen W. Wood, Cambridge: Cambridge University Press.

——(2000) *Critique of the Power of Judgement*, trans. Paul Guyer and Eric Matthews, Cambridge: Cambridge University Press.

Kierkegaard, Søren A. (1983) *Fear and Trembling/Repetition*, trans. Howard V. Hong and Edna H. Hong, Princeton NJ: Princeton University Press.

Klossowski, Pierre (1997) *Roberte Ce Soir and the Revocation of the Edict of Nantes*, trans. Austryn Wainhouse, London: Marion Boyars.

Kripke, Saul A (1981) *Naming and Necessity*, Oxford: Blackwell.

——(1982) *Wittgenstein on Rules and Private Language*, Oxford: Blackwell.

Kuhn, Thomas S. (1996) *The Structure of Scientific Revolutions* (3rd edn) Chicago IL: University of Chicago Press.

Kymlicka, Will (1995) *Multicultural Citizenship: A Liberal Theory of Minority Rights*, Oxford: Oxford University Press.

Lakoff, George and Mark Johnson (2003) *Metaphors We Live By*, Chicago IL: University if Chicago Press.

Lévinas, Emmanuel (1998) *Otherwise than Being, Or Beyond Essence*, trans. Alphonso Lingis, Pittsburgh PA: Duquesne University Press.

——(1999) *Totality and Infinity: An Essay on Exteriority*, trans. Alphonso Lingis, Pittsburgh PA: Duquesne University Press.

McCarthy, Thomas A. (1988) 'On the Margins of Politics', *The Journal of Philosophy* 85(11): 645–648.

McDowell, John (1988) *Mind, Value, and Reality*, Cambridge MA: Harvard University Press.

——(1996) *Mind and World*, Cambridge MA: Harvard University Press.

MacIntyre, Alasdair (1997) *After Virtue: A Study in Moral Theory* (2nd edn) London: Duckworth.

Marx, Karl (1998) *The German Ideology*. Includes: *Theses on Feuerbach* and *The Introduction to the Critique of Political Economy*, trans. unknown, Amherst NY: Prometheus Books.

Merleau-Ponty, Maurice (1962 reprinted from 1956 edn) *Phenomenology of Perception*, trans. Colin Smith, London: Routledge.

——(1969) *The Visible and the Invisible*, trans. Alphonso Lingis, Evanston IL: Northwestern University Press.

——(2004) *Maurice Merleau-Ponty: Basic Writings*, ed. Thomas Baldwin, London: Routledge.

Montaigne, Michel de (1993) *The Complete Essays*, trans. M.A. Screech, Harmondsworth, Middlesex: Penguin.

Moore, A.W. (2000) 'Arguing with Derrida', *Ratio* 13: 355–373.

Mulligan, Kevin (1991) 'How not to Read: Derrida on Husserl', *Topoi* 10: 199–208.

——(2003) 'Searle, Derrida and the Ends of Phenomenology' in *The Cambridge Companion to Searle*, ed. Barry Smith, Cambridge: Cambridge University Press.

Norris, Christopher (2004) *Language, Logic and Epistemology*, Basingstoke: Palgrave/Macmillan.

Nozick, Robert (1977) *Anarchy, State and Utopia*, New York NY: Basic Books.

Nussbaum, Martha (1990) *Love's Knowledge: Essays on Philosophy and Literature*, Oxford: Oxford University Press.

——(2001 revised edn) *The Fragility of Goodness: Luck and Ethics in Greek Tragedy and Philosophy*, Cambridge: Cambridge University Press.

Peirce, Charles S. (1991) *Peirce on Signs: Writings on Semiotics*, ed. James Hoopes, London: Atlantic Books.

Pettit, Philip (1997) *Republicanism: A Theory of Freedom and Government*, Oxford: Oxford University Press.

Priest, Graham (1994) 'Derrida and Self-Reference', *Australasian Journal of Philosophy* 72(1): 103–111.

——(2002 [reprinted from 1995 edn]) *Beyond the Limits of Thought*, Oxford: Clarendon/Oxford University Press.

Putnam, Hilary (1975) 'The Meaning of "Meaning"' in *Mind, Language and Reality: Philosophical Papers*, Cambridge: Cambridge University Press.

——(2002) 'Lévinas and Judaism' in *The Cambridge Companion to Lévinas*, eds Simon Critchley and Robert Bernasconi, Cambridge: Cambridge University Press.

——(2004) *Ethics without Ontology*, Cambridge MA: Harvard University Press.

Quine, Willard Van Orman (1977) *Ontological Relativity and Other Essays*, New York NY: Columbia University Press.

——(1980) *From a Logical Point of View: Nine Logico-Philosophical Essays*, Cambridge MA: Harvard University Press.

Rescher, Nicholas and Robert B. Brandon (1979) *Logic of Inconsistency: A Study in Non-Standard Possible Worlds Semantics and Ontology*, Lanham MD: Rowman and Littlefield.

Rawls, John (1999a) *A Theory of Justice* (2nd edn) Cambridge MA: Belknap/Harvard University Press.

——(1999b) *Collected Papers*, ed. Samuel Freeman, Cambridge MA: Harvard University Press.

Richmond, Sarah (1996) 'Derrida and Analytical Philosophy: Speech Acts and their Force', *European Journal of Philosophy* 4(1): 38–62.

Ricoeur, Paul (2005 [reprinted from 1981 edn]) *The Rule of Metaphor: Multi-disciplinary Studies of the Creation of Meaning in Language*, trans. Robert Czerny, Toronto: University of Toronto Press.

Rorty, Richard (1977) 'Derrida on Language, Being, and Abnormal Philosophy', *The Journal of Philosophy* 74(11): 673–681.

——(1980) *Philosophy and the Mirror of Nature*, Oxford: Blackwell.

——(1991) 'Is Derrida a Transcendental Philosopher?' in *Essays on Heidegger and Others: Philosophical Papers Vol. 2*, Cambridge: Cambridge University Press.

——(1998a) 'Habermas, Derrida and the Function of Philosophy', in *Truth and Progress: Philosophical Papers*, Cambridge: Cambridge University Press.

——(1998b) 'Derrida and the Philosophical Tradition', in *Truth and Progress: Philosophical Papers*, Cambridge: Cambridge University Press.

Russell, Bertrand (1992a) *Logic and Knowledge*, London: Routledge.
——(1992b) *Principles of Mathematics*, London: Routledge.
——(1993) *A History of Western Philosophy; And its Connection with Political and Social Circumstances from the Earliest Times to the Present Day*, London: Routledge.
Ryle, Gilbert (1953) 'The Theory of Meaning', *Philosophical Logic* 62: 167–186.
Sandel, Michael J. (1998) *Liberalism and the Limits of Justice* (2nd edn) Cambridge: Cambridge University Press.
Sartre, Jean-Paul (2002) *Sketch for the Theory of Emotions*, trans. unknown, London: Routledge.
——(2003a) *Being and Nothingness: A Phenomenological Ontology*, trans. Hazel E. Barnes, London: Routledge.
——(2003b) *Jean-Paul Sartre: Basic Writings*, ed. Stephen Priest, London: Routledge.
——(2004) *The Imaginary: A Phenomenological Psychology of the Imagination*, trans. Jonathan Webber, London: Routledge.
Searle, John (1969) *Speech Acts*, Cambridge: Cambridge University Press.
——(1977) 'Reiterating the Differences: A Reply to Derrida', *Glyph* 1: 198–208.
Sellars, Wilfrid (1997) *Empiricism and the Philosophy of Mind*, Cambridge MA: Harvard University Press.
Sonderegger, Ruth (1997) 'A Critique of Pure Meaning: Wittgenstein and Derrida', *European Journal of Philosophy* 5(2): 183–209.
Stocker, Barry (2000) 'Pascal and Derrida: Geometry, Origin and Discourse', *Symposium* IV (1): 117–41.
——(2003) 'Presence and Immediacy in Analysis and Deconstruction', *Yeditepe' de Felsefe* 2: 41–69.
Tran, Duc Thao (1986) *Phenomenology and Dialectical Materialism*, trans. Daniel J. Herman and Donald V. Morano, Berlin: Springer.
Unger, Peter (1978) *Ignorance: A Case for Scepticism*, Oxford: Oxford University Press.
——(2002) *Philosophical Relativity*, Oxford: Oxford University Press.
Wheeler, Samuel C. (1985) 'Indeterminacy of French Interpretation: Derrida and Davidson' in *Truth and Interpretation: Perspectives in the Philosophy of Donald Davidson*, ed. Ernest Lepore, Oxford: Blackwell.
——(2000) *Deconstruction as Analysis*, Stanford CA: Stanford University Press.
Wheeler, Michael (2005) *Reconstructing the Cognitive World: The Next Step*, Cambridge MA: MIT Press.
Wittgenstein, Ludwig (1961) *Tractatus Logico-Philosophicus*, trans. David Pears and Brian McGuinness, London: Routledge.
——(2001) *Philosophical Investigations* (3rd edn) trans. G.E.M. Anscombe, Oxford: Blackwell.
Zahavi, Dan (1999) *Self-Awareness and Alterity: A Phenomenological Investigation*, Evanston IL: Northwestern University Press.

INDEX

etymology: 'hospitality' 238, 244, 258–60, 262
event and structure 210–11, 217, 219
'exemplar' and friendship 273, 274–75, 294
exemplary witnesses 348–49
existence and imagined word 100–102
experience: and language 157–58; lived experience and expression 87–88, 95, 96, 100; and pragmatism 240; transcendental experience and language 164; *see also* mental experience
explicit 214, 215
expressive/expression 85, 86, 90–102, 142, 143–44; complete and incomplete expression 173–74; objective expressions 144, 146–47, 151, 152–53; pre-expressive stratum 158–59, 175–77; and self-presence 92–93, 96, 97, 143, 159; as stratum of experience 164–71, 172
extended mind 160–61
exteriority 90–91, 139; of writing 42, 57–58, 68, 70, 75; *see also* interior/exterior opposition
'external realism' 240
externalism 139

facial expressions 92–93, 94
factual knowledge 184
failure and performative 125–27, 128
faith and friendship 284–85, 286
fake art works 402
fallen writing 43, 44–45
Farrell, Frank 60, 108, 139, 140
fascination: Mandela's admiration 337–38, 339
federalism 303
feminist philosophy 18
Feuerbach, Ludwig Andreas 318, 322, 393–94n
Feyerabend, Paul 13
Fichte, Johann Gottlieb 138, 300, 301, 312–17, 320, 323
finitude 203, 229
Fink, Eugen 47, 191
Flaubert, Gustave 367, 386, 389–90, 391–92n

force: in aesthetics 400; of breaking 119, 120; and law 108, 327, 333–36, 342; and performative 124; of reflection 330–31; and signification 355–98
forgeries 402
forgetfulness 189, 193, 194, 197, 203, 388; and writing 70–71
form: conceptual form 173–74, 174–75; and force 363; and meaning 157–80, 163, 379–81, 399–400, 408–9; and sense 150–51; and work of art 389–90
formalism and justice 328
Foucault, Michel 3, 6, 7–8
foundation metaphor 158, 165, 166
foundationalism 88–89, 215, 240; *see also* logos/logocentrism
foundationalist epistemology 212–13, 214
frame/framing and art 400, 405, 409, 410
framework of science 186, 187
France: critique of French socialism 321–22; *see also* French philosophy
Freedom Charter of ANC 326, 332, 333, 336
Frege, Gottlob 20, 87, 158, 168, 214, 301
French philosophy 6–7, 15–19, 308–9, 405–6
Freud, Sigmund 75–76, 137, 159, 219, 221
friendship 265–95

Gadamer, Hans-Georg 214
Galileo 44
Gallagher, Shaun 161
Garfield, Jay 59
'general will' 334; paradox of 325, 335–36
Genet, Jean 357
Genette, Gérard 7, 225
geometry 9, 375, 376–79, 380–82; Introduction to *The Origin of Geometry* 183–209
German Idealism 9, 12, 213–14, 241; *see also* Fichte; Hegel; Kant
German nationalism 299–300, 302, 312–23; national-humanism 318, 319–23

Index   433

German Socialism 318, 319–20, 321–23
gestures and expression 92–93, 94, 95
'given' 88, 213
God 43–44, 45, 241, 288–89, 367–69
Goodman, Nelson 29, 401–3
Gorgias 79–80
grafting 106, 119
grammar: and myth 228–29; *see also* pure logical grammar; universal grammar
grammatology *see* writing
'grasping' thoughts 87
Grice, H. Paul 108–9
Grün, Karl 318, 319–22
Grunberg, Teo 186
'guest' 237–38, 239, 248, 251–52
Guyer, Paul 401

Habermas, Jürgen 215, 267, 300
Hazard, Paul 391n
hedonistic ethics 241–42
Hegel, Georg Wilhelm Friedrich 3, 4, 6, 7, 13, 14, 21; aesthetics/*Lectures on Aesthetics* 39, 399, 400, 405, 406, 407, 409, 411–16, 419–20; and contradictions 58, 59; and 'différance' 137; and earth 394n; *Encyclopaedia of Philosophical Sciences* 27, 31, 52–54; and epistemology 213–14; Flaubert on 392n; *Lectures on Aesthetics* 405, 407, 411–12, 413–14, 415–16, 419–20; and nationalism 301, 321, 322; and nominalism 29; and *Of Grammatology* 31, 39–40, 47, 52–54; *Phenomenology of the Mind (Spirit)* 5, 382, 387; *Philosophy of Right* 321; and reason 326; and Sartre 16
Heidegger, Martin 3, 4, 6, 10, 13; aesthetics 399, 400, 407, 409, 414–16, 419–20; *Being and Time* 5, 15, 48–49, 159, 160; and 'différance' 137; implicit 214; and logical positivism 186; and nationalism 301, 302, 322–23; and nominalism 29; and nostalgia 238; in *Of Grammatology* 32, 38, 40, 47–52; *Origin of the Work of Art* 414–16,

419–20; pure speech 372; and structuralism 212, 219–20, 221; *Was heisst Denken?* 238–39, 255–58; *Zur Seinsfrage* 51
'heissen' 256, 257–58
heliocentric metaphysics 388
Herrick, Tim 301
Hess, Moses 318, 321
hierarchies of norms 328, 329
hieroglyphs 53, 114–15
historicism 201, 407
historicity 189–90, 193, 201, 202, 231, 389; and art 407–8; internal historicity 194–95, 196, 373
history: and being 50; and being as presence 154, 231; of concept of structure 217, 218; equivocity and univocity 199–200, 201, 202; and friendship 287–88; and interior/exterior opposition 194–95, 196; internal history of work of art 373; language as origin of 355, 362; of metaphysics 218–20, 221–22, 231; and philosophy of art 399, 405, 407–8; of science 185, 187–88; and structuralism 362, 364, 387–88; and writing 52–54, 189–90
Hobbes, Thomas 327–28
hospitality/hostility 237–64
'host' 237–38, 245, 248, 252, 260
'hostage' 252–53
'hostess' 252, 254
household, law of 245, 259
humanism: and Marxism 8, 318, 319–23; national-humanism 299–323
humanist metaphysics 304
Humboldt, Wilhelm von 9, 10
Hume, David 44, 87
Husserl, Edmund 3–4, 6, 8–9, 14–15, 107, 310; absence of referent 121–22; contents of intentionality 239; expressive and indicative 85–86, 90–102, 142, 143, 147, 158, 164–66; form 150–51, 157–59, 162–77; influence on French philosophy 15–17; and internal mental life 85–86, 90, 98–102; *Introduction to The Origin of Geometry* 9, 10, 183–209, 357, 369; *Logical Investigations* 19, 20; mathematical knowledge

logical positivism 29–30, 87, 185–86
logos/logocentrism 17–18, 21, 27–28,
    30, 31–32, 36; absolute logos 41;
    epoch of the logos 40–43, 48, 51;
    logos and consciousness 157, 159;
    logos as 'pharmakon' 79–81; and
    meaning 38, 39; and Nietzsche 47,
    48; and present 78–79; 'stratum of
    the logos' 164–65, 166; writing and
    communication 132, 133
'lovence' 277, 278–79
lover and beloved 266, 277–83
Luthuli, Albert 343–44
Lyotard, Jean-François 6, 161, 401

McCarthy, Thomas 267–68
McDowell, John 23, 213–14, 269
McGee, Vann 59
McIntyre, Alasdair 327
magic 63, 79–80
Mallarmé, Stéphane 357, 368–69,
    385, 392n
Mandela, Nelson 324–52
manifestation of experience 96, 97, 98
Marion, Jean-Luc 6
Marivaux, Pierre Carlet de Chamblain
    de 381–82
Marx, Karl/Marxism: and national-
    humanism 300, 301, 317–18, 319,
    320, 321, 322; and politics of
    Nelson Mandela 325, 332, 338–39
Marxist philosophy 5–6, 8
'master of the house' 259–60, 262
masterpieces 373
maternal love 281–82
mathematics: economic model
    building 329; and knowledge 183–
    209; and writing 37, 183–84
Mauss, Marcel 230
Mead, George Herbert 267
meaning 83–134; of art 407–8; and
    consciousness 85–104; and context
    11–12; and expression 144, 158,
    166, 172–77; and form 157–80,
    163, 379–81, 399–400, 408–9; and
    interior/exterior opposition 140;
    and interpretation 11; and
    intuition 145–56; and logos 38;
    and metaphor 358; parallelism with
    sense 172–74; of 'Pharmakon' 56–

57; and reference 140–41, 226;
    'Sinn' and 'Bedeutung' 20; and
    structuralism 385–87; and
    textuality 56; and thinking 256;
    writing and literature 367–70,
    369–70; see also Bedeutung
Meares, Edwin D. 59
medium 172; neutrality 171
memory and writing 52–53, 54, 57–58,
    62, 65, 67–68, 70–77; see also
    forgetfulness
mental experience: and language 85–
    104; and speech 38–40, 57; see also
    mind
Merleau-Ponty, Maurice 6, 13, 15, 16–
    17, 18, 160; communication in
    literature 369–70; interweaving
    metaphor 159; visible and invisible
    326, 401
metaphor 3, 27–28, 43–44, 216, 358;
    and creativeness 366; darkness and
    light metaphor 387; foundation
    metaphor 158, 165, 166; organic
    metaphor and art 413;
    seductiveness 171
metaphysics 2, 10–11, 25–82; and
    aesthetics 384, 400, 413–16;
    analytical philosophy's critiques of
    Derrida 19–20; contradiction in
    58–60; Derrida's rejection of 28–
    30, 31–32; and empiricism 329;
    and form 163; history of 218–20,
    221–22, 231; humanist
    metaphysics 304; and logic 185,
    186; lover and beloved 266; and
    oppositions 57, 138–41, 220–21,
    266, 379; 'Pharmakon' 56–82;
    phenomenology and restoration of
    162; of presence 21, 28, 37, 40, 51,
    153–56, 220; of the proper 54; and
    structuralism 7, 10, 218–21, 356;
    and writing 27–55; see also inside/
    outside opposition
Mill, John Stuart 22, 301
mimesis and art 402
mind: extended mind 160–61;
    metaphysics of art 400, 411–12,
    413, 414–16, 420; and speech 38–
    40; see also consciousness; mental
    experience

Vienna Circle 29–30, 185, 186
violence: of law 325–26, 327, 333–36;
    violent protest in South Africa
    342–43, 350–51
virtual communication 189–90
virtue and friendship 269, 291–93
visible and invisible 325–26, 352, 401
vision *see* sight
'Voice of Being' 48, 50
voluntarism and writing 371–72
voluntaristic philosophy 85, 91, 92

Warburton, T. 113, 114
Wheeler, Michael 160
Wheeler, Samuel 139–40, 215
'white thing': perception of 168–69
whites in South Africa 333, 334–36,
    337, 342–45
Widersinnigkeit 145
will 85, 371–72; *see also* 'general will';
    intentionality
William of Ockham 29
Wirtbarkeit 244, 245
Wittgenstein, Ludwig 10, 20, 22, 107,
    214, 269–70; and analytical
    philosophy 358; anti-metaphysics
    29–30; language games 87, 187;

and nationalism 301; *Philosophical
    Investigations* 30, 87; 'private
    language' 87, 88, 139, 141;
    Tractatus Logico-Philosophicus 30,
    186
writing: and absence 106–7, 114, 115–
    18, 120–22; anguish of 367–68;
    and communication 112–23; and
    context 112; corporeality 184,
    190–92, 193–94, 197; and dancing
    390; exteriority of 42;
    grammatology as science of 31–54;
    and ideal Objectivity of sense 189–
    204; and mathematical knowledge
    183–84; meaning and literature
    367–70; and metaphysics 27–55;
    mirror writing 168–71; and
    'Pharmakon' 56–82; and signifier
    and signified 27–28, 38–40; and
    simultaneity 385; and speech 367–
    68, 371; and structuralism 355–56;
    and will 371–72

yoke effect and friendship 286, 287

Zahavi, Dan 161
Žižek, Slavoj 300